MEMORY AND AFFECT IN SHAKESPEARE'S ENGLAND

This is the first collection to systematically combine the study of memory and affect in early modern culture. Essays by leading and emergent scholars in the field of Shakespeare studies offer an innovative research agenda, inviting new, exploratory approaches to Shakespeare's work that embrace interdisciplinary cross-fertilization. Drawing on the contexts of Renaissance literature across genres and on various discourses including rhetoric, medicine, religion, morality, historiography, colonialism, and politics, the chapters bring together a broad range of texts, concerns, and methodologies central to the study of early modern culture. Stimulating for postgraduate students, lecturers, and researchers with an interest in the broader fields of memory studies and the history of the emotions – two vibrant and growing areas of research – it will also prove invaluable to teachers of Shakespeare, dramaturges, and directors of stage productions, provoking discussions of how convergences of memory and affect influence stagecraft, dramaturgy, rhetoric, and poetic language.

JONATHAN BALDO is Professor of English at the Eastman School of Music, University of Rochester, and the author of *Memory in Shakespeare's Histories: Stage of Forgetting in Early Modern England* (2012). His essays on Shakespeare and the interplay of remembering and forgetting have appeared in numerous journals and essay collections.

ISABEL KARREMANN is Professor of Early Modern Literature at the University of Zurich and the author of *The Drama of Memory in Shakespeare's History Plays* (2015). She has published widely on Shakespeare, early modern drama, and memory culture, and is the editor-in-chief of the *Shakespeare-Jahrbuch*.

MEMORY AND AFFECT IN SHAKESPEARE'S ENGLAND

EDITED BY

JONATHAN BALDO
University of Rochester

ISABEL KARREMANN
University of Zurich

Shaftesbury Road, Cambridge CB2 8EA, United Kingdom

One Liberty Plaza, 20th Floor, New York, NY 10006, USA

477 Williamstown Road, Port Melbourne, VIC 3207, Australia

314–321, 3rd Floor, Plot 3, Splendor Forum, Jasola District Centre, New Delhi – 110025, India

103 Penang Road, #05-06/07, Visioncrest Commercial, Singapore 238467

Cambridge University Press is part of Cambridge University Press & Assessment, a department of the University of Cambridge.

We share the University's mission to contribute to society through the pursuit of education, learning and research at the highest international levels of excellence.

www.cambridge.org
Information on this title: www.cambridge.org/9781009048330

DOI: 10.1017/9781009047111

© Cambridge University Press & Assessment 2023

This publication is in copyright. Subject to statutory exception and to the provisions of relevant collective licensing agreements, no reproduction of any part may take place without the written permission of Cambridge University Press & Assessment.

First published 2023
First paperback edition 2026

A catalogue record for this publication is available from the British Library

Library of Congress Cataloging-in-Publication data
NAMES: Baldo, Jonathan, editor. | Karremann, Isabel, editor.
TITLE: Memory and affect in Shakespeare's England / edited by Jonathan Baldo, Isabel Karremann.
DESCRIPTION: Cambridge ; New York, NY : Cambridge University Press, 2023. | Includes bibliographical references and index.
IDENTIFIERS: LCCN 2022057796 (print) | LCCN 2022057797 (ebook) | ISBN 9781316517697 (hardback) | ISBN 9781009048330 (paperback) | ISBN 9781009047111 (epub)
SUBJECTS: LCSH: Shakespeare, William, 1564-1616–Criticism and interpretation. | Memory in literature. | Affect (Psychology) in literature. | English drama–Early modern and Elizabethan, 1500-1600–History and criticism. | English drama–17th century–History and criticism. | LCGFT: Literary criticism. | Essays.
CLASSIFICATION: LCC PR3069.M46 M46 2023 (print) | LCC PR3069.M46 (ebook) | DDC 822.3/3–dc23/eng/20221212
LC record available at https://lccn.loc.gov/2022057796
LC ebook record available at https://lccn.loc.gov/2022057797

ISBN 978-1-316-51769-7 Hardback
ISBN 978-1-009-04833-0 Paperback

Cambridge University Press & Assessment has no responsibility for the persistence or accuracy of URLs for external or third-party internet websites referred to in this publication and does not guarantee that any content on such websites is, or will remain, accurate or appropriate.

Contents

List of Figures *page* vii
Contributors viii
Acknowledgments xiv

Introduction 1
Jonathan Baldo and Isabel Karremann

PART I ARS MEMORIAE, ARS AMATORIA

1 Allegories of Love: Affect and the Art of Memory in Shakespeare's *Sonnets* 25
 Rebeca Helfer

2 *Twelfth Night* and the Rites of Memory 44
 Brian Cummings

3 The Lustful Oblivion of Widowhood in *The Insatiate Countess* 68
 Grant Williams

PART II THE POLITICS OF MEMORY AND AFFECT

4 "Gathered again from the ash": Traumatropism, Memorialization, and Foxe's *Acts and Monuments* 89
 Devori Kimbro

5 "To take on me the payn / Ther fall to remember": *Metrical Visions* and the Dangerous Memory Networks of Complaint 106
 William Kerwin

6   Jesting, Nostalgia, and Agonistic Play   124
    Indira Ghose

PART III AFFECTIVE MEMORY: TEMPORAL AND
SPATIAL MODALITIES

7   "My despised time": Memory, Temporality, and Disgust
    in Shakespearean Tragedy   143
    Johannes Schlegel

8   Remembering Water in Robert Yarington's *Two
    Lamentable Tragedies*   162
    Katharine A. Craik

9   Mourning Memory in *Cymbeline*   181
    Daniel Normandin

PART IV MEMORY, AFFECT, AND STAGECRAFT

10 The Tug of Memory: Affect and Invention in
    Shakespeare's Drama   201
    William E. Engel

11 Memory, Text, Affect: The Deaths of Gloucester 220
    Rory Loughnane

12 Memory, Affect, and the Multiverse: From the History
    Plays to *The Merry Wives of Windsor*   238
    Evelyn Tribble

13 Cut Short All Intermission: Sound, Space, Memory,
    and Macduff's Grief   251
    Lina Perkins Wilder

CODA

14 Remembering Shakespeare   271
    Peter Holland

Bibliography   283
Index   308

Figures

8.1 Baynards Castle at the outfall of the Fleet Ditch. Undated lithograph after John M. Thorp (?) *page* 167

Contributors

JONATHAN BALDO is Professor of English in the Eastman School of Music, the University of Rochester. He is the author of *Memory in Shakespeare's Histories: Stages of Forgetting in Early Modern England* (Routledge, 2012) and *The Unmasking of Drama* (Wayne State University Press, 1996). His essays on Shakespeare have appeared in a wide range of essay collections and journals, including *Shakespeare Quarterly*, *Renaissance Drama*, *English Literary Renaissance*, *Shakespeare: A Journal of the British Shakespeare Association*, *Borrowers and Lenders*, *Criticism*, and *Modern Language Quarterly*. He is coeditor, with Isabel Karremann, of *Forms of Faith: Literary Form and Religious Conflict in Shakespeare's England* (Manchester University Press, 2017).

KATHARINE A. CRAIK is Research Lead and Professor of Early Modern Literature at Oxford Brookes University. She has edited two volumes on the history of emotion and sensation: *Shakespeare and Emotion* (Cambridge University Press, 2020) and, with Tanya Pollard, *Shakespearean Sensations: Experiencing Literature in Early Modern England* (Cambridge University Press, 2013). Her book *Reading Sensations in Early Modern England* (Palgrave, 2007) is a study of the connections between reading and interiority. She is the author of a number of essays on early modern literature and embodiment including "Sorting Pistol's Blood: Social Class and the Circulation of Character in Shakespeare's *2 Henry IV and Henry V*," in *Blood Matters: Studies in European Literature and Thought, 1400–1700* (Pennsylvania University Press, 2018), and "Sympathetic Sonnets," in *Shakespeare Survey* (2016). Her current project is a book for Oxford University Press on vividness and artificial life entitled *Lifelike Shakespeare*.

BRIAN CUMMINGS is the Anniversary Professor of English at the University of York. He has published widely on sixteenth-century religion and literature, including an edition of *The Book of Common*

Prayer: The Texts of 1549, 1559, and 1662 (Oxford University Press, 2013). His book *The Literary Culture of the Reformation: Grammar and Grace* (Oxford University Press, 2002) has profoundly influenced scholarly thinking about the poetics of religion. His latest book, *Mortal Thoughts: Religion, Secularity and Identity in Shakespeare and Early Modern Culture* (Oxford University Press, 2013), considers the debate around secular and post-secular concepts of culture. He has also published widely in journals such as *Shakespeare Survey*, *English Literary Renaissance*, and *Studies in Church History*, and published essays on memory and religion such as "Of Shakespeare and Pastness," in *On Religion and Memory* (Fordham University Press, 2013), and "Remembering the Dead in *Hamlet*," in *The Cambridge Companion to Shakespeare and Religion* (Cambridge University Press, 2019).

WILLIAM E. ENGEL is the Nick B. Williams Professor of Literature at Sewanee: The University of the South. He is the author of numerous essays, including "Handling Memory in the Henriad," in *The Routledge Handbook of Shakespeare and Memory* (Routledge, 2017), and "Shakespeare's Historical Context," in *The Shakespeare Handbook* (Continuum, 2009). He also has published six books on literary history and applied mnemonics, including *Death and Drama in Renaissance England* (Oxford University Press, 2002) and, most recently, *The Printer as Author in Early Modern English Book History* (Routledge, 2022); as well as *The Shakespearean Death Arts: Hamlet among the Tombs*, coedited with Grant Williams (Palgrave Macmillan, 2022), and a critical anthology, coedited with Rory Loughnane and Grant Williams, *The Death Arts in Renaissance England* (Cambridge University Press, 2022).

INDIRA GHOSE is Professor Emeritus of English Literature at the University of Fribourg, Switzerland. From 2011 to 2018 she was Partner Investigator at the Australian Research Council Centre of Excellence for the History of Emotions (Europe 1100–1800). Her research focuses on humor, wit, and comedy, both early modern and contemporary. She has written *Shakespeare and Laughter: A Cultural History* (Manchester University Press, 2008) and, most recently, *Shakespeare in Jest* (Routledge, 2021). She is currently working on a book on civility and the early modern theater.

REBECA HELFER is an Associate Professor in English at the University of California, Irvine. She has published widely on the ways in which this mnemonic poetics pervades English writing, including "The State of the Art of Memory and Shakespeare Studies," in *The Routledge Handbook of Shakespeare and Memory* (Routledge, 2017), and "Arts of Recollection and Cultural Transmission," in *Translatio, or the Transmission of Culture in the Middle Ages and the Renaissance* (Brepols, 2008). She is also the author of *Spenser's Ruins and the Art of Recollection* (University of Toronto Press, 2012). Her current research project provisionally titled *The Art of Memory and the Art of Writing in Early Modern England: Poetics of Ruin and Recollection* focuses on mnemonic poetics and early modern English texts.

PETER HOLLAND is the McMeel Family Professor in Shakespeare Studies at the University of Notre Dame. He was the editor of *Shakespeare Survey* for nineteen years and is a General Editor of a number of series, including *Oxford Shakespeare Topics* (Oxford University Press), *Shakespeare in the Theatre* (Arden), *Great Shakespeareans* (Bloomsbury Academic), and the Arden Shakespeare Fourth Series. Among his books are *English Shakespeares: Shakespeare on the English Stage in the 1990s* and a major study of Restoration drama, *The Ornament of Action*. He has also edited many Shakespeare plays, including *A Midsummer Night's Dream* for the Oxford Shakespeare series and *Coriolanus* for the Arden Shakespeare Third Series, as well as coediting Ben Jonson's *The Alchemist* with William Sherman. He has published well over 100 articles and book chapters, mostly on topics Shakespearean. His most recent monograph is *Shakespeare and Forgetting* (Arden, 2021) and he is currently editing *King Lear* for the Arden Shakespeare Fourth Series.

ISABEL KARREMANN is Professor for Early Modern Literature at the University of Zurich. She is the author of *The Drama of Memory in Shakespeare's History Plays* (Cambridge University Press, 2015) and has coedited, with Erica Sheen, *Shakespeare in Cold War Europe: Conflict, Commemoration, Celebration* (Palgrave, 2015) and, with Jonathan Baldo, *Forms of Faith: Literary Form and Religious Conflict in Shakespeare's England* (Manchester University Press, 2017). She is currently preparing an essay collection on *Shakespeare/Space* for the Arden Shakespeare Intersections series. In 2022 she was appointed editor-in-chief of the *Shakespeare Jahrbuch*. Her current research project explores the spatial, cognitive, affective, and perceptual ecologies of early modern drama.

WILLIAM KERWIN is an Associate Professor at the University of Missouri. His current research projects involve early modern satiric poetry, especially the epigram and the complaint poem, as it relates to different forms of memory. Apart from a focus on Shakespeare, Renaissance drama, and early British poetry, he is also interested in literature and medicine. He is the author of the monograph *Beyond the Body: The Boundaries of Medicine and English Renaissance Drama* (University of Massachusetts Press, 2005), which brings together the interrelated topics of medical instability and Renaissance drama. He is also the director of the Missouri Prison Outreach Program.

DEVORI KIMBRO is an Associate Lecturer at the University of Tennessee, Chattanooga. In her work, she focuses particularly on the Protestant Reformation, investigating the link between anti-Catholic rhetoric and religious as well as cultural trauma. Her research culminated in her 2015 dissertation "Trauma, Typology, and Anti-Catholicism in Early Modern England 1579–1625." She is also the author of four entries in *The Literary Encyclopaedia* and has published journal articles, including "'A cardinalles red-hat, and a kings golden crowne': Pamphlet Anti-Catholicism and Fabricated Authority in Thomas Milles's *The Misterie of Iniquitie* (1611)," in *Prose Studies* (2015). She has work on *Macbeth* and equivocation forthcoming from Palgrave-Macmillan, and is currently coediting a special issue of *Shakespeare* discussing public humanities and new media.

RORY LOUGHNANE is Reader in Early Modern Studies at the University of Kent. He is the author or editor of nine books, including, most recently, *The Death Arts in Renaissance England* (Cambridge University Press, 2022). In his role as Associate Editor of the *New Oxford Shakespeare*, he has edited more than ten of Shakespeare's plays. He is a General Editor of the forthcoming *Oxford Marlowe: Collected Works*, a General Editor of The Revels Plays series (Manchester University Press), a General Editor of the CADRE database (cadredb.net), and a Series Editor of Studies in Early Modern Authorship (Routledge) and Cambridge Elements in Shakespeare and Text (Cambridge University Press).

DANIEL NORMANDIN is an Instructor in English at Marshall University, West Virginia. His research explores the intersection of the colonial and antiquarian imaginations in early modern England. His current book project examines how representations of ancient Britain in texts such as William Shakespeare's *Cymbeline*, Edmund Spenser's *Faerie Queene*, and Thomas More's *Utopia* helped to generate a new historical memory that provided the materials to justify dominion over new territories. His articles on Spenser and Marvell have appeared in *Modern Philology* and *Early Modern Literary Studies*.

JOHANNES SCHLEGEL is a senior research fellow at Würzburg University. His research focuses on time and temporality, literature and media theory, mediality, materiality, and cultural techniques. He is coeditor of *The Institution of English Literature* (Vandenhoek Ruprecht, 2017) and has published several articles on Shakespeare including "'Minded like the Weather, most unquietly': Inquietude, Nature, and *King Lear*," in *Shakespeare Seminar* (2016) and "'Disjoint and Out of Frame': *Hamlet* and the Problem of Synchrony," in *Zeitschrift für Anglistik und Amerikanistik* (2018).

EVELYN TRIBBLE is a professor at the Department of English at the University of Connecticut. She has published extensively on Renaissance literature, early modern drama, memory studies, and cognitive approaches to literature. She is the author of *Cognition in the Globe: Attention and Memory in Shakespeare's Theatre* (Palgrave Macmillan, 2011) and *Early Modern Actors in Shakespeare's Theatre: Thinking with the Body* (Bloomsbury, 2017). Together with Nicholas Keene, she published *Cognitive Ecologies and the History of Remembering Early Modern England* (Palgrave, 2011). She also authored numerous articles including "Affective Contagion on the Early Modern Stage," in *Affect Theory and Early Modern Texts. Politics, Ecologies, and Form* (Palgrave, 2017), and "'The Raven o'er the infectious house': Contagious Memory in *Romeo and Juliet* and *Othello*," in *The Routledge Handbook of Shakespeare and Memory* (2017). Current research projects include the Arden 4 edition of *Merry Wives of Windsor* and a book on magic and performance in early modern England.

LINA PERKINS WILDER is Professor of English at Connecticut College. She is the author of *Shakespeare's Memory Theatre: Recollection, Properties, and Character* (Cambridge University Press, 2010), which explores stage props ranging from Yorick's skull to Desdemona's handkerchief as mnemonic objects helping audiences recall, or imagine, staged and unstaged pasts; and is coeditor of and contributor to *The Routledge Handbook of Shakespeare and Memory* (2017). Her research into memory theater and performance in Renaissance England has also produced multiple articles including "Shakespeare and Memory," in *Literature Compass* (2012), and "Towards a Shakespearean 'Memory Theater': Romeo, the Apothecary, and the Performance of Memory," in *Shakespeare Quarterly* (2005). Her current book project explores connections among science, mathematics, and language in seventeenth-century England.

GRANT WILLIAMS is an Associate Professor in the Department of English at Carleton University. He has coedited five collections: *Forgetting in Early Modern English Literature and Culture: Lethe's Legacies* (Routledge, 2004), *Ars reminiscendi: Memory and Culture in the Renaissance* (CRRS, 2009), *Taking Exception to the Law: Materializing Injustice in Early Modern English Literature* (University of Toronto Press, 2015), *The Shakespearean Death Arts: Hamlet among the Tombs* (Palgrave, 2022), and *Memory and Mortality in Renaissance England* (Cambridge University Press, 2023). He has also coedited two critical anthologies with William E. Engel and Rory Loughnane: *The Memory Arts in Renaissance England* (Cambridge University Press, 2016) and *The Death Arts in Renaissance England* (Cambridge University Press, 2022). With Donald Beecher, he is coeditor of Henry Chettle's *Kind-Heart's Dream and Piers Plainness: Two Pamphlets from the Elizabethan Book Trade* (CRRS, 2022).

Acknowledgments

From start to finish, this book has been a collaborative endeavor in many respects, and we are grateful to all the people who have played a role in its development. It originated from an SAA seminar entitled "Washed in Lethe: Renaissance Cultures of Remembering and Forgetting" in Washington, DC, where the lively discussion among participants made clear the need for a sustained exploration of the connections between memory and affect. The idea for the volume did not precede the seminar, but rather grew organically from it. We are indebted to our seminar participants for revising their essays in such a way as to foster dialogue between the study of memory and affect, and we are delighted that other colleagues followed our invitation to contribute their current work to the publication. Our editors at Cambridge University Press, Emily Hockley and George Paul Laver, have been supportive throughout. We are especially grateful for their readiness to accommodate changes to the production process, necessitated by the constraints of the pandemic. Our thanks go to the anonymous readers who enthusiastically embraced our idea of bringing the fields of memory studies and affect studies together and whose thoughtful responses helped shape the volume. Ann-Sophie Bosshard and Isabelle Koch have done a wonderful job at copy-editing and hunting down quotations, and we are grateful for the diligence and care with which they helped turn this volume into a book.

Introduction
Jonathan Baldo and Isabel Karremann

Memory Studies and the Affective Turn

In a recent book on "the new science of memory," Charles Fernyhough reminds us of a familiar fact about memory: "that emotional events are remembered more clearly and in greater detail than neutral ones. They may also stick in our minds for longer."[1] Far from a new discovery, the intimate relation between memory and affect has been widely appreciated since at least the ancient world. Their relation was fundamental to the memory arts, whose classic texts – Cicero's *De oratore*, Quintilian's *Institutio oratoria*, and the *Rhetorica ad Herennium* – all advocated the use of emotionally compelling imagery on the grounds that it would be longer retained in the memory. A survey of contemporary research in memory studies and affect studies, however, reveals surprisingly little interaction between them. Each area has its own journals, associations, and conferences.[2] There are signs of change, however. They include a recent online, interdisciplinary conference entitled "Memory, Affects and Emotions," which advises, "We are particularly interested in exploring the potential of [an] affective turn in memory studies."[3] And Harriet Phillips writes in her recent monograph, *Nostalgia in Print and Performance, 1510–1613: Merry Worlds*, of the "rich affective legacy of pre-Reformation memory in the later sixteenth century."[4] Our volume seeks to add to what we hope becomes a sustained, productive trend by exploring potential pathways between these two areas of inquiry, as well as their relationship to questions of individual personhood and collective identity in the analysis of culture and its expression in literature. It is the premise of this collection of new essays that the study of memory and affect stand in need not of uniting but of reuniting.

In his account of *memoria*, Aristotle stressed memory's emotional dimension. For Aristotle and his medieval Islamic proponent Averroes, according to Mary Carruthers, "recollection was understood to be a reenactment of experience, which involves cogitation and judgment, imagination, and emotion."[5] Memory for Aristotle "is a *state* or *affection* ... that follows on perceiving, apprehending, experiencing, or learning."[6] Deeply influenced by Aristotle, medieval thinkers held that the close connection between memory and affect was crucial for the "shaping of moral judgment and excellence of character," and hence for granting memory its "central place in medieval ethical life."[7] Carruthers writes, "Pre-modern psychologies recognized the emotional basis of remembering, and considered memories to be bodily 'affects'."[8] In medieval scholastic philosophy, "there is no such thing as an emotionally detached memory."[9] Memory was held to be composed of a visual aspect (*simulacrum* or *similitudo*) and an emotional one (*intentio*). The former "serves as a cognitive cue or token to the 'matter' or *res* being remembered"; the latter is the "'inclination' or 'attitude' we have to remembered experience"[10] and "serves to 'hook' a particular memory into one (or perhaps more) of a person's existing networks of experience."[11] *Intentio* does not merely correspond to the emotional state of the person who remembers; it refers also to that person's "attitudes, aims, and inclinations ... , as well as to the state of physical and mental concentration required." Without *intentio*, memories would be "tossed into storage at random," rather than put in "places" and "'colored' in ways that are partly personal, partly emotional, partly rational, and mostly cultural."[12] For some modern researchers, the way in which a medieval model of memory took into account emotional and motivational aspects in addition to cognitive ones has prefigured "modern ideas about memories as inherently emotionally coloured."[13]

The age of Shakespeare that is the focus of this collection shared with the Middle Ages the related beliefs that remembering has an emotional basis and that the mind is essentially embodied. As the essays in this volume confirm, for the early modern period as well as for the medieval, "each memory involves some kind of emotion; each memory is thus to an important degree a physiological, bodily phenomenon."[14] The extensive and foundational work on the humors by Gail Kern Paster and others has demonstrated the degree to which mind and body were connected in the medical and psychological thinking of the period. Emotions were conceived not as private mental events but as "visibly written on the body."[15] In spite of these widely held assumptions, in early modern studies memory and affect have largely been treated as distinct areas of inquiry. This volume aims to remedy that situation by helping to open new lines of inquiry between the study of memory and affect in the early modern period. While "emotion" tends to be employed as an umbrella term for the linguistic and nonlinguistic expression of feelings – for instance, in literature and the arts – we follow Lauren Berlant in conceptually privileging the term "affect" in order to highlight that feeling has not only a personal but a sociopolitical dimension as well: an insight that has long been acknowledged with regard to the interplay of individual and collective memory.[16] This is particularly relevant with regard to the study of early modern culture and literature, as the early modern understanding of selfhood is much more overtly social and draws on memory as well as affect – alongside reason – as sources of individual and communal senses of self.[17]

The study of memory and of affect has been siloed not just in research on the early modern period, but more generally. Two of the most flourishing and broadly interdisciplinary trends across the humanities, social sciences, and neurosciences, affect studies and memory studies have developed concurrently since the mid-1990s. The rise of the "affective turn" is often traced to political philosopher Brian Massumi's influential essay "The Autonomy of Affect" (1995),[18] which draws heavily on his work of translating Deleuze and Guattari's *A Thousand Plateaus*, the second volume of *Capitalism and Schizophrenia*. According to Ruth Leys, author of *The Ascent of Affect: Genealogy and Critique* (2017), the widely shared interest in affect among scholars in the humanities and social sciences represents a reaction against a perceived overvaluation of "the role of reason and rationality in politics, ethics, and aesthetics."[19] In her introduction to the volume *The Affective Turn: Theorizing the Social*, Patricia Ticineto Clough observes that the turn to affect across a number of disciplines coincided with "a time when critical theory is facing the analytic challenges of ongoing war, trauma, torture, massacre, and counter/terrorism." She speculates that the affective turn constitutes a "shift in thought," one that registers "a change in the cofunctioning of the political, economic, and cultural."[20] For Michael Hardt, too, attention to affects, besides shifting attention to emotions and to the body, promises syntheses of various kinds, "because affects refer equally to the body and to the mind; and … because they involve both reason and the passions."[21]

At about the same time as the growth of affect studies, the study of memory across an equally broad range of disciplines gained momentum from the culture wars in the United States in the 1990s and the proliferation of new digital technologies for recording and preserving the past, as well as from the inevitable tendency to look backward at the end of a century and a millennium. Alison Landsberg postulates about the explosion of memory studies near the turn of the century:

> It should come as no surprise that at the beginning of the twenty-first century, memory has once again emerged as an urgent topic of debate for scholars in a wide variety of disciplines. As in the past, this interest in memory might be attributable to ontological insecurity at the start of the new century or anxiety about the shape of the "new world order."[22]

The fast-rising interest in memory across cultural studies has been driven in part by the foundational work of Jan and Aleida Assmann, whose concept of "cultural memory" has been transformative, hailed by some as a new paradigm for cultural studies. Building on the work of Freud and especially of the philosopher and sociologist Maurice Halbwachs' concept of collective memory in *Les cadres sociaux de la mémoire* (1925) – the idea that a society may possess a group memory beyond that of any individual memory, though an individual's memory is influenced by and in turn may influence the collective memory – Jan and Aleida Assmann demonstrate how what they call cultural memory serves as the foundation of shared identities.[23]

Like twins separated at birth, the two fields of research known as memory studies and affect studies have had comparatively little influence on or communication with one another.[24] While the role of affect for the constitution of individual subjectivity and collective identity in the early modern period has been frequently addressed,[25] the specific links between affect and memory have gone largely unnoticed. It would be misleading to suggest that study of the literature and culture of early modern England has witnessed absolutely no traffic between affect studies and memory studies. In particular, studies of the impact of the Reformation on rituals of commemoration, most notably Stephen Greenblatt's *Hamlet in Purgatory* (2001), demonstrate how powerfully the two areas are connected. Recent work by Alexandra Walsham, Alison Shell, Gillian Wood, and Harriet Phillips likewise explores the intimate connections between personal recollection, social memory, and nostalgia in the aftermath of the Reformation.[26] But there has been no widespread and systematic communication between studies concentrating on either memory or affect in the period; independently, each represents a growing and immensely fertile area of research into the literature and culture of early modern England.[27] Memory studies in the early modern period, for the most part, have focused on epistemological and cognitive issues, on questions of belief, evidence, skepticism, confirmation, and perception.[28]

We often forget that, in the view of early modern faculty psychology, the faculty of memory powerfully governs and is governed by affects such as suffering, pain, or shame but also laughter and love, and by actions with strong causal ties to affect, such as revenge or forgiving. Mnemonic phenomena like trauma or nostalgia cannot be separated from their affective impact on the individual and collective psyche.

Reviving as well as revising Halbwachs' oppositional distinction between memory and history, Pierre Nora distinguishes "between real memory – social and unviolated, exemplified in but also retained as the secret of so-called primitive or archaic societies – and history, which is how our hopelessly forgetful modern societies, propelled by change, organize the past."[29] Commenting on the now familiar distinction, Alison Landsberg concedes that, while agreeing with Marita Sturken's assertion that memory and history are "more entangled than oppositional," they "have different modes of address. Memory always implies a subjective, affective relationship to the past, while history strives to maintain a sense of distance from the past."[30] In this sense, Shakespeare's plays about England's medieval past are not "history plays" but rather "memory plays," whose intent was to enhance an affective relationship between audiences and their collective, national past. They are among the period's most indelible demonstrations of the close working relationship between memory and affect. By contrast, in our own time, the recent global rise of populist politics has only seemingly reunited affect with memory by harnessing a rhetoric of emotion to a nostalgic invocation of the geopolitical world of yesteryear that, however, aims at consigning to oblivion the lessons of history: caught up in the here and now of anxieties, fears, and resentments, populist rhetoric privileges affect over memory, to the exclusion of memory's cognitive fellow, reason.

Memory and Affect in the Early Modern Period: Conceptual Frameworks

We take our cue for uniting the study of memory and affect from Shakespeare. When Shakespearean characters speak of "hateful memory" (*Antony and Cleopatra*, 4.10.9) or "sad remembrance" (*Twelfth Night*, 1.1.31; *Richard III*, 4.4.252), they suggest a deep connection between memory and affect that has been neglected so far by students both of cultural memory and of the history of the emotions. Hamlet's exhortation of Queen Gertrude to remember her first husband is so cruelly effective because it instills in her feelings of shame and self-loathing. Henry's St.

Crispin's Day Speech casts its spell by forging patriotic pride with the ritualized remembrance of military triumph into a national holiday. Sorrows often take root in the fertile soil of memory, as Macbeth suggests when he challenges the Scottish Doctor, "Canst thou not minister to a mind diseased, / Pluck from the memory a rooted sorrow . . . ?" (5.3.43). Shakespeare also casts memory in the part of rescuer, a bringer of joy rather than sorrow, as an astonished Prospero suggests when he questions Miranda about a childhood memory, "how is't / That this lives in thy mind?" (1.2.49). Miranda's memory serves as prototype for all the play's subsequent acts of recovery, restoration, and redemption.

Specific states of feeling that are inherently intertwined with memory, such as mourning, vengefulness, or nostalgia, drive the plots of many Shakespearean tragedies and problem plays. The number of examples that can be found not just in Shakespeare but in the literature of his contemporaries suggests that this conjunction of memory and affect is more than a rhetorical conceit that forges two distant concepts through the power of poetic language; rather, it is a conjunction made possible and familiar by early modern notions of human physiology, psychology, and philosophy which suggest that memory and affect, while in themselves different, were thought of as related modes of embodied knowledge.[31] This becomes particularly evident in texts that warned against the perilous influence of each on the other. The stenographer John Willis, for instance, warned in his handbook on the memory arts that "natural memory," that is, the brain's disposition for retention, can be harmfully impaired by emotional disturbances such as "anxious care, fear, grief, too much bashfulness, covetous hope, Jealousie, &c." or by "Filthy desires, as avarice, envy, thirst of revenge, lust, love of harlots and the ardent Passion, *Love*."[32] And clergyman William Perkins' theological-rhetorical manual on *The Arte of Prophecying* warned that the striking nature of memory images, which made them memorable in the first place, could too easily lead to an "impious" arousal of the passions: "The animation of the image, which is the key of memory, is impious, because it requireth absurd, insolent, and prodigious cogitations, and those especially which set an edge upon and kindle the most corrupt affections of the flesh."[33] These warnings, we do well to note, do not speak to an opposition between mind and body, between intellect and emotion, but are rather a testimony to the entanglement of memory and affect.

The premodern perspective thus provides a more holistic understanding of cognitive processes as grounded in the body and influenced by its sense perceptions and passions. Such an understanding can be approached through the three conceptual frameworks of faculty psychology, Galenic humoralism, and, in modern parlance, distributed cognition. The first framework located the human psychological faculties of imagination, judgment, and memory in three different "ventricles," or regions, of the brain. As such, these cognitive faculties are linked to the material disposition of the brain, as the standard metaphor for the memory also suggests: like a wax tablet, the brain must be of the right kind of material quality – moist but not too moist, warm rather than cold – in order to receive a lasting imprint.[34] Moreover, imagination, judgment, and memory as the higher faculties of intellection were also affected by the passions of the soul, which, in the Aristotelian tradition, was thought of as an embodied entity.[35] The Jesuit Thomas Wright signaled this in the title of his *Passions of the Minde* (1604), a treatise which explains the complex entanglement of the faculties and the passions. What emerges from his description is, primarily, that both are kinds of embodied cognition:

> First, then to our imagination commeth, by sense or memorie, some object to be knowne ... the which being knowne (for *Ignoti nulla cupido* [we do not know what we do not desire]) in the imagination which resideth in the former part of the braine, (as we proove) when we imagine any thing, presently the purer spirites flocke from the brayne, by certayne secret channels to the heart, where they pitch at the doore, signifying what an object was presented.... The heart immediately bendeth, either to prosecute it, or to eschewe it; and the better to effect that affection, draweth on other humours to help him ...; and not onley ... the heart draweth, but also the same soule that informeth the heart residing in other partes, sendeth the humours vnto the heart.[36]

Wright describes here a multi-tiered communication between sense perception, material brain, the heart as seat of the passions, and the soul as the seat of imagination as well as judgment and memory. The overall effect is "affection," a psychological or physical change happening in the body or involving the body;[37] or, in Wright's own words borrowed from Ovid's *Ars amatoria*, a knowledge born of passion: "we do not know what we do not desire." The passions thus are not unmediated responses to external sense perceptions but constitute a kind of cognitive processing, as Benedict Robinson points out: passions are "ways of seeing, and therefore also perceptions and modes of cognition."[38] According to Wright, passions may also be aroused by "memorie," another indicator that the embodied nature of knowledge in faculty psychology made the conjunction of memory and affect familiar. When Wright describes the imagination, drawing on "sense or memorie," as the operative faculty that sends outs "spirits" which affect both heart and soul, he formulates a key principle of the arts of rhetoric and of literary creation that is also acknowledged, for example, in Sidney's *Defense of Poesie* and especially the many contemporary defenses of as well as attacks on the theater.[39]

The second conceptual framework through which memory and affect were understood as related in the early modern period is Galenic humoralism. The pioneering work by Gail Kern Paster, begun in *Humoring the Body: Emotions and the Shakespearean Stage* (2004), has firmly established the centrality of the material body for a "premodern ecology of the passions" that connected the body and affect. In Paster's "psychophysiological" account, the early moderns understood "the passions and the body that houses them in ecological terms – that is, in terms of that body's reciprocal relations to the world."[40] Paster explains that, for early modern individuals, "the passions actually were liquid forces of nature, because, in this cosmology, the stuff of the outside world and the stuff of the body were composed of the same elemental materials."[41] The humors also feature in Wright's description quoted above, where they have the role of a medium through which passions are transported and communicated through the body. Humoralism thus goes a step further than faculty psychology by linking embodiment to the environment in reciprocal relations, thereby adding a dimension to the holistic notion of embodied perception and experience as not only embodied, but also embedded.[42]

Modern scholarship on Galenic humoralism, however, tends to neglect the subject's agency in favor of the passivity of sense perceptions and somatic experiences. Yet if "the passions are what connects our minds to the world outside us," as Cummings and Sierhuis argue,[43] then this insight urges us to understand early modern emotions as intersubjective: they allow us to connect with the other human beings who inhabit the world. This is where the philosophy of the passions in the early modern period can usefully complement the psychophysiological understanding provided by Galenic humoralism to help us see the political and ethical dimension of the emotions. As such, the passions are necessarily more than bodily impulses. They form one of the many kinds of embodied knowledge about ourselves and our relations to the environment, as Miranda Anderson remarks: "physical processes and wider environments play manifold cognitive roles, including enabling or constituting phenomena now identified by terms such as mind, thought, reasoning, experience, emotions, memory, imagination, and perception."[44] The framework of 'distributed cognition' as "an activity that is always both embodied and extended into the world"[45] is particularly relevant for linking memory and affect with the environment the embodied subject inhabits. Although "the term originates in our own period," Anderson affirms that "distributed cognition was more widely manifest in the sixteenth- and early seventeenth-century early modern belief system than it has become in current times."[46] Both memory and affect were conceived of as modes of cognition extending beyond the individual body, which was embedded in a material, social, and cultural environment. Thus, the memory arts encouraged the imaginative creation of "repositories," spatial environments through which the orator might walk in his mind to retrieve memorized facts, sentences, or names. These repositories were typically imagined as built environments, rooms, galleries, palaces, or – particularly relevant for our collection – theaters. Put into practice, especially by professional play-actors, the art of memory also relied on material artifacts like textbooks, plots, and props and on the material environment constituted by the other players and the playhouse itself, which extended the working field of recollection beyond the brain to material, tangible objects.[47] Importantly, material objects could become "triggers and sites of cognitive activity in their own right," as Sophie Duncan has recently shown in a study of props and cognition in early modern plays, actively forcing memories on figures: the handkerchief in *Othello* or the miniature portraits in *Hamlet* would be examples.[48] From the perspective of distributed cognition, memory thus not only functions *like* emotion: as externally stimulated modes of embodied knowledge, both are entangled in meaningful ways.

Early modern scholarship has been pushing toward a rapprochement between affect and memory not only from the perspective of the history of the emotions and historical phenomenology. Memory studies, too, have recently begun to shift their focus to "the affective, experiential and immanent aspects of memory, attending, in particular, to the way they foreground questions about gender and embodiment," as the authors of a review article in *Memory Studies* point out.[49] Attention to the physiology of memory itself is not new, of course: the early modern memory arts typically included quasi-medical regimens with dietary recommendations designed to improve the retentive faculties of the brain, and this has been part of scholarly discussions of the *ars memoriae*. When Amanda Bailey and Mario DiGangi state in the introduction to *Affect Theory and Early Modern Texts* that "[humoralism] understood the interrelated components of mind, psyche, soma, climate, food, and air,"[50] then something very similar can be said about the memory arts. While ostensibly focused on intellectual cognition and its training, the memory arts combined the disciplines of ancient rhetoric and humoral medicine in order to effectively manage the process of recollection by manipulating the disposition of the material body which enables it. Looking on the reception side, the memory arts were in the service of rhetoric that aimed at both cognitively persuading and affectively touching the audience, often at the same time. The recent affective turn within the field of memory studies expands this notion of embodied memory from "practices of memory cultivation" and "written and printed documents ... to objects and places, to religious discourses and to a wide range of embodied, sensory and emotive experiences."[51] Prominent examples of such scholarship include Ann Rosalind Jones and Peter Stallybrass's *Renaissance Clothing and the Materials of Memory* (2000), which reconstructs the ability of clothes to "mold and shape [subjects] both physically and socially ... through their power as material memories"; Alexandra Walsham's *The Reformation of the Landscape* (2011), which examines how religious assumptions influenced contemporary perceptions of the physical environment, and how in turn the reformed landscape shaped and commemorated the theological, political, and cultural transformations of the Reformation; or Patricia Phillippy's *Shaping Remembrance from Shakespeare to Milton* (2018), which explores textual, visual, and material forms of commemoration, often as gendered practices, including manuscript and printed memorials, portraits, jewelry, textiles or 'rarities.'[52]

This scholarship is interested in the individual and collective forms of cultural memories and affects, and in their transmission through various media and artifacts. If, in such studies, "[m]emories are formed and expressed by means of intersubjective social interactions,"[53] what must be acknowledged and conceptualized more systematically is the role that affect plays in shaping those intersubjective social interactions which produce cultural memory. Garrett A. Sullivan has shown how memory is "an embodied process that presupposes involvement with the environment" and that is also impacted by socially proscribed affects like shame or honor; hence, remembering must be understood not only as a cognitive act but as a social performance determined at least in part by affect: "Remembering is not recollection; it is instead an action or set of actions that arises out of the subject's response to specific social circumstance and a particular imperative to remember (that is, the imperative to behave in a certain way)."[54] The collection of essays edited by Cummings and Sierhuis examines the role of the passions for both subjectivity and intersubjective relations, ethics, and politics, although the only example of emotional collective memory touched on is the phenomenon of nostalgia. Nostalgia is indeed the best-studied intersection of memory and affect in early modern culture to date.⁵⁵ More recently, Amanda Bailey and Mario DiGangi have acknowledged the sociopolitical dimension of affect, arguing that "affect can illuminate the role of embodiment in early modern representations of political subjectivity and agency,"⁵⁶ a role which becomes particularly interesting when we consider the politics of memory. Patricia Cahill's chapter in that volume, for instance, reads Marlowe's *The Massacre at Paris* (1592/3) as an affective immersion in the past and its atrocities. Investigating contemporary eyewitness accounts and political pamphlets on the historical event alongside the play-text and props used to activate somatic responses, she reconstructs the affective intensity of violence enacted on stage through which Marlow's play "simulates" and reenacts rather than represents the past.⁵⁷ Exploring how history is apprehended in affective rather than merely cognitive or intellectual terms allows for a new approach to the links between trauma, memory, and history. Part II of this volume, "The Politics of Memory and Affect," pursues these links in a systematic fashion but adds reparative affects like laughter to the range of emotions through which collective memories, in particular of potentially traumatic experiences, were negotiated.⁵⁸

This Collection: Topics, Issues, Questions

Comprising four parts, each with a particular thematic focus, our volume seeks to demonstrate the range of issues, concepts, and readings made possible by the partnership of memory and affect studies. Part I, situated at the intersection of the *ars memoriae* and the *ars amatoria*, considers the emotionally inflected interplay of remembering and forgetting. Love and desire feature significantly in classical theories and practices of memory, which are in turn allied to the art of rhetoric. Rebeca Helfer examines the poetics of memory in Shakespeare's *Sonnets* in dialogue with Plato's *Phaedrus* and *The Symposium*. She argues that the sonnets at once ruin and remember the ideal that Platonic love leads to recollection, with the paradoxical twist that Shakespeare's poetry likewise embraces an aesthetic of willful forgetting and pleasurable oblivion. Like Engel's and Holland's chapters in later parts of this volume, Helfer's is interested in the ways in which the devastating emotional impact of the traumatic ur-scene of the art of memory – the poet Simonides naming the dead by remembering seating arrangements in the collapsed banquet hall – both is and is not contained in the practice of memory itself. Brian Cummings' contribution, too, builds on a classical theoretical framework – the "term *anamnesis*, or 'recollection,' familiar from Plato and Cicero"⁵⁹ as well as Erasmus' rhetorical handbook *De copia* – that is central to his exploration of both Shakespeare's *Twelfth Night* and *The Winter's Tale*. Remembering love, Cummings points out, is always bound up with the experience of loss, with saying goodbye, with the danger of forgetting love: a danger that is both imagined and countered through the recuperative deployment of rhetoric and poetry, embodied in the ancient myth of the poet Orpheus and his wife Eurydice. The final chapter in Part I takes the paradoxical imperatives of remembering love to the extreme by examining the ways in which desire may induce oblivion. Reading Marston's *The Insatiate Countess* alongside medical, moral-philosophical, and religious texts, Grant Williams shows how female corporeality – much as in the "Dark Lady" sonnets – disturbs hegemonic notions of masculinity. The depiction of Isabella invokes the seductress Circe, one of Odysseus' lethal adversaries who in the early modern period is held up as a source of forgetting oneself; her interactions with men are figures of an 'emotional contagion' that affects their powers of recollection, a major prop of selfhood in early modern culture. Williams' analysis thus complements Helfer's examination of the Trojan mythos underpinning the affective power of love on Shakespeare's mnemonic poetics.

The chapters in Part II are connected by a shared focus on the ethical challenges posed by the politics of memory. Together they explore how language and literary form can both express and contain painful memories. They confirm that limits placed on what can be said led to innovative uses of conventions in genres as diverse as hagiography, complaint, and jestbooks. Moreover, the chapters in this part demonstrate how the suppression of an individual's affective memories is often linked to political power structures: the twinned energies of memory and emotion were charged with political meaning in an England that ceaselessly reread, and remade, its past. The authors of the first two chapters in this grouping further the conversation around the study of memory and emotion in the early modern period by unmooring trauma from a purely individual, psychoanalytic context. They also explore ways in which trauma puts pressure on form and language. Part II opens with Devori Kimbro's chapter on Foxe's *Acts and Monuments*. Turning hagiographical tradition into a traumatic historiography, Foxe paradoxically but nevertheless effectively draws on a decidedly Catholic form in order to construct a traumatic origin narrative that serves as a rallying point for Protestant resolve and communal identity. The presentation of accurate historical information is here secondary to a desire to remember affectively and remember selectively in order to create a lasting impact. Traumatic historiography memorializes the mutual grieving of individuals *and* the nation in the wake of tragedy or near-tragedy. A similar dynamic informs William Kerwin's chapter, although he sees a stronger tension at work between national memory and individual trauma, one that troubles the state's memorial apparatus. In a mid-Tudor collection of complaint poetry, George Cavendish's *Metrical Visions*, affect and memory are intertwined in what Kerwin terms "the imagined testimonies of trauma victims, speaking from the grave."[60] Modeled on older narratives of confession and penance, complaint offers a poetic tradition for articulating memories of loss, shame, guilt, and fear, which are here filtered through a recorder and an author-figure. The structure of complaint both replicates and overcomes the strictures of memory-oppression under censorship in the Protestant nation. Giving us memories entangled with both individual and collective experiences of ruin and its repercussions, complaint poetry can take on different affective and political functions, ranging from release and consolation to curse and political critique. In the final chapter in this part, Indira Ghose explores the interaction between memory and the affect of pleasure in the early modern culture of jesting. In our own time, the political force of jokes has become glaringly apparent. Did jokes have a similar dimension in the Renaissance? Ghose helps us answer that question by exploring ways in which the genre of the Renaissance jestbook tapped into the collective memory of pre-Reformation festive culture. Jestbooks, Ghose observes, were frequently "marketed as vehicles of nostalgia"[61] for an illusory "Merry England" of supposed unity and amity. She emphasizes the power of jestbooks not to divide further a people whose collective memory was fractured by the Reformation but to transpose antagonism into a shared and pleasurable competition. Jests, with their sometimes anarchic spirit and energy, become advocates of civility in Ghose's thoughtful and attentive reading.

The chapters in Part III consider the relation of memory and affect to time and space, respectively. Drawing on recent affect theory, Johannes Schlegel discusses the workings of affect on temporality in *Hamlet* and *Othello*: guilt and melancholy, jealousy and disgust dilate time, just as they tend to twist the remembrance of the object eliciting these emotions. His chapter examines disgust as the affective response to the conflicting and paradoxical temporalities of the two tragedies, enacted through the plays' fundamental dramatic conflicts. Katharine A. Craik's discussion of the "London plot" of Yarington's *Two Lamentable Tragedies* examines onstage acts of memorialization that add up to a portrait of emotional life in the early modern city. Oddly, this affective cityscape is characterized by an emotional indifference, a detachment from one's affective responses that signals disordered personhood. Instead, emotions are projected onto the city, which emerges as a prosthetic version of the self. In particular, the River Thames figures as a site of local memory-making and as a model for a 'fluid memory' that acknowledges the transformative forces of both remembering and forgetting. The river's mnemonic ambivalence is invoked in the plot about Beech's murder, as the emotional catharsis the murderers experience is constantly undercut by traces of the crime washed up by London's waterways. The affective temporality of nostalgia occupies the center of Daniel Normandin's chapter on *Cymbeline*. He reads the memory of ancient British settlement as an uncomfortable topical engagement with early seventeenth-century colonial expansion. Remembering Britain's past offers a point of affective identification with indigenous peoples that sits in uneasy tension with the future promise of imperial greatness. Mapping ancient Britain onto Jacobean colonies like Virginia, nostalgia weds memory and emotion in not just a temporal but also a spatial dimension.

Part IV considers the ways in which stagecraft produces particular configurations of memory and affect. William Engel's chapter discusses the uses of emotion for mnemonic dramaturgy: affect-laden allusions and mnemotechnical cues in the playworld evoke an experiential world outside the play. Engel examines how certain moments in *Henry V* particularly invite audiences to imaginatively recreate a memory – be it based on historical events or on collective memory encapsulated in proverbial sayings – to come up with a plausible "backstory" that informs the affective actions and behavioral patterns of a character enacted on stage. He coins the intriguing phrase "tug of memory"[62] to describe the way in which plays guide audiences' memories and thereby their affective responses. History plays are a particularly productive genre for this approach, due to their characteristic temporality that encourages analogies between memories of the past and their emotional as well as topical and political significance for the present. That this topicality always already constitutes a selective memory is demonstrated by the next chapter. Rory Loughnane's contribution explores the tensions between historical narrative and a mythology of dynastic contestation that is highlighted through emotionally affective dramaturgy: in this case, the dramatic rendering of Duke Humphrey's death in two different versions (the quarto of *The First Part of the Contention* and the folio of *2 Henry VI*). By doing so, Loughnane persuasively demonstrates the importance of textual scholarship to the interpretation of memory and affect in early modern drama. The subsequent chapter, by Evelyn Tribble, continues the consideration of "backstories" and alternative dramatic narratives by examining the affect-laden recollection and return of characters from the second tetralogy in *Merry Wives of Windsor*, most notably the figure of Falstaff. Working with the concept of the multiverse as a "set of mutually incompatible story-worlds,"[63] Tribble argues that the generic shift to comedy amounts to a deliberate amnesia, a desire to forget the painfully violent (back)stories of the history plays, which are nevertheless kept in the audience's mind through recurring moments of recollection within the play. Lived and remembered affective experience becomes a source of resistance in the final chapter on the entanglements of pain, love, and memory in *Macbeth*. Focusing on the figure of Macduff, Lina Perkins Wilder traces the silences and "linguistic loops" generated by trauma. This phenomenon has received attention in the field of affect studies, on which Wilder draws to explain how Shakespeare's play carves out a space of individual affective-memorial responses to traumatic loss that cannot be subsumed under narratives of national healing, one of the aims of Foxe's *Acts and Monuments*. As Macduff's individual grief calls the play's narrative conclusion into question, affect in combination with memory wins out over politics, if only momentarily.

In the Coda to the volume, Peter Holland traces both the trauma of individual victims, whose voices Cavendish and Shakespeare allow to be heard, and the broader cultural trauma of the martyrology that Foxe so extensively charts. Its focus, however, is not on the standoff between affect and politics, but rather on how forgiveness and forgetting act as negotiations with the trauma detailed in plays like *The Winter's Tale*. Starting from the insight that forgiveness and forgetting share linguistic roots that have made them proverbial twins, the chapter revisits occurrences of the phrase "forgive and forget" in a range of Shakespeare plays to consider how it intersects with structures of political power. Like Wilder, Holland draws on trauma studies rooted in contemporary scenarios of oppressive political regimes, contributing in turn a historicized critical perspective onto the conjunction of remembrance and trauma.

Readers will no doubt already have noticed that in spite of several chapters on nondramatic texts, drama is particularly well represented in our collection. This, we believe, is a sign of the degree to which the composition of plays and their performance grant a centrality and prominence to questions of both memory and affect. Our contributors have seized upon the particularly rich opportunities afforded by drama for studying the interplay of memory and affect. Might drama have a special relationship to the dialectic of remembering and forgetting, one that makes it particularly hospitable to the critical analysis of memory and affect? Czech novelist Milan Kundera reflects on the difference that genre makes to this dialectic: "each art has a different relation to forgetting." Contrasting lyric poetry with the novel, he observes that lyric poetry's relation to memory is "privileged": "A person reading a Baudelaire sonnet cannot skip a single word." Indeed, a reader who falls in love with the sonnet may "read it several times and perhaps aloud" and even "learn it by heart." Lyric poetry is a virtual "fortress of memory." By contrast, the novel is a "poorly fortified castle."[64] Often read over the period of a week or more, a novel contains thousands of details that are already erased by the time reading is complete: "Someday, years later, I will start to talk about this novel to a friend, and we will find that our memories have retained only a few shreds of the text and have reconstructed very different books for each of us."[65]

Although Kundera refers only to the polarized examples of lyric poetry and the novel, and not to drama, we might observe that in terms of remembering and forgetting a play occupies an intermediate position. Experienced over a stretch of two or three hours and lacking the mountainous details that test the memory of the reader of novels, a play offers many more opportunities for forgetting than a lyric poem, but far fewer than a novel. A play is even more hospitable than the novel to those aspects of composition that counteract forgetting: "the echoes of phrases already pronounced, themes already set out," which "will multiply and, brought together into chords, ... will resonate from all sides."[66] In addition, live performance, with its engagement of so many of a spectator's senses, makes an enormous difference to the retention of the details of a play. Visible, tangible elements such as stage properties, especially because they were relatively few on uncluttered early modern stages, as well as costumes bore the potential to serve as powerful aids to memory. In drama, therefore, the forces of remembering and forgetting are somewhat equalized, more comparable and competitive than they are in either the fortress of memory that is lyric poetry or the poorly fortified castle that is the novel: one reason, perhaps, that both remembering and forgetting are regularly cast in such dynamic, variable, and contested roles in early modern plays. Live performance boosts affective responses as well as memory.[67] The collective experience of theatergoing, which allows responses to spread contagiously through an audience, as well as the bodied presence of actors and the use of music and sound effects, also give theater certain advantages in both the conveyance of emotions and the work of recollection. For all these reasons, drama strikes us as particularly hospitable to the analysis of memory and affect and their interactions.

Our contributors consider a broad but certainly not comprehensive range of affects and states of emotion that impact on individual and collective memory and notions of selfhood. Affects not given prolonged attention in this volume include frustration, boredom, aggression, anger,[68] compassion,[69] admiration, happiness, pleasure, amazement, bafflement, disapproval, anticipation, disappointment, and shame. But exhaustiveness has not been our aim. Rather, through this collection we hope to open new pathways and help foster further dialogue between the study of memory and affect in the literature and culture of the early modern period.

Notes

1 Charles Fernyhough, *Pieces of Light: How the New Science of Memory Illuminates the Stories We Tell about Our Pasts* (New York: HarperCollins, 2013), 176.
2 For example, the Memory Studies Association (www.memorystudiesassociation.org/), the International Conference on Memory Studies series, or the journal *Memory Studies* (since 2008); the Society for the Study of Affect (https://affectsociety.com/), the Conference of the International Society for Research on Emotion (www.isre.org/), and *Capacious: Journal for Emerging Affect Inquiry* (https://capaciousjournal.com/) as well as *Emotions: History, Culture, and Society* (https://societyhistoryemotions.com/journal/), the latter two established in 2017.
3 Fourth "Memory, Affects and Emotions" International Interdisciplinary Conference Online; https://call-for-papers.sas.upenn.edu/cfp/2022/02/03/4th-memory-affects-and-emotions-international-interdisciplinary-conference-online.
4 Harriet Phillips, *Nostalgia in Print and Performance, 1510–1613: Merry Worlds* (Cambridge University Press, 2019), 16.
5 Mary Carruthers, *The Book of Memory: A Study of Memory in Medieval Culture*, Cambridge Studies in Medieval Literature 70 (Cambridge University Press, 1990), 60.
6 *Aristotle on Memory*, ed. and trans. Richard Sorabji (Providence, RI: Brown University Press, 1971), 1.
7 Carruthers, *Book of Memory*, 68, 122.
8 Mary Carruthers, *The Craft of Thought: Meditation, Rhetoric, and the Making of Images, 400–1200*, Cambridge Studies in Medieval Literature 34 (Cambridge University Press, 1998), 14.
9 Mary Carruthers and Jan M. Ziolkowski, "General Introduction," in *The Medieval Craft of Memory: An Anthology of Texts and Pictures* (Philadelphia: University of Pennsylvania Press, 2002), 8. See also Janet Coleman, *Ancient*

and Medieval Memories: Studies in the Reconstruction of the Past (Cambridge University Press, 2010).
10 Carruthers, *Craft of Thought*, 14.
11 Carruthers and Ziolkowski, "General Introduction," 8.
12 Carruthers, *Craft of Thought*, 15.
13 Corinne Saunders and Charles Fernyhough, "The Medieval Mind," *The Psychologist: Journal of the British Psychological Association*, 29.11 (November 2016), 881. Citing a news article on recent developments in neuropsychology, Carruthers also observes, "This link of strong memory to emotion is, interestingly enough, also emphasized by at least some contemporary observation" (*Craft of Thought*, 14). On similarities between medieval *memoria* and modern neuroscience, see Fernyhough, *Pieces of Light*, 123.
14 Carruthers and Ziolkowski, "General Introduction," 8.
15 Saunders and Fernyhough, "The Medieval Mind," 881.
16 Lauren Berlant and Jordan Greenwald, "Affect in the End Times: A Conversation with Lauren Berlant," *Qui Parle*, 20 (2012), 71–89. See Ruth Leys, "The Turn to Affect: A Critique," *Critical Inquiry*, 37 (2011), 434–72, for an extended discussion of "why many of the new affect theorists make a distinction between affect and emotion and why I think the distinction cannot be sustained" (434, n. 2).
17 Garrett A. Sullivan, Jr., for instance, argues in *Memory and Forgetting in English Renaissance Drama: Shakespeare, Marlowe, Webster* (Cambridge University Press, 2005) that memory and forgetting were "central to the dramatic depiction of subjectivity" (2), while the volume of essays edited by Brian Cummings and Freya Sierhuis, *Passions and Subjectivity in Early Modern Culture* (Farnham: Ashgate, 2013), explores the "connections between embodiment, selfhood and the passions" (6).
18 Brian Massumi, "The Autonomy of Affect," *Cultural Critique*, 31 (1995), special issue on "The Politics of Systems and Environments," 83–109. That same year saw the publication of Joseph M. Jones' *Affects as Process: An Inquiry into the Centrality of Affect in Psychological Life*, vol. 14 in the Psychoanalytic Inquiry Book Series (Hillsdale, NJ: Analytic Press, 1995). Jones argues that Freud marginalized the constitutive role of affects in early childhood development through his emphasis on "primary process." *Freud and the Passions*, ed. John O'Neil (University Park: Pennsylvania State University Press, 1996), is an intriguing collection of essays on the role affect plays in Freudian psychoanalysis. For a study disputing the perception that Lacan neglected the study of affect in his work, see Colette Soler, *Lacanian Affects: The Function of Affect in Lacan's Work*, trans. Bruce Fink (London: Routledge, 2016).
19 Leys, "The Turn to Affect," 436.
20 Patricia Ticineto Clough and Jean Halley, eds., *The Affective Turn: Theorizing the Social* (Durham, NC: Duke University Press, 2007), 1.
21 Michael Hardt, "Foreword: What Affects Are Good For," in ibid., ix.

22 Alison Landsberg, *Prosthetic Memory: The Transformation of American Remembrance in the Age of Mass Culture* (New York: Columbia University Press, 2004), 18–19.
23 See, for example, Jan Assmann, *Cultural Memory and Early Civilization: Writing, Remembrance, and Political Imagination* (Cambridge University Press, 2011); and Aleida Assmann, *Cultural Memory and Western Civilization: Functions, Media, Archives* (Cambridge University Press, 2011).
24 Whereas memory studies all too frequently neglect questions of affect, work on the emotions in early modern studies has had comparatively little to say on the subject of memory, from Gail Kern Paster's seminal study *Humoring the Body: Emotions and the Shakespearean Stage* (University of Chicago Press, 2004) and the collection she coedited with Katherine Rowe and Mary Floyd-Wilson, *Reading the Early Modern Passions: Essays in the Cultural History of Emotion* (Philadelphia: University of Pennsylvania Press, 2004), to recent collections like Katharine A. Craik and Tanya Pollard's *Shakespearean Sensations: Experiencing Literature in Early Modern England* (Cambridge University Press, 2013) and Richard Meek and Erin Sullivan's *The Renaissance of Emotion: Understanding Affect in Shakespeare and His Contemporaries* (Manchester: Manchester University Press, 2015).
25 Recent collections of essays reflecting the influence of the "affective turn" on early modern studies include Ronda Arab, Michelle Dowd, and Adam Zucker, eds., *Historical Affects and the Early Modern Theater* (London: Routledge, 2015); Katharine A. Craik, ed., *Shakespeare and Emotion* (Cambridge University Press, 2020); and Carol Mejia LaPerle, ed., *Race and Affect in Early Modern English Literature* (Tempe, AZ: ACMRS Press, 2022). Monographs include Matthew Steggle, *Laughing and Weeping in Early Modern Theatres* (Aldershot: Ashgate, 2007); Jennifer C. Vaught, *Masculinity and Emotion in Early Modern English Literature* (London: Routledge, 2008); David Wood, *Time, Narrative and Emotion in Early Modern England* (Farnham: Ashgate, 2009); Allison P. Hobgood, *Passionate Playgoing in Early Modern England* (Cambridge University Press, 2014); Bridget Escolme, *Emotional Excess on the Shakespearean Stage: Passion's Slaves* (London: Bloomsbury, 2014); and Erin Sullivan, *Beyond Melancholy: Sadness and Selfhood in Renaissance England* (Oxford University Press, 2016). Relevant collections of essays on early modern Europe include Susan Broomhall, ed., *Gender and Emotions in Early Modern Europe: Destroying Order, Structuring Disorder* (Farnham: Ashgate, 2015); Susan Broomhall and Sarah Finn, eds., *Violence and Emotion in Early Modern Europe* (Abingdon: Routledge, 2016); Barbara Rosenwein, *Generations of Feeling: A History of Emotions, 600–1700* (Cambridge University Press, 2016); and Susan Broomhall, ed., *Early Modern Emotions: An Introduction* (London: Routledge, 2017).
26 Alexandra Walsham, *Church Papists: Catholicism, Conformity and Confessional Polemic in Early Modern England* (London: Royal Historical Society Studies in History, 1993); Alison Shell, *Oral Culture and Catholicism in Early Modern*

England (Cambridge University Press, 2007) and *Catholicism, Controversy and the English Literary Imagination, 1558–1660* (Cambridge University Press, 1999); Gillian Wood, *Shakespeare's Unreformed Fictions* (Oxford University Press, 2013); and Phillips, *Nostalgia in Print and Performance*.

27 The literature on memory in the early modern period is vast and growing. Useful places to start are the anthology *The Memory Arts in Early Modern England: A Critical Anthology*, ed. William E. Engel, Rory Loughnane, and Grant Williams (Cambridge University Press, 2016), and the collection *The Routledge Handbook of Shakespeare and Memory*, ed. Andrew Hiscock and Lina Perkins Wilder (London: Routledge, 2016). For a thoughtful investigation of "crucial differences and commonalities between memory studies and early modern studies," see Kate Chedgzoy, Elspeth Graham, Katharine Hodgkin, and Ramona Wray, "Researching Memory in Early Modern Studies," *Memory Studies*, 11 (2018), 5–20; this citation, 5.

28 Examples of this general trend include Evelyn Tribble and Nicholas Keene's *Cognitive Ecologies and the History of Remembering: Religion, Education and Memory in Early Modern England* (London: Palgrave Macmillan, 2011) and Anita Gilman Sherman, *Skepticism in Early Modern English Literature: The Problems and Pleasures of Doubt* (Cambridge University Press, 2021).

29 Pierre Nora, "Between Memory and History: *Les lieux de memoire*," trans. Marc Roudebush, in Genevieve Fabre and Robert O'Meally, eds., *History and Memory in African-American Culture* (Oxford University Press, 1994), 285.

30 Landsberg, *Prosthetic Memory*, 19.

31 See the introduction to Cummings and Sierhuis' *Passions and Subjectivity* (1–5), which traces the intellectual history of the passions in relation to cognition: while early modern thought in the tradition of Platonic philosophy viewed the emotions with a good deal of suspicion, neo-Stoic philosophers and Christian writers built on the Aristotelian legacy that places the passions at the center of self-knowledge and moral decision-making, of subjectivity and sociability. In these accounts, the emotions are not separate from cognition (reason, thinking, persuasion) but linked to it since both were thought of as embodied, if to different degrees.

32 John Willis, *Mnemonica; or, The Art of Memory* (1618; Engl. 1621), 141.

33 Qtd. in Evelyn Tribble, "Memory in the Early Modern Context: Practices and Theories," in D. Jalobeanu and C. T. Wolfe, eds., *Encyclopedia of Early Modern Philosophy and the Sciences* (Cham: Springer, 2021), n.p. https://doi.org/10.1007/978-3-319-20791-9_601-1.

34 The metaphor was already in use in Ancient Greece and influenced Aristotle's and Plato's discussions of memory and recollection: see Peter Agócs, "Speaking in the Wax Tablets of Memory," in Luca Castagnioli and Paola Ceccarelli, eds., *Greek Memories: Theories and Practices* (Cambridge University Press, 2019), 68–90.

35 Benedict S. Robinson, "Thinking Feeling," in Amanda Bailey and Mario DiGangi, eds., *Affect Theory and Early Modern Texts* (New York: Palgrave, 2017), 109–127, here 112.

36 Thomas Wright, *The Passions of the Minde in Generall*, ed. Thomas O. Sloan (1604; repr., Urbana: University of Illinois Press, 1971), 45.
37 See Kirk Essary, "The Renaissance of *affectus*? Biblical Humanism and Latin Style," in Juanita Feros Ruys, Michael W. Champion, and Kirk Essary, eds., *Before Emotions: The Language of Feeling 400–1800* (New York: Routledge, 2019).
38 Robinson, "Thinking Feeling," 111.
39 For example, Thomas Heywood writes in *The Apology for Actors* (1612) that "so bewitching a thing is lively and well spirited action, that it hath power to new mold the hearts of the spectators and fashion them to the shape of any noble and notable attempt"; in Brian Vickers, ed., *English Renaissance Literary Criticism* (Oxford: Clarendon Press, 1999), 474–501, citation 487.
40 Paster, *Humoring the Body*, 9, 12, and 18.
41 Ibid., 4.
42 We refer here to the terms that have become established around the concept of distributed cognition: that cognition is embodied (shaped by bodily forms, movements, states, and processes), embedded (influenced by the extra-bodily environment), extended (beyond the body to objects and other people), and enactive (brought forth through continuous reciprocal interactions between an organism and its environment). Miranda Anderson, "Distributed Cognition in the Early Modern Era," in Jalobeanu and Wolfe, eds., *Encyclopedia of Early Modern Philosophy and the Sciences*.
43 Cummings and Sierhuis, *Passions and Subjectivity*, 7.
44 Anderson, "Distributed Cognition," n.p.
45 Ibid.
46 Ibid.
47 Evelyn Tribble, *Cognition in the Globe: Attention and Memory in Shakespeare's Theatre* (New York: Palgrave, 2011).
48 Sophie Duncan, *Shakespeare's Props: Memory and Cognition* (London: Routledge, 2019), 24.
49 Chedgzoy et al., "Researching Memory in Early Modern Studies," 7.
50 Amanda Bailey and Mario DiGangi, "Introduction," in Bailey and DiGangi, eds., *Affect Theory and Early Modern Texts*, citation 10.
51 Ibid., 13.
52 Ann Rosalind Jones and Peter Stallybrass, *Renaissance Clothing and the Materials of Memory* (Cambridge University Press, 2000); Alexandra Walsham, *The Reformation of the Landscape: Religion, Identity and Memory in Early Modern Britain and Ireland* (Oxford University Press, 2011); Patricia Phillippy, *Shaping Remembrance from Shakespeare to Milton* (Cambridge University Press, 2018).
53 Chedgzoy et al., "Researching Memory," 13.
54 Garrett A. Sullivan, Jr., *Memory and Forgetting in English Renaissance Drama: Shakespeare, Marlowe, Webster* (Cambridge University Press, 2005), 7, 11.
55 A good starting point is Kristine Johanson's introduction to the special issue of *Parergon* edited by her: "On the Possibility of Early Modern Nostalgias," *Parergon*, 33.2 (2016), 1–15.

56 Bailey and DiGangi, *Affect Theory and Early Modern Texts*, 5–6.
57 Patricia Cahill, "The Feel of the Slaughterhouse: Affective Temporalities and Marlowe's *The Massacre at Paris*," in Bailey and DiGangi, eds., *Affect Theory and Early Modern Texts*, 157.
58 On negative and positive affects, and the necessity of countering traumatizing experiences that might induce fear, hatred, shame, and grief with reparative attitudes of hope, pleasure, community, and (self-)care, see Eve K. Sedgwick, "Paranoid and Reparative Reading, or, You're So Paranoid You Probably Think This Essay Is about You," in Sedgwick, ed., *Touching Feeling: Affect, Pedagogy, Performativity* (Durham, NC: Duke University Press, 2003), 123–51.
59 The quote is from Helfer's chapter, page 31 in this volume.
60 See page 107 in this volume.
61 See page 133 in this volume.
62 See pages 202 and following in this volume.
63 See pages 238 and 244 in this volume.
64 Milan Kundera, *The Curtain: An Essay in Seven Parts*, trans. Linda Asher (New York: HarperCollins, 2007), 149.
65 Ibid., 150.
66 Ibid., 150.
67 See Allison P. Hobgood, *Passionate Playgoing in Early Modern England* (Cambridge University Press, 2014); Katharine A. Craik and Tanya Pollard, *Shakespearean Sensations: Experiencing Literature in Early Modern England* (Cambridge University Press, 2013).
68 See Karl A. E. Enenkel and Anita Traninger, eds., *Discourses of Anger in the Early Modern Period* (Leiden: Brill, 2015).
69 See Steve Mentz, "Is Compassion an Oceanic Feeling?," *Emotions: History, Culture, Society*, 4.1 (2020), 109–27.

PART I

Ars memoriae, ars amatoria

CHAPTER 1

Allegories of Love
Affect and the Art of Memory in Shakespeare's Sonnets

Rebeca Helfer

In Sonnet 122, Shakespeare's poetic persona "Will" promises to remember his beloved, the beautiful young man usually referred to as the "fair youth," in paradoxical, even perverse fashion – that is, by denying the memorializing power of his own love poetry:

> Thy gift, thy tables, are within my brain
> Full charactered with lasting memory,
> Which shall above that idle rank remain
> Beyond all date, even to eternity;
> Or, at the least, so long as brain and heart
> Have faculty by nature to subsist,
> Till each to razed oblivion yield his part
> Of thee, thy record never can be missed.
> That poor retention could not so much hold,
> Nor need I tallies thy dear love to score;
> Therefore to give them from me was I bold,
> To trust those tables that receive thee more:
>   To keep an adjunct to remember thee
>   Were to import forgetfulness in me.

The speaker recalls the classical boast that monuments of writing, unlike those of marble, never fall to ruin and so offer "lasting memory," but with the intent of upending it. Replacing outer writing with inner writing, this book with his body, the speaker makes himself into the place of "lasting memory" that writing only pretends to be, constructing himself as a memorial to love. To make this case, the speaker evokes the art of memory through its most common mnemonic metaphors, books and buildings, and in ways that make the speaker sound remarkably like Hamlet: just as Hamlet promises to "remember" his father by wiping the "table of my memory" so that his father's command will be in "the book and volume of my brain, / Unmixed with baser matter" (1.5.103–4), so the speaker of Sonnet 122 writes upon the "tables ... within [his] brain" and "heart," constructing himself as a living memory theater that merges the architectural and scribal as metaphoric storage spaces for memory.[1] Nevertheless, "Will" also indirectly acknowledges that his mnemonic structure is only human, and thus also time-bound and destined to decay, along with the memory of his beloved and the poetic memorial fashioned for him. The immortality of poetry topos thus collapses twofold, as both internal and external locations for memory are subject to inexorable ruin – inevitably reduced to "razed oblivion" – despite the obvious irony that Shakespeare's speaker makes this claim in writing and as poetry.

Shakespeare treats the relationship between affect and the art of memory in Sonnet 122, as throughout the *Sonnets*, in far more significant ways than these mnemonic metaphors might suggest. With Sonnet 122, the speaker presents a palinode, a "taking back poem" in action, which symbolically retracts the very poem before its readers and indeed, it seems, this poetry writ large. It is also a palinode to another poet's palinode, I will argue, one which Shakespeare remembers and rewrites, and which is central to his poetics of memory. The speaker's rejection of writing as an "adjunct" that will "import forgetfulness" recalls the cautionary tale that Socrates gives to another "fair youth" in Plato's *Phaedrus*: the story of the Egyptian king Theuth, who rejects the "gift" of writing from the god Thoth, precisely as a deceptive aid-to-memory that would "import forgetfulness" by creating a dependence on external rather than internal remembrance, on artificial rather than natural memory, from which Socrates concludes that writing is nothing more than a mere "reminder."[2] Crucially, this story about remembering and forgetting caps Socrates' "palinode" to the God of Love, which he performs as though a poet remembering another poet's palinode to love: a story about how love, like writing, can serve as a crucial "reminder" because of its power to lead the fallen, forgetful soul from ruin to recollection, repair, and even rebirth, from *anamnesia* to *anamnesis*. The tale of Theuth thus serves as an ironic reminder of the importance of reminders in Socrates' palinode, an allegory of love that doubles as a teaching tale for philosophy as a love of wisdom. With this tale, moreover, Plato underscores the clear irony that he memorializes Socrates' teachings in writing despite his apparent rejection of it, both as a love story and as an art of memory. Plato's allegory of love in the *Phaedrus*, as in the *Symposium*, remakes mnemonic poetics for philosophy in ways that profoundly influence the Platonic sonnet tradition and shape Shakespeare's *Sonnets*.

This essay explores the relationship between affect and the art of memory, the psychological and physiological responses at the heart of such personal and poetic remembrance, written into Shakespeare's *Sonnets* as Platonic and anti-Platonic allegories of love and poetry.[3] The art of memory – a colloquial term for an art which goes by many names, including artificial memory, mnemonics, and locational or spatial memory systems – is more than a rhetorical method of memorization or aid-to-memory, as it has been understood historically. Rather, the art of memory represents first and foremost a poetics whose principles derive from epic poetry and performance, and whose affective power – the emotional force which makes it memorable, which moves and marks the mind, body, and soul – is drawn from memories of love, paradigmatically, and stories about it. The *ars memorativa* meets the *ars amatoria* in Shakespeare's *Sonnets*, as throughout the poetic tradition explored here, represented in metapoetic fashion: as an allegory of love that returns to ancient poetics by rewriting the origin story of the art of memory, the tale of the ancient Greek poet Simonides, who discovers the art of memory when he memorially reconstructs an edifice from its ruins. More than marking the decline and fall of the immortality of poetry topos, Sonnet 122 repudiates and in effect 'ruins' the ideal of Platonic love and poetry which has governed the *Sonnets* from the start, and which Shakespeare represents as an allegory of love: the speaker's doomed desire for the rebirth of antiquity in his poetry, and the early modern poetics that emerge from the failure of this fantasy. The personal is poetic, the speaker's "passions" partially veiling Shakespeare's allegory of love as an art of poetry and an art of memory.

*   *   *

What is the art of memory?[4] This colloquial term is usually understood as meaning an "art" in the technical sense – a technique or teachable method – in the context of ancient Greek and Roman rhetoric and pedagogy, as a strategy by which orators could memorize speeches. The mnemonic method is fairly simple: orators would construct a mental structure – either real or imagined, most often as a building or book – and then furnish and fill this space with images designed to spark and spur recollection. The orator would mentally traverse these spaces, 'walk through' or 'read from' them during the course of delivery, the places creating an order for topics and the images prompting the remembrance of them. And the more striking the images, the more memorable. As classical sources on the art of memory attest, this art depends upon the affective response that these mental images produce: upon the clear causal relationship between being 'moved' by emotion and its effects on memory.[5]

Yet this mnemonic method associated with rhetoric has a more complicated relationship to poetics, to literary theory and practice. Philip Sidney suggests as much in his sixteenth-century *Apology for Poetry*: "Even they that have taught the art of memory have showed nothing so apt for it as a certain room divided into many places," he asserts, which describes "verse in effect perfectly, every word having his natural seat, which seat must needs make the words remembered."[6] Scholars have long recognized the place of the *ars memorativa* in representational art: the use of the mnemonic places and images to construct a literary work as a memorial structure, a poetic monument of sorts, which houses complex and vivid images – often densely allegorical and symbolic, violent and erotic – designed to be memorable by producing a powerful affective response. We remember best through provocations to the imagination – and, of course, few things are more memorable than love and stories about it.

In contrast to most historical accounts of mnemonics, I want to approach the art of memory less as a rhetorical method used to construct a literary monument than as a poetics of ruin and recollection, less a product than a process of art.[7] The art of memory bears an intimate relationship to the art of poetry from the start, as the origin story of the art of memory suggests: the tale of the ancient Greek poet Simonides. As the story goes, Simonides discovered the importance of place to memory when he narrowly escaped being crushed to death in the collapse of a banquet hall in which he had just delivered a poem. When everyone there was "buried in the ruins" and their bodies crushed beyond recognition, Simonides alone was able to identify the deceased "from his recollection of the place in which each had sat, to have given satisfactory directions for their interment."[8] The dramatic and traumatic nature of this tale – depicting recollection born from ruin, rebirth from death – lends it its affective power: makes it unforgettable. Simonides memorially reconstructs the ruined banquet hall and the dead therein, a tale from which the rules of the art of memory derive: the construction of places by which to remember topics, the 'heads' of subjects linked to the heads of the dead. The story of Simonides demonstrates and indeed dramatizes the very method it teaches, the architectural mnemonic, and it points to a central pun of the *ars memorativa* tradition: "edify" and "edifice" are linked in rhetorical education. But this is also a poetry lesson, I would argue. The tale of Simonides joins the art of memory to the art of poetry not simply because the origin story involves a famous poet, but because the story itself dramatizes the poetic principles – the creation of vivid, evocative images and places with which to frame them – upon which the art of memory is built. Simonides is credited with formulating the idea that "painting is silent poetry, poetry a speaking picture," and thus drawing a relationship between the visual and the verbal; conceptually, this is at the heart of the art of memory as, metaphorically, internal writing or drawing that leaves its mark both psychologically and physiologically.[9] The tale of Simonides introduces a lesson in the art of memory in Cicero's *De oratore*, a dialogue on the art of rhetoric which explicitly reenacts and rewrites Plato's *Phaedrus*. Cicero gestures to his complex emulation of Plato by introducing the tale of Simonides with another tale, an ironic version and inversion of Socrates' tale of Theuth: a story of the ancient Greek general Themistocles, who rejects being taught the art of memory because he longs for an "art of forgetting." However, the art of memory ultimately has a far greater role to play in *De oratore*, which Cicero dramatizes by reenacting the tale of Simonides as the frame tale for his dialogue. Albeit indirectly, Cicero plays the part of a poet, that of a new Simonides, by recollecting the "ruins" of Rome and the death of the speakers as a "memorial to posterity," and explicitly in imitation of "the dialogues of Plato, in ... which the character of Socrates is represented" (III.ii, iv). By treating the art of memory as a poetics, the means by which he constructs a literary memorial that remembers the ruins of the past, Cicero implicitly reveals the art of memory's role in Plato's *Phaedrus* and its twin dialogue, *Symposium*.

Simonides is an important subject and subtext throughout Plato's dialogues, and nowhere more clearly than in the *Republic*. Here, Simonides' sense of poetic justice (tellingly introduced by a story about Themistocles) inspires the seminal debate about poetry's place in an ideal Republic about how the passions poetry inflames are at odds with reason and the larger critique of the 'lies' of poets, elements of what Socrates calls the "ancient quarrel between poetry and philosophy."[10] The initial debate about Simonides' poetry leads both to poetry's expulsion from this imagined Republic – itself, of course, a poetic construct – and to poetry's conditional return to this place in a new form: that is, as philosophical allegory, which Socrates dramatizes by telling the tale of the warrior Er's rebirth from the underworld through recollection, his journey from *amnesia* to *anamnesis*. And though Socrates never tells *the* tale of Simonides per se in the *Phaedrus*, he nevertheless writes a version of it with the tale of Theuth, which represents an earlier origin story of artificial memory in writing. Socrates treats the art of memory as an oral art – that of the poet in performance, telling epic tales of ruined cities and ruinous love. Even as he scorns artificial memory, openly mocking "the inventor of ... mnemonic verse," Socrates nevertheless appropriates mnemonic poetics for philosophy as an allegory of love.[11] He remakes artificial memory into a form of natural memory, into an internal mnemonic rather than an external aid-to-memory, thus returning it to its original form. To do so, Socrates tells two competing love stories, of 'wrong' and 'right' love, which also represent the competing disciplines of rhetoric and philosophy. In the process of marking this division, he nevertheless conflates rhetoric with poetics, implying throughout that both fields use the poet's mnemonic method – the art of memory – to tell or perform the same old love stories: tales of love as a destructive, ruinous force, which amount to political and pedagogical allegories about power and remembering the past. Socrates rejects this perspective with a palinode to the God of Love, self-consciously adopting the role of the poet in the process, which 'takes back' this false idea of love, or ideal of false love. Socrates credits the palinode that he claims to remember and reenact to the poet Stesichorus, who retracted his false accusations against Helen of Troy; thus the archetypal story of love's ruinous effects is transformed into one of recollection, one that represents the love of wisdom, philo-sophia. Imagining the soul as a chariot drawn by two horses of desire (one wanton and wild, the other tame and temperate), Socrates describes how the soul "burdened with a load of forgetfulness ... sheds her wings and falls to earth" (248c), but regrows them and re-ascends to the heavens when reminded by love, a transformation that elevates reason over passion, subduing desire through dialectic (249c). Whereas the 'wrong' kind of love leads to love sickness, "perplexed and frenzied," driven by "madness" and desire that leads the soul to "forget ... all" else, the 'right' kind of love, the love of wisdom, leads to the soul's remembrance of things past and the reformation of the soul (251d–e). The "sight" of the beloved spurs the chariot "driver's memory [back] to that form of beauty," and when passion is tamed it results in the "friendship of a lover" (254b). Calling his palinode "perforce poetical, to please Phaedrus," Socrates confesses that he plays the part of a poet, adapting the art of memory as an allegory of love about the love of wisdom (257a). In the context of this role, Socrates contends that no "man [can] come to the gates of poetry without the madness of the Muses" (345a), and that the madness of the lover is that of the poet and, in turn, the philosopher.[12] Such allegory is the means by which Plato justifies poetry's place in society: rather than mere love stories about ruin, his are edifying tales that reform poetics for new, higher purposes, and which represent deeper truths beneath the veil of 'lies.'

The *Symposium* extends this allegory of love as defining the love of wisdom by rewriting the tale of Simonides anew. In this implicit poetry competition dedicated to praising the God of love as something more than a dangerous and deranging force, Socrates tells the story of his education in the philosophy of love, a tall tale which he represents as remembrance. As he recounts it, his teacher Diotima defined love as a "longing for the endless fame," a desire for "immortality" shared by all, from parents and poets to philosophers. Some pursue immortality through procreation and others through poetry, but those "whose procreancy is of the spirit" beget "wisdom": "it is the office of every poet ... to beget them, and of every artist whom we may call creative," which includes Socrates.[13] In this allegory of love, beauty is the reminder which allows the soul to ascend "the heavenly ladder" from the physical to the philosophical in pursuit of immortal memory (211c). This recollected story of the soul connects with that of the *Phaedrus*, partly through direct address to that dialogue's title character: "So you may call this my eulogy of Love, Phaedrus," Socrates concludes (212c). The dialogue ends with the narrator's memory of Socrates arguing that "the tragic poet might be a comedian as well," or a satirist such as himself (223d). Described as a "giant exercise in oral recall," the *Symposium* implicitly reenacts the tale of Simonides through its framing device: a banquet hall, a space of poetry and performance, is imaginatively recreated after the death of Socrates and the other interlocutors, by a person who had learned the story from another.[14] Standing as a symbolic memorial to Socrates, the *Symposium* is a mnemonic space through which Plato plays the part of Simonides, remembering the dead and recollecting the ruins of time.

Albeit indirectly, Plato's treatment of the art of memory *as* art, a poetics transformed for philosophy and rendered as teaching tales about remembering, underlies the allegorical sonnet tradition. To remember and forget Platonic love, and to be divided between the right and wrong kinds of love, is foundational to Dante's and Petrarch's sonnets and the mnemonic poetics they fashion; this is especially clear in their mutual debt to Augustine, who in *Confessions* appropriates the Ciceronian and Platonic art of memory for Christianity, 'converts' it, in effect, for his love story about divinity.[15] Augustine's autobiographical allegory of divine love recounts the reformation of his fallen, forgetful soul as a "house in ruins," which he rebuilds as a house of God.[16] His spiritual conversion turns on mnemonic poetics, his transformation of artificial memory – memory as a "spacious palace, a storehouse for countless images" – into a Platonic allegory of his journey from amnesia to *anamnesis*, the recollection of divine love through 'reminders' in writing, from Socrates to scripture (X.8). In their poetry, Dante and Petrarch grapple with Augustine's dismissal of poetry as representative of the wrong kind of love – famously, he "wept for Dido" while forgetting himself – but also to emulate his reformation of poetics in their own allegories of love (I.13). For both poets, to remember love is to remember Rome from ruins, secular and sacred, as immortalized in the palindrome *roma summus amor*.[17] Their allegories of love – divine and human, personified through Beatrice and Laura – double as allegories of poetry, and their sonnet sequences suggest how the poetry's "pretty rooms" (as Donne describes the stanzas of the sonnet in poem "The Canonization") create a space for reflecting in metapoetic ways about how poetry remembers the past.[18]

Yet Dante and Petrarch remember (and forget) Augustine's allegorical justification for poetry in very different ways. Dante writes an Augustinian "Book of Memory" with the *Vita nuova*, a confessional collection of sonnets and a statement of allegorical poetics made to reconcile the secular with the sacred, the sonnet with the soul and salvation, and which begins the journey of the allegorical Everyman to Paradise in *The Divine Comedy*.[19] By contrast, Petrarch "ruins" what Dante reconciles by imagining poetry as "ruinae": spaces for recollection, but ones which could never reconstruct the past or fully reform the poet's soul.[20] In an ironic turn on the conversion narrative, Petrarch remains divided between times, past and present, and between loves; the love of Laura (and laureate poetry) remains in tension with the love of God, the immortality of the soul with literary immortality. In other words, love leads Petrarch not to remember or reform his soul but rather to "forget" himself.[21] And although Petrarch is usually credited with the temporal creation of the "Renaissance" – as the rebirth of an idealized antiquity through which he sought to illuminate his own dark age – the failure of this fantasy ultimately defines Petrarch's poetry and the afterlife of Petrarchism in the English sonnet.[22] To remember and forget Petrarchan love and by extension Platonic love is also, in Shakespeare's *Sonnets*, a way to remember the art of memory and the art of poetry in new ways.

* * *

Shakespeare puts these mnemonic poetics into practice in the *Sonnets* in metapoetic fashion: he ruins and recollects, reconstructs, and deconstructs the fantasy of classical rebirth associated with the sonnet tradition, using an old method to tell a new love story. The failure to remember, and the pain and pleasure of love associated with forgetting, lies at the heart of Shakespeare's Platonic allegory of love poetry.[23] Returning to Sonnet

122, recall that the speaker symbolically retracts the "gift" of his writing to and about the "fair youth" – ironically, the very poems before the reader and, it seems, the sonnet collection writ large – on the grounds that, as he ruefully concludes, "To keep an adjunct to remember thee / Were to import forgetfulness in me" (122.13–14). Evoking mnemonic metaphors, the speaker asserts that only poetry written in the book and volume of his "brain" and remembered by his "heart" will last until "eternity," a boast he then qualifies by admitting that both book and body ultimately will fall to "razed oblivion" (122.4–7). Shakespeare's poetic persona thus rejects his own writing as an agent of forgetting, which he attempts to forget himself, as though rewriting or reenacting Socrates' tale of Theuth. Yet this rejection of writing as a mere "reminder," as Socrates puts it, acts as an ironic reminder of Socrates' palinode to the God of Love: his 'taking back' poem about how the right kind of love – like writing – can be a reminder, guiding the forgetful soul from ruin to recollection, an allegory of love as *anamnesis*. However, Sonnet 122 instead moves in the opposite direction from the *Phaedrus*: the speaker's "palinode" not only retracts his own poetry; it also retracts Socrates' palinode to love, recuperating the love it repudiates.

Sonnet 122 thus marks the fall of the immortality of poetry topos and the ideal of Platonic love that it has been built upon, which has shaped the *Sonnets* up until this point and defined its poetics of memory. Love has led "Will" not to recollection but to ruin, oblivion, love sickness, madness, the very dangers and derangements described in the *Phaedrus*, which Socrates refutes. With this failure of Platonic love and poetics, Shakespeare ironically draws attention to the allegorical nature of his sonnets as a love story about poetry over time: classical, medieval, renaissance, and, ultimately, something distinctly 'early modern.' The speaker's anachronistic desire for the rebirth of antiquity, and the madness that accompanies his quixotic attempts to realize it, lies at the heart of this allegory of love. The project of the *Sonnets* is partly revealed in Sonnet 122: to rewrite the allegorical love stories of the twin Platonic dialogues, the *Phaedrus* and the *Symposium*, as a new art of memory. This sonnet also highlights the divide between the speaker's "forgetfulness" and Shakespeare's remembrance, the ways in which the poet stands apart from his poetic persona. Sonnet 122 is a crucial pivot point in this sequence, from which I will look in two directions: first back to the ideal of Platonic love and poetry that defines the *Sonnets* up to this point, and then forward to the anti-Platonic love by which Shakespeare reimagines poetics.

The *Sonnets* begins with a version of ideal Platonic love and poetry that verges on satire: the speaker's ardent belief that ideal love *should* lead to recollection and that poetry *should* repair the ruins of the past, immortalizing both love and poetry in a monumental architecture. But he takes Platonic love too literally, indeed to the point of caricature, in his self-conscious reenactment of Plato's dialogues. The "procreation sonnets," addressed to the "fair youth," recall the fair youth of the *Phaedrus*, and the speaker repeats a version of Socrates' story in the *Symposium* about Diotima's love lesson as a "desire for immortality" – a desire to live on in "memory" and for "fame" – usually pursued through procreation or poetry. Misreading Platonic love – as he later admits, "thy great gift, upon misprision growing" (87.11) – "Will" enacts his 'will' as a transaction based upon these two paths to remembrance: he exhorts the "fair youth" to procreate in order to immortalize himself, and in turn promises that he will immortalize the youth's beauty, and his own love, with these sonnets. The speaker sees his poetry as an art of memory in a limited sense, as the creation of a memorial space – a book-as-building – which he furnishes with images of the beloved. As in Socrates' palinode to the God of Love, the image of the beloved's beauty spurs the speaker's recollection, the affective force of love guiding his memorialization of him. The speaker describes this art of memory in pictorial and architectural terms evocative of Simonides' dictum, "painting is silent poetry, poetry a speaking picture." As though himself a "speaking picture," the speaker urges his love to "learn to read what silent love hath writ: / To hear with eyes belongs to love's fine wit" (23.13–14). He portrays himself as a "painter" of his beloved and constructs a gallery for his art of memory, a portrait hall of images painted in his imagination and rendered in writing: "Thy beauty's form in the table of [his] heart," his "body" the "frame wherein 'tis held," his "bosom's shop" where his "true image pictured lies" and "is hanging still" (24.2–3, 5–7).[24] But the speaker's view of the art of memory depends on a clichéd "misprision" that results in him "mistaking" Platonic love, as Shakespeare suggests.

This is Platonic love perforce, as the speaker suppresses and sublimates his passion into poetry, 'wills' it into being, and in ways that recall the central myth of the Petrarchan sonnet: Daphne's transformation into the laurel tree, the crown of poet laureate as compensation for that unrequited love of the past that Petrarch's "Laura" represents. From the very start, the speaker's procrustean efforts to shape his passion and poetry to this ideal, and his failure to do so, exposes the fantasy of Renaissance or rebirth as just that: an impossible dream. The speaker suggests that his homoerotic desire is out of place and time – "the master-mistress of [his] passion" has by "Nature" been "pricked … out for women's pleasure" – and that his love truly belongs to another place and time, that of an idealized antiquity (20.2, 13). Will's divided will (his desire and determination that, for the sake of posterity, the youth must procreate and he must write poetry that will perpetuate his memory) speaks to his anachronistic desire for the past reborn: the Renaissance as a cliché. Yet instead of a backward-looking Petrarchan gaze, the speaker looks to preserve the present for the future. When he considers how all "wear their brave state out of memory," he declares war on Time: "And all in war with Time for love of you," he tells his beloved in Sonnet 15, "As he takes from you I ingraft you new" (15.8, 13–14).[25] This "war with Time for love" is ultimately allegorical: an allegory of poetry and poetics over time, represented as a love story (of a kind) about remembering the past and poetry born from ruin.

The speaker imagines his doomed attempt to defeat "Time," whether through progeny or poetry, through mnemonic metaphors: memory as 'buildings' and 'book.' By not reproducing, the youth is willfully erasing his own memory, "Seeking that beauteous roof to ruinate / Which to repair should be thy chief desire" (10.7–8). The only "defence" of the youth "'gainst Time's scythe" is to "breed" (12.13–14), lest he "lets so fair a house fall to decay, / Which husbandry in honour might uphold / Against the stormy gusts of winter's day / And barren rage of death's eternal cold" (13.9–12). As the speaker describes his own limbs as "Bare ruined choirs, where late the sweet birds sang," he suggests that this desire is directed as much toward himself as his muse (73.4). Grandiose claims to literary immortality find their teetering apex in Sonnet 55, which reiterates Horace's boast that he has built an eternal monument to his beloved's memory. "Not marble nor the gilded monuments / Of princes shall outlive this pow'rful rhyme," or "sluttish time" erase "The living record of your memory," the speaker declares, but then qualifies this promise: his memory "shall still find room / Even in the eyes of all posterity / That wear this world out to the ending doom" (55.1–12). His sonnets' "pretty rooms" stand as a monument built to last the ravages of time, but only until the end of time. Whereas in Sonnet 122 the speaker marks the end of his memory with his own death, here his evocation of end-time creates a jarring juxtaposition between old and new views of time: the temporal framework of pagan antiquity in which time could be imagined as endless, cyclical rather than linear, contrasted with Christian revelation, the time when time itself ends. In Sonnet 64, the speaker poignantly admits that his war to defeat time inevitably will end with his own defeat by time: "When I have seen by Time's fell hand defaced . . . / When sometime lofty towers I see down rased, / . . . Ruin hath taught me thus to ruminate: / That Time will come and take my love away" (64.1–3, 11–12).

However, "Time" is not only the enemy of his Platonic love; it is also his unwilling muse. The failure of the speaker's will to temporal rebirth is figured as personal and poetic betrayal – most notably through the presence of the "rival poet," whose arrival in Sonnet 77 occasions a reframing of the speaker's Platonic bargain. Sonnet 77 (the midpoint of the 1609 edition of the *Sonnets*, as for most modern editions) is a mirror for Sonnet 122, as the speaker retracts his original 'will' through a return to the *Symposium* and Diotima's lesson on love and immortality therein. With a threatening memento mori addressed to the fair youth about "Time's thievish progress to eternity" (77.8), the speaker inverts the initial bargain of the sonnet sequence and tells the beloved to immortalize *himself*:

> Look what thy memory cannot contain
> Commit to these waste blanks, and thou shalt find
> Those children nursed, delivered from thy brain,
> To take a new acquaintance of thy mind.
>   These offices, so oft as thou wilt look,
>   Shall profit thee, and much enrich thy book.
>   (77.9–14)

In effect, the speaker relinquishes his role as memorializing poet, offering a blank book in place of his own poetry. Diotima's lesson in the *Symposium* is recalled here but inverted, such that this "book of memory" is meant to substitute for the youth's own progeny – "Those children nursed, delivered from thy brain" – but one that the speaker seemingly refuses to write. His beloved is now the source of another poet's memory, and this rival poet inspires bitter ruminations on the fair youth's infidelity to the speaker's vision: "my love was my decay" (80.14), he says, and despairs of his now "forgetful Muse" (100.5). The beautiful youth willfully refuses to reproduce himself, and thus in effect forgets himself, as in turn does the speaker-poet. With this acknowledgment that the Platonic bargain of the procreation sonnets has failed, in the poems that separate Sonnet 77 from Sonnet 122 the speaker increasingly reframes his love of the "fair youth" as what Socrates' first poem in the *Phaedrus* calls the 'wrong' kind of love: love as passion rather than reason, forgetting rather than remembrance, ruin rather than repair: "What potions have I drunk of Siren tears . . . / What wretched errors hath my heart committed, . . . / In the distraction of this madding fever!" the speaker says of his "ruined love" (119.1, 5, 8, 11).

This dramatic decline and fall sets the stage for Sonnet 122, and the palinode to Platonic love therein, which deliberately ruins the memorial of the speaker's own poetry and recants his idea of Platonic love. In Sonnet 123, a crucial adjunct to Sonnet 122, Shakespeare uses this recantation in order to reframe what the art of memory means. He creates a new allegory of time that juxtaposes fantasies of poetic permanence with the reality of ruin, suggesting that poetics is a perpetual art, and act, of both forgetting and remembering. Pairing the immortality of poetry topos with the architectural mnemonic, the speaker reimagines monuments of both stone and writing as so many ruins that are continually rebuilt and ruined yet again. "No! Time, thou shalt not boast that I do change," the speaker charges in an apostrophe, "Thy pyramids built up with newer might / To me are nothing novel, nothing strange; / They are but dressings of a former sight" (123.1–4). Denying the novelty of new edifices built upon the ruins of the past, "Will" comes to see his own willful misprision of Platonic love and poetry as an expression of a universal dilemma and delusion wrought by time. "Our dates are brief, and therefore we admire / What thou dost foist upon us that is old, / And rather make them born to our desire / Than think that we before have heard them told," the speaker asserts, while denying this deception: "For thy records, and what we see, doth lie" (123.5–8, 11). With this recognition comes a new vision of poetry: his sonnets cannot be ruined by time because they *are* ruins, and anything built from them has been built before. Poetic monuments, like material ones, are not permanent but perpetual, always fashioned and refashioned from ruin.

Tacitly, the speaker admits that his poetry too is "nothing novel, nothing strange." Indirectly, he addresses the fantasy of rebirth that has driven his poetry – the way that authors and audiences remake "old" things "born to our desire" and believe them to be new – and rejects his former fantasy of "renaissance" itself as the rebirth of an idealized antiquity (123.6–7). That's a "lie," he says, while promising to remain "true" to his love despite time's deceptions (123.11, 14). Sonnet 123 suggests that monuments of both stone and poetry find a form of immortality within ruin itself and the cyclical process of reedification, an architectural metaphor that gestures to the shared etymology of "edify" and "edifice," and which would seem to encapsulate the speaker's poetry lesson. Separating himself from "the fools of Time," as he derisively calls naïve architects in Sonnet 124, the speaker redefines himself against them in Sonnet 125: unlike those who "laid great bases for eternity, / Which proves more short than waste or ruining," he embraces the ruins of time (124.13,

125.3–4). Casting aside former immortal longings, he affirms that no "Renaissance" is ever possible, declaring such rebirth to be fantasy – a seductive fiction to delude or deceive oneself or others.

These poems inaugurate a profound shift in the *Sonnets*: to an anti-Platonic allegory of love that rejects fantasies of Renaissance – the rebirth of antiquity and the love/poetry that it represents – and embraces one that is medieval in form but made thoroughly (early) modern.[26] This new understanding of poetry in ruins is then reapplied to the love allegory through the creation of a new beloved – one who is explicitly imperfect, mutable, and 'ruined' herself. The speaker's own 'middle age' is represented as an allegory of love/poetry, which turns from an idealized homoerotic Platonic love to an anti-Platonic heterosexual desire, driven by irrational passions rather than reason. In this context, the speaker of the *Sonnets* finally and formally introduces himself: "Make but my name thy love, and love that still, / And then thou lovest me for my name is Will" (136.13–14). The speaker and Shakespeare, poet and persona, come together in this name and in this attitude toward love and poetry. This name also matters not only because of its various meanings – desire, determination, the future and its inheritance, and more – but also because of its allegorical significance as the name of a medieval Everyman: the allegorical "Will" of *Piers Ploughman*, who represents the willful sinfulness of mankind in search of salvation. Shakespeare treats this allegorical name irreverently, to say the very least: "I am that I am," the speaker proclaims in a parody of playing God, ironically to affirm that "All men are bad" – himself, above all (121.9, 14).

The so-called dark lady poems that conclude the *Sonnets* represent the medieval sonnet tradition minus the morality, from which emerges a kind of "immorality of poetry" topos. Shakespeare borrows the language of sin and salvation, the ruin and remembrance of the soul, central to the sonnet tradition – "Love is my sin, and thy dear virtue hate, / Hate of my sin, grounded on sinful loving" – but here emptied of sacral significance (142.1–2). Petrarchan paradoxes are used to describe the speaker's divided loves, his "better angel" and "worser spirit," as though in a morality play but without any moralizing meaning – a perversion of the conversion narrative, which in some sense emulates and extends the secular turn in Petrarch's own poetry (144.3–4). The speaker confesses to less-than-Platonic loves, having relinquished the spiritual for the sexual: "Th'expense of spirit in a waste of shame / Is lust in action," desire "Past reason," "Mad in pursuit, and in possession so," "the heaven that leads men to this hell," an anatomical pun on the afterlife (129.1, 7, 9, 14). Yet he remains unrepentant in any religious sense, and his expressions of regret serve only to highlight an ironic irreverence, indeed, a satire of the Catholic sonnet.[27] And though it is perfectly Petrarchan to be torn between two loves that allegorically represent two time periods and perspectives on poetry, Shakespeare turns this trope into a twisted temporal love triangle – "I have confessed that he is thine, / And I myself am mortgaged to thy will, ... / Him have I lost, thou hast both him and me" – which is an allegory of poetics as erotics, copulative in every sense (134.1–2, 13). The speaker's own long 'middle age' subsumes what comes before and after, an allegory of love and poetics over "Time" clearly charged with corrupting the morals of the medieval sonnet sequence.[28] The ardent embrace of the 'wrong' kind of love-as-poetry, driven by passion rather than reason, reaches its apex in Sonnet 147. In an ironic return to the palinode to the God of Love of the *Phaedrus*, "Will" implicitly performs anti-Platonic love by reenacting the love story that Socrates first rehearses and then recants. The speaker reiterates Socrates' first love story, the tragic tale that inspires his palinode to the God of Love, which he remembers as another poet's palinode:

> My love is a fever, longing still
> For that which longer nurseth the disease, ...
> My reason, the physician to my love, ...
> Hath left me, and I desperate now approve
> Desire is death, which physic did except.
> Past cure I am, now reason is past care,
> And, frantic mad with evermore unrest,
> My thoughts and my discourse as madmen's are,
> At random from the truth vainly expressed.
> (147.1–2, 5, 7–11)

This kind of love – love as destructive desire and the madness that it manifests – leads him to forget himself, as the speaker admits: "Do I not think on thee when I forgot / Am of myself, all tyrant for thy sake?" (149.3–4). As "Will" embraces the 'wrong' kind of love, so he also embraces a poetics of deception, the 'lies' of the poets which he epitomizes in himself and his poetry: "For I have sworn thee fair: more perjured eye, / To swear against the truth so foul a lie" (152.13–14). The final two sonnets underscore this anti-Platonic allegory by recalling the poems that praise the God of Love in the *Phaedrus* and *Symposium*, but as parody. Here "Cupid" (153.1), "The little Love-god" (154.1), offers "no cure" (153.13) for this deadly love-sickness: the passion of "Love's fire," the love which "conquers all" reason, leads not to wisdom but to willful ignorance, to disease and death rather than "rebirth," to ruin rather than recollection (154.14).

As "Will" willingly submits to his passion, this affective turn in Shakespeare's allegory of love would seem to reframe poetry not as an art of memory but as an "art of forgetting." But this will to oblivion also necessarily and paradoxically remembers what it seeks to forget: a Platonic ideal of love-as-allegory which must conceal the shame of poetry and defend its value as more than pleasurable, as more than mere stories designed to seduce readers into falling in love with their own destruction. However, Shakespeare clearly prefers the naked truth, and, in the end, he unveils this poetic allegory of love as a kind of anti-allegory. The *Sonnets* implicitly refutes the idea that poetry must represent a higher spiritual truth designed to make readers more virtuous, which amounts to an indirect defense of poetry as precisely the 'wrong' kind of love. It's not that poetry does nothing, Shakespeare suggests, just not what readers might expect: allegory neither justifies poetry nor makes us better than we are. Art may hold a "mirror up to nature; to show virtue her own feature, scorn her own image," Hamlet says, but it cannot change that nature; or as Ophelia, the fair maid quintessentially 'ruined' by love, sanely observes in the midst of her mad "remembrance": "we know what we are, but know not what we may be" (3.2.18–19, 4.5.174, 43–44). Yet, as I have suggested, Shakespeare's art of forgetting ultimately depends on an art of remembering, dressed up as his own allegory of love. To reject Platonic love and poetry is also to remember it, and creating a persona who contends that his poetry is "nothing new" is also a way to be novel, original by dint of denying originality. "Will's" determination to forget serves as an ironic reminder of Shakespeare's profound remembrance of the past and poetics, through allegories of love both old and new. And though the speaker of Sonnet 122 rejects writing as that which will "import forgetfulness" in himself and readers, the poem itself involves its audience, present and future, in the perpetual recollection of its ruin (122.14). Even as Shakespeare ruins the fantasy of monumental permanent poetry, his *Sonnets* are a written reminder that poetry's ruins are places for remembering – for the time being, if not forever.

Notes

1 On *Hamlet* and the art of memory, see Adam Max Cohen, "Hamlet as Emblem: The *Ars Memoria* and the Culture of the Play," *Journal for Early Modern Cultural Studies*, 3.1 (2003), 77–112; James Schiffer, "Mnemonic Cues to Passion in *Hamlet*," *Renaissance Papers* (1995), 65–80; Lina Perkins Wilder, *Shakespeare's Memory Theatre: Recollection, Properties, and Character*

(Cambridge University Press, 2010), chapter 4; and Hester Lees-Jeffries, *Oxford Shakespeare Topics: Shakespeare and Memory*, ed. Peter Holland and Stanley Wells (Oxford University Press, 2013), chapter 2.

2 *Phaedrus*, 274c–b, in Edith Hamilton and Huntington Cairns, eds., *Collected Dialogues of Plato* (Princeton University Press, 1961). My reading of Sonnet 122 contrasts with that of Vendler and Booth, both of whom in their commentaries understand the speaker to be referring to a physical book given to him by the beautiful young man – seemingly the same book which the speaker gave to the fair youth in Sonnet 77 when exhorting him to memorialize himself – a book which the speaker in Sonnet 122 has now seemingly lost or cast away; see Vendler, *The Art of Shakespeare's Sonnets* (Cambridge, MA: Harvard University Press, 1997), 518–20; and Booth, ed., *Shakespeare's Sonnets* (New Haven, CT: Yale University Press, 1977), 412–13. I read "thy book" (77.14), material and memorial, as referring to the sonnet collection before us.

3 My use of the phrase "allegory of love" clearly draws upon C. S. Lewis' seminal study, *Allegory of Love*, which focuses primarily on medieval poetry and poetics. However, my understanding of the relationship between the art of memory and allegory has been influenced primarily by Michael Murrin's work, *The Veil of Allegory* (University of Chicago Press, 1969), which offers an illuminating account of the relationship between mnemonics and poetics, especially chapter 3. On the early modern sonnet sequence as social and political allegory, see Arthur F. Marotti, "'Love Is Not Love': Elizabethan Sonnet Sequences and the Social Order," *ELH*, 49.2 (1982), 396–428.

4 Seminal studies on the history of the art of memory include Frances Yates' *The Art of Memory* (University of Chicago Press, 1966); Mary Carruthers' *The Book of Memory: A Study of Medieval Culture* (Cambridge University Press, 1990); Lina Bolzoni's *The Gallery of Memory: Literary and Iconographic Models in the Age of the Printing Press*, trans. Jeremy Parzen (University of Toronto Press, 2001); and Paolo Rossi's *Logic and the Art of Memory: The Quest for a Universal Language*, trans. Stephen Clucas (University of Chicago Press, 2000). On the range of the memory arts, see *The Memory Arts in Renaissance England: A Critical Anthology*, ed. William E. Engel, Rory Loughnane, and Grant Williams (Cambridge University Press, 2016). For recent work on Shakespeare and the memory arts, see *The Routledge Handbook of Shakespeare and Memory*, ed. Andrew Hiscock and Lina Perkins Wilder (London: Routledge, 2018), including my chapter on "The State of the Art of Memory and Shakespeare Studies."

5 The major classical discussions of the art of memory – Cicero's *De oratore*, the pseudo-Ciceronian *Rhetorica ad Herrenium*, and Quintillian's *Institutio oratoria* – all describe the method and importance of creating striking images that impress themselves upon the memory. On the strategies of the memory artist in creating affecting mnemonic images, see work by Yates, Carruthers, Rossi, and Bolzoni, the latter of whom explores how "eros and memory are deeply related" in the memory arts (Bolzoni, *Gallery of Memory*, 145–62).

6 Philip Sidney, *An Apology for Poetry*, ed., Forrest G. Robinson (New York: Macmillan, 1970), 54.
7 See Rebeca Helfer, *Spenser's Ruins and the Art of Recollection* (University of Toronto Press, 2012), chapter 1, where I offer a fuller account of the memory arts.
8 Cicero, "De oratore; or, On the Character of the Orator," in J. S. Watson, ed., *Cicero on Oratory and Orators* (Carbondale: Southern Illinois University Press, 1970), II.l.xxxv.
9 On Simonides' analogy between poetry and painting, see William E. Engel, "Mnemonic Criticism and Renaissance Literature: A Manifesto," *Connotations*, 1.1 (1991), 12–33.
10 Plato, "Republic," in Hamilton and Cairns, eds., *Collected Dialogues of Plato*, I–III, X.
11 Plato, "Phaedrus," in Hamilton and Cairns, eds., *Collected Dialogues of Plato*, 267a.
12 On the *Sonnets* and Platonic love, see Ronald Gray, *Shakespeare on Love in the Sonnets and Plays in Relation to Plato's Symposium, Alchemy, Christianity and Renaissance Neoplatonism* (Newcastle upon Tyne: Cambridge Scholars Publishers, 2011). See also Danijela Kambaskovic, "'Of comfort and dispaire': Plato's Philosophy of Love and Shakespeare's Sonnets," in R. S. White, Mark Houlahan, and Katrina O'Loughlin, eds., *Shakespeare and Emotions: Inheritances, Enactments, Legacies* (Basingstoke: Palgrave Macmillan, 2015), 17–28.
13 Plato, "The Symposium," in Hamilton and Cairns, eds., *Collected Dialogues of Plato*, 207a–209a.
14 Murrin, *Veil of Allegory*, 91.
15 See, for example, R. G. Spiller, *The Development of the Sonnet: An Introduction* (New York: Routledge, 1992). My understanding of Dante's and Petrarch's treatment of memory in their sonnets focuses on the influence of Augustine's Christianized art of memory in *Confessions*, written as a Neoplatonic allegory of love about the soul's *anamnesis*; see Helfer, *Spenser's Ruins*, 48–59.
16 Augustine, *Confessions*, trans. R. S. Pine-Coffin (London: Penguin, 1961), 1.13. See Yates, *The Art of Memory*, and Carruthers, *The Book of Memory*, on Augustine's complex relationship to the art of memory.
17 As Greene and Hui both suggest, Petrarch's mnemonic poetics might be said to begin with a walk through the ruins of Rome (a walk he remembers in a letter), and in this journey through memory, Petrarch articulates his love of a lost past that translates allegorically into his love poetry. See Thomas Greene, *The Light in Troy: Imitation and Discovery in Renaissance Poetry* (New Haven, CT: Yale University Press, 1982), especially chapter 5; and Andrew Hui, *The Poetics of Ruin in Renaissance Literature* (New York: Fordham University Press, 2017), chapter 3.
18 In "The Canonization," when Donne writes, "We'll build in sonnets pretty rooms," he connects the meaning of "stanza" in Italian as "room" or "stopping place" to the architecture of the poem, figured metaphorically as a "well-wrought urn" and monument to the memory of sinful-lovers-turned-

saints. This innovative and irreverent metaphysical conceit, I would argue, turns a conventional trope about the sonnet as a space for memory – and, indeed, as a kind of architectural mnemonic – in two directions: back to the sonnet's Catholic and confessional origins, and forward to a sexualized and secular context.
19 See Dante's *Vita nuova*, XXV, on the relationship between "Love" and allegory as a poetics.
20 Petrarch suggests as much when he refers to his poetry as *rime sparse* or "scattered rhymes." On Petrarch's view of poetry as "ruinae," see Greene, *Light in Troy*, 92.
21 Petrarch, *Petrarch's Lyric Poems: The Rime Sparse and Other Lyrics*, ed. Robert M. Durling (Cambridge, MA: Harvard University Press, 1976), Poem 23.
22 On Petrarchism in relation to Shakespeare, see Heather Dubrow, *Echoes of Desire: Petrarchism and Its Counterdiscourses* (Ithaca, NY: Cornell University Press, 1995), chapter 4; Thomas P. Roche, Jr., *Petrarch and the English Sonnet Sequences* (New York: AMS Press, 1989), chapter 8; Richard Strier, *The Unrepentant Renaissance: From Petrarch to Shakespeare to Milton* (University of Chicago Press, 2011), chapter 1.
23 On forgetting and/as remembering in the *Sonnets*, see Garrett A. Sullivan, Jr.'s "Voicing the Young Man: Memory, Forgetting, and Subjectivity in the Procreation Sonnets" and Amanda Watson, "Full character'd: Competing Forms of Memory in Shakespeare's *Sonnets*," both in Michael Schoenfeldt, ed., *A Companion to Shakespeare's Sonnets* (Malden, MA: Blackwell, 2007), 331–42, 343–60. See also Peter Holland, *Shakespeare and Forgetting* (London: Bloomsbury, 2021).
24 Bolzoni examines the gallery as mnemonic trope in *Gallery of Memory*, 204–13.
25 See Raymond B. Waddington on the art of memory in "Shakespeare's Sonnet 15 and the Art of Memory," in Thomas O. Sloan and Raymond B. Weddington, eds., *The Rhetoric of Renaissance Poetry: From Wyatt to Milton* (Berkeley: University of California Press, 1974), 96–122.
26 On the de-idealized poetics of the *Sonnets*, see Joel Fineman's classic account, *Shakespeare's Perjured Eye: The Invention of Poetic Subjectivity in the Sonnets* (Berkeley: University of California Press, 1986), where he argues that Shakespeare's anti-Platonism is the source of his new poetics of subjectivity.
27 See Strier, *The Unrepentant Renaissance*, chapter 1, on Shakespeare's treatment of this theme.
28 Shakespeare's art of memory, by which he represents a medieval poetics-turned-early modern, is reinforced in *A Lover's Complaint*, the narrative poem appended to the *Sonnets* and its de facto conclusion. A 'ruined' maid remembers her seduction and destruction by a deceptive lover, described through metaphors of mnemonic poetics, by which Shakespeare defends poetry as the 'wrong' kind of love: as 'lies' that seduce both maid and reader alike, but which both desire all the same. In the end, the maid confesses that she would do it all again, and allow her poet-seducer to "new pervert a reconciled maid" (*A Lover's Complaint*, 329).

CHAPTER 2

Twelfth Night *and the Rites of Memory*

Brian Cummings

For the first festivities of her reign, at Twelfth Night in 1559, less than two months after accession, Queen Elizabeth approved a masque at which cardinals, bishops, and abbots were caricatured by crows, asses, and wolves, respectively.[1] Twelfth Night was the realm of the Lord of Misrule. At the Temple in London in 1561 and 1562, a Prince Palaphilos was picked apparently at random: shrewdly, the lawyers identified Lord Robert Dudley. He rode to the inn shod in gilded armour, attended by eighty knights, including twenty-four as constant companions, clad entirely in white. Prince Dudley presided over his Queen's misrule from dusk on Christmas Eve until Twelfth Night.[2]

That Shakespeare's *Twelfth Night* originated in such social festivities has long been assumed. The first recorded performance of the play is 2 February 1602, at Middle Temple Hall:

> At our feast we had a play called 'Twelve Night, or What You Will', much like 'The Comedy of Errors' or 'Menaechmi' in Plautus, but most like and near to that in Italian called 'Inganni'. A good practice in it to make the steward believe his lady-widow was in love with him, by counterfeiting a letter as from his lady, in general terms telling him what she liked best in him and prescribing his gesture in smiling, his apparel, etc. and then, when he came to practice, making him believe they took him for mad.[3]

The feast in question was Candlemas, not Twelfth Night. However, in 1954, Leslie Hotson appeared to discover a smoking candle for a first performance of the play at court on the last day of Christmas, 6 January 1601. The Florentine Duke of Bracciano, Virginio Orsini, scion of the famous Roman family and Knight of the Golden Fleece, was a supporter of the Earl of Essex and is recorded attending the Christmas revels. He wrote home reporting *una commedia mescolata, con musiche e balli*.[4] This "mixed play" was performed in the hall, richly hung with tapestries. From here, Hotson was quick, perhaps too quick, to find in the name Duke Orsino a courtly homage.

Since Hotson's brave conjecture in the heyday of the ransack of the archives for direct allusions to Shakespeare's life and works, the significance of the holiday setting has moved into the background. The classic account remains C. L. Barber's *Shakespeare's Festive Comedies* (1959), a contender for best book on Shakespearean comedy ever written. Barber makes the play a farewell exercise in "holiday humor," providing a process of "clarification" to audiences through "release" via revels.[5] After Barber, a revival of interest in religious contexts for theatre suggested a different explanation for the meaning of Twelfth Night in the play. Here, nostalgia for the traditions of the old religion holds sway. The historian Ronald Hutton's lament in *The Rise and Fall of Merry England* (2001) describes the decline of Twelfth Night from the late Middle Ages, when it was marked by a religious office. In some parishes a Star of Bethlehem, "sometimes gilded, sometimes made of brass," was suspended from the rood loft. It was more an urban festival than a rural one, although there are no surviving accounts for it in London parish records.[6] Hutton details a courtly memory of Twelfth Night rituals after the Reformation, not only in the reign of Elizabeth but also of James and into the court of Charles I.[7] Ben Jonson saw his *Christmas his Masque* performed on Twelfth Night 1616. Only with Charles II did the masque disappear, with secular festivities, and especially gambling, encouraged instead.[8]

Decline may be mirrored in Restoration performances of Shakespeare's play. *Twelfth Night* was among eight titles by Shakespeare granted to Sir William Davenant by the king in December 1660 for the right to perform at the Duke's Theatre in Lincoln's Inn Fields.[9] The first staging followed on 11 September 1661, with Thomas Betterton starring as Sir Toby Belch; revivals appeared in 1663 and 1669. Samuel Pepys remembers in his diary seeing it twice. The first time, he says, "I took no pleasure at all in it."[10] On 6 January 1663, he enlarges: "And after dinner to the Dukes house and there saw Twelfth night acted well, though it be but a silly play and not related at all to the name or day."[11] Pepys makes no mention of the dramatist by name, and it is not altogether evident how far the performance reflected Davenant's revision. The consensus is that it was "staged with little or no textual revision," although the evidence is largely negative, in that unlike *Hamlet*, *Macbeth*, and *The Tempest*, Davenant did not publish an adaptation.[12] A 1720 edition of a comedy, *The Half-Pay Officers*, an alteration of Davenant's *Love and Honour*, with "some scenes borrowed from Shakespeare's *Twelfth Night* and *Henry V*," suggests more hybrid action.[13]

Pepys' remark on "a silly play and not related at all to the name or day" perhaps reflects what Hutton describes as a desacralisation of Catholic

England into a world of secular merriment and social trivia. Yet this view is contradicted by the fact that the play was performed in 1663 on the feast day and that Pepys feels the absence of direct reference to it. Pepys in fact shows a persistent engagement with the holy day. In 1660 after eating all day and playing the viols he descends on a party at his cousin Stradwick's. There is a "brave cake" with the traditional bean, received by the Twelfth Night 'Queen,' who is played by Pepys' unmarried sister Paulina, and her 'King' (Mr Stradwick).[14] In 1663 Pepys mixes "great pleasures" with new year's resolutions to do his duty and increase his own good name and money.[15] In 1668 the Twelfth Night play at the Duke of York's is *The Tempest* in the adaptation by Davenant and John Dryden; it is followed by dancing and then home to another party with music, singing, and a Twelfth Night cake. This all goes on until two in the morning and later, after which Pepys reflects that "going to a play or the like, to be the greatest real comforts that I am to expect in the world."[16] In 1669 there is another cake and they draw lots for who is queen and king; Pepys gets to be Queen. The play the next day is John Fletcher's *The Island Princess*, in an anonymous adaptation.[17]

How do plays imitate the world of ritual? At the heart of this argument lies Stephen Greenblatt's famous statement that in King Lear we find "a sense of rituals and beliefs that are no longer efficacious, that have been *emptied out*."[18] This chapter suggests rather that the structures of ritual – social as well as religious – are still present, even when they are not explicitly mentioned. In this way the play is not (as Greenblatt calls it) part of a "swerve from the sacred to the secular."[19] Religious ritual is mimetic as well as sacramental. In that way it evades the strict dichotomy Greenblatt proposes between performance and belief. Theatre, too, shares in key aspects of ritual: mimesis, repetition of the past to generate a future, and the possibility of imaginative redemption. Central to this is the realization that memory includes affect. Ritual performs memory over and over again, and in this way keeps memories and emotions alive, even when they cannot be fully understood or grasped. On different occasions the same ritual may be felt as more and less metaphorical, more and less meaningful. *Twelfth Night* as a play is a sublime example of how fragile and fleeting this experience of emotional memory can be.

I

"It is amazing how little happens in *Twelfth Night*," comments Barber with dry astuteness.[20] Indeed, the lawyer John Manningham's memory of seeing the play emphasizes its stock comic plots from Plautus, such as *Menaechmi*, with its twin brothers, its comic servant, domineering wife, doddering father-in-law, and quack doctor, plus the farcically named Peniculus (the parasite), Erotium (the charming courtesan), and Cylindrus (the cook).[21] The action in Plautus takes place in the Illyrian seaport of Epidamnus. His *prologus* sets a familiar Shakespearean scene: "There was a certain old merchant in Syracuse. Two twin sons were born to him, boys of such similar looks that their wet nurse who gave them the breast could not tell them apart."[22] The twins inevitably become separated, and it is Plautus' task to reunite them and to solve their sexual adventures in the process. So far, so predictable. Manningham, though, is the more taken with the similarities between Shakespeare's new play and *Gl'Ingannati*, a humanist comedy of intrigue from a Siena academy, the Accademia degli Intronati. First performed on the last day of carnival in 1531, the play was based on *commedia dell'arte*. Concerned with the romantic status of its heroines, and including witty problems, jests, cants, and inventions, this play, like others from the academy, was aimed at a female Sienese public.[23] The Articles of the Accademia, dating from 1532, emphasized how literary exercises in the service of the philosophy of love would convey "liberty to everyone."

Translations of *Gl'Ingannati* appeared in Latin, French, and Spanish. Yet for the part Manningham liked best, where the Steward is persuaded by means of a counterfeit letter to believe his mistress is in love with him, Shakespeare had no source.[24] Here, Leo Salingar suggests a different product of the Accademia in Siena is pertinent. This is a play called *Il Sacrificio*, printed with *Gl'Ingannati* in some editions.[25] In a mock-ceremony, thirty members of the Intronati (which is a canting pun between enthronement and 'thunderstruck') advance in turn with joke names (*Lo sdegnoso*, 'Indignant'; *Il Soppiatone*, 'Secret Whisperer') to burn a love token in a sacrificial urn. Freeing their hearts of error, they lead the women to redemption, having wasted "the flower of their years" in "the prison of amorous sufferings." One of them, Messer Malevolti, places a carved Cupid as an offering from his lady, and recites a poem to mark his disillusionment. In this manner, the priest of Minerva offers to release them all from love. "You are surely not worth calling a god any longer."[26]

Hotson as well as Salingar noted the similarity of the name to Malvolio.[27] The curious point is that the occasion of the *sacrificio* made to Minerva on behalf of "the charming ladies of Siena" is itself Twelfth Night. Does this suggest that Shakespeare favours a pagan secularization of the traditional Christian feast? Certainly, the feast was under attack within the Elizabethan Protestant church. Archbishop Grindal in 1576 made visitation articles instructing his bishops to uncover

> whether the ministers and churchwardens have suffered any lord of misrule or summer lords and ladies, or any disguised persons, or others, in Christmas or May games, or any morris-dancers, or at any other times, to come unreverently into the church or churchyard, and there to dance, or play any unseemly parts, with scoffs, jests, wanton gestures, or ribald talk.[28]

Earlier, while Archbishop of York, Grindal in 1570 extended a similar ban to summer lords and other disguised persons, prohibiting feasts and dances in the church or churchyard.[29] In *Twelfth Night*, Shakespeare represses any direct memory of Christmas games or even of a masque or dance, leaving perhaps only the songs – and the name – of Feste as a residual survival.

Twelfth Night opens with an Italian Duke, Orsino, discoursing on pleasure and art, and in particular on the relationship of music and melancholy, a familiar Renaissance trope:[30]

> ORSINO: If music be the food of love, play on.
> Give me excess of it, that surfeiting,
> The appetite may sicken and so die.
> That strain again, it had a dying fall.
>
> (1.1.1–4)

The play throughout speaks in terms of unspeakable emotion: here, of desire; later, of trauma and loss; by the end, of joy and happiness.[31] The word 'surfeit' suggests emotional excess, but also of an embodied kind. Sensuousness is conveyed by a synaesthesia of ear, breath, and smell:

> ORSINO: O it came o'er my ear like the sweet sound
> That breathes upon a bank of violets,
> Stealing and giving odour
>
> (1.1.5–7)

Orsino elaborates a miniature theory of the senses which also embodies a theory of emotional responsiveness. This emphasizes directness but also a kind of submerged erotic thrill. The bawdy comes upon the audience as if unaware, in "scoffs, jests, wanton gestures, or ribald talk," not so much the result of the unseemly intrusion of Morris dancing imagined by Grindal within the Elizabethan churchyard, as an Italianate homily on the dangers of the flesh. Olivia, Orsino declares, has been overcome by the excesses of mourning for her recently deceased brother. What if the overcharge of the memory of grief could be transferred into the realm of the body? Neither language nor, paradoxically, the body can properly "contain" the emotion, which is overdetermined.

> ORSINO: O she that hath a heart of that fine frame
> To pay this debt of love but to a brother,
> How will she love, when the rich golden shaft
> Hath killed the flock of all affections else
> That live in her; when liver, brain, and heart,
> These sovereign thrones, are all supplied and filled
> Her sweet perfections with one selfsame king!
> Away before me to sweet beds of flowers:
> Love-thoughts lie rich when canopied with bowers.
>
> (1.1.33–41)

Everything comes together: Cupid's arrow of desire ('shaft' equals 'erection' as well as 'bow'). A theory of affections combines with the erotics of the body in adumbrating the human organs of "liver, brain, and heart" which unite in a "sovereign" power. The reading "selfsame" comes from the Second Folio of 1632; like 'same' it is used as an intensive, but Shakespeare uses the form 'selfsame' more frequently elsewhere, and it reiterates the self-generation of love in "Love-thoughts." Orsino's hymn to the goddess of love culminates with a reduplicated synaesthesia of flowers in love's bower. This is an interleaved metaphorics of affection.

"We are neural beings," state George Lakoff and Mark Johnson in *Philosophy in the Flesh*. "Our brains take their input from the rest of our bodies."[32] The "cognitive turn" has become the prevailing philosophy of emotion and memory at the beginning of the twenty-first century. Emotion is made to be akin to sensation and sense perception; memory to a methodical transcript of previous experience.[33] This has also made a profound impression on the way we read metaphor, as a product – even an affect – of the body. Bodies feel, bodies remember, and the mind takes note, using a language itself imprinted by the body's cognitive networks. "The mind is inherently embodied. Thought is mostly unconscious. Abstract concepts are largely metaphorical," Lakoff and Johnson conclude.[34]

The problem might be said to lurk in the passage from each of these blank, undeniable, and inherently banal sentences to the next. Sixteenth-century rhetoric and theory of the passions suggests a less linear and one-directional trajectory from experience to language. In particular, memory and language become redundant in Lakoff and Johnson's account, since they are subordinate to a bodily experience already known. Yet in Orsino's speech, language does not flow from experience into memory, since the body is itself infected by his metaphor. Rather, his metaphoric language just as much inflects his self-conception of his own body. This is the staple of classical rhetoric, as in the exposition of metaphor in *Rhetorica ad Herennium*: "A similitudine, sic: 'Corpore niveum candorem, aspectu igneum ardorem adsequebatur.'"[35] The examples in this standard textbook of the Elizabethan grammar-school are taken from Homer's *Iliad*.[36] Orsino's dense conceits take for granted a discrepancy between experience and emotion which is typical of the Elizabethan concept of "mixed metaphor." Puttenham in *The Arte of English Poesie* defines this as "sensable figures altering and affecting the mynde by alteration of sence or intendements."[37] This is how we come to dissemble, "or speake otherwise then we thinke," a concept almost unimaginable in the cognitive world of Lakoff and Johnson.

Mixed metaphors prevail in *Twelfth Night*, as do also its penchant for mixed genres (*commedia mescolata*), whether from New Roman comedy of identity and stereotype, or medieval mumming of festive misrule, or Tuscan humanist plays of manners. Perhaps this also helps to explain what happens to social rites in the sixteenth century. As E. K. Chambers comments in his extraordinary documentary history of *The Elizabethan Stage*: "Tudor kings and queens came and went about their public affairs in a constant atmosphere of make-believe, with a sibyl lurking in every courtyard and gateway, and a satyr in the boscage of every park."[38] The language of "making him believe" is found in Manningham's diary of the play in performance, showing the cross-over between courtly ritual and theatrical fantasy. Chambers calls this with acute sensitivity a "mimetic dialogue" between "ceremonies of welcome and farewell." The fullest scope for social performance, Chambers averred, lay in the annual progresses from London to the countryside, and also in the feasts of the year's cycle. "The chief mask of the year," he cites, "which every ambassador intrigued to attend, was traditionally danced on Twelfth Night."[39] What takes place in the masque, of course, is not some direct memory of pre-Reformation liturgy, but an elaborate fantasy of the past, a celebration of holiday itself.

Here we may juxtapose the uncanny timbre of reflexive memory in Act 1, scene 2:

VIOLA: What country, friends, is this?

(1.2.1)

This is a scene of belatedness, or of unbelongingness. Since the performances of John Philip Kemble in the eighteenth century it has been a custom to reverse the sequence of 1.1 and 1.2, since 1.2 is so powerfully the initiator of the play's action. Indeed, the first production I saw, also the first Shakespeare play I ever saw (unless this is some trick of my memory), placed Viola first on stage. Viola begins by remembering, or is it mis-remembering, or half-remembering?

Viola is the beginning and end of the play. Yet what does Viola remember? She is always in some sense a cipher, even before she becomes Cesario, a blank personality, tabula rasa, virgin territory, without memory. Arrival in Illyria acts as some kind of primal scene, re-enacting the strange twin birth from which she is now all too consciously separated, in the unknown place Messaline:

CAPTAIN: This is Illyria, lady.
VIOLA: And what should I do in Illyria?
   My brother, he is in Elysium.
   Perchance he is not drowned: what think you, sailors?
CAPTAIN: It is perchance that you yourself were saved.
VIOLA: O my poor brother! And so perchance may he be.

(1.2.2–7)

The Captain certainly remembers where he is: "This is Illyria, lady." Yet where is that? Somewhere between Dalmatia, Ragusa, and Croatia, Illyria represents a medley of coastlines, in a tesserated, spiralizing infinity. Illyria is not quite a real place but an imaginary of the originary, the ur-place where myth ends and time begins.[40] It is half in Homer and half in Plautus, caught between the Adriatic and Aegean of the imagination and a very real Roman and post-Roman empire. Viola's birthplace, Messaline, too, is an onomastic no-man's-land between Mytilene in Greece and Messina in Sicily.

The Captain attempts to impose his fragmentary memories of a place he has sailed to and from in the past onto Viola's bewildering sense of disturbance and displacement. Throughout the play the Captain is assaulted by flashbacks, by a menace of unfinished business and unfulfilled punishment. The split selves of Viola and Sebastian are thrown about by this mental turbulence of past and present. Yet in any case, the Captain's projection does not constitute Viola's own shaken memory, which is divided instead between mourning for her recently lost brother and reinvention of her long-lost father. What she experiences, perhaps, are what Freud called "screen memories." Her lost and unremembered childhood exists only in shards of memory to be assembled figuratively or apparently unconsciously. Freud's own extraordinary account in his seminal paper *Screen Memories* (1899) has always been understood as at least partly autobiographical. Contemporary with his full statement of the theory of *Traumdeutung*, it also comes thick and fast on his elaboration of Hamlet in his memories of his own father. Freud recounts an analysis of a thirty-eight-year-old patient, an educated man interested in psychology. His early memories are fragmentary: a meadow, a bunch of flowers, some children playing, including a young girl in a yellow dress, a delicious loaf of bread. Was it a repeated memory, Freud asked, or one suddenly recalled later? The patient, surprised by the question, begins to connect these memories with later ones, in adolescence, of holiday, and his father's decline: "There then followed long years of hardship; I don't think there was anything about them worth remembering. I never felt really at ease in the town. I don't think I ever ceased to long for the glorious woods of my childhood."[41] What is the source of this unacknowledged and misunderstood longing? Freud locates the patient's problem in latent sexuality. "This holiday, when I was seventeen, was the first I'd spent in the country." Seventeen years old, he fell hopelessly in love with a daughter of the family where he was staying, herself fifteen. After a few days the girl went to school, so that separation becomes the inevitable concomitant of the memory of holiday. He passes his time in solitary walks in lovely woods, building castles in the air. A key to interpretation lies in the dandelion flower which he cannot get out of his mind: a synaesthesia of the yellow of the girl's dress. It is hard not to feel that this explains beautifully the puzzle of memory and forgetfulness in Viola's displacement from her childhood fantasies to the shores of Sicily.

II

Why should time proceed only in a forward direction, or emotion always lead outwards from experience? Twelfth Night is a screen memory for a society's unconscious. Of course, Freud's holidays need to be differentiated from the "holy days" of the church calendar. Nonetheless, as David Cressy demonstrated at length, there is a continuity between the two, alongside a continual ideological struggle over the concept throughout the post-Reformation period. Cressy describes a "calendar of layers as well as passages." The medieval Christian year, divided formally between the everyday and the festival (*feria* and *festiva*), with its ample accumulation of saints' days, coexisted with an agrarian calendar of the harvest year, the law calendar, and an increasingly complex repository of regnal, political, and religious anniversaries endorsed by the Tudor state. "The calendar was a lesson in history and a reminder of duties" with no obvious distinction between what is necessary more for spiritual welfare or for due maintenance of order.⁴²

Epiphany always is and was a boundary rite: the foundational ceremony of welcome and farewell, or of appearance surpassing reality. This is surely the reason why Shakespeare advertises his play as belonging to the ritual that marks the end of the feast of Christmas. If Pepys misses the point of the connection, the fact that he notices a discrepancy shows the persistence as well as porousness of the culture of festivity. Theophany is recognized in the mysterious narrative of three eastern magi guided by the star to the birthplace of God in an impoverished stable. A scattering of references in the New Testament (2 Thessalonians, 1 and 2 Timothy, Titus) to a "glorious appearing" (or "brightness of the coming") is readily embellished by a Christian poetics of a God that dies but was therefore also born, and is fixed to the natural cycle of the year and its balance between winter and summer, awakening and falling. Antiquarians fully understood the relationship of such rites to older pagan traditions. Ralph Holinshed's *Chronicles* treat as synonymous "Christenmasse, otherwise called Yule": a midwinter feast combined with a wild hunt. Holinshed's citation is from a Scottish source.⁴³ In his account of Northumberland, Thomas Fuller considered Yuletide a northern English dialect word for Christmas (with cognate terms such as 'yule-block', 'yule-oakes', and 'yule-songs').⁴⁴ In either version, the festival period is twelve days and nights long. Twelfth Night thus marks the end of festival, the terminus of the boundary, where play comes to an end. Holinshed and Camden were aware that behind Yuletide lay the even more venerable Greek and Roman celebration of Saturnalia. In his account of the invasion of Britain under Claudius, Holinshed cites Dio Cassius to quote the general Aulus Plautius crying, "O Saturnalia," in declaring the triumph of his coming.⁴⁵ In Sir James Frazer's *Golden Bough*, Saturnalia is joined to the Christian story of the dying and reviving god in the myth of "the Scape-Goat," in which carnival freedom marks out the liminal history of sacrifice.⁴⁶

The argument made by Barber is that festive forms are neither remembered nor repressed in the theatre but sublimated. In this sublimation, the limits of misrule (or dissent) are marked, as are also the boundaries of acceptable ritual and memory. In this way, Twelfth Night is reappropriated in native form. Barber assimilates Athenian Old Comedy to Shakespeare without needing a clear line of humanist scholarship to justify it: the forms of insult in Aristophanes easily re-emerge in the flyting of Sir Toby Belch. Like Chambers, Barber sees in festivity a form of mimesis rather than direct cultural memory. Yet in any case, even seen through the historical lens of Hutton, Twelfth Night does not correspond to a simplistic narrative of decline and fall from religion to secularization. In fact, Twelfth Night *increased* in importance after 1400, even as New Year declined.[47] In the reigns of Edward II and Edward III, a King of Twelfth Night was chosen by dropping a bean into the cake mix and crowning the man who found it.[48] This then disappeared from royal festivities but was revived (for example) in Merton College, Oxford, in the late fifteenth century. In the reigns of Henry VIII and Edward VI, there is an element of the invention of tradition, rather than the casualness either of forgetting or of nostalgia. Both appointed lords of misrule at court.[49] Morris dancing formed a frequent part of the Christmas and Shrovetide celebrations of Henry VIII, and in the case of the fifth Earl of Northumberland, Twelfth Night.[50] While Elizabeth does not appear to have employed a lord of misrule, there is evidence of her reviving the King of the Bean at Twelfth Night.[51] Outside the royal festivities, Machyn records a visit to the court of a lord of misrule from the city of London in 1561.[52]

And so we enter into the third scene of Shakespeare's play: a third world with a third company of characters. Prose takes over from poetry as popular culture does from amorous humanism. Ostensibly this is the household of the mourning Olivia, but it is presided over by the maid Maria (who comes to us straight out of Plautus) and her uncle Belch of monstrous bladder:

SIR TOBY: What a plague means my niece to take the death of her brother thus? I am sure care's an enemy to life.

(1.3.1–2)

If winter suggests grief and death, it also suggests the counter-measures of drink and oblivion. Sir Toby implies memorialization is a curse. Memory is the spur to an overspill of passion to which he counter-proposes carousing as its death knell. If Feste is the Fool of the play, Belch is its unconscious, a self-proclaimed Lord of Misrule. Bacchic excess mingles with sexual innuendo:

SIR TOBY: Fie, that you'll say so! He plays o' th' viol-de-gamboys, and speaks three or four languages word for word without book, and hath all the good gifts of nature.

(1.3.21–23)

This is Toby's introduction to his fellow boyo and boozing companion Sir Andrew Aguecheek, "as tall a man as any's in Illyria," dismissed by Maria as "a fool and a prodigal" (1.3.16 and 19). Toby comes straight back with a counter-punch in which he attempts to best Maria not only with fake learning ("three or four languages word for word without book"), but also with the sexual connotation of the viola da gamba. This musical instrument, which to be played must be held firmly between the legs and stroked with a piece of wood, is a stock-in-trade for bawdy. Here the word-play in "gamboys" also draws attention to the fact that Maria and all the other women on the stage are played by boys. The 'viol' also acts as a travelling metonym for Viola, the eunuch cum absently present vagina of the play now unfolding in front of us. Linguistically, by the 'book,' and in action, in an elaborate interplay of gestures of the hand, the mock-ritual continues:

SIR ANDREW: And you part so, mistress, I would I might never draw sword again. Fair lady, do you think you have fools in hand?
MARIA: Sir, I have not you by th'hand.
SIR ANDREW: Marry, but you shall have, and here's my hand.
MARIA: Now, sir, thought is free. I pray you bring your hand to th' buttery-bar and let it drink.
SIR ANDREW: Wherefore, sweetheart? What's your metaphor?
MARIA: It's dry, sir.
SIR ANDREW: Why, I think so: I am not such an ass but I can keep my hand dry. But what's your jest?
MARIA: A dry jest, sir.
SIR ANDREW: Are you full of them?
MARIA: Ay, sir, I have them at my fingers' ends; marry, now I let go your hand, I am barren. *Exit.*

(1.3.53–66)

A ritual, any ritual, whether sacred or festive, makes a connection between the future and the past, to make the future feel the same as the past. Ritual performs an act of memory, in order to efface the ordinary neural networks of memory, so as to create in performative tradition a formal invention of how the present has always been, and indeed the future will be. The court's extravagant displays of plenty at Twelfth Night, in venison and pork and wine, create a not-so-subtle counterpoint to the rites of body and bread invoked in the holy communion of incarnation. The divine rites of the Book of Common Prayer contain a whole playbook of gestures indicated in the rubrics or often simply in the implication of the prayers themselves (here from the 1559 rite of baptism): "for he embraced them in his armes, he laied his hands upon them, and blessed them, doubt not you therefore, but earnestly beleve ...."[53] In the masque, the fool plays the part of priest: "Fair lady, do you think you have fools in hand?" (1.3.54). Sir Andrew offers his hand to Maria, but she does not take it. She proffers an alternative: "Now, sir, thought is free. I pray you bring your hand to th' buttery-bar and let it drink." The phrase "thought is free" sounds liturgical yet meets with an overly familiar leer. The phrase of course is proverbial rather than doctrinal, as in John Lyly's *Euphues*: "Why then quoth he, doest thou thinke me a fool, thought is free my Lord quoth she." Free thought also includes the vivacity of metaphor; metaphors ready to hand, hands exchanged for metaphors. This is the miracle of liturgy, to turn things into something else, in masques as well as masses.

Sir Andrew punningly exchanges other bodily fluids: "I am not such an ass but I can keep my hand dry." Hands, we remember, are for grasping or groping, as well as for grieving or laying on in blessing. Andrew's hand keeps his mouth wet with drink, but his hand is also at the ready to wipe his own "ass." The free play of Sir Andrew's and Sir Toby's hands is all too apparent throughout. The women are wise to keep their bodies to themselves, avoiding too much in the way of hands. Maria outwits them, here and elsewhere, exiting with a final single finger in the face of Andrew and the revellers. The rest of the scene after she leaves is all "legs and thighs" (1.3.114), dancing, capers and galliards, all the man-talk they can muster after her come-downs.

If Barber indicates a decline of Christmas rule under Mary and Elizabeth, he also cites via Chambers the easy familiarity in university colleges or inns of court with both terminology and traditions.[54] It is this cross-reference between solemnity and mirth that is striking. Grindal's visitations attest to the nervousness of church authorities in relation to festive traditions. Later, Lewis Bayly, in *The Practice of Pietie*, recommended suppressing all recreation and sports on Sundays, revealing rampant anxiety about retention of saints' days. George Abbott, Archbishop of Canterbury, and John King, Bishop of London, curried favour with the evangelical wing by supporting such measures, at least in outward statements. Early in his reign, James I attempted to soothe the grievances of the English commons by forbidding Sunday performances of plays, baiting of animals, "or other like disordered or unlawful exercises."[55] However, he clearly did not intend the ban to cover court pleasures: he expected a play on almost every one of the twelve days, with a masque on the Twelfth. In relation to the Millenary Petition, he ignored the pressure to reduce the number of holy days, although he made some compromise on the issue of the sabbath. There is thus little change in policy from the Elizabethan proclamations, except for a certain sympathy with Sabbatarianism, and even Charles I continued masques on Twelfth Night.

Yet on the matter of religion and festivity, it may be that too rigid a division is mistaken, either between pre- and post-Reformation, or between sacred and secular leanings.⁵⁶ The Book of Common Prayer retained a Collect and Proper Prefaces from the Sarum Missal for the feast of Epiphany.⁵⁷ Doctrinal mindfulness merges into a lyrical element of fantasy: "O God, who by the leading of a star didst manifest thy only begotten son to the gentiles."⁵⁸ Puritans objected to merriment, but then there were plenty of examples of medieval disapproval of popular festivities. What is also significant is how merriment shows the open edge of ritual in action. An example is Phillip Stubbes' *Anatomy of Abuses* (1583), where Stubbes reveals the inhibitions of London tradesmen in relation to the countryside, as much as he does confessional conflicts:

> Against *May, Whitsonday* or other time, all the yung men and maides, olde men and wiues run godding ouer night to the woods, groues, hils & mountains, where they spend all the night in plesant pastimes, & in the morning they return bringing wᵗ them birch & branches of trees, to deck their assemblies withal.⁵⁹

The lord of misrule is conflated with Satan, and the Maypole is called a "stinking idol." Stubbes strays into the carnivalesque in his execration of carnival. Moreover, in the same decade, a Puritan of a different stripe is well able to assimilate the lord of misrule within an attack on conformist religion. Martin Marprelate, that dandy arch-heretic and scourge of the bishops, uses the techniques of flyting and burlesque to turn the conformist world upside down: "But what then / should you therefore take him vp for it / as though he were the veriest asse in a countrie."⁶⁰ In order to mock Archbishop Whitgift and Bishop Aylmer of London, Martin openly invokes Erasmian forms of the grotesque: "By this time I hope / they see their folly."⁶¹ Puritan though he is, Marprelate has a lively ear for obscene wordplay: *Howe say you now M. cuntry Parsons & Fickers*.

Marprelate calls himself "courtier Martin" in mockery of the airs and graces of "my lord bishops" who hypocritically veer between sober church government and the delights of office. In similar vein he plays on the lines between erudition and popular culture: "Tushe / I would not haue you claime all the skill / in Barbarismes and Solecismes vnto your self."⁶² To counter the upstart prophet of the fields, Whitgift and Aylmer first tried censorship. But when Martin's books popped up out of nowhere in Warwickshire and Northamptonshire, evading the metropolitan gaze, Whitgift turned to a cleverer form of suppression: counter-mockery, itself produced via the clandestine press. Thomas Nashe talked the same language as the Martinists and paid them back in kind, writing a "counter-cuffe" to Martin Junior in the name of Pasquill the Cavaliero.[63] He mocks Old Martin for assuming that his piety is above the law, he who "newlie knighted the Saints in heauen," but who all along is a drunkard, crying, "rise vp Sir Peter and Sir Paule" for all the world like a tavern drinking game, later quoted in Nashe's own *Summer's Last Will and Testament*: "Rise vp, Sir Robert Tospot."[64] Nashe averred that Marprelate was himself no better than a country braggart living "Betweene the skye and the grounde, VVithin a myle of an Oake, and not many fieldes of, from the vnpriuiledged Presse." He promises to supply instead:

> The Anotamie latelie taken of him, the blood and the humors that were taken from him, by launcing and worming him at *London* vpon the common Stage; The maine buffets that are giuen him in euery corner of this Realme, are euident tokens, that beeing thorow soust in so many showres, hee had no other refuge but to runne into a hole, and die as he liued, belching.[65]

The conventional story of the post-Reformation literary scene pits the stage against the pulpit, the sophisticated university or urban wit against the choleric anti-theatrical Puritan. However, Nashe and Marprelate demonstrate a mingled and promiscuous counter-culture in which opposites attract and infect each other, in behaviour and in language. This, surely, is the world of Shakespeare's *Twelfth Night*, where Marprelate, running into a hole to "die as he liued, belching," bumps into Sir Toby. Except that in the conventional world of literary history Martin is Malvolio, not Belch. Among the many wonders of *Twelfth Night* are its proliferation of inversions among characters and fools. If Sir Toby thinks of himself as a winningly unruly lord, he is also an ass like Sir Andrew. He is just one fart away from becoming a permanent Aguecheek. Malvolio, too, prim as he is, plays the ass as he cross-dresses as the lover. In the metamorphosis of madness he also accrues some sympathy. Both Sir Toby and Feste appear as forms of clown, yet it is never clear whether Toby is fool or knave. For, as Enid Welsford comments, "sometimes they were treated as synonyms, sometimes emphasis was laid on the distinction between them."[66] Butt swaps cheek with butt, so that the audience is always having to adapt to the volatile directions of the comedy. Meanwhile, Feste plays the fool apparently above everyone, only to exchange roles constantly with Maria and even sometimes with Olivia. The play is Erasmus' folly incarnate.

III

The lord of misrule is a lord of mediation, mitigation, and mime. In one of Barber's simplest and most brilliant footnotes, he rejects the search for literalism, "on a one-to-one sort of basis," in some primal occasion for *Twelfth Night* as "a court revel."[67] A contrast may be drawn with Nashe's *Summer's Last Will and Testament*, where the surviving text more directly suggests a singular festive event. "Fair words want giving hands," sings Summer, whose manual and verbal gestures perform a ritual to redeem sorrow with pleasure, including fragments of a semi-religious formal litany:

> Come, come, the bells do crye.
> I am sick, I must dye:
> Lord, haue mercy on vs.[68]

"Tis no play neither, but a show," states the Prologue. Nashe writes to the event, in a pageant or game, in a way that is different from Shakespeare. Even if Elizabeth watched a masque in the first frosts of 1601, the new play is written to work on the stage, over and over and again, in the iterative performative space of theatre. Plays are always memorializations of a mimesis that exists in potential and yet also continual form, rather than single masques. Every night, or the following afternoon, the play is repeated, its passions re-enacted. The actors speak the same lines, perform the same gestures. In this way they share something with the rites of religion. For here, too, prayers are repeated word for word, and manual actions set in rubrics.

Plays and liturgies alike are therefore rites of memory. There is some interplay, nonetheless, between formality and improvisation. The words are to be repeated by rote, but actors (and even priests) make mistakes; in any case they inflect with subtle differentiation of intonation, since they time their actions anew on each occasion of performance. Actors, Peter Holland reminds us, forget their lines as much as memorize them.[69] Priests use bookmarks and choirboys as props to help them but still muff their lines. There is an innate tension of memory, then, in both forms of ritual action. It may be countered that religion and theatre are different things and that comparing the two risks making something too light of the one and too serious of the other. Yet the mutual anxieties of performance enlist an important form of understanding even if the comparison cannot be drawn too far. Puritans complained that formal written prayer lacked sincerity, that it was mere verbal show. Only extemporary prayer was "true" prayer. God would tell the difference. The whole problem, they said, with the Book of Common Prayer is that it makes apes of every believer. Yet theatre, too, is prone to such doubts. If the action is too rehearsed, if it feels performed rather than meant, the magic is dispelled, and the audience is reminded all too vividly that it is sitting in broad daylight (or, these days, more often in the dark) only pretending to "make believe." Darkness and daylight are both agents of disenchantment.

Anne Barton perhaps wrote best on the distinction between plays and liturgies, describing how in medieval theatre "audience and actors shared the same ritual world," while the Elizabethan theatre disturbed this boundary.[70] The actor playing Orsino investigates this via a monopoly claim on genuineness of feeling:

> ORSINO: [To Curio and Attendants]
> Stand you awhile aloof. [To Viola] Cesario,
> Thou know'st no less but all: I have unclasped
> To thee the book even of my secret soul.
>
> (1.4.11–13)

Emotion is an open book. It cannot be faked, it is said (or so it is hoped). And yet the exposition of emotion is indeed found precisely in books, books of rhetoric especially. Rudolph Agricola's *De inventione dialectica*, in its third book, described emotion as the aim and result of rhetoric correctly practised. There are three ways, Agricola says, of treating emotion in rhetoric. The first is by means of speech, "to employ the words of someone who is angry, fearful, in love, or grieving."[71] This is the technique of comedy and tragedy: fiery feelings in tragedy, milder ones in comedy, but in both, "language itself should imitate the tumult and disturbance of an excited mind."[72] The second is "to describe someone who is aroused by some emotion," for which Agricola gives the example of the Messenger's speech in Seneca's *Oedipus*. This kind of emotional arousal is more overtly mimetic, in that it represents the feelings of another person. It is the third sort, however, that is the most striking for drama: "our speech does not strive to make our own emotion evident, but seeks to elicit and excite that of another person."[73] By expressing the emotion in one person, a similar emotion is inculcated within another.

This perhaps explains in retrospect one of the strangest and most original comments on emotion in Agricola's work, from the previous chapter: "It makes no difference to the emotions whether something actually is the case, or just seems so."[74] This is seemingly counter-intuitive, and certainly contradicts Lakoff and Johnson's assertion that emotion is a bodily affect, from which language takes its cue. Their view is the one asserted by Orsino, that he says only what he feels. And yet Orsino uncovers his "secret soul" in front of someone who is overtly playing a part. Viola indeed goes on to give a beautiful rendition of Agricola's argument. First, in reply to Orsino, she states that acting is sometimes a better rendition of emotion. In the next scene (1.5) she gives a demonstration of the point by comparing with Olivia two kinds of rhetoric, one of which is a failure, and the other, successful. Success, however, is not a concomitant of mere bodily reality:

VIOLA: Make me a willow cabin at your gate,
And call upon my soul within the house

(1.5.223–24)

While she calls this a more natural type of speech, it is emphatically mimetic, a reflection all the while of the central dramatic trope of the play, that she is playing the part of two bodies and two genders. In the beautiful scene 2.4, Viola acts this out the more tellingly by appeal to a sense of her past. This is rendered not as a direct axiom of memory but as a fictional retelling of her self. What is her history, Orsino asks? "A blank, my Lord" (2.4.106).

Twelfth Night above any other play involves play for its own sake. Nothing happens, and yet is it true that nothing is felt? Paradoxically, it is also transparently a play of feeling: the frankest of the comedies, the least open to accusation of mere courtliness or drollery. It fulfils Agricola's indifference, in the arousal of emotion, to "whether something actually is the case, or just seems so." The actors, pretending to feel, nonetheless, in any performance worth the name, make the audience feel something real, as indeed Agricola insists is the third main technique of emotion in literature. More than any other Shakespeare play, then, the actors need to get it right. Take away feeling and there is nothing there, it is what you will or what you won't. In obverse, though, *Twelfth Night* emerges as truly a theatre which risks everything, since nothing is at stake.

What could be more and less consequential here than the problem of identity resting in the twins? Here, emotion is put to a memory test. In 4.1 there is a strange encounter between folly in the form of Feste and the emotional sinecure that is Sebastian. He has no experience of the events we have seen in the audience, but has to improvise as if he has no memory at all:

SEBASTIAN: What relish is in this? How runs the stream?
Or I am mad, or else this is a dream.
Let fancy still my sense in Lethe steep

(4.1.53–55)

To what extent is identity formed by memory? A philosophical interest in experiments involving twins goes back to ancient times: if we put two twins into varying lives, are they identical still or not? In 4.1 Sebastian is catapulted into instantaneous experience as Olivia seizes him in love at first sight. The audience has a brief interlude of misrule within Maria's household in 4.2 before coming across Sebastian again in 4.3, still lacking the time even for self-acknowledgement:

> SEBASTIAN: Yet doth this accident and flood of fortune
> So far exceed all instance, all discourse,
> That I am ready to distrust mine eyes,
> And wrangle with my reason that persuades me
>
> (4.3.11–14)

Do we mean what we feel? Do we feel what we say? Emotion has become the modern byword for sincerity, but it was not always so, as Renaissance rhetoric shows us. Can we trust our senses when even our memories are prone to imagination and belief?

We might think that emotion more than identity is linked to memory, but Sebastian and Viola reassess emotion at will, even when not based on viable memories. Freud after all suggests that memory is inaccessible in its original form, that there is a gap between memory and experience. We do not have, he says, memories *from* childhood, only memories *of* childhood. "These show us the first years of our lives not as they were, but as they appeared to us at later periods, when the memories were aroused."[75] It is not that they are invented as such, as transferred from one place to another, say from Sicily to Illyria. Shakespeare's play thus counterposes fictions of selfhood versus cognitive accumulation. This, possibly, is the true location of the festive, not in remembered religious rites of the past but in intimations of the imagination in the construction of a festive present and future.[76] Not for nothing does Erasmus talk in terms of folly having a *culturae ritus*, or cultic rites.[77] The feast of Twelfth Night stands outside of time, where the past is present, and the future already happening:

> VIOLA: If nothing lets to make us happy both,
> But this my masculine usurped attire,
> Do not embrace me, till each circumstance,
> Of place, time, fortune, do cohere and jump
> That I am Viola.
>
> (5.1.243–47)

In 5.1, a world of misrule and a world of emotion fully juxtapose in a scene of staggering wonder. Things happen differently; a woman falls in love without knowing, a master elopes with his male servant. Why should we believe any of it? Viola invites Orsino to meet the sea Captain and yet also to recall him from long past in different "circumstance / Of place, time, fortune":

ORSINO: That face of his I do remember well;
 Yet when I saw it last, it was besmeared
 As black as Vulcan, in the smoke of war.

(5.1.41–42)

Is Antonio's multiple experience of shipwreck in some sense a synecdoche for Odysseus' scar in the *Odyssey*? The play enforces the recognition of experiences as sequential, which in our apprehension of them are jarringly discontinuous. As Terence Cave writes: "There is an important sense in which the things we see in literature are not there until we see them."[78]

An audience can see straight off that the twin characters, so carefully kept apart until now, are *not* the same. Yet the play nonetheless treats them still as interchangeable, in a way that is much more disturbing even than the confusions of gender.[79] Experience of twenty years past is thrown off as inconsequential, while meantime Sebastian and Viola are forced to consider the fictions of an instant as replacing a previous lifetime. Why not marry someone after thirty seconds?

When Summer reconciles with Spring in *Summer's Last Will and Testament*, Will demands "a reckoning at thy hands." Gesture brings forth redemption, even in festive form. In this conjuration, accomplished in *Twelfth Night* by the counter-cultural logic of saturnalia, it is appropriate that the marriage is consecrated by a counterfeit ritual performed by an actor-priest:

PRIEST: A contract of eternal bond of love,
 Confirmed by mutual joinder of your hands,
 Attested by the holy close of lips,
 Strengthened by th'interchangement of your rings

(5.1.145–48)

Mistaken identities, which also include mistaken experiences, contingencies, and epistemologies, are summed up in a realignment possible only according to theatrical rites of memory:

SEBASTIAN: And say, 'Thrice welcome, drownèd Viola.'
VIOLA: My father had a mole upon his brow.
SEBASTIAN: And so had mine.
VIOLA: And died that day when Viola from her birth
 Had numbered thirteen years.

SEBASTIAN: O that record is lively in my soul!
             He finishèd indeed his mortal act

                                                              (5.1.225–31)

Twelfth Night is a play of unexplained loss and mourning and grief, the occasion of which cannot be recalled except by imaginative redress or displacement. On a night that takes place only once a year, and even then in a dream or a fiction, emotions can be put to rights. At some point the ritual experience of the church passes over into the world of the stage. Yet it is not in the process ossified or emptied out: it is felt to live on again in mimesis. Mimesis is not an after-effect of ritual disenchantment. It is the precondition of memory and of forgetfulness, and of feeling in the first place.

Notes

1 E. K. Chambers, *The Elizabethan Stage*, 4 vols. (Oxford: Clarendon Press, 1924), vol. I, 155.
2 Ronald Hutton, *The Rise and Fall of Merry England: The Ritual Year 1400–1700* (Oxford University Press, 2001), 114.
3 Bruce R. Smith, *Twelfth Night: Texts and Contexts* (Boston: St. Martin's Press, 2001), 2.
4 Leslie Hotson, *The First Night of Twelfth Night* (London: Rupert Hart-Davis, 1954), 202.
5 C. L. Barber, *Shakespeare's Festive Comedies: A Study of Dramatic Form and Its Relation to Social Custom* (Princeton University Press, 1972), 6.
6 Hutton, *Rise and Fall of Merry England*, 15–16.
7 Ibid., 197.
8 Ibid., 241.
9 Emma Depledge, *Shakespeare's Rise to Cultural Prominence: Politics, Print and Alteration, 1642–1700* (Cambridge University Press, 2018), 53.
10 *The Diary of Samuel Pepys*, ed., Robert Latham and William Matthews, 11 vols. (London: G. Bell, 1970–83), vol. II, 177.
11 Ibid., vol. IV, 6.
12 Amanda Eubanks Winkler and Richard Schoch, *Shakespeare in the Theatre: Sir William Davenant and the Duke's Company* (London: Arden Shakespeare, 2022), 83.
13 British Library, shelf mark: 161.a.63. It is possible the BL is mistaken and the source is *Much Ado about Nothing*.
14 *Diary of Samuel Pepys*, vol. I, 10.
15 Ibid., vol. IV, 6.
16 Ibid., vol. IX, 12–13.
17 Ibid., vol. IX, 409.
18 Stephen Greenblatt, *Shakespearean Negotiations: The Circulation of Social Energy in Renaissance England* (Oxford: Clarendon Press, 1988), 126.

19 Ibid., 126.
20 Barber, *Shakespeare's Festive Comedies*, 242.
21 See Robert Miola, *Shakespeare and Classical Comedy: The Influence of Plautus and Terence* (Oxford University Press, 1994), 182.
22 Plautus, *Menaechmi*, 18–20; *The Two Menaechmuses*, ed. and trans. Wolfgang de Melo, Loeb Classical Library (Cambridge, MA: Harvard University Press, 2011), 430–31.
23 Leo Salingar, *Shakespeare and the Traditions of Comedy* (Cambridge University Press, 1974), 212.
24 E. K. Chambers, *William Shakespeare: A Study of Facts and Problems*, 2 vols. (Oxford: Clarendon Press, 1930), vol. II, 327–28.
25 *Il Sacrificio de gl'intronati, celebrato nei givochi d'vn carnevale in Siena et Gl'Ingannati, commedia de I medisimi* (Venezia: Plinio Peitrasanta, 1554).
26 Salingar, *Shakespeare and the Traditions of Comedy*, 214.
27 Hotson, *The First Night of* Twelfth Night, 108.
28 E. K. Chambers, *The Medieval Stage*, 2 vols. (Oxford: Clarendon Press, 1903), vol. I, 181 (n. 1).
29 Hutton, *Rise and Fall of Merry England*, 127.
30 On music and melancholy, see Mary Ann Lund, *A User's Guide to Melancholy* (Cambridge University Press, 2021), 211.
31 See Bridget Escolme, *Emotional Excess on the Shakespearean Stage: Passion's Slaves* (London: Bloomsbury Arden Shakespeare, 2014), 98.
32 George Lakoff and Mark Johnson, *Philosophy in the Flesh* (New York: Basic Books, 1999), 18.
33 Ibid., 412.
34 Ibid., 3.
35 "From equivalence, as follows: 'His body was as white as snow, his face burned like fire'"; *Rhetorica ad Herennium*, 4.33.44, ed. and trans Harry Caplan, Loeb Classical Library (Cambridge, MA: Harvard University Press, 1954), 340–41.
36 *Iliad*, 1.104 and 10.437.
37 George Puttenham, *Arte of English Poesie*, Book III, chapter xviii (on "mixt allegorie"); *The arte of english poesie contriued into three bookes: The first of poets and poesie, the second of proportion, the third of ornament* (London: Richard Field, 1589), 155.
38 Chambers, *The Elizabethan Stage*, vol. I, 107.
39 Ibid., 205.
40 Ivan Lupić is currently working on the concept in *The Illyrian Renaissance: Literature in the European Borderlands*.
41 Sigmund Freud, *Über Deckerrinerungen* (1899); "Screen Memories," trans. David McLintock, in Adam Phillips, ed., *The Penguin Freud Reader* (London: Penguin Books, 2006), 550.
42 David Cressy, *Bonfires and Bells: National Memory and the Protestant Calendar in Elizabethan and Stuart England* (London: Sutton Press, 2004), 1.
43 Raphael Holinshed, *The Chronicles of England, Scotland and Ireland*, 2 vols. (London: Lucas Harrison, 1577), vol. I, 285.

44 Thomas Fuller, *Historie of the Worthies of England* (London: Thomas Williams, 1661), 304.
45 Holinshed, *Chronicles*, vol. I, 48.
46 James George Frazer, *The Scape-Goat*, chapter 8 ("The Saturnalia and Kindred Festivals"; see abridged edition, *The Golden Bough* (London: Penguin Books, 1996), 700–703.
47 Hutton, *Rise and Fall of Merry England*, 62.
48 Ibid., 60. See also Barber, *Shakespeare's Festive Comedies*, 25.
49 Chambers, *The Elizabethan Stage*, vol. I, 124.
50 Hutton, *Rise and Fall of Merry England*, 33. See Lancashire, "Orders for Twelfth Day and Night," 15–16.
51 *Calendar of State Papers and Manuscripts, Relating to English Affairs, Existing in the Archives and Collections of Venice*, ed. R. Brown et al. (London: Public Record Office, 1865–1947), vol. VII, 374 (6 January 1566).
52 *Diary of Henry Machyn, Citizen and Merchant-Taylor of London*, ed. J. G. Nichols, Camden Record Society Old Series (London: Camden Society, 1848), 273.
53 Exhortation on the gospel, Baptism (1559); *The Book of Common Prayer: The Texts of 1549, 1559, and 1662*, ed. Brian Cummings (Oxford University Press, 2011), 148.
54 Barber, *Shakespeare's Festive Comedies*, 26; referring to Chambers, *The Medieval Stage*, vol. I, 407–19.
55 Hutton, *Rise and Fall of Merry England*, 154.
56 Frances E. Dolan, *Twelfth Night: Language and Writing* (London: Bloomsbury Arden Shakespeare, 2014), 29–30.
57 *Book of Common Prayer*, ed. Cummings, 700.
58 Collect for Epiphany; *Book of Common Prayer*, ed. Cummings, 282.
59 Philip Stubbes, *The anatomie of abuses containing, a discouerie, or briefe summarie of such notable vices and imperfections, as now raigne in many countreyes of the world* (London: John Kingston for Richard Jones, 1583), M3v.
60 *Oh read ouer D. iohn bridges, for it is worthy worke: Or an epitome of the fyrste booke, of that right worshipfull volume, written against the puritanes, in the defence of the noble cleargie, by as worshipfull a prieste, iohn bridges, presbyter, priest or elder, doctor of diuillitie, and deane of sarum wherein the arguments of the puritans are wisely prevented* (Fawsley: Robert Waldegrave, 1588), F4v.
61 Ibid., G1r.
62 Ibid., F5r.
63 Thomas Nashe, *A countercuffe giuen to martin iunior by the ventruous, hardie, and renowned pasquill of england caualiero* (London: [John Charlewood], 1589), title page.
64 *The Works of Thomas Nashe*, ed. Ronald B. McKerrow, rev. ed. F. P. Wilson, 5 vols. (New York: Barnes and Noble, 1966), vol. III, 267.
65 *A countercuffe giuen to martin iunior*, A2r.
66 Enid Welsford, *The Fool: His Social and Literary History* (London: Faber & Faber, 1935), 237.

67 Barber, *Shakespeare's Festive Comedies*, 241.
68 Nashe, *Summer's Last Will and Testament*, in McKerrow, ed., *Works*, vol. III, 283.
69 Peter Holland, "On the Gravy Train: Shakespeare, Memory and Forgetting," in Holland, ed., *Shakespeare, Memory and Performance* (Cambridge University Press, 2006), 211.
70 Anne Righter [Barton], *Shakespeare and the Idea of the Play* (London: Chatto & Windus, 1962), 19.
71 Agricola, *De inventione dialectica*, III, c. 2; in Wayne A. Rebhorn, ed., *Renaissance Debates on Rhetoric* (Ithaca, NY: Cornell University Press, 2000), 51.
72 Ibid., 52.
73 Ibid., 53.
74 Agricola, *De inventione dialectica*, III, c.1; trans. Rebhorn, 50.
75 Freud, "Screen Memories," 559.
76 The festive use of music in the play is discussed in K. R. Parker, "Wassailing and Festive Music in Shakespeare's *Twelfth Night*," *Australasian Drama Studies*, 76 (2020), 160–82.
77 Erasmus, *Encomium moriae*, 40; ASD IV/1.
78 Terence Cave, *Recognitions: A Study in Poetics* (Oxford: Clarendon Press, 1988), 10.
79 Daisy Murray, *Twins in Early Modern English Drama and Shakespeare* (London: Routledge, 2017), 161.

CHAPTER 3

The Lustful Oblivion of Widowhood in The Insatiate Countess

Grant Williams

The Insatiate Countess (1613) examines a formidable affect defined in the period by its inordinate excess: lust. Incapable of controlling her concupiscent urges, Isabella, the dowager-Countess of Swevia, abandons her newlywed husband for Guido, Count of Arsena, only to leave this lover soon after for Gniaca, Count of Gazia. She then charms a Spanish colonel into assassinating her first jilted paramour and she receives from the Duke of Medina the death penalty, but not just for a single crime. The Duke's judgment centers on punishing her for – as well as preempting – her voracious and dangerous libido: "her lust / Would make a slaughter-house of Italy" (5.1.54–55).[1] And, with Isabella's execution, the Duke wishes that a similar "fate / Attend all women so insatiate" (5.2.230–231).

John Marston, responsible for a substantial draft of the tragedy,[2] took the basic plot and characters of his cautionary tale from either William Painter or Geoffry Fenton. In 1567, both had published English translations of François de Belleforest's *Histoires tragiques* (1565), itself based on Matteo Bandello's *Novelle* (1544), from which originated the story of Bianca Maria, the Countess of Cellant. Carefully comparing these sources with *The Insatiate Countess*, Giorgio Melchiori, the foremost editor of the text, sensibly affirms Marston's designs to follow Painter's lead in thematizing "the tragic effects of the 'soul-killing' sin of lust."[3] Melchiori, however, does not scrutinize lust's depiction in the different versions of the narrative, concerning himself almost exclusively with Marston's modifications to events and character names. As a result, he overlooks the playwright's innovative revision of the source material.

In warning about the dangers of female concupiscence, *The Insatiate Countess* portrays Isabella's plethoric body as oblivion incarnate and offers new scenes – no signs of which exist in the sources – that significantly and sustainedly engage with memorial culture. Marston's strategy is to ramp up the menace of the Countess so that he can puncture the male fantasy of the lusty widow, which flourished on the stage at the time.[4] Such a fantasy held out to an unattached male spectator the prospect of refashioning himself: a gentleman could acquire a fortune, secure his social status, and fulfill his erotic desires with the promise of an heir all through winning the hand of a dowager. Not so for Marston, who demonstrates the lusty widow's detrimental effects on spouses and suitors by way of two memory arts for perpetuating male identity: commemoration and *nosce te ipsum*. Forgetting her dead husband and inducing forgetting in her suitors, Isabella prevents men from being remembered and from self-remembering.

Marston's reframing of female lasciviousness as a threat to male remembrance is a bold move, but its realization leaves something to be desired. *The Insatiate Countess* fosters cultural fears of the lusty widow impeding men from knowing themselves and at once disarms these fears by imagining the male community overcoming the danger, particularly through act five's scaffold scene, where capital punishment appears to contain and control Isabella's malignancy. But the finale's staged victory on behalf of homosocial memorialization fails to smooth over the trauma posed by Isabella, a trauma poignantly articulated at the play's opening when she profanes the obsequy for her first husband by using ritual to pledge her love to Roberto. The play cannot resolve the troubling contradiction that the lustful female body, an incarnated oblivion which induces men to forget themselves, is simultaneously the vessel upon which patriarchal mnemonic culture desperately depends for its continuity.

Nosce te ipsum

When Guido is dissuading Gniaca from attacking him, we hear his account of how Isabella's lust poses a serious threat to male self-knowledge:

> Thou dotest upon a devil, not a woman,
> That has bewitched thee with her sorcery,
> And drowned thy soul in Lethy faculties,
> Her ruthless lust has benumbed thy knowledge,
> Thy intellectual powers oblivion smothers,
> That thou art nothing but forgetfulness.
>
> (4.2.60–65)

The speech blames Isabella's charms for leaving Gniaca in an animal-like stupidity and, with its allusion to sorcery, casts her in the role of Circe, the mythological enchantress from *The Odyssey*. It was an accepted early modern reading, as Garrett Sullivan demonstrates in his discussion of

Shakespeare's Cleopatra, to take the enchantress's transformation of men into swine as an exemplum of self-forgetting.[5] Spenser capitalizes on this aspect of the myth in Book II of *The Faerie Queene*, where the hog Gryll refuses to be restored to human form after Guyon has defeated the Circean figure of Acrasia.[6] Lust provoked by the seductress makes the male subject abandon his reason and forget who he should be. Spenser allegorizes the loss of identity through forgetting with Verdant's shield from which Acrasia's seduction has "fowly ra'st" the "old moniments" – that is, his heraldic arms.[7] Such an effacement of masculine selfhood, epitomized by the popular phrase "forgetting thyself," was understood during the period as the dialectical counterpart of the famous humanist injunction "know thyself," that is, *nosce te ipsum*, an important type of ethical remembering.[8] What the romance hero in Spenser's case – or the epic hero in Odysseus's case – does symbolically is to help besotted men regain knowledge of who they are supposed to be. And so Guido, when exposing Isabella as a Circean figure, puts himself in that heroic position vis-à-vis Gniaca, who finally breaks free from her spell only after Guido compels him to reflect upon his eventual memorialization: "And infamy shall write thy epitaph: / Thy memory leaves nothing but thy crimes, / A scandal to thy name in future times" (4.2.71–73). Guido's verbal intervention of urging Gniaca to understand the consequences of remembering has the intended effect of helping him to know himself: he listens to his friend's reasoning and realizes his grave error.

This scene of ethical self-remembrance does not occur in the play's sources, where the two counts, disregarding Isabella's vengeful request,[9] prefer friendship over the wicked demands of a person whom they treat more like a fling than a serious beloved. Marston or the subsequent playwrights add the situation of Gniaca overcoming his unethical forgetting through his comrade's assistance. Consequently, the process of *nosce te ipsum* that the play advances lays most of the burden of blame for the psycho-physiological experience of male lust on Isabella, as though her lovers were not fully accountable for their thoughts and actions. Of course, this deviates widely from Protestant ethics, wherein the faithful were expected to manage their own inner stirrings, given the currency of Christ's famous injunction: "But I say unto you, That whosoever looketh on a woman to lust after her, hath committed adulterie with her already in his heart" (Matt. 5:28, KJV). *The Insatiate Countess* ignores such moral responsibility over personal interiority. The scene clearly minimizes Gniaca's cognitive complicity in his infatuation, since his own humors have not drowned his "soul in Lethy faculties" (4.2.61). Instead, his intellectual powers have been smothered by Isabella's fluidity, and "her ruthless lust has benumbed [his] knowledge" (4.2.63). Knowing thyself is a male activity of shoring up homosocial bonds against the onslaught of lustful female corporeality. Conversely, the play sustains no interest in the possibility of the titular protagonist struggling to gain her own self-knowledge. Unlike her lovers, Isabella is never depicted prior to her wanton ways. Her lust is self-originating. In her soliloquies we hear her concupiscent commentary on men's bodies without the pangs of conscience or the inner turmoil of self-doubt. Spectators are not meant to sympathize or identify with this horrific obstruction to men knowing themselves. The play, instead, builds its dramatic tensions around the ways in which her sex-crazed corporeality threatens to dissolve male identity.

Fearful Fluidity

Despite occasionally indulging in the metaphorical language of witchcraft, the play does not treat Isabella as a genuine supernatural threat. Her deleterious effects emanate from her mortal female body, the playwrights sustaining a Galenic explanation of her actions as if all women were capable of being insatiable. And yet her fearful fluidity mentioned by Guido does not manifest itself in phlegm, the predominant humor in women that explained the inferiority of their memories relative to men's.[10] Again, the play appears to be less concerned with Isabella's own forgetting than with how she makes the lovers forget themselves. When impulsively lusting after Guido on her wedding day, she soliloquizes, "My blood, like to a troubled ocean, / Cuffed with the winds, incertain where to rest, / Butts at the utmost shore of every limb" (2.3.42–44). Upon first seeing Gniaca, she is so swept away by her hot blood that she confesses that in her frenzy she would be willing to commit incest (3.2.49). Her superabundant and volatile fluidity is a sign of her weak gender, for the early modern humoral economy judged women to be naturally plethoric. That is why women menstruated, as Gail Kern Paster explains, because their periods were a natural way for their colder and moister bodies to evacuate the excremental humor.[11] Their blood unlike that of men was undigested, unrefined, and unstable, thus making them more inclined to diseases,[12] one of which was lovesickness or love melancholy, the medical explanation for lust and compulsive venery.[13] In the words of an early modern commentator, lust is "that boyling damned putrification of the bloud."[14]

Although the play remains silent on how Isabella's plethoric body could ever be held directly responsible for making men forget themselves, humoral discourse suggests two means by which her blood could overwhelm their interiority. First, the sanguine complexion predisposed an individual to sexual intercourse. Since seed, common to women, as well as men, was actually blood refined by concoction, its surplus specifically fostered an "amorous disposition."[15] Isabella's appetite would have been further primed by her widowhood, for, as Joseph Swetnam asserts, "[I]t is more easy for a young man or maid to forbear carnal act, than it is for a widow."[16] Considering the presupposition that women are by nature plethoric and widows crave sex, a dowager would place extraordinary demands on a lover and eventually harm his memory. According to Galenic medicine, "the immoderate use of venery and carnal company of women" dried out the brain with lust's heat, hardening the faculty so that it could not receive impressions.[17] Second, Isabella's fearful fluidity may gesture toward the commonplace that immoderate venery drains a man of his life force. The male body, which uses an abundance of blood to distill a modicum of seed, cannot keep pace with the naturally plethoric female, let alone a wanton one. Every ejaculation "harmeth a man more, then if hee should bleed forty times as much," impelling him closer to death and literal oblivion.[18] The play's subplot alludes to this popular belief of male consumption through copulation (3.3.44–45).

Even more fearfully, Isabella's fluidity does not need direct sexual contact to inundate male interiority. When she prepares him for dalliance, Gniaca boasts of how his "youthful veins, / Like a proud river, overflow their bounds" (3.4.72–73) and unknowingly describes himself in the same language used to characterize Isabella (2.3.42–44; 2.4.96–99). Have her raging humors flooded his body? Such a corporeal invasion would not have been fanciful during the period. According to Ficino's theory of fascination, a person's eyes transmit his or her spirits, originally refined in the heart out of the sanguine humor; that is why Ficino, citing Aristotle, says that the gaze of menstruating women stains mirrors with bloody drops.[19] Isabella's rarefied spirits have entered the eyes of the doting suitor and then sought out his heart, where they have reverted back to a fluid state.[20] Upon seeing Gniaca for the very first time, Isabella exclaims, "My blood is violent, now or else never / Love me" (3.2.99–100); initially resistant to her overture, he quickly becomes enamored by her beauty, admitting, "[M]y blood burns like fire" (3.3.110). Her rioting blood may have triggered in her suitors a lovesickness that would eventually deteriorate their mental faculties, particularly corrupting their imagination and memory.[21] Thought to have inferior memories compared with those of men, women have the power to emasculate them by invading their bodies with a sanguine plethora.

The Lustful Oblivion of Widowhood in The Insatiate Countess

Near the end of the narrative, fascination explicitly yields more dire consequences. Lust rankles into bloodlust. After Isabella ditches him, Guido prophesizes that women, who are composed of mere blood yet lack souls, ultimately seek bloody acts (3.4.190). Isabella later substantiates his dictum while seducing Sago into plotting the deaths of her two former lovers (4.2.218–251). When repentantly apostrophizing Guido's bleeding corpse, Sago encourages the audience to connect together the grim chain of events through blood:

> O cease to weep in blood, or teach me too,
> The bubbling wounds do murmur for revenge:
> This is the end of lust, where men may see
> Murder's the shadow of adultery
> And follows it to death.
>
> (5.1.23–27)

A corpse was said to hemorrhage in the presence of its murderer because its blood would reunite with those spirits that the dying man had transmitted to the murderer at the time of death.[22] This reference to Ficino's theory of fascination dramatizes the extraordinary menace of Isabella, whose fluidity flows through a series of male bodies. The wounds that "murmur for revenge" could very well be issuing Isabella's humors, symbolically perverting the principle of hereditary succession, the common metonym of which was blood. If patriarchy enables male subjectivity to create a bloodline that perpetuates memory through offspring, Isabella's fluidity might be said to generate a lust line that tears through the homosocial fabric. As the constitutive matter of seed, her blood has engendered no sons but only murderous strife among the male characters.

Oblivion Incarnate

Isabella's personification of liquid lust puts on display humoralism's involvement in the female imaginary, especially as conceived by the feminist philosopher Luce Irigaray. Western women, for Irigaray, have formed their identities according to a mechanics of fluids – not that of solids, which subtends the masculine imaginary. For the early modern period, her scheme is not so cut and dry. Humors, whose elemental liquidity affects both genders and their interactions in various ways, bring nuance to the Irigarian economy, which overprivileges contemporary scientific assumptions about states of matter.[23] Isabella's metonymic connection with oceanic flows and lunar or menstrual fluctuations emphasizes the turbulence that the female imaginary generates for male identities. In postcoital rapture, Gniaca wallows in his experience of Isabella's body: "I have swum in seas of pleasure without ground, / Vent'rous desire past depth itself hath drowned" (3.4.85–86). She has left him groundless, bearingless, dissolved in marine enjoyment. Guido later puts his pleasure in perspective when he warns that Gniaca will be "Devourèd in her gulf-like appetite" (4.2.70) if he does not escape her.[24] The image of Charybdis lies behind his curious expression in that "gulf," being a watery depth or whirlpool, was often applied to a voracious appetite:[25] Zeus punished the daughter of Poseidon and Earth for exceptional greediness by smiting her with a thunderbolt and hurling her into the ocean, where, transformed into a monster, she three times daily swallowed great volumes of seawater with everything in it.[26]

Besides comparing her appetite with the boundless sea (2.1.238–39; 4.2.82–83), the playwrights project onto Isabella the image of Charybdis most notably during the final phase of Isabella's marriage masque. This metatheatrical episode is yet another narrative addition with which the playwrights entrench the thematic affinity between forgetting and lust.[27] Upon executing a lavolta or galliard, Guido "falleth into the bride's lap, but straight leaps up, and danceth it out" (2.1.153–54, stage directions). The accident arouses Isabella: "Was I not deep enough, thou god of lust, / But I must further wade?" (2.1.158–59), suggesting that her vulva has tried to draw the handsome dancer into its depths. The comment about wading may either contradictorily indicate Isabella's own slow progress in fulfilling her lust or be a faulty rendering of "wait." But Guido is mortified by his tumble: "Let me depart unknown, 'tis a disgrace / Of an eternal memory" (2.1.169–70). His words foreshadow his warning to Gniaca that "Devourèd in her gulf-like appetite, / . . . Thy memory leaves nothing but thy crimes, / A scandal to thy name in future times" (4.2.70, 72–73). Isabella's emblematic staging of Charybdis could not occur at a more consequential moment for the play's preoccupation with the male imaginary. The main masque shows each masquer presenting to his mistress a shield decorated with an impress, a personalized emblematic motto, whose meaning she has to decipher. In effect, it stages a Tudor variant of a helm show, a public display of coats of arms, in which knights who wished to compete in a tournament had to demonstrate their aristocratic credentials before heralds.[28] For Guido, the helm show – a ritual of the male imaginary through which the gentleman validates his social status before the court – spells, instead, an utter catastrophe, bringing shame and disgrace upon himself.

As the accidental dumbshow suggests, Isabella's monstrous appetite and menacing gulf threaten to obliterate male selfhood, drawing out the vaginal in oblivion and oblivion in the vaginal. Early modern representations of forgetting reveal its latent gender assumptions by superimposing Charybdis on the voracious orifice. *Richard III* mentions "the swallowing gulf of dark forgetfulness and deep oblivion" (3.7.127–28) and, in a poem apostrophizing everlasting oblivion, Marston requests that this "mighty gulfe," this "insatiate cormorant" "devoure" him quickly,[29] again blurring forgetting with lust. A vagina is also a place of deep oblivion as well as oblivion's sinister source. In the opening scene, Mizaldus addresses to his comrades a series of puns on Isabella's genitalia: the first line of the play is "What should we do in this Countess's dark hole?" (1.1.1); and in response to Roberto's stellar praise for Isabella, Mizaldus warns, "Marry, I fear none of these will fall into the right ditch" (1.1.16–17), anticipating Guido's tumble; and Mizaldus assures Roberto that "the way into your ladyship is open" (1.1.20). As Richard Scarr observes in a discussion of Marston's punning, Isabella is very much "The Insatiate C[o]unt[ess]."[30] Forgetting shares with female lust the same vaginal-oral image when it comes to imperiling male identity.

The Insatiate Countess urges the spectator to see beyond her alluring exterior to the underlying Charybdian horror – the feminine life-force as a site of oblivion, which Slavoj Žižek names in another context "the lamella, the libido as organ, the inhuman–human 'undead' organ without a body."[31] The play pushes Isabella to the margins of everyday social relations, dehumanizing her as the monstrous embodiment of the voracious appetite of forgetting. Her fluid, plethoric nature is, to use Žižek's appropriation of Lacanian terms, an organ without a body – pure drive incarnated, whose insatiability both fascinates and repels the male onlooker. The organ's horror comes from confounding the sexual drive with an oral one, no doubt an elaboration of the premodern coupling of lust with gluttony.[32]

By attributing lustful forgetting to Isabella's fearful fluidity, the play casts the blame for male lechery squarely on the female body and turns male ethical self-remembrance into a heroic struggle. As we have seen, Guido brings Gniaca out of his Lethe-like stupor through the discipline of *nosce te ipsum*, and on the scaffold of the main plot's last scene, the Duke of Medina stirs Sago to repentance – another form of self-knowledge – for having murdered Guido (5.1.1–30). That the male lovers are not accountable for their actions when benumbed by her fearful fluidity is forcefully demonstrated by Sago receiving a pardon just before Isabella's execution. If

Sara Eaton is correct in noting that *The Insatiate Countess* is the only early modern English play that has an aristocratic heroine killed on the tragic scaffold for her sexual transgressions, then the drastic punitive measures taken reveal the extent to which Isabella is considered a threat to mnemonic culture and indicate a confidence in patriarchal institutions to restore stability to male and female identities.[33] It is with the spectacle of execution that law and punishment effectively contain any further danger her body poses to the male characters, while publicizing a warning to other insatiate women.

The Wife's Commemorative Duty

Just before the axe falls, however, Isabella does the unthinkable for a play that has channeled so much energy into portraying her as oblivion incarnate. A miracle occurs: Isabella remembers. Does the plot finally acknowledges the tragedy as her own, especially given that this eponymous character delivers over 550 lines, one of the longest female speaking parts in the whole of Jacobean drama?[34] Does the play take its cue from Painter's translation, where the narrator actually claims that on the scaffold Bianca Maria, confessing her faults and praying to God, "began to know hir selfe?"[35] No, it definitely does not. Isabella arrives less at knowing herself than at knowing her other. On the scaffold, she comes to remember her husband.

Upon entering the scene, Isabella does not recognize her surroundings, and when told that her death draws near, she replies that her physician says she is in good health. Afterward, when hearing her vengefully exulting over Guido's bloody murder, the Cardinal pleads with her to accept his guidance, for he fears for her soul (5.1.95–96). He tries to shrive her until her second husband Roberto, now a friar, ascends the scaffold. The playwrights have again added something new to the narrative, which Melchiori calls "the major departure from the source."[36] In Painter and Fenton, the second husband leaves the plot for good, after Bianca Maria abandons him; in the play, Roberto, disgusted with his wife's infidelity, renounces worldly living to become a beadsman (2.4.52–53), a calling which, Melchiori asserts, allows him to reappear later at the execution "to bring about the repentance and pardon of the countess."[37] Melchiori's reasoning, however, seems tenuous, since the Cardinal could have easily and more efficiently performed the role of facilitating her absolution.

Marston, I contend creates instead a scene much like the one he creates between Guido and Gniaca, where a mindful companion, an ethical amanuensis if you will, leads a forgetful individual back into a state of remembrance. But there is one crucial difference. Roberto assists Isabella into knowing him, her husband. Roberto says, "Lady it seems your eye is still the same, / Forgetful of what most it should behold. / Do not you know me then?" Isabella replies, "Holy sir: so far you are gone from my memory, / I must take truce with time, ere I can know you" (5.1.155–59). What follows this exchange is a speech in which Roberto, as if talking about another couple in third person, brings Isabella into full remembrance of him. It is only through knowing her husband – not herself – that Isabella is then able to repent of her shameful deeds and receive from him pardon. Why must Isabella, puppet-like, perform an act of remembrance, when for most of the play she's been demonized as the embodiment of an oblivion dangerous enough to dissolve male identity?

The scaffold scene can be understood as a spectacle of a wife's duty to her husband, a spectacle that forces closure upon the troubling problematic raised in the play's opening scene. Isabella is punished for several crimes, but her disorderly life stems from an initial violation of a wife's vows: as one critic puts it, she commits "an unparalleled triple infidelity to a marriage that was already an act of infidelity to the memory of her former husband."[38] At the play's beginning, Isabella profanes the mourning ritual of the "month's mind" that she is supposed to carry out for the Count of Swevia, her first husband. In other words, Marston introduces Isabella's first harmful act as a violation of the memory art of commemoration. Prior to any action occurring, the stage directions set the scene by indicating that the Countess is to be discovered "sitting at a table covered with black, on which stands two black tapers lighted, she in mourning" (1.1.sd). The month's mind took place around a similar piece of furniture, which symbolized the deceased "in the form of a draped hearse surrounded by candles."[39] The ritual commemorated the dead person with obsequies, frequently a requiem mass, on the thirtieth day following the funeral or death,[40] extending the duration of the funeral as if mourning were as heartfelt as on the day of interment.[41]

When Roberto approaches her during her obsequies, she offers feeble resistance to his argument that mourning cannot change what fate has determined. After a courtship of fifty lines or so, Isabella confesses, "I had a month's mind unto you, / As tedious as a full-riped maidenhead" (1.1.91–92). Her wordplay overwrites the ceremony with another signification, an amorous fancy for a person as in Robert Tofte's subtitle *The months minde of a melancholy lover*,[42] and her simile of the "full-riped maidenhead" suggests monthly menstruation, looking forward to her later blood-fueled lusts. Commemoration has been eliminated, obliterated by new desire.

When Guido and Mizaldus hear the announcement of Isabella's hasty second marriage, their exclamations provide the audience with an affective script of how it should respond to what she has done. Citing the slaughter of Priam at the hands of Pyrrhus, Guido vows to believe a "player's passion" (1.1.120) before he will trust a mourning woman; and echoing Hamlet's sarcastic quip, "the funeral baked meats / Did coldly furnish forth the marriage tables,"[43] Mizaldus declares with cynicism, "The tapers that stood on her husband's hearse / Isabel advances to a second bed" (1.1.130–31). The clear allusions to *Hamlet* magnify anxieties around the remarrying widow. Indeed, Marston's opening goes further than Shakespeare in imagining the primal scene of the widow's lustful betrayal of her dead husband. Isabella blasphemes the rites of the month's mind by using the candles to perform, in her words, a "subtil conjuration" (1.1.97). Before the Reformation, testators would regularly make bequests for memorial tapers to be maintained at funeral and anniversary services. Considered to have apotropaic powers,[44] candles protected the deceased during the first thirty days after burial, when it was believed that the soul remained in the neighborhood of the body. A lit candle materialized the intercession of the living on behalf of the deceased and externalized the mourner's mindfulness to keep alive the deceased's memory. *The Insatiate Countess* begins with Isabella deliberately betraying this sacred trust in order to pledge her lust to Roberto: "And as this taper, due unto the dead, / I here extinguish, so my late dead lord / I put out ever from my memory, / That his remembrance may not wrong our love" (1.1.98–101). The scandal of her actions depends on the spectator accepting the month's mind as a valid expression of mourning. The opening scene dilutes the Catholic overtones by appealing to the memorial ends of patriarchy rather than explicitly referring to the masses and prayers for departed souls, which would invoke the potentially objectionable doctrine of purgatory.[45] As though casting a diabolical spell, Isabella obliterates the memory of her first husband, and in liturgical response Roberto snuffs out the other taper, but soon enough, finding himself likewise abandoned, will ironically wail, "To let the nuptial tapers give light to her new lust, / Who would have thought it?" (2.4.28–29).

Because the narrative sources mention no such event and ritual, the inclusion of the maimed rites reveals Marston's determination to situate Isabella's lust within commemorative culture. The scene of the widow's betrayal initiates the plot of *The Insatiate Countess* with what would have been a narcissistic shock for that culture. To be forgotten by a loved one must be the most painful of blows to an early modern man's sense of self. In his advice on choosing maids, written seven years after the play, Alexander Niccholes expresses outrage over a widow's conjugal treachery:

> Who can love those living that he knows will so soon forget him being dead, that are but summer swallows for the time of felicity, that will hang about one's neck as if they had never arms for other's embracing, or as though extreme affection without control could not but thus manifest itself and break out and yet decease[d], and such a Lethe of forgetfulness shall so soon overtake thee as if thou hadst never been, nay so little a quantity of time shall confine it, that she shall not lie in her month but she shall be churched again, and open to another all thy fruitions, with as fresh and plenteous an appetite as the harlot to her next sinner.[46]

Coupling menstruation with the month's mind, the wife's lapse in loyalty after thirty days provokes social anxieties over the woman being a slave to her body at a time when she should be grieving. Violating much more than affection's bonds, the widow's lust has plunged her erstwhile mate and his estate into the waters of Lethe as if he had never existed.

The Lusty Widow as a Site of Remembering

In eliciting male fears over a wife's failure to perform her primary duty to her husband, the opening scene sounds an alarm against the allure of the lusty widow. *The Insatiate Countess* appears at a moment when this stock character had been flourishing on the Jacobean stage.[47] Comedies exploited the lusty widow as a plot device, since her sexual appetite, unfettered by parental control, gave a dispossessed or younger son access to the marriage market. Jennifer Panek argues that this theatrical stereotype, far from promoting a stigmatized social category, belonged to a male fantasy that arose from the "common fact" of widows remarrying in the period and would have "appealed to at least a portion of the theatre patrons of early modern London."[48] Her theatrical embodiment provided younger sons as well as poor unmarried men with the opportunity to fantasize the windfall of socioeconomic privilege, which normally smiled upon primogeniture in establishing a patrimony – the material legacy designed to preserve the gentleman's name for future generations.

The entire main plot of *The Insatiate Countess* can be read as delivering a riposte to the male fantasy of the lusty widow, notwithstanding the high degree of Isabella's hapless suitors. Marston's alarmism disallows his less privileged male spectators from indulging in escapist wishful thinking. The play makes it clear that, far from fulfilling a suitor's desires, the lustful widow is a site of forgetting destructive to male identity. Marston develops this argument, as we have seen, in conjunction with two different memory arts: the lusty widow jeopardizes both the commemoration of the husband and the male lover's self-remembrance. Given that the memorialization of the dead is linked to a Catholic ritual which had been suppressed by the Church of England, the play's replacement of maimed rites with a struggle for self-knowledge encourages the audience to associate the *nosce te ipsum* with Protestant remembering. The plot thus enacts a kind of reformation of memory. Should we then believe the playwrights that the mnemonic stakes have been raised by this religious turn? No; I would argue, instead, that they effect here a theatrical ploy to salvage male identity. On closer inspection, the two memory arts diverge from one another rather significantly along gendered lines: commemoration depends on female remembering, while *nosce te ipsum* depends on male remembering. The plot's pivot from the opening scene's maimed rites to the struggle for self-knowledge, that is, from men being forgotten to men having forgotten, empowers patriarchy within the play. The unannounced shift enables the male characters to reassert their agency over memory threatened by lust, for Isabella's grave danger to society is no longer that she forgets each successive lover but that she impedes each from remembering himself.

With the final scene, Marston attempts to resolve the threat that the lusty widow poses to commemoration in the same way that he deals with her threat to *nosce te ipsum*: through discipline and punishment. In making a spectacle of her execution, the play endeavors to prove that the judicial system can handle irruptions of Charybdian horror and set a firm deterrent for other licentious women. And yet the full weight of the law along with the authority of religion fails to effect convincing closure. Isabella's last-minute repentance, in light of her consistently irreligious behavior, sounds improbable, and the spectacle of her remembering Roberto can hardly rectify the problem of widows neglecting their memorial duties. Though, in a manner of speaking, dead to the world, Roberto, the former count turned beadsman, is still very much alive. His actions thus fall flat as a deterrent, since deceased husbands lack the wherewithal to return in the flesh and reprimand their unfaithful wives. Even more pointedly, Roberto's enforcement of his marital privilege elides the simple fact that he is Isabella's second husband. The Count of Swevia, her first betrayed spouse, has been literally forgotten by Isabella as well as by Marston in this concluding scene. The inadvertent irony is stunning: in trying to reestablish a husband's authority over the negligent wife, the juridical finale only underscores the utter powerlessness of husbands to ensure that their widows will become faithful custodians of their memories.

A man had no legal means of guaranteeing that his wife would remain dutiful to him when he was gone. After being dependent on men her whole life, a widow would gain for the first time considerable independence, not available to maids and wives. Neither reverting back to the authority of her father nor passing to the supervision of a son, the bereaved woman could now choose a sexual partner by herself.[49] No longer under the jurisdiction of a husband, she was allowed to own property and possessed legal rights according to ecclesiastical and civil law.[50] When it came time to make her own will, a privilege which she could perform only as a widow, she could bequeath property to younger sons and stepsons, circumventing the first born altogether.[51] At the vulnerable moment when primogeniture relied most heavily on a wife to preserve patrimony, the widow had options available to her that she did not have when married. Walter Raleigh thus advises his son to remember that when bequeathing his estate to his wife, he "givest it to an enemy, and most times to a stranger, for he that shall marry thy wife shall despise thee, thy memory, and thine, and shall possess the quiet of thy labor, the fruit which thou hast planted, enjoy thy love, and spend with joy and ease what thou hast spared and gotten with care, and travail."[52]

And this is what the play cannot fully admit about mnemonic culture's dependence on the widow. It was within her power to perpetuate or discontinue whatever legacy her husband left. The male imaginary needed the widow, not out of any premodern equivalent to romantic love or courtly devotion, but because it was only through her compliant custodianship that a dead patriarch could keep his genealogical line from slipping into oblivion. As Raleigh asserts in his advice to his son, "wives were ordained to continue the generation of men, [not] to transfer them and diminish them either in continuance or ability."[53] If she outlived her master – a likelihood in all classes, especially the upper where wives could be considerably younger than their husbands[54] – an aristocratic woman was expected to remember him through a wide range of material practices and observances, for, according to Amy Erikson, the most common executor between the fourteenth and early eighteenth centuries was an executrix.[55] At the beginning of *The Insatiate Countess*, Isabella is very likely following instructions left by the Count's last will and testament. Besides safeguarding property for heirs and raising children to find suitable mates, aristocratic widows had long administered their husbands' legacies, "arranging and paying their husbands' funerals, building their tombs, fulfilling their religious bequests, collecting their debts and paying their creditors."[56] Just as significantly, her spoken and written reminiscences also prevented his unoccupied locus from sliding out of the social order: "The virtuous widow by her behaviour continued to honour her husband, and she kept his memory alive by constantly rehearsing his merits far more effectively than brass or stone or gilded monument."[57] Her indispensable memorial role is epitomized by the word "relict," a premodern English synonym for widow that semantically overlaps with "relic." The encroachment of relict's more recognizable homonym would not have been lost on early modern individuals when glossing the word.[58] A widow actively preserved the remains of her husband.

The Insatiate Countess, however, avoids confronting patriarchy's anxious dependence on wives. Its attack on the male fantasy of the lusty widow strategically portrays her concupiscent body as a manageable site of oblivion. Marston seeks to maintain male agency over memory by displacing the problem of commemorating the husband with that of ethical self-remembrance. Yet, in its attempt to restore the security of mnemonic culture with the spectacle of the law, the play's finale of remembering and forgetting inadvertently exposes the fragility of the early modern male imaginary. The widow's desire ultimately determines her husband's legacy – determines whether or not his identity is borne into the future.

Notes

1 I would like to thank the collection's editors for their excellent comments on this chapter. All in-text citations are taken from John Marston and others, *The Insatiate Countess*, ed. Giorgio Melchiori (Manchester University Press, 1984).
2 Marston wrote his draft at some point between late 1607 and early 1608, before he left the theatrical profession to take holy orders, and William Barksted and Louis Machin were likely hired to finish the draft for the first performance in 1608 or early 1609. See Melchiori, ed., *The Insatiate Countess*, 16–17.
3 Melchiori, ed., *The Insatiate Countess*, 17.
4 Take, for example, George Chapman's *The Widow's Tears*, Thomas Middleton's *A Trick to Catch the Old One*, Middleton's *The Puritan Widow*, and Lording Barry's *Ram Alley, or Merry Tricks*.
5 Garrett A. Sullivan, *Memory and Forgetting in English Renaissance Drama* (Cambridge University Press, 2005), 91–93.
6 Edmund Spenser, *The Faerie Queene*, 2nd ed., ed. A. C. Hamilton et al. (Harlow: Pearson Education, 2007), 2.12.86.6–9.

7 Ibid., 2.12.80.3–4.
8 See "Introduction," in Christopher Ivic and Grant Williams, eds., *Forgetting in Early Modern English Literature and Culture: Lethe's Legacies* (London: Routledge, 2004), 1–18; 6–7.
9 William Painter, *The second tome of the palace of pleasure* (London: Nicholas England, 1567; STC 19124), GGG3^r–GGG3^v. M. Bandello, *Certaine tragicall discourses* (London: Thomas Marshe, 1567; STC 1356.1), U7^r–U8^v.
10 Sullivan, *Memory and Forgetting*, 44.
11 Gail Kern Paster, *The Body Embarrassed: Drama and Disciplines of Shame in Early Modern England* (Ithaca, NY: Cornell University Press, 1993), 79.
12 Ibid., 81.
13 Jacques Ferrand, *A Treatise on Lovesickness*, ed. Donald Beecher and Massimo Ciavolella (Syracuse, NY: Syracuse University Press, 1990), 250.
14 Alexander Niccholes, *A discourse of marriage and wiving* (London: Leonard Becket, 1620; STC 18515), E3^v.
15 Lawrence Babb, *The Elizabethan Malady: A Study of Melancholia in the English Literature from 1580 to 1642* (East Lansing: Michigan State College Press, 1951), 129–30.
16 Joseph Swetnam, *The araignment of leuud, idle, froward, and vnconstant women* (London: Thomas Archer, 1615; STC 23534), E4^r.
17 Levinus Leminus, *The Touchstone of Complexions*, trans. Thomas Newton (London, 1576; STC 15446), P8^r.
18 Qtd. in Babb, *The Elizabethan Malady*, 130. Gniaca suggests this idea when discussing sex (3.4.91).
19 Marsilio Ficino, *Commentary on Plato's Symposium on Love*, trans. Sears Reynolds Jayne, 2nd ed. (Woodstock, CT: Spring Publications, 1999), 160.
20 Ferrand, *A Treatise on Lovesickness*, 92–93.
21 Ibid., 101–2; 115.
22 Ficino, *Commentary on Plato's Symposium*, 163.
23 Luce Irigaray, *This Sex Which Is Not One*, trans. Catherine Porter and Carolyn Burke (Ithaca, NY: Cornell University Press, 1985), 106–18.
24 Gulf appears in the sources but does not carry the rich associations with forgetting that Marston assigns to it: Painter, *The second tome of the palace of pleasure*, JJJ1^r; Bandello, *Certaine tragicall discourses*, T3^v, U4^r.
25 "gulf, n.," OED Online, October 2021.
26 Natale Conti, *Natale Conti's Mythologiae*, trans. John Mulryan and Steven Brown, 2 vols. (Tempe, AZ: ACMRS, 2006), vol. I, 748.
27 No such scene exists in the sources.
28 Alan R. Young, *Tudor and Jacobean Tournaments* (London: George Philip & Son, 1987), 46.
29 "Cormorant" could be a greedy person, not just a bird. John Marston, *The Scourge of Villainy* (London: Iohn Buzbie, 1598; STC 17485), I2r. See also the gulf of greediness in Spenser, *The Faerie Queene*, 2.12.3–5.

30 Richard Scarr, "Insatiate Punning in Marston's Courtesan Plays," in T. F. Wharton, ed., *The Drama of John Marston: Critical Re-visions* (Cambridge University Press, 2000), 82–99; 97.
31 Slavoj Žižek, *The Parallax View* (Cambridge, MA: MIT Press, 2006), 117–18.
32 Thomas Wright, *The Passions of the Minde* (London: 1604; STC 26040), J8ᵛ.
33 Sara Eaton, "Defacing the Feminine in Renaissance Tragedy," in Valerie Wayne, ed., *The Matter of Difference: Materialist Feminist Criticism of Shakespeare* (Ithaca, NY: Cornell University Press, 1991), 181–98; 198, n. 48.
34 Melchiori, ed., *The Insatiate Countess*, 39.
35 Painter, *The second tome of the palace of pleasure*, JJJ1ʳ.
36 Melchiori, ed., *The Insatiate Countess*, 25.
37 Ibid.
38 Leonora Leet, *Elizabethan Love Tragedy, 1587–1625* (New York University Press, 1971), 85.
39 Jennifer Woodward, *Theatre of Death: The Ritual Management of Royal Funerals in Renaissance England, 1570–1624* (Woodbridge: Boydell Press, 1997), 41.
40 See Clive Burgess, "A Service for the Dead: The Form and Function of the Anniversary in Late Medieval Bristol," *Transactions of the Bristol and Gloucestershire Archaeological Society*, 105 (1987), 183–212.
41 Christopher Daniell, *Death and Burial in Medieval England, 1066–1550* (London: Routledge, 1997), 62.
42 Robert Tofte, *Alba* (London: Matthew Lownes, 1598; STC 24096).
43 William Shakespeare, *Hamlet*, 2.2.503–5; 1.2.180–81.
44 Woodward, *Theatre of Death*, 45.
45 During the Elizabethan period, the month's mind "had a customary half-life in many parts of England." See David Cressy, *Birth, Marriage, and Death: Ritual, Religion, and the Life-Cycle in Tudor and Stuart England* (Oxford University Press, 1997), 398.
46 Niccholes, *A Discourse of Marriage and Wiving*, F2ʳ.
47 See note 4.
48 Jennifer Panek, *Widows and Suitors in Early Modern English Comedy* (Cambridge University Press, 2004), 10–11. Panek asserts, "Nearly all the well-known theatrical names of the first quarter of the seventeenth century produced at least one comic remarrying-widow plot" (5).
49 Stephen Collins, "A Kind of Lawful Adultery: English Attitudes to the Remarriage of Widows, 1550–1800," in Peter C. Jupp and Glennys Howarth, eds., *The Changing Face of Death: Historical Accounts of Death and Disposal* (London: Macmillan and St. Martin's Press, 1997), 34–47; 42; Barbara J. Todd, "The Virtuous Widow in Protestant England," in Sandra Cavallo and Lyndan Warner, eds., *Widowhood in Medieval and Early Modern Europe* (New York: Addison Wesley Longman, 1999), 66–83; 66.
50 Theodora A. Jankowski, *Women in Power in the Early Modern Drama* (Urbana: University of Illinois Press, 1992), 35–36.

51 Barbara Jean Harris, *English Aristocratic Women, 1450–1550* (Oxford University Press, 2002), 168.
52 Walter Raleigh, *Sir Walter Raleighs instructions to his sonne and to posterity* (London: Beniamin Fisher, 1632; STC 20641.5), C4^r–C4^v.
53 Raleigh, *Sir Walter Raleighs instructions*, C6^r.
54 Amy Louise Erickson estimates that "up to 45 per cent of all women could expect to be widowed some time in their lives." See *Women and Property in Early Modern England* (London: Routledge, 1993), 154.
55 Ibid., 156–57.
56 Harris, *English Aristocratic Women*, 152.
57 Collins, "A Kind of Lawful Adultery", 36.
58 For an early modern gloss on "relict" as "relic," see Todd, "The Virtuous Widow in Protestant England," 82.

PART II

The Politics of Memory and Affect

CHAPTER 4

"Gathered again from the ash"
Traumatropism, Memorialization, and Foxe's Acts and Monuments

Devori Kimbro

In the summer of 2013, I attended two conferences in England focused on the Catholic/Protestant divide during the early modern era. While there, conference attendees toured various sites around Lewes, Sussex, with significant bearing on the Reformation – including the ruins of a Cluniac priory that stood for nearly four centuries before the violence of the Dissolution. As a native of the western United States, I marveled at the layers of physical history around me. As a scholar of the English Reformation, I marveled at the continued presence of the violence of that era through various means of memorialization. Plaques and images strewn throughout the city commemorated the sacrifice of a group of seventeen Protestant martyrs burned during the Marian Reaction, and I learned through both conference presentations and discussion with residents that these acts of martyrdom are one of the primary inspirations for Lewes' continued observance of Bonfire Night on November 5 each year.[1] As a scholar, I primarily study these events from afar, safely ensconced in the glow of my computer screen as I gaze in horror at the graphic woodcuts depicting these martyrdoms for authors like John Foxe and others. But as I walked the streets of Lewes and looked at the totems of memorialization, the trauma of the period was omnipresent. All around me were scars, psychic and physical, serving as reminders of a nearly 500-year-old event.

In this chapter, I will undertake an examination of what is now designated "cultural trauma" and how similar forces likely helped create one of the Protestant Reformation's most enduring texts: John Foxe's (1516/17–1587) *Acts and Monuments*, more colloquially known as the *Book of Martyrs*. How then can an exploration of the first edition of *Acts and Monuments* through the lens of cultural trauma help us garner a more fulsome understanding of its genre, occasion, and legacy? Many scholars have questioned to what extent Foxe's Protestant martyrologies differ from their Catholic and early Christian forebears. One may also posit that Foxe (as well as other reformers) sought to position the Protestant Reformation within a framework familiar to them as former Catholics, and Catholics knew their martyrologies and hagiographies. I wish to position this awareness and purposefulness of genre within the context of early modern trauma studies and explore how an early modern understanding of cultural trauma often situated itself in religion, since both trauma and certain religious ideologies relied on common knowledge of a series of events from texts memorializing said events.

Scholars of the early modern period have been hesitant to engage with trauma theory in purely modern contexts and considerations.[2] This is not without good cause. Currently, "trauma" is most readily identified with Freudian psychoanalysis. Additionally, there is anxiety when it comes to probing too deeply into individual mindsets of any long-past time, especially when not much private confessional writing survives. As Judith Pollmann reminds us, "Most memories are personal and private, and inaccessible to the historian."[3] Much of the use of trauma in the field of early modern studies revolves around examinations of how trauma and traumatic events, as broadly defined by the Freudian school, impacted literary expression, character development, and narrative structure in the era.[4] According to this definition of trauma, a traumatic event is one that continually and without invitation reinscribes itself on the psyche of an individual. Trauma often manifests as amplified memory divorced from the physical reality of the originating event. In this vein, trauma and memory are intimately connected, as memory itself, in its accurate *and* hyperbolized states, is the interlocutor of trauma. To be traumatized is to remember against one's will and suppressive instincts, and to remember is to endure trauma yet again. So far removed as we are from the actual events of England's Reformation, it is difficult to say whether religious upheaval produced trauma, as Freud understood the term, in individuals.

However, scholars of early modern literature and history have become invested in developing means to apply broader inquiries surrounding trauma to pre-modern texts. In their impressively wide-ranging collection, *Early Modern Trauma: Europe and the Atlantic World*, Erin Peters and Cynthia Rogers remind us that while trauma may seem a uniquely modern phenomenon, "trauma and its residual evidence [are] historically and contextually specific and may take different names."[5] This license to conceptualize trauma outside the lens of modernity allows for imposition of current theoretical traumatic frameworks to be retroactively applied toward a better understanding of the way trauma was *likely* expressed prior to the development of our terminology. As such, this chapter relies heavily on a convergence of theories of cultural trauma. Where cultural trauma differs from individual trauma is that while individual trauma is an interloper – an unwanted and difficult-to-banish reminder of an event – cultural trauma is usually intentionally deployed on a public with limited individual access to the actual event. Cultural trauma is often deemed "memorialization" or "commemoration." An event occurs, and through documenting and commentary through writing or other means, it creates a traumatic resonance for individuals not present for the original incident. Likewise, memorialization and trauma can be associated when the outcome of that commemoration serves to highlight the emotional resonance of past violence as a means of shocking and horrifying the public, sometimes as a deterrent. Jeffrey C. Alexander's examination of the social elements of trauma underscores the way this mechanism works without undermining the depth of affect and emotion that can surround these commemorative events: "Collective traumas are reflections of neither individual sufferings nor actual events, but symbolic renderings that reconstruct and imagine them." Alexander also argues that trauma, in a collective sense, is not rational but still intentional: "It is people who make traumatic meanings, in circumstances they have not themselves created and which they do not fully comprehend."[6] Cultural trauma is often seen through a lens of "memorialization" or "commemoration," which are acts Dominick LaCapra deems "traumatropic."

Borrowed from the biological term for an aberration in a root structure brought on by physical harm, LaCapra describes "traumatropism" as a convergence of cultural trauma and historiography wherein memory and affect conjoin. An event occurs, and through documentation and commentary, it comes to create a traumatic affective resonance for individuals not directly impacted by the original incident. The tales of martyrs, both Protestant and Catholic, are the best surviving evidence we have of the impact of these changes on individuals. Their documented statements and the records of their suffering are powerful. As Brad S. Gregory notes, the number of actual recorded martyrs throughout all of Europe during the period is minuscule compared with the overall population, coming in somewhere around 5,000 during the entirety of the sixteenth century, yet these figures loom large in the popular imagination and subsequent generations.[7] An analysis of Foxe's martyrologies as a document of religious sentiment through the lens of cultural trauma in the early modern period shows us that even in the early modern period, there was an awareness of the effect *and* affect of cultural trauma as a motivating force, and there was a willingness to deploy this trauma accordingly. The adaptation and continued use of something that might have been discarded as a remnant of "popery," such as the martyrologies that formed a cornerstone of the Catholic tradition, became a critical tool for demonstrating the importance of the work of carrying on the Reformation to other citizens. This is significant because it gives us insight as to why the conventions of the martyrology not only remained but were elevated in their importance and visibility, often appearing alongside the Bible itself. It is because, as is demonstrated in biblical exegesis like typology, polemicists understood that, tapping into a history of pain and fear associated with the delicate balance of religion and rule, of personal belief and proscribed dogma, their readers may be more inclined to understand the stakes of the argument at hand and be properly motivated to act on those fears to keep the Reformation moving forward and pure.[8] Although there may not have been a cultural concept of trauma as we understand it now, the impulse to deploy trauma as an effective means of harnessing public outrage and anxiety to push a political and social agenda is an old one.

Martyrologists writing during the tumultuous period of European religious upheaval during the Protestant Reformation were making Alexander's "traumatic meanings." Many martyrologies included narratives of martyrs and saints who had died decades, if not centuries, before the collection was put together. This is certainly true of Foxe's tome, which includes lengthy retellings of the ordeals of early Christian martyrs as a means of connecting their deaths to the sufferings of those who perished during the Marian Reaction. Furthermore, the martyrologies and the traumatic details shared in *Acts and Monuments* were meant to foster the resolve of Protestants facing the continuation of the Reformation in England under the reign of Elizabeth I. As Foxe himself says in his dedicatory epistle to Elizabeth in the 1563 edition, he hopes that the volume will "encourage, by the same your princely benignitie, both me and all other my fellowe brethren to proceade (the grace of the Lorde so assisting vs) in further trauayle, to accomplyshe that whiche our diligence can extende vnto for the vse of Christes churche, vtilitie of your Realme, and the glorie of his holy name."[9] But that resolve, as far as Foxe was concerned, had to be fostered by a wariness of the consequences should the Reformation fail or backslide, or at the very least by an awareness of the sacrifices that had ushered England's Protestants through the Marian era into the (potentially) more tolerant Elizabethan era.

Critically, though, the Marian martyrologies created a sense of shared identity separate from the Catholic identity for English Protestants. Trauma, in a cultural sense, results in an event deemed "traumatic" by a group of people which is then reexplored through memorialization in literature and other forms, even as the event itself fades into the past. As a result, situating Foxe's work in a framework of cultural trauma and exploring the way the text worked on the memory of his readers sheds light on what Foxe may have viewed as a necessity for a text of this sort at this historical moment. For his readers to understand the importance of finishing the work of the Reformation, he had to make them understand the consequences of leaving it unfinished. This connection is significant because we usually struggle to apply the boundaries of trauma to the premodern period. Cultural trauma, however, represents a more concerted transmission of ideas than an organic traumatic incitement. Indeed, cultural trauma is often codified and deployed by apparatuses (the state, the church, etc.) that by their very natures keep expansive records of their doings. By its definition, cultural trauma is not something that happens spontaneously, stemming from the impact of an isolated incident on an isolated individual or group of individuals.

Foxe's compendium bore great affective import for generations of English Protestants who understood it as an artifact of suffering and national identity. First published in 1563, five years after Elizabeth became queen, Foxe's tome soon became as ubiquitous in England as the Bible. In 1571, Elizabeth's Privy Council ordered Foxe's book placed in many cathedrals and churches.[10] Inspired by its initial popularity, Foxe went on to publish several more expanded editions during his lifetime, and versions of the text remained popular well into the eighteenth century as England's long Reformation continued.[11] *Acts and Monuments* occupied a unique place in the documentary history of England's Reformation under Elizabeth. Although it was seemingly held in equal esteem with the vernacular Bible, it is not really a text of Protestant doctrine. Rather, it is a narrative of torment. After presenting a brief history of the Christian church until Thomas à Becket's death in 1170, Foxe moves rapidly into a history of John Wycliffe and his translation of the Bible to English in the fourteenth century. The bulk of Foxe's original text and its subsequent editions are stories of the trials and executions of English Protestants during the reign of Mary Tudor. Similar to earlier martyrologies, these accounts were meant to both horrify and inspire. David Loades notes that the immediate impact of the publication of *Acts and Monuments* was that "its vivid and gruesome stories entered into the public imagination, combining the appeal of the horrific with a gratifying moral and religious message."[12] In spite of its prohibitive cost and its horrifying contents, *Acts and Monuments* nevertheless became a defining presence in the English Protestant imagination during the Elizabethan era and beyond. What then can account for *Acts and Monuments*' enduring legacy in English literary and ecclesiastical traditions? Most simply, the content of the text is unshakably memorable. As the Reformation continued, booksellers' stalls became flooded with tracts and pamphlets focused on doctrinal debates on issues ranging from royal supremacy to transubstantiation. Foxe instead relied on the familiarity of the martyrology genre and on the residual trauma of England's brush with the Counter-Reformation to create a narrative of English Protestantism that was at once recognizable while at the same time placing Elizabeth's reign in a new phase of both Christianity and Reformation alike. In doing so, his argument becomes self-evident: the Protestant martyrs who suffered so cruelly under the reign of Mary I shared an ideological lineage with those who sacrificed their lives for Christianity since the earliest days of the faith under the Roman Empire. There are myriad reasons why Foxe, a devout Protestant who had spent much of Mary's reign in exile on the continent, would choose to make his mark on English Protestantism with a book of martyrology rather than a doctrinal tract or otherwise. During Edward VI's reign, Foxe was a friend and pupil of John Bale, who "encouraged" him to compile his first martyrology.[13] Strategically, a text placing Protestant martyrs in the company of early Christian martyrs also had a legitimizing effect. Furthermore, it could be argued that a book cataloguing the traumatic deaths of those who stood strong against the forces of tyrannical superstition and "popery" could help stiffen the resolve of Elizabethans tempted to backslide into the old ways in the face of Elizabeth's Settlement, which would nominally promote a more religiously tolerant England. Cultural trauma provides a critical lens for assessing the contemporary and cultural import of martyrdom as expressed through texts like Foxe's *Acts and Monuments*. Cultural trauma bears some similarities to individual trauma in a psychoanalytical sense. Primarily, as we see from evidence of martyrdom during the period, the sense of loss or damage is often outsized to the reality of the event. Many Europeans, Protestant or Catholic, never personally knew any martyrs to the Reformation. Thanks to the rhetoric of martyrologies and the ubiquity of printed polemical texts, however, a literate person could examine a broadsheet or pamphlet detailing the horrors of martyrdom. Graphic and evocative woodcuts both supplemented the text for the literate and conveyed the concepts to the illiterate.

The traumatic text or artifact is not created in a vacuum, of course. For the purpose of exploring Foxe's role in creating a Protestant narrative of cultural trauma, we can turn to Alexander's incorporation of Max Weber's discussion of the sociology of religion. Since cultural trauma is a cultural construct, it relies on cultural architects. Drawing on Weber, Alexander identifies these individuals with the term "carrier groups." The specific demographics of a carrier group depends entirely on the situation at hand; in the case of this faction of the Protestant Reformation that exploited the traumatic ends of religious martyrs, martyrologists such as Foxe constitute a specific "carrier group." Alexander notes, "Carrier groups have both ideal and material interests; they are situated in particular places in the social structure; and they have particular discursive talents for articulating their claims for 'meaning-making' in the public sphere."[14] Much of the text of a martyrology such as *Acts and Monuments* is designed to be a testimonial to carrier groups and "meaning-making." Nearly every figure presented in the text, from the early Christian martyrs defiantly professing their faith while being led into the coliseums of Rome to figures more contemporary to Foxe like John Wyclif (d. 1384) and William Tyndale (c. 1494–1536), can be described as a meaning-maker. Foxe explores all these figures through the context of their ability to make meaning either through sacrificial, public acts and the testimonies that precede them or through radical acts of translation that move the Bible out of Vulgate Latin into vernacular tongues to support the development of the priesthood of all believers. Both Wyclif and Tyndale, who were afforded special status as meaning-makers of the English Reformation, are given their own narrative spaces within *Acts and Monuments*, with Wyclif's story dominating much of the second book of the 1563 edition, and Tyndale's being singled out for telling in the third book.

We can easily identify martyrologists as a unique but pervasive carrier group in the workings of the Protestant Reformation. Martyrologies as a tool of doctrinal and evangelical work are endemic to every era of Christianity, but they were of distinct use when it came to building hagiographical conceits throughout the growth of Christianity. Helen Constance White notes in her comprehensive study *Tudor Books of Saints and Martyrs* that martyrs have their feet "in two worlds, the world of historic fact and the world of spiritual significance," which denotes their traumatropic place, made of both history and the affective response to that history.[15] White also notes, time and again, that the accuracy of these accounts was very seldom the aim for their creation, instead reminding us that "From the beginning the saint's or martyr's legend was an instrument of propaganda for convert-making, designed to convey the wonder and excitement of conversion and the subsequent missionary zeal of the convert."[16] Whether or not martyrologies are intentionally traumatropic perhaps cannot be easily decided. The rhetoric of the stalwart martyr, coming from the Greek term for "witness," in the face of mocking questioning and torture is paramount to the documentation of the martyr's experience across time and implies a corresponding reader response.

Since Alexander draws on Weber's work that situates cultural trauma within a socioreligious framework, it is uniquely suited to our ability to understand the modus operandi of martyrologists like Foxe during England's religious conflicts. In continuing this analysis, Alexander positions trauma as a "social performance," developing rhetorical meaning between the situation (the Marian Reaction and Elizabeth's ascension), the audience (Protestant readers), and the authors (martyrologists). Given Elizabethan censorship practices, carrier groups during Foxe's publication tenure were effectively arms of the state. The traumatropic and propagandistic texts produced by Foxe and his contemporaries were state-sanctioned if not state-issued.[17] The intentional goal on the part of the carrier group as referenced above would be to communicate the trauma to the audience. Alexander notes that the carrier group "makes use of the particularities of the historical situation, the symbolic resources at hand, and the opportunities provided by institutional structures."[18] While the tradition of the martyrology was long-established in the Christian/Catholic world, the use of a decidedly Catholic trope bordering on a hagiography to convey Protestant trauma is unique and demonstrates the willingness of Foxe and other writers to make use of the "historical situation" endemic to the Protestant Reformation and the Marian Reaction, as well as the "symbolic resources" of the genre. As Elizabeth Mazzola notes, "sacred ... practices still powerfully organized the English moral imagination in the sixteenth and seventeenth centuries," even once Catholicism had nominally fallen out of favor.[19]

According to Alexander the first step in the transmission of this cultural trauma is that "the performance of trauma is projected to the members of the carrier group itself. If successful, the members of this originating collectivity become convinced that they have been traumatized by a singular event. Only with this success can the audience for the traumatic claim be broadened to include other publics."[20] Foxe certainly fits this criterion as a member of a carrier group for cultural trauma. Foxe's biographers note that he was a "committed evangelical" as early as the 1540s, during the latter years of Henry VIII's reign. After Henry's death, the nobility charged with the protectorate of Edward VI pushed forward with more drastic and complete reforms than the prior king had been willing to undertake. Foxe had access to England's Protestant elite through his duties as tutor for the children of the earl of Surrey, which also put him in the company of powerful Protestant families like the Howards. He authored a few controversial tracts during his remaining time in England but fled to the Continent on Mary's accession in 1553. During this time, he joined with other English exiles in Protestant countries and began the work of compiling a series of Latin martyrologies and defending the activities of other notorious evangelicals such as John Knox (c. 1514–1572) and John Bale (1495–1563). As Foxe suffered the rigors of self-exile for the safety of himself and his family as the Marian Reaction continued apace, he often received vivid accounts from those remaining in England, detailing the tortures and deaths they had witnessed among their Protestant brethren. These narratives found their way into the last of Foxe's Latin martyrologies, *Rerum in ecclesia gestarum*, published in late 1559, which was his first broad commercial success. When he returned to England in October 1559, almost a year into Elizabeth I's reign, he had money and a new reputation as a chronicler of the Protestant martyr experience.[21]

Foxe uses his dedicatory epistle to Christ to frame the carrier-group narrative for his readers in the opening of *Acts and Monuments*, although that text originally appears in untranslated Latin.[22] He spends much of the opening of this dedication extoling the strength he got from Christ through his myriad trials, saying that he was "agitated with so many and such great toils as would wear out even some burden bearing donkey." The process of compiling the work at hand "has cost [him] unbearable cares, sleeplessness and worries." Through his dedication to Christ, Foxe shares with his readers that the act of compiling these tales has been, in and of itself, traumatic. This act of compilation serves the purpose of investing a form of immortality in the martyrs themselves and steeling the resolve of those who are tasked with carrying on the hard work of the Reformation. Additionally, Foxe further completes the carrier group agenda by formulating a relationship with the audience as participants in both the trauma and the continuing Reformation by referring not to himself and his travails alone, but to a more universal "we," noting that the narratives contained therein are the "way *we* [emphasis mine] see with how much greater glory Cranmer, Ridley, Latimer, John Hooper, Bradford, and the rest of the prize fighters in the same company, died fighting in [Christ's] army." Later, Foxe extends the obligation of memorialization to his readers in a true embodiment of the carrier-group-to-public by commenting that the martyrs, "in whose names we rightly and constantly owe," are embodiments of England's "thanks to [Christ's] goodness." Although Foxe, through the compilation of the text, has been the primary receiver of the trauma, he is now, through the act of publication, placing the traumatic burden of memorialization on his readers.

As an archivist, Foxe seemed to be acutely aware of the differences between history and historiography – and the latter was rhetorically significant in Elizabethan England.[23] Those supportively documenting the Protestant Reformation at home and abroad had to make a case that Elizabeth's succession was righteous and in England's best interest as a means of settling decades of religious upheaval precipitated by her father's need for a divorce. Documentary evidence from Mary's reign indicates that while she certainly drew a firm line of what constituted heresy and treason, executing nearly 300, her approach to the counter-Reformation was decidedly more measured than the resulting 200 years of Protestant historiography would have one believe. *Acts and Monuments* is above all historiography rather than history. John King notes that while Foxe attempted to serve purely as a compiler for the works he brought together under the banner of his magnum opus, there is a fair amount of editorializing through selection: "Although belief that Foxe willfully falsifies documents is groundless, because he carefully transcribes texts and confines editorial additions to clearly demarcated commentaries and glosses, he is often highly selective in his choice of material. Like Spenser, Foxe subscribes to a historical standard whereby invented fiction may conform to moral and religious truth."[24] There is, however, a significance to Foxe's particular use of historiography. The very essence of Foxe's chosen form, a martyrology, has typological connotations since, with England's first steps into a long Reformation only three decades past, those reading Foxe would certainly have known of the importance of martyrologies and hagiography in the Catholic tradition.

Much of the sense of occasion of *Acts and Monuments* is documented in the actual tales of the martyrs that form the latter part of the text, creating a timeline connecting the martyrs from the early Christian church and the works of Eusebius to those who died under Mary's reign. Foxe also spends a great deal of time exploring his purpose and function in the text's front matter. As was common in the era, there are two dedicatory epistles in the 1563 edition – one addressed to Christ, the other to Elizabeth. The address to Elizabeth at once embraces the significance of the martyrological tradition while attempting to remove the provenance of martyrdom from the clutches of the Catholic tradition. This would have been a requisite move given that the English reformers were again anxious to "complete" the work begun under Henry and stalled after the death of Edward. Foxe and his fellow reformers were desirous to give the appearance that there would be no tolerance for any vestiges of "popery," but the connection between martyrdom and the Catholic tradition of hagiography and sainthood would have been hard to ignore.[25] One of Henry's earliest reforms involved stripping traditional English religion of saints' days, federally sanctioned holidays that religious detractors argued not only elevated common men and women through idolatry, but also inhibited England's economic growth by frequently stopping work in exchange for feasting and frivolity.[26] As a result, Foxe must find a way to argue for the importance of martyrologies – and he does so by forming a direct link not to Catholic martyrologies but to early Christian martyrologies. Foxe casts himself as a modern Eusebius to Elizabeth's Constantine: not a humble Christian chronicler who desires to elevate the status of these men and women to heretical sainthood, but rather a historian of a tortured past from which the Reformation may rise triumphant. He tacitly compares the two by saying, "At length the Lord sent this mild Constantinus, to cease bloud, to staye persecutiom, to refreshe his people." Like Constantine at the end of the period of great Christian persecution under the hand of the Roman empire, Elizabeth, argues Foxe, is sent to England to bring a temperate hand that "cease[s] bloud" of the Protestant martyrs who suffered similarly to their forbears.[27]

Although Mary Tudor is not directly named in the text, her presence is felt in this particular narrative as Foxe reminds Elizabeth and his other readers of the cyclical nature of such religious trauma and strife, saying that, though God "suffer[s] sometyme the Tyraunt to rage, and the Hypocrite to reigne for the iniquitie of the people, yet some tyme againe, the same hande of the Lorde whiche woundeth, healeth: that presseth, refreseth: that striketh, salueth againe, to make amendes withal."[28] Noticeably, Foxe does not present the trauma of martyrdom as an instance to be solely overcome and left in the past. It is important to him that his readers recognize the traumatic nature of each discrete recurrence. They must realize that their faith will be challenged again and again, but with faith like that possessed of both the early Christian martyrs and their brothers and sisters lost during the Marian Reaction, movement into a new era of the Reformation is possible.

A lot of this work occurs in the narratives themselves, where Foxe diligently uses typeface to signal how Protestant martyrs viewed the role of their faith in the world as they were facing down Catholic detractors. For instance, in the narrative of the martyrdom of John Rogers, an early victim of Mary's attempts at counter-reform, Foxe sets apart the description of the two churches in the dialogue between inquisitor and martyr.

When asked about his allegiance to the "Catholike Church ... in England, hauing receaued the Pope to be supreame head," Rogers typographically replies, "know none other head but Christ, of his catholike Church, neyther wil I acknowledge the Byshop of Rome to haue any more autority, then any other Bishop hath, by the word of God, and by the doctrine of the old & pure Catholike Churche. iiii. hundreth yeares after Christ."[29] Here Foxe significantly sets Roger's faith as "(c)atholic" in opposition to the "(C)atholic" faith adhered to by his inquisitors. This differentiation is not attributable to the vagaries of early modern typesetting and spelling alone, but instead signifies the prominence given to the Protestant faith as a purportedly original form of Christianity. Literally drawn from the Greek *kaθolikós* for "universal" or "in respect of the whole," the term came to be applied to the Roman Catholic Church once it was established as a state religion to reflect its encompassing of the known, Roman world. With his typographical difference, Foxe argues for a positioning of the Protestant faith as a truly Catholic faith: something universal in its totality as opposed to the purely dogmatic, nominal positioning of the "Catholike" faith, which is but a denomination associating itself with Christianity's universality.

Cynically, one may argue that Foxe "editorialized" historic and documented accounts from the Marian martyrdoms for the sake of promoting a larger propagandistic purpose. Violence sells, after all. Foxe outlines his purpose in his dedicatory epistle and argues for the significance of the project, offering some insight into how he not only served as an archivist of sorts for these martyrdom narratives, but also undertook sharing them with the English public. The dedicatory epistles of the first edition of *Acts and Monuments*, however, exemplify LaCapra's theory of traumatropism. The first dedicatory epistle is addressed to Christ and offers up praise for the current success of the English Reformation, as well as strong intimations that Foxe acknowledges that the work is far from over. Throughout this dedication, Foxe frequently conflates the sense of history and the sense of memory, arguing that they serve a dual purpose. Foxe asserts that, within the context of salvation, the martyrologies are unnecessary in an earthly frame of reference, since the stories of their subjects are already well known to Christ. Foxe writes, "[E]ven if no record of them were to exist here, those whose names have been inscribed in the book of your life could not fail to be the most illustrious in every way." Here, he expresses the innate tension between "memory," wherein slippage may render the bravery of the martyrs forgotten, and "history," using the representation of the "book of life" to express a form of documentary or archival existence of these deeds that serves the purpose of allowing them entry to God's kingdom. Indeed, Foxe almost exclusively uses derivations of the term "history" to describe the contents of *Acts and Monuments*. In a way, the early modern vision of history, as embodied in Foxe and described by Daniel R. Woolf, reminds us that those who wrote history in the period were less concerned with the accurate description of past events, and more so with "history's *story* delivered principally for the purposes of moral edification or entertainment."[30] Foxe even asserts that the mere act of compiling the narratives was sacred in its origination: "the propitious favor of your [Christ's] mercy has been present also with us as we were sweating in compiling their history." In this way, Foxe allows the martyrologies he has compiled to exist in the dual space of LaCapra's traumatropism, which owes much to the same slippage of genre and meaning as described by Woolf. The purpose of relaying these martyrdoms is not necessarily to create a completely faithful rendering of the events surrounding the deaths of the martyrs. Foxe never asserts that to be his motivation. Rather, he acknowledges throughout his epistle that he desires to compile these "histories" as a means of achieving affective resonance. Foxe desires to cast the suffering of the martyrs not as emulative inspiration, but rather as a means of coaxing those still living in Elizabeth's new Protestant state into greater resolve. Foxe expresses this partnership of memory and history by evoking the image of the dead martyrs as a form of incitement of the continuing Reformation, praising Christ for thinking it "worthy to recall to light anew and reveal to the notice of your church the cause and innocence, as if gathered again from the ash, of your blessed Martyrs, whom the perversity of this world reduced to flames and ashes."[31] Even though the ensuing pages of martyrologies will provide sufficient violent narratives, Foxe feels pressed to engage with the affective resonance even in his introduction, asking readers to root their resolve in the very ashes of the men, women, and children who were executed under Mary.

Additionally, Foxe asserts a dual purpose for the martyrologies that involves not just commemorating and elevating the memories of the Protestant dead, but also imposing permanent ignominy on those who interrogated, tortured, and put them to death. This cuts to the heart of what was perhaps a most Protestant use of traumatropism not just in Foxe's text but also in much of the work that sought to expose purported Catholic superstition and cruelty throughout the next two centuries of English polemical production.[32] In essence, it was not enough that history and memory should conjoin to memorialize the valorous, but that some of that space be allocated to condemn Catholicism. For Foxe and his readers, the text performs as an externalized memory that uses typology to impart significance. This mirrors the process of cultural memory that Jan Assmann reminds us is institutional in that it is "exteriorized, objectified, and stored away in symbolic forms."[33] In the dedicatory epistle, Foxe envisions this exteriorized future for *Acts and Monuments* as it will let the reader "look on the opposite side at your adversaries, of whom it is generally agreed that there were so many murders, injustices, cruelties against your own people, and likewise many crimes perpetrated secretly and wickedly by the same people, which they never expected would be publicly known."[34] Foxe deems that the text can even transcend the memory of the Marian Reaction by providing information heretofore unknown by the public who are reading it.

It is hard to parse Foxe's precise reasoning for choosing a series of martyrologies as a text meant to legitimize Elizabeth's succession and to position English Protestantism as a form of "true" Christianity, especially given the genre's favored status in the Catholic tradition. Likely, though, Foxe understood that the potent blend of cultural trauma and traumatropism melded the affective resonance of trauma with the selective narrative-building of historiography. This combination produced the effect of tying Protestant history more concretely to early Christian history by using a form that would have been well known to former English Catholics. Cultural trauma, even prior to its theoretical identification, was an important tool in creating and sustaining national narratives that centered on memorialization in service of continuing engagement with the Protestant cause. Foxe demonstrates time and again that attentiveness to the historical truth of martyrdom narratives springing from the Marian Reaction is secondary to the affective reaction garnered from exploiting residual cultural trauma. This reaction is ultimately Foxe's aim. Protestants reminded viscerally and repeatedly of the dangers of England falling once again into Catholic hands would be more inclined to press for a more permanent Reformation, one that matches Foxe's vision. Additionally, Foxe understood the importance of rooting the relative newness of Protestant reforms in the long-distant past, forging a deep connection between those who perished during the Marian Reaction and the martyrs of early Christianity and their sufferings. Foxe, and other Protestant martyrologists, understood the binding ties of cultural trauma and memorialization and the benefits that martyrology as a genre offered in conveying these messages to readers eager for both spiritual sustenance and visceral titillation – a combination that has proved popular and effective ever since.

Notes

1. In recent history, the terms "Marian Restoration" and "Marian Reaction" have been used to describe the period between the death of Edward VI and the ascension of Elizabeth I. I will be using the term "Marian Reaction" since its affective resonance hews truer to the argument of this chapter discussing Elizabethan Protestantism.
2. Scholarship exploring trauma in the early modern period includes Thomas P. Anderson's *Performing Early Modern Trauma from Shakespeare to Milton* (Burlington ,VT: Ashgate, 2006) and Lisa S. Starks-Estes's *Violence, Trauma, and Virtus in Shakespeare's Roman Poems and Plays: Transforming Ovid* (Houndmills: Palgrave Macmillan, 2014).
3. Judith Pollmann, *Memory in Early Modern Europe, 1500–1800* (Oxford University Press, 2017), 1.
4. Some important critical texts in the exploration of trauma and literary studies include Gert Buelens et al., eds., *The Future of Trauma Theory: Critical Literary and Cultural Criticism* (New York: Routledge, 2014), and Cathy Caruth, *Unclaimed Experience: Trauma, Narrative, and History* (Baltimore, MD: Johns Hopkins University Press, 1996).
5. Erin Peters and Cynthia Rogers, "Reading Historical Trauma: Moving Backward to Move Forward," in Peters and Rogers, eds., *Early Modern Trauma: Europe and the Atlantic World* (Lincoln: University of Nebraska Press, 2021), 5.
6. Ibid., 4.
7. Brad S. Gregory, *Salvation at Stake: Christian Martyrdom in Early Modern Europe* (Cambridge, MA: Harvard University Press, 1999), 6.
8. Typology is one of the four most prominent means of biblical exegesis used in the period. Typology situates past and present in the biblical/religious narrative by understanding figures and events as "types" of one another. For instance, Moses is a type of Christ since they both elevate a population imprisoned by a superstitious and worldly realm to a "promised land" as a result of their sacrifices. I recently explored this connection in *Trauma, Typology, and Anti-Catholicism in Early Modern England, 1579–1625* (Tempe: Arizona State University Press, 2015).
9. Foxe, *Acts and Monuments* (London: John Day, 1563), B2r.
10. John King, "Introduction," In King, ed., *Foxe's Book of Martyrs: Selected Narratives* (Oxford University Press, 2009), xi–xii.
11. In this chapter, I will be focusing entirely on the first edition of *Acts and Monuments* since all other subsequent editions underwent significant additions rather than amendments.
12. David Loades, "Introduction," in Loades, ed., *John Foxe and the English Reformation* (Aldershot: Ashgate, 2002), 5.
13. Thomas S. Freeman, "Foxe, John," in *The Oxford Dictionary of National Biography* (2008).
14. Alexander, *Trauma*, 16.

15 Helen Constance White, *Tudor Books of Saints and Martyrs* (Madison: University of Wisconsin Press, 1963), 4.
16 Ibid., 21.
17 For more information on the way the Elizabethan state monitored and challenged publication, see Cyndia Clegg's *Press Censorship in Elizabethan England* (Cambridge University Press, 1997).
18 Alexander, *Trauma*, 16.
19 Elizabeth Mazzola, *The Pathology of the English Renaissance: Sacred Remains and Holy Ghosts* (Leiden: Brill, 1998), 3.
20 Alexander, *Trauma*, 17.
21 Freeman, "Foxe, John."
22 I will be using the English translation of this passage drawn from the critical website, John Foxe's *The Acts and Monuments Online* sponsored by the University of Sheffield. This translation is provided by John Wade, University of Sheffield. All additional quotes from *Acts and Monuments The Unabridged Acts and Monuments Online* or *TAMO* (1563 edition) (The Digital Humanities Institute, Sheffield, 2011). Available from: www.dhi.ac.uk/foxe.
23 This is not to suggest that other cultures are not and have not been equally reliant on historiography rather than history. Indeed, a historian would argue that most history *is* historiography.
24 John King, "Fact and Fiction in Foxe's *Book of Martyrs*," in David Loades, ed., *John Foxe and the English Reformation* (Aldershot: Ashgate, 2002), 15.
25 For more information on the way that Catholic traditions were often ensconced into English Protestant practice, see P. A. Schwyzer, "Fallen Idols, Broken Noses: Defacement and Memory after the Reformation," *Memory Studies*, 11.1 (2018), 21–35, and Mazzola, *The Pathology of the English Renaissance*.
26 For further analysis on how England's Reformation altered holidays and other celebrations, see David Cressy, *Bonfires and Bells: National Memory and the Protestant Calendar in Elizabethan and Stuart England* (Berkeley: University of California Press, 1989).
27 Foxe, *Acts and Monuments*, B1v.
28 Ibid.
29 Ibid., YYy2v.
30 Daniel R. Woolf, "From Hystories to the Historical: Five Transitions in Thinking about the Past, 1500–1700," *Huntington Library Quarterly*, 68.1–2 (2005), 33–70; 36.
31 Foxe, *Acts and Monuments*, *2v, trans. John Wade. See note 23 above.
32 For further reading on the tradition of English anti-Catholic literature and its lasting legacy, see Peter Lake and Michael Questier, *The Antichrist's Lewd Hat: Protestants, Papists, and Players in Post-Reformation England* (New Haven, CT: Yale University Press, 2002); Leticia Alvarez-Recio, *Fighting the Antichrist: A Cultural History of Anti-Catholicism in Tudor England* (Brighton: Sussex Academic Press, 2011); Frances E. Dolan, *Whores of Babylon: Catholicism, Gender, and Seventeenth-Century Print Culture* (Ithaca, NY: Cornell

University Press, 1999); and Arthur F. Marotti, *Religious Ideology and Cultural Fantasy: Catholic and Anti-Catholic Discourses in Early Modern England* (University of Notre Dame Press, 2005).
33 Jan Assmann, "Communicative and Cultural Memory," in Astrid Erll and Ansgar Nünning, eds., *Cultural Memory Studies: An International and Interdisciplinary Handbook* (De Gruyter, 2010), 109–18; 110.
34 Foxe, *Acts and Monuments*, *2r, trans. John Wade.

CHAPTER 5

"To take on me the payn / Ther fall to remember"
Metrical Visions *and the Dangerous Memory Networks of Complaint*

William Kerwin

Early modern English literature provides stirring examples of the empowering possibilities of sharing a memory. Perhaps the most famous:

> He that shall see this day and live old age
> Will yearly on the vigil feast his neighbors,
> And say, "Tomorrow is Saint Crispian."
> Then will he strip his sleeves and show his scars,
> And say, "These wounds I had on Crispin's day."
> Old men forget; yet all shall be forgot
> But he'll remember, with advantages,
> What feats he did that day.
> (*Henry V*, 4.3.44–51)

Henry, in his speech before the battle of Agincourt, prophesies a glorious and still generative future memory: a time when people will look back, embellishing the truth in a mixture of recollection and fiction, all in the service of spreading pride and communal good-feeling. The memory will serve the rememberer, but it will also have a social function, spreading to the neighbors and elevating the speaker in their eyes. The memory will transfer not just the past but emotions in that future present, as the power of memory, according to the youthful king, will spread fraternal happiness to people not yet alive. Memories will work, he predicts, like actors on a stage, in a performance that generates and transfers affects both within the speakers and between those remembering speakers and their listeners.

But other early modern texts present memory's generative emotional powers in a quite different light, when testimony spreads affects and ideas with darker purposes, working like infection or curse. When the source of the memory is not accomplishment but suffering, betrayal, or death, how does it persist in the holder, how does it spread into the hearer, and how can it unsettle the status quo? What different motives would drive verbal artists to present this process? On the stage and in early modern complaint poetry, we can find powerful examples of how memory can carry and spread painful affects, caused by social injustice or personal pain, that move in a wide range of directions. Certain literary forms are particularly well suited for presenting memories that transfer painful feeling from rememberer to the audience.

This chapter looks at one such site of dark memory, in the workings of the mid-century complaint movement, and argues that complaint is a key part of early modern memory culture. In particular, it explores George Cavendish's collection of individual stories, *Metrical Visions*, which was part of a new wave of complaint poetry, and participated in a shift in the representation of those charged moments where people from the past remember. These complaint poems work quite differently from medieval tragic poetry, as they remember in terms that combine individual affects – including guilt, shame, fear, and indignation – and political critique. Often cloaked in an outward conservativism, one that affirms traditional hierarchies, on closer examination the mid-century complaint poem demonstrates much more complicated networks of power. Composed of the imagined testimonies of trauma victims, speaking from the grave, complaint is one form where individual emotion and politics converge, and then spread. Less famous than its almost-contemporary complaint collection *The Mirror for Magistrates*, Cavendish's *Metrical Visions* (composed, conjecturally, between 1552 and 1554) transforms the *de casibus* tradition of individual tragic stories by borrowing from Lydgate's *Fall of Princes* but creating a completely different sense of individual character. Cavendish complicates and modernizes the medieval tragedies, primarily by combining the traditional protest complaint with an awareness of the various facets of an individual memory, and the role that networks play in those memories. He invents a way of speaking which exists first in this poetic genre and then evolves into the Shakespearean soliloquy. As such, complaint poetry acts as a bridge between medieval tragic poetry and early modern dramatic tragedy.

The idea of the network, developed by a range of theorists but powerfully brought into literary study by Caroline Levine, creates a productive opening for considering the nexus of memory and affect in Cavendish's poetry, and, more broadly, for reconsidering formalism and its relationship to history. Levine, in her 2015 book *Forms: Whole, Rhythm, Hierarchy, Network*, has opened up numerous critical readings which challenge either new critical or new historicist readings that move toward narrative closure. She considers linkages between literary forms and social forms, organizing her study around the four terms in the title's list.[1] Network is a form, both social and literary, that interacts with other forms in conflictual ways. In addition, Levine stresses the importance of looking at how multiple networks are at play in any given text or historical moment.² At the core of her version of a "new formalism," Levine sees these four forms as each multiple and colliding. The collisions of various social rhythms, for example, in a historical setting, means that no one such form ever produces complete closure. Literary forms, she argues, are cut from the same cloth as historical forms, though they can be used to challenge or support the historical forms they interact with.³

Metrical Visions can fruitfully be seen through the prism of the concept of network, which reveals things not only about this text but about early modern memory culture as a whole. Networks appear here in two ways: through the networks of characters within the volume itself, where the memories of a complaining speaker spreads affect to listeners and readers, and within a network of complaint poems and collections across the Tudor period. From medieval tragic poetry to politically directed mid-century collections like *The Mirror* and Cavendish's *Metrical Visions* to the end of century erotic complaints shaped by Ovidian complaints, the genre evolves in ways that reflect all of the century's titanic shifts. One key part of that transformation is memory, and what people do with it. Cavendish's collection is situated in, and responds to, a number of social webs: the power networks of Henry VIII's court, the punitive reaches of royal authority, the cloak-and-dagger resistance of Catholic opposition to the Reformation, the growing spy system, and an ornate and growing web of people sending, delivering, and receiving letters.⁴ And the poets writing these complaint collections – like the playwrights who would follow them in the 1580s and 1590s – had a fascination for the historical struggles before and at the start of the Tudor dynasty, with their vast and competing networks of connected and conflicting power sources, as well as for the individual tragedy that could occur within those competing systems. In its uses of the past, *Metrical Visions* shares with those history plays a demanding sense of how power flows across multiple networks, and how memory and transfers of memory are crucial parts of that power flow.

As poetry, *Metrical Visions* molds a new shape for both memory and emotion, finding a complex form that voices interiority, political protest, and fear. In showing the various ways that memory works, the performances of individual speakers and their interactions with the frame narrator let us see how memory can trigger these multiple experiences, serving as radically different affordances while playing dramatically different roles: release from pain, burden from the past, alliance-building for the future, political critique in the moment, consolation for both speaker and listener, dishonest guise for self-protection, danger for those who hear it, weapon for those who receive it, or curse on anyone involved. In addition to creating a complex set of subjectivities, Cavendish's collection moves outward to create networks, as it puts memory into roles and onto a stage, emphasizing how the lyric side of complaint, voicing an individual's trauma, soon metamorphoses into a representation of group interaction. The volume is as much about how the complaints affect the listeners as it is about the speakers. To use two of Levine's keywords, memories "sprawl" and "collide," breaking through the forms of the "whole" and the "hierarchy" in ways that violate any drive toward closure.

Complaint stands as a nexus of individual and collective ruination, and complaint collections embody the most far-reaching sense of the idea of the network.[5] Recently, rich studies of Ovidian-inspired complaints from the last quarter of the sixteenth century have explored individual and social identity, especially in relation to women's roles as both authors and poetic subjects. Both the literary production of those so-called female complaints and historical narratives of women's voices in the period serve as colliding networks.[6] But less critical attention has been paid recently to the complaint from earlier in the century, less centered on erotic isolation and more focused on boundary-invading stories linking groups. Responding in many ways to medieval predecessors, *Metrical Visions* and *The Mirror for Magistrates* transform the political complaint into a more hybrid form, breaking new ground in both political theory and poetic form, creating a character-based commentary that grew out of medieval modes but also made distinctive and powerful innovations.[7] Cavendish's characters tell their own tales, to a recorder, and in doing so they actively sort through their own memories, and make the listening author-figure and any eventual readers sort through theirs as well. Mike Pincombe writes, contrasting Lydgate and Cavendish, that with the latter "*de casibus* tragedy is marked precisely by the fact that it takes the form of a complaint spoken in the first person."[8] The poems spend time pointing out destructive forms of memory, connected to injustice, shame, and ingratitude, which are all connected to social forms and institutions. So in addition to asking us to sympathize with the speakers' memories, both major complaint collections, *Metrical Visions* and the *Mirror for Magistrates*, voice a memory network, turning us away from the speaker's story to those of a linked group of social actors, leading a reader to link individual pain with social interdependency.

A key part of residual cultural memory conveyed through mid-century complaint is medieval poetic tradition, which mid-century complaint, including Cavendish's, engages with in complex ways.⁹ English elegiac traditions that feed complaint include poems like "The Wanderer" and Chaucer's "Anelida and Arcite"; these more personal, even primal lyrics represent the *cri de coeur* function that continues into Tudor complaint. Lydgate's fifteenth-century *The Fall of Princes* represents complaint's political directions, and as Maura Nolan has recently pointed out, the collection gives us complex poems that rely on the medieval concept of "*chauntepleure*," or singing and weeping.¹⁰ Tasked by his patron Humphrey of Gloucester to write a moral poem showing that tragedy comes from vice and can be avoided by virtue, Lydgate complicates that simple calculus by providing multiple narrations of events and allowing their inconsistent memories to coexist. Over a century later, Cavendish borrows heavily from Lydgate throughout his collection, both in his selection of passages and in this aesthetic of mixing.¹¹ But Cavendish's development of *chauntepleure* goes in a different direction, intensifying the individual history of the complainer, and *Metrical Visions* emphasizes the flow of memory and its attendant affects from those speakers to the narrator and to the reader. Complaint is still mixed memory, but in a new, post-medieval and post-Reformation way.

Cavendish's collection narrates events very close to the time of its publication, and it captures some of the most traumatic memories of the English Reformation. We hear a set of stories that begin during the reign of Henry VIII, and then travel through Edward's tenure and the perilous early years of Mary's reign.¹² Cavendish is more famous for his *Life of Wolsey* (composed between 1554 and 1558), sometimes called the first major English biography. *Metrical Visions*, perhaps because it pointed to contemporary political figures or perhaps because of its generally Catholic sympathies, was not published until 1825. Very much a battle of memory and counter-memory, set in the wars of religion and politics, the collection captures the fears of a conspiracy-driven, political, dangerous world. Especially in recusant circles, people were reluctant to talk openly or write down politically sensitive things, because they feared the operations of state power. Even as they passionately want to be remembered, they simultaneously fear their words being remembered, and so now memory, as testimony, was deeply dangerous, which adds to complaint poetry's strong connection with the ideas of ruin and trauma. These complaints remember the fallen, and they also remember the sin, and the series of interactions between the complaining speaker and the dream-led interlocutor/recorder enacts and reforms confessional rituals and rhythms. Those testimonies and interactions create a purgatorial place for the suffering dead to mingle with the living, in the spectrum of grief and anger that is always part of elegy. They resonate with an older tragic mode, the *de casibus* tragedies, with a moral thrust blaming suffering on individual sin or on forces beyond the individual's control – the fickle fate of the world, the vice before a fall, the universality of the wheel of fortune. These tones are undercut, however, by a sometimes implicit and sometimes explicit commentary on the individual stories and the emerging politics of the Tudor world. In these stories, political power creates suffering as often as individual vice or blind fate does, a flow of responsibility that the remembering speakers try to get us to believe. Their testimony of trauma is wrapped up in protest. And the confessional nature of the poetic encounter – the complainants tell their tale to the listening recorder, and to us – as well as the purgatorial nature of their status as dead but not yet in heaven or hell bring powerful memories of Catholic ways of organizing feeling and memory into the experience of the poem.[13]

The sprawling nature of memory grows out of another key element of this collection, shared with the *Mirror for Magistrates*: the frame component, where the "auctor," not the complainants, speaks. Imitating Lydgate again, Cavendish employs what his predecessor called "l'envoys" in short sections that usually are entitled "Thauctor/GC." He comes to life as an organizing scribe, but not one without his own feelings to note and to share. And in his comments, both before and after individual complaints, we are given an outsider to the dramatic speeches with whom we can identify, which means the experience of memory – of the transfer of the emotion from one moment to its aftermath – involves the reader as well as the narrator.

For the remainder of this chapter, I will consider one group of poems from the collection, those that tell the stories of the Pole family and their political cohorts. This is a small section of the volume's complaints but one that is representative of the culture's contested and colliding memory networks, as the complaints from the Pole family weave a tapestry of social forms, including the cloak-and-dagger politics of the Henrician court, the traumatic violence inflicted on recusants, the erasure of female agency within the legal system, and the recreation of rituals of confession and penance. Each of the individual speeches involves a transfer of the affect of memory from the complainer to a group of other individuals.

Historically, the Pole family was caught up in the anti-Reformation politics of the 1530s. The matriarch of the Pole family, Lady Margaret of Salisbury, was the daughter of Clarence, Duke of Gloucester, and as such a continuer of the Yorkist line of succession and arguably the last of the Plantagenets. She also had been a friend of Henry's first wife, Catherine, and governess to their daughter Mary, and she was close to figures active in Catholic resistance movements, those keeping alive the beliefs and memories of Catholic culture.¹⁴ These Catholic affiliations were made much more dangerous by the choices of Margaret's son Reginald Pole, who became a cardinal, lived in exile in Rome, and vociferously attacked Henry's proposed divorce and the ecclesiastical changes of the Reformation.¹⁵ The Exeter conspiracy of 1538, centering on allegations that Henry Courtenay, Marquess of Exeter and first cousin of the king, was seeking to usurp the throne at the head of a group of Catholic dissidents, added pressure on the Pole family. The cardinal was the most flamboyantly rebellious family member, but by no means the only one suspected of supporting Catholic rebellion.¹⁶ Henry and his advisors turned on the family members remaining in England, eventually arresting Margaret's other sons Geoffrey and Henry (Baron Montague), an associated nobleman Henry Courtenay (Marquis of Exeter), as well Margaret Pole herself. Part of the evidence came from the few letters sent by family members that they were not able to destroy; these messages, like many in Tudor England, constituted a newly prominent memory network, that of an expanding system of letter-writing.¹⁷ Other parts of the evidence came via the state police apparatus, from Geoffrey, the younger son. Under the pressures of isolation and then torture, Geoffrey testified – that is, provided his memories – against his family, and then attempted suicide.¹⁸ Montague and Exeter were executed in 1538, with Margaret falling to the axe in 1541. Taken as a whole, these complaints, and the cultural narratives they bring into play, let us hear the emotional power and the political protest released by the transfer of memories. The capstone poem of this network, Margaret Pole's appearance with "corage impotent" (1029), is eerily elliptical, resisting the passion and direct challenge to authority found in the poems by others in her circle. This set of complaints exemplifies the competing networks of Tudor culture and of the evolving complaint tradition.

Cavendish shapes them with framing materials and spatial separation. They come in two sections, with Margaret's complaint coming after several intervening ones, adding to the feeling of mysterious isolation in her character. Before that, Montague and Exeter follow Thomas Cromwell, and they in turn follow the narrator's interjection of his own feelings as he becomes a character in the play that is about to begin:

> Pawsying a whyle / reforming of my penne /
> Ffordulled with writing / and feobled was my brayn
> Thus sitting in a muse / I saw too noble men
> Present byfore me / redy to complain
> Desiring me bothe / to take on me the payn

> Ther fall to remember. / dissendyd of oon Race
> Whome to behold it was a pityous case.
>
> (743–49)

The first three lines point to the narrator – his material practice of pen-maintenance, his "ffordulled" and "feobled" state after listening to previous sorrows, and the general passivity of "sitting in a muse." The effect is to take us into this man's feelings. When the two beheaded men appear, they prepare for their own speeches, but they also initiate a transfer of their pain, into the tired narrator, and into us. The word "bothe" points in two directions: back to both of the men, but also ahead to the realities of transferred pain and remembrance. Listening to or reading complaints is no easy task, as "to take on me the payn" makes clear. Like young Hamlet receiving the charge from his father, "Remember me" (1.5.91), any listener to what is to come better get ready for the heavy lifting of memory.

Although they want to be remembered as falsely accused, and the narrator has just told us that remembering their fall is the painful task he'll take up, Montague and Exeter turn much of their complaint against Geoffrey, first summarizing his crimes in the third person and then addressing their absent relative directly. Their words about Geoffrey dominate this complaint, giving it the power of a courtroom drama. Montague and Exeter play roles as witnesses, as prosecuting attorneys, and as sentencing judges. Memory of the past slides out of a legal diction and into the religious as prophecy, as their memories get transferred to their family member, to the narrator, and to the reader.

The transfer of this multi-vocal memory depends on the multi-temporality of the exchange, which makes memory a field that shifts across time, and not always, as in Hal's speech before Agincourt, in good ways. At first they lay out the charge, saying of Geoffrey:

> That so against nature / onnaturally hathe wrought
> Distroyeng all his blood / and brought hymeself to nought
>
> (804–5)

This very quickly tells his history chronologically, from beginning to empty end: "Nature" – because of Geoffrey's actions – begets "onnaturally," and then "blood" devolves into "nought." This process starts with the grand world of nature before shifting to the more local and familial web of blood relationships. After this opening, their speech briefly turns to their memory-as-testifying, before the main thrust of their complaint becomes accusation and prophecy, which eventually wend themselves into other memory forms.

Their own memories of who they were and the fall they experienced quickly turns to their shame about other peoples' memories of them in the future. Memory transfers not only from them to us, but from their past selves to their future selves, which are figured as living in the future but still living in and suffering through the very same memories:

> The blast of our Cryme / is greatter shame
> Than is the losse / of all our bryttell glorye
> That we / alas / shold bere the slaunderous name
> Of traytors falce / in any boke or storye
> What is he of our bloode /./ that would not be sory
> To here our names. / with vile ffame so detected
> Wherwith our posteritie / shall allwayes be suspected
>   (771–77)

Shame here is an affect dependent on the memories of others. "Blast," "name," "boke," "story," and "fame" provide us a string of speech-acts. "Blast" combines the sense of nature, in a strong wind, with the withering effects of a curse. The contrast of "shame" and "glorye" – a mild variation on the genre's seemingly endless deployment of the "shame"/"fame" rhyme – show their terror over the future's alleged misreading of their lives. The thoughts and feelings of how they will be remembered dominate their complaint.

But if shaping how they themselves will be remembered is outside their powers, they do want to shape how another will live on in future memories. They turn to the story of Geoffrey, brother of Montague and close connection with Exeter, whom they want to be remembered in specific ways, with particular affects. They address Geoffrey directly:

> O cruell accuser. / thy malice was too strong
> Our fall to conspyer / by falshod brought abought
> Ayenst all nature / thou hast don vs great wrong
> Therfore frome shame / we put the[e] owt of dought
> Thou shall never escape. / it is so ferre blowen owt
> Ffor of all kind of vices. / shortly to conclude.
> The worst ayenst God / is ingratitude.
>   (806–12)

Their accusations come from multiple fronts, and in different temporalities, as they charge Geoffrey with the past sins of attempted suicide, the shame-worthy act of family betrayal, and the vice of ingratitude. The middle of the stanza moves into the present tense – announcing that at the moment of speaking they are doing something specific to

Geoffrey – and then to the future, in the prediction of an unending period of shame. Finally, the two men move into a generalization that aspires to timelessness. Ranking ingratitude as the worst vice seems exceptional, given the usual "deadly sins" lists and hierarchies, but if you consider ingratitude as essentially a faulty sense of memory, it fits with Montague and Exeter's general attack and the central concerns of the genre. Memory isn't just a medium that serves to transport the story; it is a long-living force that the story was, is, and will be.

This particular memory evolves until it transforms, in a cerebral-Ovidian way, into a kind of infernal curse. Notice the flow of movement and agency within this speech:

> Thoughe thy necligence / bryngythe vs to this end
> Yet that thou mast haue therof remembraunce
> We / God humbly besech / suche grace to the[e] send
> That thou mayst repent / or he on the[e] take vengaunce
> Ffor thy great ingratitude / take this for thy penaunce
> Allwayes in thy hart / call to thy memory.
> That by thy oonly meane hedles here we lye /
>
> (813–19)

The stanza works through a sequence of temporalities. Negligence on Geoffrey's part has caused one thing; Exeter and Montague then act in the present by their beseeching; in the immediate future God, they hope, will send grace, which may lead Geoffrey to repent or may lead to a punishment of unending memory, in a future without limit. The two speakers' memories will be transferred, at some point, to the other people who will remember Geoffrey and to Geoffrey himself, but those processes will be quite different. The memories people will have about Geoffrey, Montague and Exeter charge, will never be separated from shame. And the memories that Geoffrey will have, they say at the end of this passage, will be his assigned form of penance. "Allwayes in thy hart," they curse, will be this awful memory of family slaughter. They are telling their tale and enacting not their confession but the confessions (both the one to the law officials that was false, and this imagined one, which would be true) of Geoffrey. And what is his penance? His penance is memory. Here we have the representation of a future memory – what Geoffrey will remember in the future; this passage is akin to Henry V's Crispin's Day exhortation, with its call to imagine a future where veterans remember their day of glory. But here, the memories that lie ahead will not console and comfort – they will burden.

In the comments after the two men depart – labeled "Lenvoy de / auctor G.C." – Cavendish turns back to the *de casibus* rhetoric of universal and unchanging movements of fortune. But this move contains something of a feint, as the universal and timeless are placed in a historical moment. Here those generalized patterns mirror patterns originating not in a wheel of fortune but in the erratic behavior of the king:

> Ffor if a prynce hathe caught / a deadly sauor
> Of indygnacion / ffarewell all treuthe and nobleness
> To the bloke ye must / it is remedyles.
>
> (831–33)

As Cavendish asks us to attend to this particular prince, and those particular blocks, he gives this poem a sharp dissenter's edge. The dissent comes in insisting on a memory of a prince who caught "a deadly sauor."

Memory works quite differently in the case of the family matriarch, Lady Margaret Pole, Countess of Salisbury.[19] Historically, she was a figure of striking originality, which makes it all the more surprising to see how within this collection her speech rarely ventures beyond the conventional. Anyone in the know – who knew of her historical death, and the possible connections to seditious Catholic politics – would have felt the gap between the cultural complexity of that story and the safe position of her complaint. Historically, Margaret Pole's execution was a mystery, a scandal, and a horror story. She is not accused by any historian of any vice or conspiracy, though that might be because of her circumspect role-playing. Her position is surveyed thoroughly by Hazel Pierce in her academic historical study,[20] but we get a sense of the limits of historical understanding from Hilary Mantel, who writes:

> Her life, marked by stunning reversals of fortune, is an irresistible subject, but it presents a familiar difficulty for the historian. Was she, at this point or that, doing nothing of interest at all – or was she doing everything, in a way that was almost supernaturally discreet? Margaret's later life, at least, is well documented, but we cannot approach her story from the inside.[21]

In fact, Cavendish does attempt to approach her from the inside, but the portrait is much more restrained than those of the other family members. It connects with many historical networks, but maintains strict silence on the anti-reformation conspiracies going on all around her. Cavendish's separation of her speech from that of her family members also elides the family network. None of Margaret's networks plays a major role in her complaint.

The historical Margaret lived a life of enormous vicissitudes. Due to her status as the daughter of George the Duke of Clarence, she and her brother were under threat from the beginning of Henry VII's reign. In 1499, when she was twenty-six, her brother Edward was executed by the king's order, and she lost all of her lands. The wheel turned, however, in 1513, when she was created Countess of Salisbury, and in 1515 her family's previously seized lands were restored to her. On her husband's death, she became one of the richest people in England.[22] Her political fortunes, tied for decades to her alliance with Queen Catherine and Princess Mary, for whom she was a principle guardian, kept her in far-reaching but still tenuous wealth and power. As Catholic threats to Protestant England, real or perceived, became more prevalent, the Countess was arrested in 1538, and interrogated on numerous occasions. Transferred to the Tower, she languished there until 1541, when she was beheaded in a famously gruesome fashion.[23]

Cavendish's introduction of Margaret is, like her speech to follow, determinedly reticent. Before she speaks, the narrating Cavendish describes her as she approaches as "Of corage impotent" (1029), an inward state mirroring her position at the end of her life, when she was executed without any charge to fight against. He introduces her and her story as a warning to other nobles, and he recalls her origins – "Of the blood Royall / lynyally dissendyd" (1033) – before turning to England's reigning nobility, pointing to Fortune in words suggesting a revolution:

> Wherfore ye nobles / beware of hir cruell hate
> Non hathe more need / than ye of great renown
> Ffor whan ye are most highest / than dothe she throwe you down
> And tomblyth you hedlesse / from your hyghe stages
>
> (1037–40)

But what exactly is it that these nobles "hathe more need" of? "[O]f great renown" describes who they are, not what they need; the need of the nobles is left unnamed. Perhaps nobles, especially Catholic nobles, need to remember that they live in peril. In contrast to most of the other speeches, Margaret's speech is followed by no after-speech envoy, and the editor Edwards notes that the manuscript page has a gap where perhaps an after-comment was intended. "Certainly," he writes, "the transition to the following lament is extremely abrupt."[24] Margaret, one of the country's most powerful women, has a tale with very little power. But perhaps this is in keeping with her treatment in other literary tragedies, as in Shakespeare's *Richard III* where she is listed in the dramatis personae merely among the "Children of Clarence (Boy *and* Girl)."

Her sixty-three-line speech in *Metrical Visions* confesses nothing about her recent past, and so is not in any way a memoir of sin; nor is it an accusation directed in a focused way about what has happened to her. Instead, as Margaret stays largely aloof from her end, we get an autobiography, a lofty recall of events from the earlier parts of her life, beginning with her childhood and the murders of her father and brother, moving then to the moment of her return to power, and finally to her time as a powerful figure in English society. The memories that others make of this woman feel quite distinct from the memories in the spoken complaint. When she testifies, she describes her lineage; gives an interestingly hesitant memory of her brother's fate; narrates a staunch defense of the probity of her life as a leader and as a governess of princess Mary, daughter of Catherine of Aragon; tells of her assault by "cruel" Fortune; and then offers a closing warning to other women of high estate. As Mantel has noted of traces of her in the official record in general, this verbal legacy gives no voice to the political machinations and sectarian rivalries that lead to her fall – no hint of her family's decisions, and their sometimes subversive acts.

Margaret's family memories are steeped in a sense of injustice; her genealogy is a chart of political persecution, one that she transfers to us in her memories without specifically linking them to her own fate. Her first memory is of her father, the murdered Clarence of Shakespeare's historic tragedy, but the wording suggests she is also indirectly talking about herself:

> My ffather a duke / of Claraunce was hys stille
> And brother to king Edward / the iiiith of that name
> Who was condemned also / alas / alas the whyle
> By subtill accusation / and he no thyng to blame
> Ffor a prophane prophecy / of whome than ran the ffame /
> Condempned therefore to dye / and drowned in a butt of wynne
> Thus by Crewell ffortune / brought he was to Rewyn /
>
> (1049–55)

In relating her father's fall, her memory is full of anger at "subtill accusation," and not just at "Crewell ffortune," suggesting a very human agency in his fate. This causation points to human agency, not Fate. She also narrates how political actions caused the downfall of her brother, who was killed, "bothe bought and sold" (1059). But strikingly, she offers no similar charge against her own prosecutors, beyond the subtle allegiance with her father in the word "also." The historical record suggests she was struck down not by an apolitical Fortune but, like her father, by "subtill accusation"; however, you would barely know that from her testimony, which departs from a universalizing lament against Fortune only when she points at procedural injustice and her lineal place: "I was condempned / withowt examynacioun / Of the Plantagynttes last of that generacio" (1094–95). Within the same sentence she notes both the unfairness of her arrest and her connections to the much-persecuted Plantagenets.

From the network of her family she shifts to the network of her contemporary female group, aristocratic women. "O ye matrons / that be of noble race / A myrror make of me / trust not to your estate" (1098–99). These women are not named; they are an anonymous caste, and we do not know if the manuscript was circulated within particular groups and families. But Margaret Pole asks that they look on her and remember; through her memories, she is attempting to transfer to them an awareness of the dangerous clash of networks around them.

Margaret Pole was canonized by the Catholic Church in 1886, giving her a place in another network of memories. Gratitude, at last, but not a real voice.

**

What does reflection on *Metrical Visions* have to offer for a consideration of what memory does in the specific cultural spaces of Tudor England? What affects get spread through this collection? And specifically in this small segment of the collection, the laments and accusations of Margaret Pole and her circle, how are we asked to feel and think as we hear their complaints? As a part of the mixture of old and new forms of memory in the period preceding the flourishing of English drama, *Metrical Visions* shows us an evolutionary stage in the history of memory writing, a stage in which moralism meets protest, and elegy meets history. Mike Pincombe calls Cavendish "one of the great founding fathers of … a dissident tradition," and we hear that dissent rising out of memories of loss.[25] The reasons for the suffering are not all of a type: the sometimes tiresome rhyme of "shame" and "blame" conveys an important point: some of the speakers come across as having sinned, and readers are asked to remember those failures, and here memories serve as warnings and admonishments. But more often the rememberers appear as having been sinned against, and testify that what we need to remember is injustice. The abstract moralism of the *de casibus* tradition mingles with protest, especially as the poems become particular and localized, where the poems remember networks of oppression and suffering. These speakers ask to be remembered, and they ask that the systems that did them in – the networks of power – be part of the culture's shared memories.

In the relationship between the interlocutor and the individual speakers, complaint carries with it traces of a confessional culture. Confession, liturgically, is supposed to ease the pain of one's one sins, and the shame and guilt that come from them.[26] But complaint doesn't just reenact confession – it recasts it, in another generic metamorphosis. Being remembered replaces being absolved, and traumatic pain becomes incorporated into the experience of the narrator and the reader. And while the poems echo the rituals of confession, they do *not* point to an authorizing scriptural or early Christian lineage, where figures explicitly connect themselves to recognized saints: unlike the stories in *Foxe's Book of Martyrs*, these stories' only community is the one created in the telling and listening. They are not redeemed by being part of any broad tradition. Their testimony is more spectral, and the absence of an immediate publication of these stories adds to this feeling of ephemerality. But their contemporary-Tudor cultural irrelevance doesn't make them any less moving and revelatory. The collection overall provides a window onto both collective and personal trauma, and the affect of the transferring of pain from memory to memory. The poetic form of the complaint goes a long way toward reshaping poetry's – and eventually the theater's – power to convey the contested and contagious passions of memory, and to locate those affects within networks. For example, in the Shakespeare play most directly connected to the Pole family network, *Richard III*, one can see speeches that reflect the lyric advances evident in *Metrical Vision*. Clarence's account of his dream to the jailer, and Hastings' pre-execution speech about the error of his trust in Richard of Gloucester, both follow the complaint tradition.[27] Linked by familial webs to Margaret Pole, these speakers can be seen as part of the network of political complaint poems that moved into the forefront of English literary culture in the 1550s.

Imagine Memory as a character. This Memory meets other characters, who are themselves their own Memories. *Metrical Visions*, with its transfer of tales, is a memory stage, a memory "super-spreader" event, a network that pits memory against memory in the creation of systemic injustice.

Notes

1 Caroline Levine, *Forms: Whole, Rhythm, Hierarchy, Network* (Princeton University Press, 2015). She begins with theoretical thinking on network thinking, including the writings of Deleuze and Guattari, for their thinking on the rhizome, and Bruno Latour, and the idea of actor-network theory. Her innovation is to put network theory – and especially the idea of network sprawl or overlapping networks – at the service of her new formalism.
2 Ibid., 114. Emphasizing the existence of "overlapping networks," Levine argues that a "formalist approach advocates paying careful attention to the multiplicity of networks and especially to their differences."
3 Ibid., 129: "We can never apprehend the totality of the networks that organize us," and 131: "a formalist approach reveals many opportunities, large or small, to hamper networks and their coordinating power."
4 While the spy network under Queen Elizabeth, led by Francis Walsingham, was not yet established, the cases found in *Metrical Visions*, especially those of the Pole family, as discussed below, demonstrate that surveillance, particularly of letters, was an established practice in Henrician England as well. For just one example, see Hazel Pierce's discussion of events in late 1541, connected with the downfall of the Pole family: "[O]n 17 January, Sir Thomas Wyatt was arrested under suspicion of having had 'intelligence with the King's traitor Pole.'" *Margaret Pole: Countess of Salisbury 1473–1541: Loyalty, Lineage, and Leadership* (Cardiff: University of Wales Press, 2003), 174.
5 See Rebecca Helfer, *Spenser's Ruins and the Art of Recollection* (University of Toronto Press, 2012). She surveys the idea of ruin across the period, and includes Willy Maley's witty term "ruinaissance," which aims at ruin's ubiquity.
6 The subjects surrounding gender and complaint are getting reconsidered with rigor and vigor. For a starting point, see Rosalind Smith, Michelle O'Callaghan, and Sarah C. E. Ross, "Complaint," in Catherine Bates, ed., *A Companion to Renaissance Poetry* (Hoboken, NJ: Wiley Blackwell, 2017), 339–53. For an older but still useful overview and anthology, see John Kerrigan, *Motives of Woe: Shakespeare and "Female Complaint"* (Oxford: Clarendon Press, 1991).
7 Scott Lucas, *"Mirror for Magistrates" and the Politics of the English Reformation* (Amherst: University of Massachusetts Press, 2009). Lucas sees the *Mirror* as fundamentally involved in contemporary politics, and considers it as part of a cultural movement toward individual characterization and a historiography based on causation. See also Paul Budra, *A Mirror for Magistrates and the de casibus Tradition* (University of Toronto Press, 2000).
8 Mike Pincombe, "A Place in the Shade: George Cavendish and *de casibus* Tragedy," in Mike Pincombe and Cathy Shrank, eds., *The Oxford Handbook of Tudor Literature* (Oxford University Press, 2009), 372–88; 374. Pincombe goes on to elevate Cavendish over the *Mirror* collective: "It was Cavendish who introduced the innovation, not Baldwin and his co-writers."

9 On the prose complaints of mid-century, like those of Simon Fish, see John King, *English Reformation Literature* (Princeton University Press, 1982). Also see Andrew McRae on the culture of agrarian complaints. McRae, *God Speed the Plough: The Representation of Agrarian England, 1500–1660* (Cambridge University Press, 1996). And James Simpson, *Reform and Cultural Revolution* (Oxford University Press, 2002).
10 Maura Nolan, "'Now wo, Now Gladnesse': Ovidianism in *The Fall of Princes*," *ELH*, 71.3 (2004), 531–58. She writes that "throughout the book, Lydgate tempers Humphrey's thesis with an elegiac, Ovidian, and feminine discourse of love betrayed and lost that he derived from Chaucer's *Anelida and Arcite* and the *Legend of Good Women*. What results is a distinctly mixed aesthetic, one that renders history in deeply ambivalent fashion, as both sexual and moral, providential and contingent, tragic and elegiac all at once" (532). She defines Lydgate's originality: "staging an elaborate literary negotiation of themes he finds central to English vernacular poetry, as it had been defined by Chaucer and Gower. These include the relationship between tragedy and elegy, the role of the complaint genre in history writing, and the problem of historical causality" (534). The *chauntepleure* is, she says several times, "a figure" which "functions best as an agent of disruption" (535).
11 The borrowings are meticulously charted by Edwards in his edition.
12 This essay quotes from the edition of *Metrical Visions*, ed. A. S. G. Edwards (Columbia: University of South Carolina Press, 1980). Edwards notes, "The title *Metrical Visions* is wholly without authority, being the invention of their first editor, S. W. Singer. None of the manuscripts has a title. I have, for convenience, retained Singer's title throughout, while preferring Dugdale's . . . 'diuers Elegieciall Poems upon sundry persons'" (17).
13 Elizabeth Mazzola has persuasively described the ways in which, after the Reformation, "sacred symbols and practices still powerfully organized the English moral imagination in the sixteenth and seventeenth centuries, continued to orient behaviors and arrange perceptions, and persisted in specifying to believers and non-believers alike the limits of the known world. These sacred symbols remained the primary guides to and deepest structures for feeling." Mazzola, *The Pathology of the English Renaissance: Sacred Remains and Holy Ghosts* (Leiden: Brill, 1998), 3.
14 The most thorough historical accounting of these events remains that of Madeleine Hope Dodds and Ruth Dodds, *The Pilgrimage of Grace, 1536–37, and the Exeter Conspiracy 1539*, 2 vols. (1915; revised ed., London: Frank Cass & Co., 1971). On the family matriarch see Pierce, *Margaret Pole*. On Cardinal Pole, see Thomas F. Mayer, *Reginald Pole: Prince and Prophet* (Cambridge University Press, 2000).
15 See Meyer, *Reginald Pole*, chapter 2, "The Campaign against Henry VIII," 62–102.
16 For the broader story of Catholic opposition to Henry, see vol. I of Dodds and Dodds, *The Pilgrimage*; for the Exeter conspiracy more specifically see vol. II, "The Exeter Conspiracy," 297–328.

17 On the ways that the early modern period saw a rapidly expanding culture of letter writing, see James Daybell, *The Material Letter in Early Modern England* (Houndmills: Palgrave Macmillan, 2012). For connections between letter writing, forgery, and allegations of treason, see Andrew Gordon, "Material Fictions: Counterfeit Correspondence and the Culture of Copying in Early Modern England," in James Daybell and Andrew Gordon, eds., *Cultures of Correspondence in Early Modern Britain* (Philadelphia: University of Pennsylvania Press, 2016), 85–109. For another example specifically connected to the Pole family, see Pierce, *Margaret Pole*, 174: "On 23 February Jerome Ragland and his wife Anne were also examined 'touching the burning of certain letters after the apprehension of lord Montague.'"
18 Pierce, *Margaret Pole*, 128–29 and 140. Pierce presents the divergent narratives of his mental breakdown and suicide attempt.
19 Margaret Pole has been the subject of much attention in the last decade. Hazel Pierce has the most thorough scholarly work: see Pierce, *Margaret Pole*. Pole also plays a role in the popular fiction of Philippa Gregory's *The King's Curse* (2014). Susan Higginbothom added another study in her *Margaret Pole: The Countess in the Tower* (2016). And Hilary Mantel gives Margaret very assertive, almost spunky voice in the final book of her Cromwell trilogy *The Mirror and the Light* (2020).
20 Pierce, *Margaret Pole*.
21 Hilary Mantel, "How Do We Know Her?," *London Review of Books*, February 2, 2017, 3–6; 6.
22 For thorough narrative of this life, see Pierce, *Margaret Pole*; for a briefer account, see Mantel, "How Do We Know Her?"
23 The executioner required multiple strokes, in an event that all accounts describe as shameful. See Pierce, *Margaret Pole*, 177–78.
24 Edwards, ed., *Metrical Visions*, 193.
25 Pincombe, "A Place in the Shade," 388.
26 Paul Stegner, "A Reconciled Maid: *A Lover's Complaint* and Confessional Practices in Early Modern England," in Shirley Sharon Zisser, ed., *Critical Essays on Shakespeare's* A Lover's Complaint (Aldershot: Ashgate, 2006), 79–90; Katherine A. Craik, "Shakespeare's *A Lover's Complaint* and Early Modern Criminal Confession," *Shakespeare Quarterly*, 53.4 (2002), 437–59.
27 1.4.9–63; 3.4.79–92. *The Norton Shakespeare*, ed. Stephen Greenblatt, 2nd ed. (New York, 2008).

CHAPTER 6

Jesting, Nostalgia, and Agonistic Play
Indira Ghose

In a comic interlude in *Henry IV, Part 2*, the fatuous Justice Shallow brags about his wild youth to the equally dim-witted Silence. Shallow delivers a swaggering account of his deeds in his student days at the Inns of Court and indulges in a spot of name-dropping to boot, boasting of his close acquaintance with Sir John Falstaff. "I see him break Scoggin's head at the Court gate, when a was a crack not thus high," he reminisces, declaiming nostalgically, "Jesu, Jesu, the mad days that I have spent!" (3.2.23–26).

It is apposite that Shakespeare briefly links John Falstaff, his greatest comic creation, to Scoggin, legendary court jester and protagonist of one of the most popular jestbooks of the Tudor era. *Scoggins Jests* (c. 1540), a collection of the alleged pranks of Scoggin, is thought to have been written by the physician Andrew Borde.[1] It is equally apposite that Scoggin was probably a fiction, loosely based on an amalgamation of Henry Scogan, poet at the court of Richard II (1367–1400) and friend of Chaucer, and the possibly apocryphal John Scoggin, jester at the court of Edward IV (1442–83), who reigned in England more than half a century after the death of Falstaff reported in *Henry V*.[2] Falstaff, for his part a composite of the historical knights John Oldcastle and John Fastolf, charged with heresy and cowardice, respectively, and of the emblematic figures of the Vice, the Lord of Misrule, and the *miles gloriosus*, to name only a few of his progenitors, was ironically refashioned by Shakespeare from a Lollard martyr into a symbol of "Merry England," a never-never-land of concord and endless festivity.[3] As with Shallow and his concocted memories, a remarkable number of jests recreate an image of "Merry England," capitalizing on the pleasure of nostalgia for a fabricated vision of a harmonious past as a canny marketing ploy. At times, however, jests tap into memories of a festive past and the legacy of classical wit to present quite a different scenario: a constellation in which social tension is accepted as a given, but in which antagonism is transmuted into a sparring match, evoking the shared pleasure of a competitive game. In doing so they mobilize the cultural memory of adversarial jesting and the pleasure of a sporting contest to put forward a model of agonistic civility grounded in the collective pleasure of play.

Early Modern Jesting and Cultural Memory

In 1552 the scholar and physician John Caius, one of the founders of Gonville and Caius College, Cambridge, published a treatise on the sweating sickness in which he mourns a lost age of amity and good-fellowship that flourished "in the olde world, when this countrie was called merye Englande."[4] The concept of "Merry England" encompassed a range of aspects such as harmony, conviviality, charity, hospitality, prosperity, and festive merry-making. Like all cultural myths of a golden age, it was endlessly malleable to the requirements of succeeding generations, and was wheeled out at regular intervals to allude to the pre-Reformation era, or alternatively the Elizabethan age, the early seventeenth century, or even the pre-Hanoverian age. Nonetheless, as Keith Thomas has pointed out, in the case of the early modern age, "it was an amalgam in which real social facts jostled together with the images of literary convention and the inherent nostalgia of social criticism."[5] The Reformation induced a sharp rupture with the past, and observers on both sides of the religious divide lamented the attrition of charity and the demise of rural hospitality with the dissolution of monasteries and the relocation of landlords to the metropolis.

Although Dr. Caius is using the term "merry" in its original meaning of "pleasant," by the end of the century the connotations of mirth and amusement had taken precedence.[6] In the early modern period a wide-ranging movement to reform social manners swept Europe, propelled by Reformation as well as Counter-Reformation forces.[7] The Church had always castigated popular disorder and indulgence in worldly pleasures, but the disciplinary measures adopted during the Reformation were bolstered by humanist efforts to revitalize Christianity and purge popular culture of paganism, remnants of which were excavated in seasonal festivity. Puritans inveighed against vice and vanity, and issued dire warnings about the idle recreations that distracted people from the thoughts of God and merely gratified lower-grade passions. These included jesting and the frivolous diversion offered by jestbooks. In his *Foundation of Christian Religion* (1595), the influential divine William Perkins provides a catalogue of pernicious beliefs that hinder a godly life. In the continual struggle "against the motion of the divell, and the inticements of the world," he warns explicitly of succumbing to the illusion "That merrie ballads and bookes, as *Scoggin, Bevis of Southampton, &c* are good to drive away time, and to remove hart quames."[8] In his guidelines for godly speech, Perkins lists jesting alongside "*Swearing, blaspheming, Cursed speaking, Railing, Backbiting, Slandering, Chiding, Quarrelling, Contending,*" all varieties of the abuse of language. In the mode of a catechism Perkins discusses the question of "Whether jesting be tollerable in any sort, or not?" and declares, "That jesting which standeth in quippes, tauntes, and girdes, which serveth onely for the offence of some, with the delight of others, is not tollerable: because *all speech must edifie, and minister grace to the hearers.*" Laughter, he exhorts his readers, is permissible, but is only seldom to be indulged in, reminding them that while the New Testament mentions a number of occasions on which Christ wept, "wee never read that hee laughed."[9]

At the same time, the Renaissance saw a remarkable upsurge in the prestige of jesting. The emergence of humanism in Northern Italy was grounded in a rediscovery of the legacy of antiquity. Keen to distance themselves from what they regarded as the barbarism of the Middle Ages, humanist scholars fostered the cultural memory of the classics, while their patrons believed the revival of ancient culture would reinforce their position as the putative heirs of the civic virtue and glory of Rome.[10] The study of rhetoric, cultivated in the medieval period mainly to develop the skill of writing letters in Latin, increased in importance to become one of the main subjects on the curricula of schools and universities. The recovery of complete texts by Aristotle, Cicero, and Quintilian, among others, provided access to the store of ancient wit, enthusiastically received by the leading scholars of the time. Foremost among them was Erasmus, whose towering position in the Renaissance republic of ideas was reinforced by a canny use of the new medium of print. His *Adagia*, a compilation of classical aphorisms and sententiae, first appeared in 1500, but steadily accrued new entries and grew in volume in the many reprints of the book during his lifetime. His *Apophthegmata*, first published in 1531, was a compendium of humorous tales about famous figures in classical history, from philosophers, rulers, and army commanders to orators. Witty anecdotes about the great and the good, of enduring interest to lesser mortals to the present day, were much in demand in the early modern period and were eagerly assimilated into other miscellanies. By the time of Erasmus' death in 1536, the *Apophthegmata*, originally based on Plutarch's *Moralia*, had been extended from two to eight volumes and had been enriched with material from sources such as Diogenes Laertius' *Lives of the Eminent*

Philosophers and Macrobius' *Saturnalia*. Erasmus' apothegms offered a trove of anecdotes from which later jestbooks generously helped themselves. One of the most popular examples is the following:

> Servilius Geminus was dining with Lucius Mallius, a distinguished artist at Rome. He observed that Mallius had ugly sons, and remarked, "Mallius, you don't model as well as you paint." "No wonder," said Mallius, "I model in the dark, I paint in the light!"[11]

The joke comes from Macrobius' *Saturnalia*. Written in the fifth century CE at a time when the Roman Empire was in its death throes, it is a work suffused with nostalgia for the old order. Based on Plato's *Symposium*, it recreates three days of leisurely debate during which bons mots are exchanged. Macrobius describes Lucius Mallius as "the best painter in Rome," even if he is barely remembered today. More prominent is his interlocutor, Servilius Geminus, Roman consul in the third century BCE. No doubt Erasmus would have relished the coupling of the antithesis of dark and light with the Latin quibble on *fingo/pingo* (mold or fashion, and paint), but also the way Mallius adroitly turns the jibe into an opportunity to boast of his virtuosity in a gamut of skills.

The classical legacy was not the only source of inspiration for humanist wit. The first Renaissance jestbook in print, the *Facetiae* (1470), is attributed to the humanist scholar and papal secretary Poggio Bracciolini. Poggio was an avid collector of jocular tales, which, as he tells us, he swapped with colleagues and friends at the Vatican in a club dubbed the "bugiale," or factory of lies.[12] His jests are far more ribald than those of Erasmus. Some of them have classical origins, some spring from oral narratives, but many have their origins in the Oriental stories that Petrus Alphonsus, a Spanish Jewish physician who converted to Christianity in the twelfth century, collected in the form of a handbook for preachers titled the *Disciplina clericalis*. Expanded on by later clerics, it furnished material for *exempla* that gained tremendous popularity in the late medieval period and formed the basis for *fabliaux*, exploited by writers such as Boccaccio. The first jestbook published in English was William Caxton's translation of a handful of jests from both Poggio and Alphonsus, *The Fables of Alfonce and Poge* (1484), which were fittingly appended to a volume of Aesop's fables.[13]

In England jestbooks rapidly carved out a niche for themselves in the burgeoning early modern market for print. They appeared in the form of compilations of jests, fables, and one-liners, with titles such as *Tales and Quick Answers* (1535), derived from both Erasmus' *Apophthegms* and Poggio's *Facetiae*; jest-biographies, narratives of pranks loosely attached to a jester figure, such as *Scoggin's Jests* (c. 1540); or comic *novelle*, an example of which is *The Cobbler of Canterbury* (1590).[14] Most of them exploit cultural repositories of classical jokes or medieval *exempla* or *fabliaux*; the jest biographies revolving around protagonists such as Scoggin, Skelton, Howleglas, Tarlton, Armin, George Dobson, Mother Bunch, or Long Meg of Westminster seem to have Eastern roots, and can be traced back to Marcolphus, mythical jester at King Solomon's court.[15] *A Hundred Merry Tales*, printed and probably written by the lawyer, printer, and playwright John Rastell, might be regarded as the first homegrown English jestbook. Rastell was the brother-in-law of Sir Thomas More and, along with the dramatist John Heywood, Rastell's son-in-law, belonged to the clique around More, whose own reputation as a wit became part of the lore that surrounded him after his death.[16] Availing themselves of the stock cast of characters of *exempla* – greedy priests, lascivious women, and dim-witted rustics – the jests often incorporate a satirical sting. Take, for instance, the following jest:

> A man there was that came to confess himself to a Grey Friar and shrove him that he had lain with a young gentlewoman. The friar then asked him in what place, and he said it was in a goodly chamber, all night long, in a soft, warm bed.
>
> The friar hearing that, shrugged in his clothes and said, "Now, by sweet St. Francis, then wast thou very well at ease."[17]

The humor of the punchline stems from the unexpected turn the absolution takes. The priest attempts to ferret out the prurient details of the sinful act – only to end by congratulating the penitent on his exploit. (The term "shrug" could imply "to fidget about," which would suggest a touch of envy on the friar's part.[18]) The humanist circle around More, deeply critical of the abuses of the Church and vested in restoring Christian virtue, would have delighted in a quip targeting mendicant friars, notorious for lechery. But the essence of all humor is ambiguity. Different readers might enjoy the joke for quite different reasons. Later generations might have applauded the joke as a satirical exposure of the corruption of the old Church, urgently in need of reform. Or the jest might have been enjoyed for its titillating content, for the disingenuous way the sinner whets the priest's (and the reader's) appetite without providing the details he wants to hear, or simply for the pleasurable twist in the narrative. Or it might recall a time when the clergy could be the butt of a bawdy joke, a more fun-loving age in which human weaknesses were treated with tolerant humor. In other words: it might cater to a nostalgia for Merry England.

The Purpose of Jesting

However raunchy some of Poggio's *facetiae* might appear to us, he makes it clear that his book is intended for an elite readership, not for the great unwashed. In his preface he writes, "I wish to be read by men of wit, and jolly companions," and mocks those who disapprove of the book as "too rustic."[19] Poggio also defends the unadorned style in which the jests are narrated as entirely suited to their content, intimating that those who disparage his lack of embellishment display their ignorance of classical rhetorical precepts relating to a carefully cultivated plain style.[20] In the late fifteenth and early sixteenth centuries, reading and collecting jokes, whether in Latin or in English, was a pastime of the educated, who enjoyed jests, quips, and riddles as a vehicle to reflect on paradox, the indeterminacy of language, and the delusions of fallacious logic.[21] *Serio ludere*, or a playful approach to serious themes, was much in vogue among the *literati*, attested to by the contemporary enthusiasm for Lucian shared by both Erasmus and his friend More.[22]

An example is this jest:

> A Priest was expounding to his congregation the passage of the Gospel wherein is recited that our Saviour fed five thousand people out of five loaves, and, by a slip of the tongue, instead of five thousand, said five hundred. His clerk, in a low whisper, called his attention to the mistake, reminding him that the Gospel mentioned five thousand: – "Hold your peace, you fool," said the Priest; "they will find it hard enough to believe even the number I said."[23]

Whatever their religious affinities, readers of the jestbooks in which it circulated, such as the *Tales and Quick Answers*, first published in 1535 and expanded in 1567, might have enjoyed the dig at the ignorance of the masses and the mendacity of priests. But they might also have taken pleasure at the light-hearted way in which the joke explores urgent issues with which humanists and reformers grappled: the pitfalls of literalism and the debasement of faith.

It is worth bearing in mind that a rigorous divide between elite and popular culture emerged only gradually. Apart from mining the cultural memory of the classics, much of early modern humor taps into shared memories of festive laughter and the pleasure in flyting, the competitive exchange of insults.[24] While the jestbooks that appeared in England in the sixteenth century were largely miscellanies culled from classical and Alphonsian sources, and recycled the same well-worn jokes about celebrated personages of the past, country bumpkins, and lustful women, by the turn of the seventeenth century a new generation of former university wits and hacks had turned their hand to writing jestbooks as a means of earning quick money. They included playwrights like Thomas Dekker and George Wilkins, who authored *Jests to Make You Merry* (1607); professional comedians like Robert Armin, who published a string of volumes centered on fools, including *A Nest for Ninnies* (1608); impoverished gentlemen like Anthony Copley, whose *Wits, Fits, and Fancies* (1614), largely a translated version of a Spanish jestbook, specialized in verbal quibbles; and hacks like John Taylor, a former boatman who called himself "the Water Poet" and became a one-man industry churning out cheap print. Jests became shorter and pithier; hoary chestnuts were transposed into an urban setting with additional cast members (apprentices, lawyers, stupid foreigners), and circulated in oral as well as literary culture. Humor became an important commodity in the early modern entertainment industry, retailed in taverns, theaters, and alleys.

Humanists had defended their pleasure in jokes by pointing to Aristotle's justification of the importance of relaxation. In the *Nicomachean Ethics* Aristotle declares that while pleasure is not the *summum bonum*, as the Epicureans would later have it, it is an indispensable element in life. Amusement fortifies us in our quest for the good life. Relaxation, he concludes, is not an end, but is pursued for the sake of activity.[25] Aquinas has recourse to the same passage to rationalize the notion of moderate and decorous laughter.[26] In the preface to the *Apophthegmata*, dedicated to the young William, Duke of Cleves, Erasmus writes that his work is intended to provide a digest of ancient wisdom for young princes and other noblemen who do not have the leisure to engage in study. By spicing the work with humor, he is following the example of the ancients, who "with the lure of pleasaunt delectacion emplante in tendre young wittes, thynges worthie & expedient to bee knowen, to the ende that the unbroken youngth, not yet full rype for the serious preceptes of philosophie, might even with playe & dalyyng learne suche thynges." Admittedly, some tales might appear less edifying than merely entertaining. In defense Erasmus claims that he does not "esteme it a thyng worthie blame ever now and then with laughter to refreshe the mynde with cures and maters of charge in maner tiered, so that the matter to laugh at bee pure witte and honest," taking a sideswipe at the likes of Poggio, whose fables are "voide of honestee, voide of learnying, and full of rebaudrie."[27]

For Erasmus, diversion through humor served a didactic purpose. Not everyone was convinced. In the 1550s and 1560s John Heywood published a series of collections of epigrams and proverbs whose popularity gratified the early modern taste for memorable adages and aphorisms. Rather than plundering the storehouse of antiquity, Heywood provides a wealth of folk wisdom for a London readership. As Greg Walker points out in a recent study, Heywood's work is a genial parody of Erasmus' educational project, adapted to a new, less learned audience. Heywood's collections of self-consciously contradictory witticisms are a wry take on the early modern appetite for summations of classical wisdom and mock "the naive idea that the proverb tradition will provide a source of clear, practical guidance."[28] Instead, they aim above all to entertain the readers – and confirm them in their self-assessment as urbane and witty.

With the resurgence of rhetoric in the Renaissance, wisecracks, sallies, and clever ripostes experienced a rise in stock. They were useful skills in urban life, in which quick wits and improvisation were at a premium. If the sympotic tradition, in particular Plutarch's *Quaestiones convivales*, or 'table-talk,' and Macrobius' *Saturnalia*, provides the main fund of diverting tales for Erasmus, another rich source of wit was the collection of quips by Cicero and Quintilian. In the section on wit in *De oratore*, Cicero has his speaker, Gaius Julius Caesar Strabo, list the advantages of using jokes during a speech. Cutting retorts serve to mock an opponent and ridicule his arguments. In addition, jokes serve to ease the tension of a dispute and relax the atmosphere. Last, witty speech "shows the orator himself to be refined, to be educated, to be well bred."[29] As Strabo points out, the speaker must at all costs distinguish himself from actors or buffoons. Cicero is referring specifically to actors in mimes, at the time a popular if vulgar form of drama, replete with scabrous jokes, while a buffoon was someone marked out by a fondness for clownish behavior, grimacing, and mimicry.

In underlining the importance of humor in defining social status, Cicero is drawing on Aristotle's discussion of wit in the *Nicomachean Ethics*. Aristotle lists wittiness (or *eutrapelia*) as one of the virtues of social intercourse, and regards it as a golden mean between excessive jocularity and a morose lack of humor. "Those who carry humor to excess are thought to be vulgar buffoons," he explains, while "those who can neither make a joke themselves nor put up with those who do, are thought to be boorish and unpolished."³⁰ Joking well is a sign of refinement and good breeding.

In the Renaissance wit became a mark of social distinction, avidly sought after by aspirants of all stripes. Advice on how to hone one's skills at repartee and quick-witted ripostes was purveyed in a range of texts, from rhetorics to courtesy literature to conversation manuals. Baldassare Castiglione's *Book of the Courtier* (1528), probably the most influential courtesy book, was modeled on Cicero's *De oratore*. Book 2 is devoted to jesting, and borrows liberally from Cicero's supply of jokes. In his satire of the follies of the age, Barnabe Rich pokes fun at jestmongers who are anxious to make their mark. "So there be among them that will get jestes by heart," he mocks, others "will not let a merriment slip, but they trusse it up for their owne provision, to serve their expence at some other time: and this they esteeme to be as good as a sute of Sattin, to grace themselves withall."³¹ Like fashionable apparel, jests were an asset in acquiring social status.

One of the most remarkable paeans to wit was delivered by the humanist poet and man of letters Giovanni Pontano. The larger part of his treatise on speech, *De sermone*, published posthumously in 1509, deals with wittiness. Expanding on the discussion of urbanity in Quintilian's *Institutio oratoria*, which alludes to the refined mode of expression characteristic of the denizens of Rome and encompasses humorous discourse, Pontano asserts that wit and urbanity are the hallmarks not only of polished rhetoric but of good citizenship: "wittiness," he insists, "is a moral and civic virtue, not only an oratorical and forensic or senatorial one."³² Wit, he maintains, is an art that the educated man, not just the orator, can acquire, and that serves to enrich social intercourse. Pontano highlights the notion of wittiness as a social virtue put forward by Aristotle, but relates it to civility, not merely in terms of gaining cultural capital for the purpose of enhanced prestige but also in terms of human interaction in civil society.³³

Pontano emphatically rejects wit that "is annoying and odious and tends to quarreling and contention," or jests which are "sharp and abounding with bile," "obscene, buffoonish, very bitter, or rustic, rude, unseasoned, not worthy of the city."³⁴ This does not mean that jesting should be devoid of pungency. He notes that jokes are like play, and points out that judicious retorts "often produce admiration in the minds of the listeners."³⁵ An example he recommends (borrowed from Poggio) is the following:

> A Florentine traveler, extremely fat as well as sharp-witted, journeying through the city of Siena, happened to be leaving by the gate that leads to Rome, and his raised mantle showed a very large and swollen paunch. And thereupon the guards of the gate said, joking and laughing, "This little

man is clever because he placed his bag in front, not in back." Then he, beaming for all he was worth, said, "Would you walk safely with your property through this territory of thieves and assassins in any other way?"

Pontano enthuses, "What could be more charming and witty than that?"[36] The virulent enmity between the Sienese and Florentines, reaching back to the thirteenth century, meant that violence frequently lurked beneath the surface of any encounter between the citizens of the two city-states. What is crucial for Pontano is that in a situation fraught with tension, wit is deployed in a verbal duel that by eliciting a shared pleasure in competitive wit, however reluctantly acknowledged, compels the antagonists to remain within the bounds of civil interaction.[37]

Jesting and Civility

In an age convulsed with religious violence, in which cheap print in England was awash with vicious anti-Catholic humor, few traces of communal hatred are to be found in the genre of jestbook. It is true, as Keith Thomas points out, that the period saw a number of radical changes in the culture of laughter. These include the banishment of humor from the realms of religion and politics. Jesting about religious matters and official policies was proscribed. The official disapproval culminated in the Bishops' Ban of 1599, sweeping legislation directed at both satire and pornography.[38] Francis Bacon encapsulates the key precepts with regard to humor in a few pithy lines: "As for jest, there be certain things which ought to be privileged from it; namely, religion, matters of state, great persons, any man's present business of importance, and any case that deserveth pity."[39]

But it is not merely a desire to toe the official line that palliates the rancor of jestbook humor. It is partly due to the fact that classical jests continue to be popular, serving as they do the purpose of confirming one's sophistication. But many of the jestbooks also stress their desire to foster conviviality, and are marketed as vehicles of nostalgia for an earlier age of allegedly harmonious social relations. *A Banquet of Jests*, attributed to Archie Armstrong, jester at the court of James I and Charles I, promises the reader that the jokes are "mild and gentle" and "as they bark at none, so they bite not any." Their aim is "to recollect the memories of those to whom they have been known but since forgotten."[40] Thomas Dekker and George Wilkins begin their jestbook, *Jests to make you Merie* (1607), with a definition of the jest. They write

> A Jest is the bubling up of wit. It is a Bavin which being well kindled maintaines for a short time the heate of laughter. It is a weapon wherewith a

foole does oftentimes fight, and a wise man defends himselfe by. It is the foode of good companie if it bee seasoned with judgment: but if with too much tartnesse, it is hardly digested but turns to quarrel.[41]

The images Dekker and Wilkins use conjure up an atmosphere of hospitality and conviviality: a blazing hearth, an inviting meal, and congenial company. Jests, they admit, can be trenchant, but cutting retorts should be used only in self-defense. Similarly, in a collection of vignettes centered on a figure called "Old Hobson," described as a "haberdasher of smale wares" during Queen Elizabeth's reign, the reader is informed, "here are merriments without hurt, and humorous jests savouring upon wisdome" and admonished to "read willingly, but scoffe not spitefully."[42]

A small handful of jests that touch on contemporary religious conflict have found their way into the jestbooks. Their targets are, however, often undercut by the ambiguity inherent in all humor. One example is the narrative of the old peasant at church. In John Taylor's jest miscellany, *Wit and Mirth* (1629), the story goes as follows:

> A poore Country man, praying devoutly superstitious before an old Image of S. Loy, the Image suddenly fell downe upon the poore man, and bruised his bones sorely, that hee could not stirre abroad in a moneth after; in which space the cheating Priests had set up a new Image. The Country man came to the Church againe, and kneeled a farre off to the new Image, saying: *Although thou smilest and lookest faire upon me: yet thy father plaid me such a knavish pranke lately, that ile beware how I come too neere thee, lest thou shouldest have any of thy Fathers unhappy qualities.*[43]

For all its obligatory references to "cheating" priests and "superstitious" worship, the joke is essentially a variation on the figure of the ignorant but sly rustic, in this case too obtuse to grasp that an image is merely an artifact, but crafty enough to take precautions against its potential for malice. Even the snatch of conversation the peasant indulges in with Saint Loy (or Eligius), however close it sails to the wind of blasphemy, has the charm of the tête-à-têtes between Christ and the rural priest Don Camillo, a popular comic creation of the humorist Giovannino Guareschi in postwar Italy. The barb targeted at idolatrous practices and their exploitation by conniving priests might well elicit a chortle from readers on both sides of the religious boundary. Some readers might detect an oblique comment on the religious policy of outward conformity enforced by the Elizabethan authorities – but the joke cuts both ways, and could be read as alluding to all the religious shifts England endured with the changes of regime.

As it happens, the joke is a reworked version of a much earlier jest:

> As a man kneled upon a tyme prayenge before an olde rode, the rode felle downe on him and brak his hede; wherfore he wolde come no more in the churche halfe a yere after. At lengthe, by the provocation of his nighbours, he cam to the churche agayne; and bycause he sawe his nighbours knele before the same rode, he kneled downe lyke wyse and sayde thus: well, I may cappe and knele to the, but thou shalte never have myn harte agayne, as long as I lyve.
>
> By which tale appereth, that by gentyll and courteyse entreatinge mens myndes ben obteyned. For though the people cappe and knele to one in highe autorite, yet lyttell whoteth he, what they thynke.⁴⁴

It stems from one of the earliest jestbooks in English, *Tales and Quicke Answeres* (1535). The humor derives from a similar source: a doltish but devious member of the lower orders hedging his bets with those in power. The tagline, which explicitly broadens the political import of the joke, disappears in later versions – as do most taglines.

The same anecdote appears in the 1607 collection attached to "Old Hobson." Set explicitly in Marian England, the staple allusions to Catholic superstition appear:

> In the raing of Queene Mary, when great supersticion was used in England, as creeping to the crosse, worshipping of Images and such like, it was Maister Hobsons chaunce amongst other people to be in the Church, and kneeling to an Image to pray, as it was then used, the same Image by some mishapp fell downe upon Maister Hobson and broke his head, upon which occation he came not thether in halfe an yeare after but at length by the procurement of his neighbours he came to the Church againe, and because he saw his neighbours kneele before the same Image, he kneeled downe likewise, and said thus, wel I I may cap, and kneele to thee, but thou shalt never have my heart againe so long as I live: meaning for the broken head it had given him.⁴⁵

The joke is presented as relating to the genial Hobson himself, who figures as a fool or jester, whom we simultaneously laugh at and laugh with in appreciation of his comic skill. Fools often play out collective uncertainties and anxieties while seeming to confirm the rest of humanity in our superiority to them. Recasting the Catholic simpleton as the jester-protagonist of the jestbook effectively enables a rapport to the readership – which significantly mitigates the thrust of anti-Catholic hostility.

Other jests about Catholics are similarly circumspect. The following joke is a benign version of the stupid foreigner joke popular in all cultures and in all ages:

> A Brave and valiant Captaine, whom I could name, had a scarfe given him here in England, and he sayling over into the Low-Countryes, an old Romane Catholike Lady of his acquaintaince was very importunate to beg his scarfe of him. The Captaine asked her what shee would doe with it, and said it was not fit for her wearing. Shee answered him that, if he would give it her, that Jesus Christ should weare it in the Church upon holy daies, meaning the Image. Madam, said the Captaine, if you will bring me word, that ever his father wore such a scarfe, then I will give you this for him.[46]

Idolatry is associated with a rather touching old lady. A Protestant viewpoint is represented by a manly Englishman, whose gentle mockery of the old woman is the epitome of civility.

Catholics are not the only confession to feature as the butt of a jest. Evenhandedly, Taylor includes a joke aimed at Puritans:

> One hearing a clocke strike three when he thought it was but two, said: This Clocke is like an hypocritical Puritane; for though he will not sweare, yet hee will lye abbominably.[47]

The joke exploits the stereotype of the hypocritical Puritan and mocks their campaign to eradicate blasphemous oaths. But the joke also redounds on the speaker, who, it might appear, is annoyed with both the clock and the Puritan for telling inconvenient truths.

While some jests attempt to evade the harsh realities of conflict, others acknowledge that conflict is an inevitable element in society. Drawing on the repository of witty retorts in both the classical and the medieval tradition of jesting, they put forward the thrust and parry of wit as a paradigm to emulate. In doing so, they create communities of laughter which, however fleetingly, unite adversaries in the shared pleasure of agonistic play. In the following jests, scenarios of confrontation are described in which opponents do not resolve their differences, but in which antagonism is transmuted into agonism in the form of a verbal skirmish:

> A Scholar and a Courtier meeting in the street seemd to contest for the wall; sayes the Courtier: I do not use to give every coxcombe the wall. The Schollar answered: but I do, sir; and so passed by him.[48]

The courtier attempts to foment trouble by insulting the scholar and arrogating the safer side of the street to himself. Instead of resorting to either servility or violence, the scholar deftly turns the tables on his antagonist and exposes him to the laughter of the passersby. A similar situation is presented in an encounter between a gallant and a gentlewoman:

> An impudent fellow meeting a civill gentlewoman upon a narrow cawsie [causeway], that she could not passe him without striving (in courtesie) to give way rudely brake out into this question Gentlewoman are not you a whore? She being nothing danted at his blunt behauiour but having more witte about her then he had civilitie, answered him thus, trust me Sir I am none now, nor ever was I any but once, and that was when your father being no better than a Chimny-sweeper, lay with me all night, whilest she whom you now cal mother kept the dore.[49]

The gentlewoman returns the insult but redoubles the stakes: not only does she label the man's father as a lowly menial, but additionally insinuates that his mother is nothing but a bawd. Both the scholar and the gentlewoman enact a mode of civility that consists less in elegant manners than in channeling conflict into the fierce sparring of a verbal competition.

A final example demonstrates how by using witty repartee, a Recusant scores points off her opponents and reaps all the laughs:

> A Countrey woman at an Assize was to take her oath against a party. The said party entreated the Judge that her oath might not bee taken. The Judge demaunded why he excepted against her. My Lord (quoth hee), shee is a Recusant or Romane Catholique, and they hold it no matter of conscience to sweare any thing against us. Come hither, woman, said the Judge, I doe not thinke thou art a Recusant; I am perswaded, that for fourty shillings thou wilt sweare the Pope is a knave. Good my Lord, said shee, the Pope is a stranger to mee; but, if I knew him as well as I know your Lordship, I would sweare for halfe the money.[50]

Faced with a hostile counterpart who casts aspersions on her credibility, the woman at first seems to find an ally in the judge. She is no doubt swiftly disabused of the illusion when he sneers that for a monetary incentive, surely she would be prepared to slander the Pope. The countrywoman enters into the spirit of the game – by offering to impugn the reputation of the judge instead, at a bargain price. Readers might have enjoyed the jest for quite different reasons – as exposing a cunning Catholic or as deflating a pompous pillar of the establishment. The jest does not evoke nostalgia for a cozy vision of Merry England infused with harmony and amity. Instead, it resonates with the collective memory of flyting and the classical and medieval tradition of combative wit. Jests such as these propose a mode of civility in which conflict is played out in the form of agonism. They harness a common cultural memory to create, however fleetingly, an affective community, uniting the audience in pleasure – shared pleasure in agonistic play, and shared pleasure in laughter.

Notes

1 See R. W. Maslen, "The Afterlife of Andrew Borde," *Studies in Philology*, 100.4 (2003), 463–91.
2 Douglas Gray, "Scoggin [Scogan, Scogin, Skogyn], John (*supp. fl.* 1480), Supposed Jester and Author," *Oxford Dictionary of National Biography*, Oxford University Press, www.oxforddnb.com/view/10.1093/ref:odnb/9780198614128.001.0001/odnb-9780198614128-e-24848.
3 See Jonathan Baldo, *Memory in Shakespeare's Histories: Stages of Forgetting in Early Modern England* (New York: Routledge, 2012), 51–90.
4 Cited in Ronald Hutton, *The Rise and Fall of Merry England: The Ritual Year 1400–1700* (Oxford University Press, 1994), 89. On "Merry England" also see Keith Thomas, "The Perception of the Past in Early Modern England," in David Bates, Jennifer Wallis, and Jane Winters, eds., *The Creighton Century, 1907–2007*, (University of London Press, Institute of Historical Research, 2009), 181–218.
5 Thomas, "The Perception of the Past," 207.
6 See "merry, adj..," *Oxford English Dictionary Online*, Oxford University Press, www.oed.com/view/Entry/116864.
7 See Hutton, *The Rise and Fall*, 111–52. Also see Martin Ingram, "Reformation of Manners in Early Modern England," in Paul Griffiths, Adam Fox, and Steve Hindle, eds., *The Experience of Authority in Early Modern England* (Basingstoke: Macmillan, 1996), 47–88.
8 William Perkins, *The Foundation of Christian Religion* (London: Iohn Porter and Iohn Legat, 1595), C3v, A2r. In quotations from early modern texts u/v and i/j have been modernized.
9 William Perkins, *A Direction for the Government of the Tongue according to Gods word* (London: Abraham Kitson, 1593), A2r, D1v, D2r–v.
10 On the various forces that led to the birth of the Renaissance and the emergence of humanism, see Peter Burke, *The Renaissance*, Studies in European History, 2nd ed. (Basingstoke: Palgrave Macmillan, 1997), 1–27, and Quentin Skinner, *The Foundations of Modern Political Thought*, 2 vols. (Cambridge University Press, 1978), vol. I, 28–41. The classic definition of cultural memory as a repository of texts and other artifacts that serve to underpin a society's identity was adumbrated by Jan Assman. See Jan Assman and John Czaplicka, "Collective Memory and Cultural Memory," *New German Critique*, 65 (1995), 125–33.
11 Desiderius Erasmus, *Apophthegmata*, trans. and annotated Betty I. Knott and Elaine Fantham, in Betty I. Knot, ed., *Collected Works of Erasmus* (Toronto University Press, 2014), vol. 38, no. 6.198, 652.
12 Poggio Bracciolini, *The Facetiae or Jocose Tales of Poggio*, 2 vols. (Paris: Isidore Liseux, 1879), vol. II, 230–31.
13 For a potted history of the jestbook, see P. M. Zall, "The Natural History of Jestbook: An Introduction," in Zall, ed., *A Hundred Merry Tales and Other English Jestbooks of the Fifteenth and Sixteenth Centuries* (Lincoln: University of

Nebraska Press, 1963), 1–10, and Ian Munro and Anne Lake Prescott, "Jest Books," in Andrew Hadfield, ed., *The Oxford Handbook of English Prose 1500–1640* (Oxford University Press, 2013), 343–59.
14 See F. P. Wilson, "The English Jestbooks of the Sixteenth and Early Seventeenth Centuries," *Huntington Library Quarterly*, 2 (1938–39), 121–58.
15 Zall, "An Introduction," 4.
16 He is described by the Protestant humanist Thomas Wilson as a man "whose wit even at this hour is a wonder to all the world and shall be undoubtedly even unto the world's end." See Thomas Wilson, *Art of Rhetoric (1560)*, ed. Peter E. Medine (University Park: Pennsylvania State University Press, 1994), 174.
17 John Rastell, *A Hundred Merry Tales: The Shakespeare Jest Book*, ed. John Thor Ewing (London: Welkin Books, 2018), 122. In the following I am indebted to Ewing's introduction, 14–51.
18 "shrug, v.," 5, *Oxford English Dictionary Online*, Oxford University Press, www.oed.com/view/Entry/178970.
19 "Preface to the 'Facetiae' by Poggio the Florentine," in Poggio, *Facetiae*, 5.
20 See Cicero, *Orator*, trans. G. L. Hendrickson and H. M. Hubbell, Loeb Classical Library (Cambridge, MA: Harvard University Press, 1939), 23.75–26.90.
21 See Anne Lake Prescott, "Humanism in the Tudor Jestbook," *Moreana* 24.95–96 (1987), 5–16.
22 The classic study is Rosalie L. Colie, *Paradoxia Epidemica: The Renaissance Tradition of Paradox* (Princeton University Press, 1966).
23 Poggio, *Facetiae*, vol. II, 156.
24 See Peter Burke, *Popular Culture in Early Modern Europe* (New York University Press, 1978).
25 Aristotle, *The Nicomachean Ethics*, trans. David Ross, Oxford World's Classics (Oxford University Press, 2009), 1176b33–35.
26 St. Thomas Aquinas, *Summa theologiae*, ed. and trans. Thomas Gilby (London: Blackfriars, 1972), vol. 44, 2a2ae, q. 168.
27 Desiderius Erasmus, *Apophthegmes*, trans. Nicholas Udall (London: Richard Grafton, 1542), **vii r–v, ***r.
28 Greg Walker, *John Heywood: Comedy and Survival in Tudor England* (Oxford University Press, 2020), 247. On the *Epigrams* and *Proverbs*, see 241–58.
29 Cicero, *On the Ideal Orator*, trans. James M. May and Jakob Wisse (New York: Oxford University Press, 2001), 2.236. The section on wit runs from 2.216b to 2.290.
30 Aristotle, *The Nicomachean Ethics*, 1128a4–10.
31 Barnabe Rich, *Faultes, faults, and nothing else but faultes* (London: Ieffrey Chorleton, 1606), B4v.
32 Giovanni Gioviano Pontano, *The Virtues and Vices of Speech*, ed. and trans. G. W. Pigman III, The I Tatti Renaissance Library (Cambridge, MA: Harvard University Press, 2019), 311. On Pontano, see the introduction by G. W. Pigman III in his edition of *De sermone*, vii–xxvii, and George Luck, "*Vir Facetus*: A Roman Ideal," *Studies in Philology*, 55.2 (April 1958), 107–21.

33 On the link between *eutrapelia* and civility, see Ian Munro, "Vita Energetica: Love's Labour's Lost and Shakespeare's Maculate Theater," in Kent Lehnhof, Julia Reinhard Lupton, and Carolyn Sale, eds., *Shakespeare's Virtuous Theatre* (Edinburgh University Press, forthcoming).
34 Pontano, *The Virtues and Vices*, 279, 299.
35 Ibid., 315, 323.
36 Ibid., 257. The joke appears in Poggio, *Facetiae*, vol. II, 118, this time set in Perugia, and in Castiglione's *Courtier*, who replaces the Florentine with the humanist and poet Galeotto da Narni. See Baldesar Castiglione, *The Book of the Courtier*, ed. Daniel Javitch, A Norton Critical Edition (New York: W. W. Norton, 2002), 2.60.
37 On agonism as a mode of civic practice in a pluralist society, see the work of William Connolly, especially *Identity/Difference: Democratic Negotiations of Political Paradox* (Minneapolis: University of Minnesota Press, 2002).
38 Keith Thomas, "The Place of Laughter in Tudor and Stuart England," *Times Literary Supplement*, January 21, 1977, 77–81.
39 Francis Bacon, "Of Discourse," in Brian Vickers, ed., *The Major Works*, Oxford World's Classics (Oxford University Press, 1996), 406.
40 Archie Armstrong, *A Banquet of Jest* (1657) in P. M. Zall, ed., *A Nest of Ninnies and Other English Jestbooks of the Seventeenth Century* (Lincoln: University of Nebraska Press, 1970), 169–70. I am indebted to Zall's introduction, ix–xviii.
41 T.D. [Thomas Dekker] and George Wilkins, *Iests to make you Merie* (London: Nathaniell Butter, 1607), B1r.
42 [Richard Johnson], *The Pleasant Conceites of Old Hobson the merry Londoner, full of humorous discourses, and witty meriments* (London: Iohn Wright, 1607), A4r–v.
43 John Taylor, *Taylors Wit and Mirth*, in William Carew Hazlitt, ed., *Shakespeare's Jest Books* (1864; New York: Barnes and Noble, 2007), 460.
44 *Tales and Quicke Answeres*, in *Shakespeare's Jest Books*, 97–98.
45 Johnson, *The Pleasant Conceits of Old Hobson*, F2v.
46 Taylor, *Taylors Wit and Mirth*, 468.
47 Ibid., 481.
48 [Robert Chamberlain], *Conceits, Clinches, Flashes, and Whimzies*, in *Shakespeare's Jest Books*, 512.
49 Dekker and Wilkins, *Iests*, D1v.
50 Taylor, *Taylors Wit and Mirth*, 469.

PART III

Affective Memory
Temporal and Spatial Modalities

CHAPTER 7

"My despised time"
Memory, Temporality, and Disgust in Shakespearean Tragedy

Johannes Schlegel

For quite some time now, it has firmly been established that, among a myriad of other things, Shakespeare's plays are about memory, remembrance, and commemoration. Hester Lees-Jeffreys, for instance, emphatically claims that

> Shakespeare both engaged with and changed the ways in which people remembered. Plays themselves are mnemotechnic, representing (necessarily memorable) events as something repeatable, even re-liveable; they re-present completed events, whether based on "real life" or not, in real time. Sometimes they perpetuate or promote particular memories, and even invent them. In doing so, they rely on the memories of actors, but at the same time their existence is fleeting and ephemeral.[1]

Rendering Shakespeare a key actor in a veritable "crisis of memory,"[2] Lees-Jeffreys presupposes a conceptual understanding of memory, with remembrance – and not least forgetting – as active, often conscious operations of selecting, storing, transmitting, and processing historical data which are highly dependent on the situation in which they are executed. "*Re*-membering," as Astrid Erll puts it, "is an act of assembling available data that takes place in the present."[3] In their mutual insistence on the *re*-peatable and the *re*-livable, on the *re*-presentational logic of *re*-membering, both Lees-Jeffreys and Erll address an aspect of memory work which, at least in early modern studies, has so far not received the attention it deserves: temporality. If a present operationally refers to a past, then memory serves as a medium in which the specific production, experience, and negotiation not so much of time, but rather of temporality can be observed – the difference between these two being, as Linda Charnes puts in her article "Anticipating Nostalgia," that "[t]emporality has a politics; time does not."[4] So whereas time has to be conceived of as absolute and universal – homogeneous and empty in the Benjaminian sense[5] – temporality is always already contingent, historical, and material. It is, in a word, produced in a series of cultural-technical processes.

In fact, Shakespearean drama is full of explicit references to the relation between techniques of memory and temporality. For instance, Hamlet literally overwrites and re-formats his table – "from the table of my memory / I'll wipe away all trivial fond records" (1.5.98–99) – and Claudius displaces the untimely grief for his dead brother – "Though yet of Hamlet our dear brother's death / The memory be green" (1.2.1–2). In another example, Prospero describes remembrance as the "dark backward and abysm of time" (1.2.50). While it seems odd that, despite a plethora of critical attention to either notion, their connection has seldom been discussed,[6] this seems to be changing somewhat with notable recent publications by Robin S. Stuart (2018), Jerzy Limon (2008), and Evelyn Tribble (2012).[7] In several research contributions, J. K. Barret has emphatically proposed to reframe the role of memory in early modern literature in terms of multiple and competing temporalities rather than the past alone. In her article "The Crowd in Imogen's Bedroom" (2015), she argues that visual mnemonics "make the audience retrospectively aware of [a] range of competing options"[8] as they produce a tension between what might be in the future and a counterfactual (or imaginative) version of the past, of what might have been. These alternative versions of the past "stick to the present as unforgotten prospects," thus creating "uncertainty about both the past and the present."[9]

As Barret's emphasis on "uncertainty" indicates, memory and its specific temporalities moreover trigger emotional and affective responses. Or, to put it differently, it is precisely where the alleged order of memory as a stable, linear time is exposed and experienced as potentially paradoxical temporality that affects come into play. "Memory and affect," to quote Charnes once again, "do not obey the dictates of chronology; only rarely do we process or complete our relationship to the past in a way that lets us tell ourselves, confidently, 'that was then, and this is now.'"[10] The reactions to such conflicting temporalities are, as I will argue in the following, particularly strong affects, first and foremost, disgust.

The word *disgust* did not appear in the English lexicon before the end of the sixteenth century. Prior to Florio's 1598 translation of the Italian "Sgusto" in his *World of Words* there are no recorded uses of the English word,[11] and it does not appear in any of Shakespeare's plays or poems. Benedict Robinson, however, has suggested that "the years on either side of 1600 actually invented disgust,"[12] thus heralding "the emergence of a social world in which the work of producing and maintaining social boundaries was increasingly performed by forms of cultural competence, a socioaesthetics in which the visceral judgement of the sense is linked to other forms of boundary-drawing."[13] While the word may have been unfamiliar to most of Shakespeare's contemporaries, the concept itself is crucially linked to this moment in time. What can be observed in the "crisis of memory" addressed by Lees-Jeffreys, then, is a veritable crisis of temporality, which is both product and motor of a momentous pluralization of the historical semantics of time, that is, the (possible) interplays of structural and semantic changes. The early modern period witnesses, in other words, the emergence of a new temporal regime that slowly, yet increasingly, transposes medieval, cyclical time to modern notions of linearity.[14] Shakespearean tragedy stages the resulting frictions – and reacts to them with depictions of disgust that render this affective bodily response as a kind of cognition.[15]

I

Despite his frantic endeavors to "wipe away all trivial records" of the past and to start processes of active commemoration anew, Hamlet occasionally dreads remembrance. Speaking his first soliloquy (1.2.129–59), he continues to address the problems of memory. This, however, does not happen without a notable displacement, in which memories of his mother's mourning substitute for the commemoration of his father's death, as if actual remembrance should be avoided or repressed: "heaven and earth, / Must I remember?" (1.2.142–43) What is more, Hamlet's attempts to evade dreadful memories are explicitly related to a temporal confusion – "two months dead – nay not so much, not two" (1.2.138) – finding its full articulation in the misogynist revulsion toward his mother's seemingly insatiable sexual appetite, which, to Hamlet, appears both unnatural and untimely:

HAMLET: [W]hy, she would hang on him
As if increase of appetite had grown
By what it fed on, and yet, within a month –
...
A little month, or ere those shoes were old
With which she followed my poor father's body
Like Niobe, all tears, ...
within a month, ...
She married.

(1.2.143–56)

In the rejection of the mother and her overhasty remarriage, a universal disgust comes to the fore that is the affective response to a world that appears entirely repulsive:

> Oh God, God,
> How weary, stale, flat, and unprofitable
> Seem to me all the uses of this world!
> Fie on't, ah fie, 'tis an unweeded garden
> That grows to seed, things rank and gross in nature
> Possess it merely.
>
> (1.2.132–37)

World and life appear disgusting precisely because, like Gertrude's unconstrained sexual appetite, they represent a lavish profusion of vitality. The disgust that is experienced and articulated here combines two aspects of what Aurel Kolnai has described as two facets of physical and moral disgust: "the disgust aroused by exuberant, exaggerated fertility" that "shades off into the pathological," on the one hand,[16] and an intellectual "disgust aroused by satiety," on the other, which "comes about only when a constantly repeated experience had been originally or is in normal circumstances a pleasurable one; it is then not only the object but also our enjoyment of it that becomes disgusting."[17]

It is this universal, boundless disgust that T. S. Eliot identified as the major aesthetic shortcoming of Shakespeare's play. In his essay *"Hamlet"* from 1919, he claims that Hamlet's disgust transcended any possible and plausible origin. The prince faced the difficulty that while his disgust was caused by his mother, she was not an adequate object for it; his disgust "enveloped" and "exceeded" her: "Hamlet (the man) is dominated by an emotion which is inexpressible, because it is in *excess* of the facts as they appear."[18] According to Eliot, the play was thus blatantly lacking in the correspondence between the events portrayed and the emotions that the events trigger in their main participants; it was lacking, in other words, what Eliot calls the "objective correlative." Eliot's assessment of *Hamlet* is notoriously harsh. But what if the "objective correlative" of Hamlet's disgust was not primarily his mother, but rather the temporality of memory, which, as was shown earlier, is then transferred on to the mother?

This chapter seeks to flesh out the implications that derive from the triangulation of memory and temporality with disgust as a particularly strong affect. It argues that in Shakespearean tragedy, memory becomes the contested site where the interrelation between the temporality of disgust and the disgust of temporality is acted out and negotiated.

I argue that disgust is triggered and represented by material memory objects in two of Shakespeare's tragedies for which problematic temporalities are constitutive, *Hamlet* and *Othello*.[19] My reading of these plays seeks to establish that disgust serves as affective response to the pressure of seemingly paradoxical temporalities: Hamlet's experience of a past that is embodied in the untimely object of the skull, on the one hand, and Othello's experience of a memory of the future which is mediated by and becomes manifest in the handkerchief, on the other. Given the temporal intricacies of each play, then, the temporalities of disgust can be read in two ways: both as a "presentist mode"[20] of a specific temporal experience and, by extension, as a mode of the negotiation of a "cross-temporality"[21] that constitutes the movement of experience as memory into the past. This approach, I hope, contributes not only to investigations of the relation between memory and affect in the early modern period, but also to a further understanding of the cultural functions of disgust which, in the wake of Eliot, have often been considered more or less decorative, as something that garnishes supposedly more profound negotiations of, say, sex and politics.[22]

II

Precisely due to his obsession with memory, Hamlet throughout the play, right up to his own death, is living in an anomalous temporality that Rebecca Schneider has described as "syncopated time," in which "then and now punctuate each other"[23] and which is experienced in affects. Indeed, the shift from avenging to remembering brings about a novel focus on the interiority of the protagonist. As Rhodri Lewis suggests, "[b]y the brilliant device of having his ghost instruct Hamlet not to revenge, but to remember and therefore revenge, Shakespeare bypasses such dramatic crudity [of earlier revenge tragedies] and shifts the attention of his audience to the disposition of his prince's emotional life, now at the very forefront of the play's action."[24] Remembering, however, is not reducible to merely inward, emotional processes. Rather, scholarship in recent years has established that memory, as a key factor of cognition, is in fact "distributed," that is, extended through the body and various objects of the environment.[25] It is this embodiment that memory shares with affect, for both of which a "reciprocity between body and world"[26] is constitutive. To focus on remembering in *Hamlet* is therefore to focus not only on inwardness but on social and material relations as well, which are, perhaps, responsible for the characters' insistence on verbal confirmation that they are being remembered, most unforgettably when the Ghost returns to remind Hamlet not to forget.

Hamlet seems unlikely to be in any real danger of forgetting his father, though his revenge mission seems, for five acts, at risk; indeed, as John Kerrigan argued in an influential article on memory and revenge in this play, by insisting on remembering his father through reviving him as a character in *The Mousetrap* or as an image in a portrait shown to Gertrude, Hamlet repeatedly deflects the task of revenge. In her article "Misremembering *Hamlet* at Elsinore," Kathryn Prince points out that it is striking that alongside Hamlet other characters also represent aspects of memory besides revenge:

> Polonius is associated with shameful, inadvertent forgetting, and Ophelia with shameful, inadvertent remembering, Claudius with guilty, inadvertent remembering, Gertrude with guilty, deliberate forgetting, Horatio with memory as an instrument of emotional regulation and Fortinbras with memory as an instrument of emotional mobilisation . One way of understanding these character oppositions is through the actions that the characters take to mobilise or regulate emotions through memory.[27]

This suggests that Hamlet wants to be in charge not only of what is remembered – by him, about him, and by those around him – but also of the affects these practices of remembrance as embodied cognition entail.

While memory introduces syncopy into the practice of emotions – mobilizing present emotions through the recollection of emotions associated with both the past and the future (the anticipated memory of posterity) – Kathryn Prince sees "strategies of containment" at work that "neutralize these emotional incursions."[28] The key emotions that Prince identifies are Hamlet's melancholy in the graveyard scene – which is nostalgic as it is clearly projected onto a lost past – and Claudius's guilt, which persists as a continuous haunting. It has to be noted, however, that Prince's analysis focuses on emotions for which a certain temporal durability is constitutive: both melancholy and guilt are feelings that last, that dilate time. They find their embodiment around 1600 in both the fashionable pose of the melancholic lover – "Ay me, sad hours seem long," a longing Romeo exclaims, observing the slow passage of time in the first act of *Romeo and Juliet* (1.1.152) – and the inertia of the hourglass pictured in Dürer's *Melancholia I*.[29] This, however, raises the question of which temporal relation could be observed for a strong affect such as disgust, which is characterized by sudden immediacy. Yorick's skull, after all, is not merely an untimely memory object that triggers Hamlet's melancholia, but one that provokes his disgust:

HAMLET: [A] fellow of infinite jest, of most excellent fancy, he hath borne me on his back a thousand times – and now how abhorred in my imagination it is! My gorge rises at it. Here hung those lips that I have kissed I know not how oft. . . . Prithee, Horatio, tell me one thing.
HORATIO: What's that my lord?
HAMLET: Dost thou think Alexander looked o' this fashion i' th' earth?
HORATIO: E'en so.
HAMLET: And smelt so? Pah!
HORATIO: E'en so my lord.

(5.1.157–70)

As I have argued elsewhere, the Gravedigger scene as a whole displays a profound temporal confusion that necessitates perpetual operations of resynchronization by means of diverse cultural techniques.[30] It also illustrates that a residual past which still impresses itself onto the present causes not only conflicting temporalities but also conflicting affects and emotions that cannot be sufficiently explained – and contained – as melancholia. The rhyme on "bore/abhorred" makes clear that the perceived close proximity between past and present in the medium of memory causes a physical reaction ("my gorge rises at it"), namely, disgust. At the same time, Hamlet seems to linger between the attraction of the memory – "Here hung those lips that I have kissed not how oft" – and repulsion: "Pah!" Just like "fie" in an example I quoted earlier, the plosive here indicates a breakdown of language in which the experience of disgust cannot be properly articulated. Indeed, the disarticulation is the proper expression of the experience of disgust beyond language: it is simultaneously an adequate reaction as well as an articulation of a semantic failure, it is a sound that "linger[s] somewhere between speech and gesture."[31]

This dis/articulation shows an elementary structure of disgust and of its experience, which Winfried Menninghaus, in his epochal study *Disgust: Theory and History of a Strong Sensation*, describes as follows:

> The fundamental schema of disgust is the experience of a nearness that is not wanted. An intrusive presence, a smell or taste is spontaneously assessed as contamination and forcibly distanced. The theory of disgust, to that extent, is a counterpart – although not a symmetrical one – of the theory of love, desire, and appetite as forms of intercourse with a nearness that is wanted. Appetite and erotic desire aim at the overcoming of distance – the establishment of a union. The ideal presence of this union that would dissolve unpleasurable tensions is disturbed only, if at all, by its fleeting

character. For disgust, however, it is precisely this transitoriness that offers the desperately sought release from a "false embrace," an intolerable contact or union.[32]

Whereas melancholy is a lasting emotion or mood that is not necessarily directed toward a present object – although it may be triggered by one – disgust is an immediate phenomenon of presence – the desperately sought release – that is marked by its intentionality, "the directedness of mental states and events to some object."[33] Disgust is therefore not a strategy of containment, as claimed by Kathryn Prince, but a performative disruption, withdrawal, and extraction. Here, disgust brings the body perilously close to the memory object, only then to pull away from it in the registering of the proximity as an offense.

In its ambivalence, however, this scene depicts not only the disgust of temporality, but also the temporality of disgust: it simultaneously lags behind the memory object from which it recoils and generates the object in the very act of recoiling. This is also what possibly distinguishes an affect – that is, disgust – from emotions such as melancholia or, related to this, nostalgia.[34] Concerning the latter, Isabel Karremann argues that it can be characterized by its "time-structure and its affect-structure"[35]: whereas the former describes the experiences of a deficient present in relation to a categorically different, often glorified past, it is particularly the latter that "connects memory with affect."[36] Karremann explains: "Nostalgia seems to touch one immediately, on a very personal, even bodily level, as is testified by its original, medical meaning of home-sickness. While it is primarily an effect of language and the imagination, ... its emotional and physical impact make it feel authentic."[37] Karremann's observation and description of both the temporality and the affective structure of nostalgia are helpful in further delineating the temporality of disgust in the graveyard scene. While much of it is indeed structured by a nostalgic longing of reminiscence, it abruptly changes into the sheer physical reaction of disgust. In a way, this change marks a rupture in the categorical difference between past and present which has proven to be constitutive for nostalgia. The skull as memory object, in other words, serves as a medium which brings about a paradoxical temporality, in which past and present, albeit briefly, coincide. The past is brought in close proximity to the present, and can thus be read as a disruption of linear time. Hamlet experiences both past and future in the instant: "Hamlet uses the antique matter of the skull to produce a temporality that, in disputing his present moment, reproduces the explosiveness of eschatology, but without an *eschaton*, or end."[38] Disgust, then, is the affective response to the "production of presence"[39] of a paradoxical temporality *qua* memory. The fact that disgust is a defensive affect that forcefully creates a distance is finally shown in the further course of the scene, albeit under different circumstances. Here, the active construction of memory helps to open up future prospects.

Many of the play's depictions of disgust revolve around corporeal transience, which also marks a specific immanent temporality:

HAMLET: O that this too too solid flesh would melt,
Thaw and resolve itself into a dew,
Or that the Everlasting had not fixed
His canon 'gainst self-slaughter.

(1.2.129–32)

While it has been subject to some critical debate whether flesh, as described by Hamlet here, is either "solid," as in the Folio from 1623, "sallied," as the second Quarto (1604) puts it, or "sullied," as suggested by John Dover Wilson in the 1930s,[40] nowhere in the play is this yearning for the liquidation of the flesh more fulfilled than in the death of Ophelia. It is striking, however, that her drowned body does not become an object of disgust. Rather, it is transposed into an elegiac, almost pastorale miniature by Gertrude (see 4.7.166–83).[41] As much as Hamlet takes out his misogynist loathing on her, as a dead woman, Ophelia remains remarkably untouched by his fantasies of decay. It is not Hamlet but her brother Laertes who speaks her obituary:

LAERTES: Lay her i' th'earth,
And from her fair and unpolluted flesh
May violets spring. I tell thee, churlish priest,
A ministering angel shall my sister be
When thou liest howling.

(5.1.205–9)

Hamlet's disgust, which otherwise ruthlessly exposes every glorifying embellishment, is silent here. Even his game of one-upmanship with Laertes in Ophelia's grave can barely conceal that the two men, jointly, violently pursue an act of rigorous division: Ophelia's body, whose sexuality and sensual desire were articulated in madness, is excreted and disposed of.[42] It thus represents something that operates analogously to disgust and that Julia Kristeva influentially has described as "abjection" (*Powers of Horror*, 1982), in the Latin sense of the word: the rejected, repulsive, detestable, and abominable; also, the lowly and degraded. The transfiguration of Ophelia into angelically pure innocence is possible only through this act of "abjection," of a repulsion and separation of that which simultaneously constitutes and threatens the speaking subject due to its proximity. By means of the exclusion, temporal order is restored in that the past becomes detached or severed from the present. According to Winfried Menninghaus, "the feeling of abjection or of disgust, is, in Kristeva too, essentially a function of memory; it is in no way simply dependent for its power on something that 'lies there, quite close.'"[43] As I will show in the following, it is this notion of temporality as presence that constitutes one of the most significant differences between *Hamlet* and *Othello*.

III

Memory, temporality, and disgust are also crucial to *Othello* and, as in *Hamlet*, the affective dynamics of disgust find literary expression in the structural dynamics of the tragedy. *Othello* differs, however, in its temporal orientation. The tragedy's temporal difficulties have been central to critical readings of *Othello* since the seventeenth century and have thus proven to be of remarkable endurance. Steve Sohmer even speaks of it as the "greatest crux in Shakespeare for more than 300 years."[44] The "double time" scheme describes two conflicting, contradictory temporal structures that are, however, inextricably intertwined. On the one hand, the dramatic action takes place during approximately one and a half days. Othello and Desdemona are summoned before the Senate on the first night of their elopement, and are required to depart for Cyprus immediately. Barely reunited, they are then once again called from their bed by the brawl that leads to Cassio's disgrace. The following morning, Iago successfully stirs Othello's jealousy and Desdemona drops her handkerchief, while the murder of Desdemona appears to take place that same night. Simultaneously, however, the characters in the play explicitly allude to a more extensive time frame, as in Othello's claim that Desdemona, "with Cassio hath the act of shame / A thousand times committed" (5.2.210–11), or Emilia's repeated assertion that her "wayward husband hath a hundred times / Wooed me to steal" the handkerchief (3.3.294–95; et passim).

While the "double time" scheme is summarized and addressed in almost every critical edition, there also have been influential attempts at (dis-)solving it. Graham Bradshaw, for instance, has argued that all references to the second, "longer" time frame indicate events that took place not on Cyprus, but either on the voyage there or in Venice.[45] Steve Sohmer puts forward a more elaborate explanation in arguing that the temporal confusion is due to the friction between competing, yet simultaneously valid calendars: a Venetian one that largely accorded with the Gregorian reforms of 1582, and the Cypriot Julian calendar, which accorded with the Old Style calendars of Protestant England.[46]

By and large, these and similar accounts aim at restoring notions of linear time and unilateral chronology. They follow, in other words, Othello's own assumption that "We must obey the time" (1.3.296). However, Jonathan Gil Harris has pointed out that such readings constitute a temporal fallacy of sorts: "Critics of double time in the play have confused temporality and the measurement of time; for no matter how useful chronology may be in ironing out *Othello*'s events into a credible sequence, it inevitably neglects how the play repeatedly crumples and palimpsests time."[47] The specific temporality of *Othello*, Harris continues, is constituted by several historical layers that are folded into the present. This is achieved by both the memory object of the handkerchief and the insistence on immediacy.

As theatrical prop, signifier, and actant in complex actor-networks, the handkerchief is, to say the least, overdetermined. When it is first mentioned in 3.3.293, Emilia states, "This was her [i.e., Desdemona's] first remembrance from the Moor," thus irrevocably tying it to notions of memory. The capacities of the handkerchief, however, seem to transcend those of a sentimental trinket. In the next scene, it is described as follows:

OTHELLO: That handkerchief
   Did an Egyptian to my mother give:
   She was a charmer and could almost read
   The thoughts of people. She told her, while she kept it,
   'Twould make her amiable and subdue my father
   Entirely to her love; but if she lost it
   Or made a gift of it, my father's eye
   Should hold her loathèd, and his spirits should hunt
   After new fancies....
   'Tis true. There's magic in the web of it:
   A sibyl, that had numbered in the world
   The sun to course two hundred compasses,
   In her prophetic fury sewed the work;
   The worms were hallowed that did breed the silk,
   And it was dyed in mummy, which the skilful
   Conserved of maidens' hearts.
                                            (3.4.51–71)

The value or even power Othello attributes to this piece of cloth stems not only from its exotic heritage but also from its temporality, as it promises to combine, to weave together, both past – in the form of memory – and future – the sibylline prophecies – into a single material object. In *Shakespeare from the Margins*, Patricia Parker describes this contradictory disruption of linear time as *preposterous*, which, being derived "from *posterus* (after or behind) and *prae* (in front or before) – connotes a reversal of 'post' for 'pre,' behind for before, back for front, second for first, end or sequel for beginning."[48] From here, the thrust of the temporality of disgust in *Othello* can also be explained.

After all, the handkerchief is not only an important memory object, but, first and foremost, an object that is ambivalently sexually charged as the embroidered strawberries metaphorically and metonymically represent both virginity and chastity, on the one hand,[49] and sexual activity and promiscuity, on the other. This is, of course, a well-established reading of the embroidery, which was deepened by Lynda E. Boose as early as 1975, when she suggested reading the handkerchief as "a visually recognizable reduction of Othello and Desdemona's wedding-bed sheets, the visual proof of their consummated marriage."[50] While this has inspired a number of important readings of the handkerchief, including those by Edward A. Snow (1980), Michael Neill (1989), Arthur L. Little (1993), and Emily Weissbourd (2019), I would like to further complicate such readings by considering affective and temporal dimensions. After all, it is not – at least not only – anxiety about a contagious sexuality per se that inspires disgust, but a future that preposterously informs the present. Because the handkerchief stands in for ideas of marital fidelity, it evokes future sexual intercourse in the form of a promise, and it is this temporality that is, again and again, manipulated by Iago.

From the outset of the play, he seeks to inspire time-urgency that is to direct consciousness to the present moment and thus to time's volatility. "Even now, now, very now," he shouts toward Brabantio, "an old black ram / Is tupping your white ewe" (1.1.89–90). He shapes similarly temporal responses in others. Directing Roderigo into a state of heightened expectation in the second act, Iago suggests that though "Pleasure and action make the hours seem short" (2.3.344), "How poor are they that have not patience!" (2.3.335). Iago utilizes time in his attempts to convince Othello of Desdemona's infidelity as well. When Othello demands ocular proof for his accusation, Iago denies just that:

IAGO: Would you, the supervisor, grossly gape on?
    Behold her topped? ...
    It is impossible you should see this,

> Were they as prime as goats, as hot as monkeys,
> As salt as wolves in pride, and fools as gross
> As Ignorance made drunk.
>
> (3.3.396–406)

Not only does Iago, in a series of similes, continue the bestial imagery he already deployed with Brabantio, he also inspires the simultaneous feeling of attraction and repulsion in Othello that is the hallmark of disgust.[51] This carries over, then, into the register of his moral contempt. Significantly, it is the handkerchief "[s]potted with strawberries" (3.3.436) that functions as proof, although it is not even present.

Thus, a complex temporality of the memory object is revealed, which establishes a truth in the present because it contains a memory of something that will always already have been. The temporal structure of this peculiar memory can be described as what Jacques Lacan has coined the "future anterior" in *The Language of the Self*: "What is realized in my history is not the past definite of what was, since it is no more, or even the present perfect of what has been in what I am, but the future anterior of what I shall have been for what I am in the process of becoming."[52] The future anterior, then, encapsulates the intricacies of memory in the assemblage of palimpsested time in *Othello*. Samuel Weber further explains the complex workings of the future anterior and its relation to memory as follows:

> The perfect tense is supplanted by the future anterior, thus calling into question the very foundations of subjective identity conceived in terms of an interiorizing memory. In invoking the future anterior tense, Lacan troubles the perfected closure of the always-already-having-been [des *Immer-schon-gewesen-Seins*] by inscribing it in the inconclusive futurity of what will-always-already-have-been [*Immer-schon-gewesen-sein-wird*], a "time" which can never be entirely remembered, since it will never have fully taken place.[53]

In the preposterous workings of the memory object, the disgust with temporality comes to the fore. In a final act of temporal inversion, Othello undoes his narrative of linear temporal development by describing himself as a "base Indian" (5.2.343) and, by extension, as "circumcisèd dog" (5.2.351), thus deliberately seeking a temporal order that has forever been lost. In the presence of the abject body of Desdemona, however, the immediacy of disgust can be overcome only if the future anterior of memory is fulfilled: "I kissed thee ere I killed thee: no way but this, / Killing myself, to die upon a kiss" (5.2.354–55).

IV

My readings of *Hamlet* and *Othello* have shown that in acts of remembrance and its embodiment in memory objects, conflicting, threatening temporalities come to the fore, to which no fully conscious, reflective response is available – only the affective response of disgust, which, in turn, is marked by its very own temporality, its immediacy. While in the two tragedies memory refers either to a past or, paradoxically, to a future, disgust insists on and thus generates presence, albeit an overwhelming and ultimately unpleasant one. This raises several questions, which could not be addressed in the scope of this chapter. How, for instance, is the disgust of a respective play translated to its audience? Do the playgoers necessarily share the character's affects? The history of racist receptions of, say, *Othello* seems to suggest otherwise.[54] This is the question concerning affective communities both on the stage and in the theater, which are not least constituted by simultaneity and synchronicity. And what role does genre play? While disgust is arguably no stranger to comedy, the question remains whether temporality, especially as presence and pleasure, is connected to other affects in the comedies as well.

Notes

1 Hester Lees-Jeffreys, *Shakespeare and Memory* (Oxford University Press, 2013), 6–7.
2 Ibid.
3 Astrid Erll, *Memory in Culture*, trans. Sara B. Young (Basingstoke: Palgrave, 2011), 8; original emphasis.
4 Linda Charnes, "Anticipating Nostalgia: Finding Temporal Logic in a Textual Anomaly," *Textual Cultures*, 4.1 (2009), 72–83; 73.
5 Walter Benjamin, "Theses on the Philosophy of History," in Hannah Arendt, ed., *Illuminations: Essays and Reflections* (New York: Schocken, 2007), 253–264; 261.
6 A possible reason for this neglect may be that founding theories by Maurice Halbwachs, Pierre Nora, and Frances Yates emphasized the centrality of *loci memoriae* in their respective studies, which, in turn, has led to a privileging of the spatial dimensions of the *ars memoria*. The constitutive relation between memory and temporality has been emphatically put forward by Andreas Huyssen in *Twilight Memories: Marking Time in a Culture of Amnesia* (New York: Routledge, 1995), esp. 1–101, though not for an early modern context.
7 Robin S. Stewart, "From Last Judgement to Leviathan: The Semiotics of Collective Temporality in Early Modern England," in Lauren Shohet, ed., *Temporality, Genre and Experience in the Age of Shakespeare: Forms of Time*

(London: Bloomsbury, 2018), 223–46; Jerzy Limon, "The Archaeology of Memory," *Cahier Élisabéthains*, 73 (2008), 39–47; Evelyn B. Tribble and John Sutton, "Minds in and out of Time: Memory, Embodied Skill, Anachronism, and Performance," *Textual Practice*, 26.4 (2012), 587–607.

8 J. K. Barret, "The Crowd in Imogen's Bedroom: Allusion and Ethics in *Cymbeline*," *Shakespeare Quarterly*, 66.4 (2015), 440–62; 441.

9 Ibid., 442.

10 Charnes, "Anticipating Nostalgia," 74.

11 In the first edition of *World of Words*, Florio translates "sgusto" as "disgust, distast, vnkindnes, dislike." For whatever reasons, disgust is dropped from the translation in the 1611 edition, while the other three terms are retained.

12 Benedict Robinson, "Disgust, c. 1600," *ELH*, 81.2 (2014), 553–83; 553.

13 Ibid., 555.

14 On the "rise and fall of the modern time regime," see Aleida Assmann's study *Is Time Out of Joint? On the Rise and Fall of the Modern Time Regime*, trans. Sarah Clift (Ithaca, NY: Cornell University Press, 2020). Max Weber and E. P. Thompson have seen the Reformation and ensuing forms of proto-capitalism and industrialization as driving forces behind this process of reconceptualizing time. A much-needed complication of this position is put forward by Paul Glennie and Nigel Thrift in *Shaping the Day. A History of Timekeeping in England and Wales, 1300–1800* (Oxford University Press, 2009).

15 The chapter is thus interested in what Steven Mullaney has referred to as the "Emotional Logic of the Elizabethan Stage" – that is, the relation between, on the one hand, "the historical trauma of a certain kind of dissociation, generational and affective rather than strictly theological or doctrinal, and the historical emergence of Elizabethan popular drama," on the other; Steven Mullaney, "Affective Technologies: Toward an Emotional Logic of the Early Modern Stage," in Mary Floyd-Wilson and Garret A. Sullivan, Jr., eds., *Environment and Embodiment in Early Modern England* (Basingstoke: Palgrave, 2007), 71–89.

16 Aurel Kolnai, *On Disgust* (Chicago: Open Court, 2003), 61.

17 Ibid., 63. Speaking of "moral" disgust, Kolnai does not necessarily talk about ethics, but rather about mental and/or spiritual phenomena – *geistig* in the German original – as opposed to physical ones. Shakespeare is, of course, no stranger to the disgust of excess. See, for instance, the opening lines of *Twelfth Night*: "If music be the food of love, play on; / Give me excess of it, that surfeiting, / The appetite may sicken and so die" (1.1.1–3). For a full discussion of this excess and its relation to emotional memory, see Chapter 2 in this volume.

18 T. S. Eliot, "*Hamlet*," in Frank Kermode, ed., *Selected Prose of T. S. Eliot* (London: Faber and Faber, 1975), 45–49; 48, original emphasis.

19 While disgust plays a crucial role in comedy and tragedy alike, Robert Douglas-Fairhurst has argued that it provides "a miniature" of the latter's "ambivalent narrative drive." See Douglas-Fairhurst, "Tragedy and Disgust,"

in Sarah Annes Brown and Catherine Silverstone, eds., *Tragedy in Transition* (Malden, MA: Blackwell, 2007), 58–77; 74.

20 Hans Ulrich Gumbrecht, *Production of Presence: What Meaning Cannot Convey* (Stanford University Press, 2004).

21 Lone Bertelsen and Andrew Murphie, "An Ethics of Everyday Infinities and Power: Félix Guattari on Affect and the Refrain," in Melissa Gregg and Gregory J. Seigworth, eds., *The Affect Theory Reader* (Durham, NC: Duke University Press, 2010), 138–57; 146.

22 See, for instance, R. Chris Hassel Jr.'s "Hamlet's 'Too, Too Solid Flesh,'" *Sixteenth Century Journal*, 25.3 (1994), 609–22, or, more recently, Amanda Bailey's "*Hamlet* without Sex: The Politics of Regenerate Loss," in John S. Garrison and Kyle Pivetti, eds., *Sexuality and Memory in Early Modern England: Literature and the Erotics of Recollection* (New York: Routledge, 2016), 220–36. Notable exceptions are Andreas Höfele's essay on disgust, "Der Prinz und das Fleisch: Hamlets Ekel," in Ortrud Gutjahr, ed., *Hamlet: Theatralität und Tod in Michael Thalheimers Inszenierung am Thalia Theater Hamburg* (Würzburg: Königshausen & Neumann, 2009), 95–109; the volume *Disgust in Early Modern Literature*, ed. Natalie K. Eschenbaum and Barbara Correll (London: Routledge, 2016); and the article by A. M. Balizet, "'Amend Thy Face': Contagion and Disgust in the *Henriad*," in Darryl Chalk and Mary Floyd-Wilson, eds., *Contagion and the Shakespearean Stage* (Cham: Palgrave, 2019), 127–46.

23 Rebecca Schneider, *Performing Remains: Art and War in Times of Theatrical Reenactment* (Abingdon: Routledge, 2011), 2.

24 Rhodri Lewis, "Hamlet, Metaphor, and Memory," *Studies in Philology*, 109.5 (2012), 609–41; 612.

25 This notion has influentially been put forward by, among others, Evelyn Tribble and John Sutton in "Cognitive Ecology as a Framework for Shakespearean Studies," *Shakespeare Studies*, 39 (2011), 94–103; Laurie Johnson, John Sutton, and Evelyn Tribble in *Embodied Cognition and Shakespeare's Theatre: The Early Modern Body-Mind* (New York: Routledge, 2014); and Sophie Duncan in *Shakespeare's Props: Memory and Cognition* (New York: Routledge, 2019).

26 Amanda Bailey and Mario DiGangi, eds., "Introduction," in *Affect Theory and Early Modern Text: Politics, Ecologies, and Form* (New York: Palgrave, 2017), 1–23; 10.

27 Kathryn Prince, "Misremembering *Hamlet* at Elsinore," in Paul Megna et al., eds., *Hamlet and Emotions* (Cham: Palgrave, 2019), 253–70; 259.

28 Ibid., 260.

29 For relations between time and melancholia, see, for instance, Amelia Barikin, "After the End: The Temporality of Melancholia," in Andrea Bubenik, ed., *The Persistence of Melancholia in Arts and Culture* (New York: Routledge, 2019), 107–21, and, albeit for a decidedly not early modern perspective, Anne Enderwitz, "Modernist Melancholia and Time: The Synchronicity of the Non-Synchronic in Freud, Tylor and Conrad," in Martin Middeke and

Christina Wald, eds., *The Literature of Melancholia: Early Modern to Postmodern* (Houndmills: Palgrave, 2011), 173–86.
30 Johannes Schlegel, "'Disjoint and Out of Frame': *Hamlet* and the Problem of Synchrony," *ZAA*, 66.2 (2018), 163–79.
31 Robinson, "Disgust," 559.
32 Winfried Menninghaus, *Disgust: The Theory and History of a Strong Sensation*, trans. Howard Eiland and Joel Golb (Albany: State University of New York Press, 2003), 1–2.
33 Carolyn Korsmeyer, *Savoring Disgust: The Foul and the Fair in Aesthetics* (Oxford University Press, 2011), 16.
34 In the burgeoning fields of affect theory and of the history of emotions, it has been intensely debated how emotion, affect, and feeling can conceptually be distinguished – if at all. While Eric Shouse, for instance, argues for theoretically clear-cut, unambiguous differences, claiming, "Feelings are *personal* and *biographical*, emotions are *social*, and affects are *prepersonal*" ("Feeling, Emotion, Affect," *M/C Journal*, 8.6 (2005), http://journal.mediaculture.org.au/0512/03-shouse.php, original emphasis), the pragmatic deployment of these concepts renders much of the differentiations futile. For an informed, extensive critique both of the assumption of affect as "a non-conscious experience of intensity" (Shouse, "Feeling, Emotion, Affect") – an assumption that was established by Brian Massumi and Silvan Tompkins – and of the difficulties of definition, see Ruth Leys, "The Turn to Affect: A Critique," *Critical Inquiry*, 37.3 (2011), 434–72.
35 Isabel Karremann, "A Passion for the Past: The Politics of Nostalgia on the Early Jacobean Stage," in Brian Cummings and Freya Sierhuis, eds., *Passions and Subjectivity in Early Modern Culture* (Burlington, VT: Ashgate, 2013), 149–64; 152.
36 Ibid., 153.
37 Ibid.
38 Jonathan Gil Harris, *Untimely Matter in the Time of Shakespeare* (Philadelphia: University of Pennsylvania Press, 2009), 93; original emphasis.
39 Gumbrecht, *Production of Presence* xiii.
40 On this, see Höfele's illuminating essay, "Der Prinz und das Fleisch," in which he emphasizes the play's obsession with flesh and disgust, reading it along the lines of Menninghaus's decidedly modern history and theory of aesthetics. The potential of disgust as affective reaction to specifically early modern concerns is thus not addressed.
41 For a different reading of Gertrude's narration of Ophelia's death, see Philippa Berry, *Shakespeare's Feminine Endings: Disfiguring Death in the Tragedies* (London: Routledge, 1999), 26–28, which highlights the erotic, even bawdy as well as potentially pagan aspects of the rendition, both of which lead to the dissolution of Ophelia.
42 Ophelia's agency regarding possible (self-)censorship and the possible limits of (self-)censorship has been subject to sustained discussion. Charney and

Charney, for instance, find that madness "enables her to assert her being: she is no longer enforced to keep silent" ("The Language of Madwomen in Shakespeare and His Fellow Dramatists," *Signs*, 3.2 (1977), 451–60; 456). Sandra Fischer, however, has argued that Ophelia's mad speeches and songs "seem to point to a loss rather than an assertion of self. The voice of madness is indeed louder than her earlier rhetoric, yet it fails to break through or change the constraints" ("Hearing Ophelia: Gender and Tragic Discourse in *Hamlet*," *Renaissance and Reformation*, 14.1 (1990), 1–10; 7). More recently, Caralyn Bialo has argued that Ophelia's madness constitutes a gender-based critique of the Danish court, which has to be understood as performance: since "Her madness cannot be rhetorically encapsulated; it must be performed and witnessed" ("Popular Performance, the Broadside Ballad, and Ophelia's Madness," *Studies in English Literature, 1500–1900*, 53.2 (2013), 293–309; 298). Such readings, however, render the acts of active commemoration all the more productive.

43 Menninghaus, *Disgust*, 374.
44 Steve Sohmer, "The 'Double Time' Crux in *Othello* Solved," *ELR*, 32.2 (2002), 214–38; 214.
45 Graham Bradshaw, *Misrepresentations: Shakespeare and the Materialists* (Ithaca, NY: Cornell University Press, 1993), 148–68.
46 For a cultural history of calendars and their respective temporalities as well as their political significance in early modern Europe, see Robert Poole, *Time's Alteration: Calendar Reform in Early Modern England* (London: UCL Press, 1998), and Kevin Birth, "Calendars: Representational Homogeneity and Heterogenous Time," *Time & Society*, 22.2 (2013), 216–36.
47 Harris, *Untimely Matter*, 174.
48 Patricia Parker, *Shakespeare from the Margins* (University of Chicago Press, 1996), 21.
49 In the pictorial and emblematic tradition of the enclosed garden (*hortus conclusus*) that emerged in the late Middle Ages and that persists in the early modern period, the strawberry is often used as Marian symbol. While the red fruit is reminiscent of the Passion of Christ, the three-part leaves allude to the Trinity. What is more, due to its ability to flower and to bear fruit simultaneously, it is a symbol of Mary's virginity.
50 Lynda E. Boose, "Othello's Handkerchief: 'The Recognizance and Pledge of Love,'" *English Literary Renaissance*, 5.3 (1975), 360–74; 363.
51 For William Ian Miller, "the allure of the disgusting" is the central paradox of disgust (Miller, *The Anatomy of Disgust* [Cambridge, MA: Harvard University Press, 1997], 108). Likewise, Carolyn Korsmeyer develops her aesthetic theory of disgust around the paradoxical notion of "attractive aversion" in *Savoring Disgust*.
52 Jacques Lacan, *The Language of the Self: The Function of Language in Psychoanalysis*, trans. Anthony Wilden (Baltimore, MD: Johns Hopkins University Press, 1968), 63.

53 Samuel Weber, *Return to Freud: Jacques Lacan's Dislocation of Psychoanalysis*, trans. Michael Levine (Cambridge University Press, 1991), 9.
54 On this history, see, for instance, Bernth Lindfors, "Ira Aldrich at Covent Garden, April 1833," *Theatre Notebook*, 61.3 (2007), 144–69. The essay collection edited by Carol Mejia LaPerle, *Race and Affect in Early Modern English Literature* (Tempe, AZ: ACMRS Press, 2022), explores the emotional experiences of and responses to racial formation and racist ideologies in Shakespeare's time.

CHAPTER 8

Remembering Water in Robert Yarington's Two Lamentable Tragedies

Katharine A. Craik

Two Lamentable Tragedies (1601) is a play about the stubborn persistence of a traumatic memory in the city of London: the murder on August 23, 1594, of a London chandler, Robert Beech, and his servant Thomas Winchester, by the shopkeeper Thomas Merry. As the allegorical figure of Truth says in the opening scene, in one of many references to the River Thames, the "silver stream can never wash, / The sad remembrance of that cursed deede" (A3r). The play is usually attributed to Robert Yarington, although its authorship has been the subject of much debate.[1] Part of the wave of domestic tragedies which flourished after 1580, *Two Lamentable Tragedies* relates a pair of parallel stories, each of which concerns avarice or the "desire to gaine" (D2r). The first story, often referred to as the 'London plot,' deals with Beech's murder. The second, known as the 'Italian plot,' tells a fictional story of the murder of a young boy, Pertillo, at the hands of his uncle Fallerio, a wealthy landowner. Despite Yarington's foregrounding of Truth at strategic moments throughout the action of the 'London plot,' the play's representation of real-life crime is far from straightforward. This chapter explores the complexities involved in remembering historical events on stage, particularly those which took place in the rapidly transforming environment of early modern London, and considers afresh the distinct affective character of domestic tragedy. The Thames plays a central role in Yarington's story, as well as bringing his play's metaphorical landscape to life, but its function is not, as the quotation above indicates, straightforwardly either to preserve or to erase memory from the collective psyche. Instead, the river expresses new and unfamiliar ways of sensing the presence of the past in the city and in the theater. Yarington's experimentation in the 'London plot' with the relationship between memory and affect reflects in unusual ways on the urban soma and on drama's ability to make effective and affective representation of recent historical events.

Two Lamentable Tragedies is billed on its first page as "Two Tragedies *in one*" (A2r), and scholars have suggested it may be the hasty assemblage of two separate plays.² The action takes place in two different emotional landscapes, in London and in Padua. While the 'London plot' contains passages of prose, the 'Italian plot' is written in verse. There are, however, many similarities between these two stories, not least their shared attention to the problem of how, what, and who to remember. The opening scene of the 'Italian plot' takes place in the household of Pandino and Armenia who are lying "sick on a bedde" (B1r). Armenia asks her villainous brother-in-law Fallerio to remember her by taking care of her son, Pertillo: "hear the latest words / That your dead sister leaves for memory" (B2r). Some thirty lines later, still at the bedside, Pertillo is in turn considering how best to remember his late parents: "I will erect a sumptuous monument, / And leave remembrance to ensuing times" (B2v). Remembrance of the dead also frames the opening scenes of the 'London plot.' Beech's murder had taken place within living memory of the play's first audiences since, as Yarington confirms, the crime "was done in famous London late ... [and] most here present, know this to be true" (A3r).³ The 'London plot' offers a detailed portrait of everyday domestic and professional life, and the audience is repeatedly urged to recognize its protagonists as like them.⁴ Recent scholarship on early modern domestic tragedies has focused accordingly on the realism of these household settings. Highlighting in particular their densely realized materiality, Ariane Balizet, Catherine Richardson, and Emma Whipday have advanced our understanding of the emotional intensity of domestic tragedies, and the dependency of this intensity on real-life possibility.⁵ As Richardson writes, "their impact was not of the nature of a shocking possibility, but of an appalling actuality."⁶ The events, narratives, and images represented on stage are recognizable, and a powerful sense of felt reality contributes to their memorability. But while *Two Lamentable Tragedies* draws on this realist tradition, it also departs decisively from it. "Real life" or "actuality" is not easily accessible in this play, and Yarington complicates any sense that London's ordinary citizens – whether onstage or off-stage – felt things, or forged memories, as a coherent group. The Londoners of *Two Lamentable Tragedies* indeed often seem as vulnerable to emotional detachment as they are inclined toward strong feeling. It is argued here that the traumatic events represented in the 'London plot' allow Yarington to sketch out new and unfamiliar patterns of emotion in the city and, relatedly, to develop novel techniques for triggering emotionally charged memories among audiences.

Early modern domestic tragedy involves deeply felt emotion, not least because it tends to deal with local events which mattered to its first audiences. To remember something or someone necessarily involves feeling since, as Alison Landsberg has written, "memory always implies a subjective, affective relation with the past."⁷ In Yarington's opening allegorical tableau, the figure of Homicide seeks to harness the power of this relation when he invites each audience member to keep a "hart wide open to receive, / A plot of horred desolation" (A2v), which was, in fact, already familiar to them. Later in the play, the figure of Truth anticipates that the spectators' grief will "flowe up to the brim, / And overflowe your cheekes with brinish teares" (E2v). These conventional prompts seem in keeping with Yarington's commitment to didacticism since, as Henry Hitch Adams has written, "[t]he dramatist in both stories lays great emphasis on moral and theological instruction."⁸ But the responses anticipated by Truth sometimes seem strangely at odds with the play's opening instruction that "all men ... weepe, lament and waile" (A2r) in order ultimately to reflect on, and amend, their own shortcomings. Part of the play's innovation, I argue, lies in its interruption of familiar connections between affective investment in a recognizable past, the creation of personal or cultural memory, and the delivery of strict homily. These interruptions go some way toward accounting for the fact that the play has not been much loved or performed, unlike other domestic tragedies such as *Arden of Faversham* (1592) or *A Warning for Faire Women* (1599). Both the emotional unrecognizability and the affective power of the 'London plot' lie in Yarington's disturbance of the ways events may be remembered, and his expression – often through uneasy comedy – of the difficulties involved in forgetting.

The 'London plot' of *Two Lamentable Tragedies* centers on the Thames, which, in keeping with the play's interest in urban commerce, functions as a conduit for the circulation of goods and people. Many late sixteenth- and early seventeenth-century plays are set in or around the river, which provided a flexible allegorical frame for the exploration of "the linearity of time and recovery of memory."⁹ Water pageants, such as those staged to mark the investiture of Henry, eldest son of James I, as Prince of Wales, used the river to suggest growth, progress, and enduring sovereignty. In Anthony Munday's *London's Love to the Royal Prince Henrie* (1610), the river expresses England's invincible imperialism and, more prosaically, the economic security offered by hydraulic power and engineering.¹⁰ And in Samuel Daniel's *Tethys Festival* (1610), a troupe of fantastical riverine characters bring Britain's tributaries to life by embodying the virtues of wisdom and concord.¹¹ Meanwhile a sense of time passing, and of memory's reiterative qualities, is suggested in poems such as Edmund Spenser's *The Ruines of Time* (1591) and *Prothalamion* (1596), both of which mention "silver streaming *Thamesis*"; the marriage of Thames and

Medway in *The Faerie Queene*, IV.xi (1596); and Michael Drayton's exploration of the "linearity of time and the recovery of memory" in *Poly-Olbion* (1612).[12] Here the river evokes a range of ideological or cultural scripts dealing with time's ceaseless movement, and the making or recovery of memory. But the Thames in *Two Lamentable Tragedies* stands for neither London's expansively unfurling future nor the powerful reverberations of its illustrious past. In the distinct urban landscape of the 'London plot,' the river keeps stalling or stopping altogether. It seldom facilitates purposeful acts of recognition or remembrance, but instead seems linked with careless indifference. This unusual and experimental domestic tragedy offers Yarington a platform to rethink the ways that London's citizens experience affect-laden events from the past, as well as the role of public theater in creating emotional cohesion and homiletic consensus among the living.

I

The river is at the center of the 'London plot.' The residence of the unfortunate Mr. Beech is in Thames Street, which runs east to west parallel to the river, and the play contains many references to water's metaphorical significance. Occasionally, water promises emotional catharsis since, as Truth says, "the river Thames / Doth strive to wash from all impuritie" (A3r). When it comes to absolving Merry, his sister Rachel notes that repentance, too, may "wash away thy sinne / With clensing teares of true contrition" (E2v). In one of Yarington's typical associative moves, the metaphysical question of how to rinse clean Merry's conscience blurs into the more practical but no less urgent business of scouring evidence from the scene of the crime:

> oh would to God I could
> As cleerly wash your conscience from the deed,
> As I can cleanse the house
> (D3r)

Merry himself urges Rachel to "Wipe up the blood in every place above, / So that no drop be found about the house" (D3r). Water's capacity to cleanse offers little prospect of absolution, but instead, at best, the erasure of an incriminating stain. Traces of Beech's murder nevertheless remain trapped in London's waterways, especially its ditches, "sinkes and gutters, privies, crevices" (D3r), as well as the "narrow lane" (G1v) of water at Baynard's Castle stairs in Blackfriars, to the east of the Fleet.[13] Rather than elaborating the rich symbolic vocabulary of natural sources or tides, Yarington concentrates instead on the places where the "water side" (E2v) meets the city at points of material constraint or difficulty. Despite its potential to offer spiritual purification, the Thames more often looks bluntly secular and stubbornly retentive. When Yarington lowers water's cosmological register into a domestic, urban frame, he is also showing how the river's capacity persistently to remember triggers individual anxiety and shame rather than civic pride or belonging.

Emotional extremity is expressed elsewhere in the 'London plot' through images of water running out of control. Grief involves "streames of sorrow" such as those Rachel envisages for Merry, whose despair "like a spring tide over-swels the bankes" (D2r). Such is the force of Merry's feeling, indeed, that Rachel imagines he might "make an inundation, / And so be borne away with swiftest tides" (D2r). Withholding the expression of emotion, on the other hand, involves perilous scarcity. As Master Cowley, Beech's neighbor, explains to Merry's servant Harry Williams, who finds himself a reluctant witness to Beech's murder,

> those that smother griefe too secretly,
> May wast themselves in silent anguishment,
> And bring their bodies to so low an ebbe,
> That all the world can never make it flowe,
> Unto the happy hight of former health.
> (F4r)

Sufferers whose painful emotions are stymied by their own silence end up wasted, barren, and depleted. Here the body is conceptualized as a free-flowing stream whose vigor, height, and depth suggest healthy self-expression. Emotions are registered by and reflected in liquid flow, the body in constant flux as it strives toward an ideal state of equilibrium. But while Yarington makes occasional use of this familiar humoral vocabulary, he also envisages emotions operating outside natural sources, eddies, or tides.[14] The extreme affective experiences of the play, articulated as floods and droughts, suggest the perversion of predictably systemic properties of humoral flow. And the dark or blocked urban waterways which feature so prominently in the 'London plot' sketch out new, less schematic patterns of affective response.

The river proves integral to the protracted strand of the plot concerning the disposal and recovery of Beech's "dissevered ... limbs." The murderer Thomas Merry packs his victim's torso into a salt sack, then crosses the river to give it "a watrie funerall" (F3v) in a ditch on the south bank. Two

Figure 8.1 Baynards Castle at the outfall of the Fleet Ditch. Undated lithograph after John M. Thorp (?). Wellcome Collection Library, London. Licensed by Creative Commons: https://wellcomecollection.org/works/kerzfg4f.

watermen moor their boats at an insalubrious docking point on the north bank and ready themselves for a busy morning's work on St. Bartholomew's Day.[15] Here they stumble across the rest of Beech's remains, which Merry has tossed into the Thames at "some darke place nere to Bainardes castle" (F3v), and set about piecing together (or re-membering) the events leading up to his murder (see Figure 8.1).

The watermen belong to a social order lower even than that of the retailers, day laborers, and servants who make up the rest of the cast of the 'London plot.' Tasked with ferrying passengers forward and backward between the sets of stairs dotted along the Thames, and between the north and south banks, watermen were reputationally rough, unrefined, and garrulous.[16] Sometimes regarded as the clowns of *Two Lamentable Tragedies*, they nevertheless make an important contribution to the play's portrait of affective life in the city and, especially, to the notion that any significant relationship to the past is channeled through strong feeling.[17]

The Second Waterman, whose name is Will, begins by expressing his unwillingness to work:

> By my troth I am indifferent whether I go or no. If a fare come why so, if not, why so, if I have not their money, they shall have none of my labour. (F4v)

When the First Waterman reminds his partner that "we that live by our labours, must give attendance," Will replies:

> I am indifferent, I care not so much for going,
> But if I go with you, why so, if not, why so.
> (F4v)

Even when Will falls over the bag which contains Beech's head and legs, he remains unmoved:

> 1ST WATERMAN: Good Lord deliver us, a man's legges, and a head with manie wounds.
> 2ND WATERMAN: Whats that so much, I am indifferent, yet for mine owne part, I understand the miserie of it, if you doe, why so, if not, why so.
> (F4v)

The discovery of Beech's remains fosters in Will neither fear nor sadness, as Truth's prologue had anticipated, but instead a strange kind of emotional neutrality. While his partner seems appropriately shocked by the awful discovery, Will feels nothing at all. Later the First Waterman will remark upon the "strange and very rufull sight" (F4v) which confronts them, but Will again twice replies, "I am indifferent." When the First Waterman points out that the deceased is wearing hose and shoes, making him unlikely to have died at the hands of the hangman, Will's reply remains unchanged: "I am indifferent" (G1r). And at the moment when the First Waterman finally connects their gruesome find to Beech's murder, Will is still unmoved:

> Masse I am indifferent, Ile go along with you.
> If it be so, why so, if not why so.
> (G1r)

He remains implausibly neutral even when the third neighbor offers to reward their discovery: "We are indifferent whether you give us any thing or nothing, and if you had not, why so, but since you have, why so" (G1v). Will's indifference to work, and to money, is also an indifference to others. His neutrality is not *schadenfreude*, the lack of sympathy which derives pleasure from someone else's misfortune. Instead, he expresses nothing more or less than an emotional vacuum, a stopping or absence of feeling. He simply does not care one way or the other, and feels nothing at all. Like the stoppage of the Thames in a gutter or crevice, Will experiences an absence of will, desire, or feeling. His indifference destabilizes one of the key conventions of dramatic representation: that when something happens, it matters. In the specific context of domestic tragedy, the episode disturbs the assumption that engaging with the past involves feeling. To Will, by contrast, the story of Beech's murder remains unremarkable and therefore unmarked.

As a pair, Yarington's watermen dramatize the tension between feeling and not feeling, or remembering and forgetting. If there is comedy in the scene, and in Will's unconcern, it derives from the dissonance which arises when someone feels indifferent toward that which culture suggests is worth remembering. Suspicious that Beech's body may have been "throwne into the Thames" (D3r), Beech and Merry's neighbors value the watermen as an informal police force capable of dutifully uncovering evidence of crimes which the river has failed properly to erase. The two watermen, on the other hand, reveal the problems involved in regarding acts of remembering and forgetting as opposing experiences which the movement of the Thames is equally equipped to register. As Isabel Karremann has written, "what is forgotten is not irretrievably gone but rather purposefully overlooked, put aside as insignificant or as an obstacle to signification."[18] Will's carefully chosen name confirms that his indifference to the events which led up to Beech's murder is neither casual nor inconsequential. If Will's purposeful lack of engagement with the awfulness of the discovery is a putting-aside of remembrance, this happens through a putting-aside of emotion – which changes, in turn, the way the events surrounding Beech's murder can be reexperienced in the theater. Will expresses no conventionally grief-stricken response to what he witnesses, and there are no flowing, let alone overflowing tears as Truth had advocated in the opening scene. In early modern poetry, as we have seen above, the affective register of the endlessly flowing river tends to signify remembering (eternity, permanence, ceaselessness). Its constant movement is also sometimes evoked in early modern drama to suggest actions akin to forgetting (disburdening, forgiving, washing away).[19] In the distinct, urban setting of Yarington's 'London plot', however, the river keeps stopping. And whereas liquid flow suggests robust physical and psychological health in the context of early modern humoralism, the wasting, ebbing, or indeed sheer absence of feeling suggests an altogether different experience of emotionality more in keeping with London's already heavily polluted urban waterways.[20] As we will see, Yarington's repeated disruption of the free-flowing movement associated with both memory and emotion disturbs in turn the congregational solidarity which the homiletic impulse of domestic tragedy normally presumes. Even Truth herself ends up equivocal about the possibility of delivering, through dramatic representation, an emotionally charged memory-lesson directly into the audience's conscience.

II

Many writers were committed to remembering Beech's murder – or, at least, to realizing the commercial value of keeping alive the memory of this event. The aftermath of his death witnessed the publication of a news tract entitled *A True Discourse of a Most Cruell and Barbarous Murther Comitted by one Thomas Merrey* (1594), as well as a pamphlet entitled *A World of Wonders, A Mass of Murders* (1595), and five broadside ballads. John Day and William Haughton's *The Tragedy of Merry* was performed in 1599–1600 at the Rose, and this is probably the same play which Henslowe's diary references as *Beech's Tragedy*.[21] All of these texts remember Beech's murder, although they do so in different ways and for different reasons.[22] Their sheer quantity and variety registers the fact that history's place in the public imagination, including and especially recent local history, was at this time a source of intense debate. On the one hand, those who defended the stage pointed out the usefulness of history plays for curating a shared sense of the past. Theater's detractors, on the other hand, found such claims impossible to reconcile with the risk that imaginative constructions of the past, like any other imaginative constructions, might foster mindless lethargy, forgetfulness, and oblivion.[23] At stake was the extent to which the dramatization of historical "truths" functioned as a reliable form of documentary evidence, and the capacity of such evidence to shape the present and future memories of those who encountered it. As Frances E. Dolan notes, domestic tragedies of the 1580s and 1590s tend starkly to reveal "the processes of cultural formation and transformation in which they participated."[24] *Two Lamentable Tragedies* brings such processes vividly to light, illuminating changing practices of memory-making through the inclusion of a singularly partial, interrogative relator of past events called Truth.

In many respects, Yarington seems committed in the 'London plot' to a form of documentary playmaking which makes events from the recent past easily communicable to, and recognizable by, a citizen audience. The lives of the protagonists center on keeping shop, satisfying customers, and finding ways to live thriftily – much like the lives of the citizens who would have attended the play's first performances. As Homicide notes, the Londoners represented on stage, like those in the playhouse, are generally "bent with vertuous gainfull trade, / To get their needmentes for this mortall life" (A2r) – even if scarcity makes them persistently vulnerable to "all-griping *Avarice*" (A2v). The 'London plot' vividly captures a sense of neighbors living in difficult proximity, packed together so tightly that Merry fears that the smell of Beech's corpse may be "felt throughout the streete" (D2v).[25] Like the Londoners in the theaters on the south bank, or at the Fortune, where *Two Lamentable Tragedies* may have had its first performances, Yarington's Londoners attend sermons at St. Paul's Cross, drink beer, and borrow penny loaves from their neighbors.[26] Yarington inserts a number of references to familiar local landmarks such as The Bull, where Merry settles (B4r), and the Three Cranes, where Merry's servant Williams escapes his master's "murthrous hand" (C1r). The action is brought further to life through everyday domestic details such as Beech's cutting of a piece of cheese as he prepares to meet his neighbor and soon-to-be-killer. The scene looks familiar and recognizable, folding the recent past into the living present. As Landsberg reminds us, memory involves an affect-based relationship to the past.[27] Here the triggering of emotion, and the securing of memory, both rest on the assumption that the audience will recognize and sympathetically respond to a familiar urban habitus – and then feel the force of its abrupt and traumatic dissolution.

Most critics have argued that the closely observed realism of domestic tragedy stokes up affective tension in order to deliver memorable homily. Jean Howard writes, for example, that while domestic tragedy deals with overwhelming desires, it also resolutely "counteracts the entropic force of these desires by bringing the criminals to account, eliciting their confessions, and killing them off."[28] This firm bringing-to-justice reveals London as a place where dangers exist, but in which order will prevail because the sins of its citizens will be unsparingly exposed and punished. More recently, Sheila Coursey has considered *Two Lamentable Tragedies* in parallel with contemporary 'true crime' podcasts, arguing that the play works toward a restoration of social order since it "holds the audience accountable" for the voyeuristic role they play in the consumption, circulation, and performance of Beech's murder.[29] The conclusion of the 'London plot' does indeed seem unambiguously didactic. One of Beech and Merry's neighbors, Master Cowley, notes that if he were in charge of proceedings, the murderers would be reviled in public memory: "Ide blase their shame, / And make them pay due penance for their sinne" (H3v). In fact, Rachel takes matters into her own hands by blazing her own shameful legacy: "Let me be merror to ensuing times, / And teach all sisters" (K2v). According to the allegorical figure of Avarice, it is the painful memory of her brother's wrongdoing which grieves Rachel most profoundly, so that eventually she does not even "wish to overlive, / The sad remembrance of her brothers sinne" (F3v). Within the didactic frame of domestic tragedy, the target of such admonitions was usually women. The Officer accordingly points out, at the play's conclusion, that Rachel's onstage execution will "teach all other by this spectacle, / To shunne such dangers as she ran into" (K2v). Merry's servant Harry, who helped conceal Beech's body, is spared when he pleads benefit of clergy, whereas "wretched *Rachels* sexe denies that grace" (I2v). The relentlessness of this homily, central to the affective power of the conclusion to the 'London plot,' persistently collapses the gaps between past and present, and reality and fiction, until "all sisters" (K2v) who remember Rachel are directed to feel the same way she does: properly chastened, properly disciplined.

And yet Yarington significantly disturbs this homiletic message by disturbing the process of emotional memory-making. As Balizet writes, "In somatic domesticity, power is expressed through the coherence of . . . a balanced male body."[30] In order for the homily to function, there must be some recognition of people "like us" and a household "like ours." But *Two Lamentable Tragedies* is notable for the extremity and brutality of its staged violence, amply fulfilling Truth's opening promise to offer a surfeit of "mangled bodies, and . . . gaping wounds" (A3r). First Merry dismembers Beech ("Ile cut him peece-meale . . . Fetch me the chopping-knife," E2r), then scatters his body parts throughout the city. The Third Neighbor predicts the impossibility of piecing Beech back together: "they cannot make, / That sound and whole, which a remorseless hand / Hath severed" (G2r). Much of the action is organized around the painstaking reconstruction of events surrounding the murder, a process mirrored and replicated when Beech is literally, painfully *re*-membered. One important piece of the jigsaw is supplied by a gentleman who remembers walking "betime" (G2r) near Paris Garden ditch in Southwark. Here the action returns to the dark, muddy places where the Thames meets the city as the Gentleman recalls how his spaniel plunged repeatedly into the water. Suspecting foul play, the gentleman orders that "the ditch be dragd" until Beech's torso is eventually revealed, washed up "amongst the Nettles growing near the bank" (G2v). (The dog's horrible discovery fuels a series of uncomfortable jokes about the difficulty of keeping meat fresh in the city.) In the following scenes, the citizens set about awkwardly joining up Beech's "middle mention" (E2v) with the head and legs found earlier by the watermen. "Lay them together," says Beech and Merry's neighbor Master Loney, and "see if they can make, / Among them all a sound and solid man" (G2r). Beech's body-in-parts, and its hastily improvised reconstruction, signals the breakdown of social order in London, but also the erosion of the emotional belonging, and physical cohesion, which makes the represented households look recognizable and replicable. And if Beech – and by extension his neighbors – suffers a catastrophic loss of power and agency, a parallel form of psychic fragmentation seems also to afflict the perpetrators, Merry and Rachel, who keep repeating the suggestive phrase "we be all undone" (G3v).

The spectacle of Beech's "dissevered blood besprinckled lims" (E2r), and the existential unraveling of the murderers, is a reminder that the affective impact of domestic tragedy rests not only on the audience's recognition of their own middle-class lives but also on the sense of rupture when these lives are abruptly compromised or curtailed. This disturbance continues with the protracted death of Beech's servant, Thomas Winchester, who must be killed because he witnessed his master's murder. Rachel hopes, unrealistically, that Winchester may not have registered Merry's identity:

RACHEL: Perchaunce the boy doth not remember you.
MERRY: It maie be so, but ile remember him.

(C3v)

Merry therefore delivers six blows to Winchester's head, the seventh of these "mortall wounds" (D3v) causing the weapon to lodge immovably in his skull. The half-living, half-dead Winchester then appears, according to a singularly demanding stage direction, carried "*in a chaire, with a hammer sticking in his head*" (D3v). As Loney points out, "He is not dead but hath a dying life" (D3v). If Landsberg is right in her assertion that "[m]emory remains a sensuous phenomenon experienced by the body, and ... continues to derive much of its power through affect," then the sensations ignited in the minds and bodies of the audience by this gruesome scene must surely have made it one of the most memorable of *Two Lamentable Tragedies*.[31] Its memorability arises from its spectacular breach of the bodily and somatic integrity which belongs to the familiar contours of home. The play dramatizes, with maximum suddenness, the splintering of a familiar and recognizable urban habitus.

The homiletic strategy of the 'London plot' is to ensure such splintering never occurs again by consigning these events to the past. And yet the action of these key scenes is structured around the indistinct spaces between remembering and forgetting. The events leading up to and subsequent to Beech's murder are recollected slowly, imperfectly, and only with great difficulty. The salter's servant is sent around the city to identify the customer (Rachel) who purchased the sack, but confesses he does "not well remember" (G3r) her identity. A maid reports that she remembers seeing two people running away from the door of Beech's shop after Winchester has been attacked, but then says it was too dark for her to see anyone clearly (C4v). The cutler recalls lending his hammer to someone, but when this same hammer is found with Winchester in his almost-alive "extremitie" (D4r), the cutler "remembers not, who borrowed it" (G1v). Meanwhile the wounds which Merry inflicts on Beech are described as "sound memorials" (C3v), even though their intention is to bring Beech into oblivion. And Merry kills Winchester not only to remove him as a witness, but also, more strangely, so that "he shall quite forget who did him harme" (C3v). If the 'London plot' sets out to memorialize a brutal double murder, and to impress it into the memories of his audience so that it never happens again, Yarington nevertheless everywhere emphasizes the risk and likelihood of forgetting.

Just as Merry is undertaking the "barbarous deed" (E2r) of dismembering Beech onstage, the allegorical figure of Truth unexpectedly reappears. Having berated the moon for shedding light on Merry's grisly task, she turns directly to the audience, whom she addresses as the "sad spectators of this Acte" (E2v). Earlier Truth had assured the audience that the play presents an accurate record of real-life events: "Would truth were false, so this were but a tale" (A3r). Here she acknowledges the scene's affective power by noting that their hearts must surely now "taste a feeling pensivenesse" (E2v) – before unexpectedly advising the audience to invest no more emotion in what they are witnessing:

> I see your sorrowes flowe up to the brim,
> And overflowe your cheekes with brinish teares,
> But though this sight bring surfet to the eye,
> Delight your eares with pleasing harmonie,
> That eares may counterchecke your eyes, and say,
> Why shed you teares, this deede is but a playe.
> (E2v)

The 'London plot' may be true, insofar as it really happened, but Yarington foregrounds an equal and competing truth: *Two Lamentable Tragedies* is a work of imaginative fiction, played by what Homicide calls "purple actors" (F3v) and, as such, deserves scant emotional investment.[32] The audience's eyes may be full "to the brim," but Truth offers a "countercheck" to any such emotional excess. Just as the Second Waterman, Will, had seemed resolutely indifferent to the piteous sight of Beech's remains, Truth's intervention encourages emotional detachment at the very moment when the audience is most likely to be affectively engaged. While this is interesting for what it suggests about the complexity of Londoners' responses to the fictional reenactment of a true crime which had taken place within living memory, it is also an important corrective to the assumption that domestic tragedy delivers memorable homily. A powerful homiletic impulse, which depends (in the case of domestic tragedy) on sympathy with and fearful recognition of events from the recent past, is difficult to reconcile with Truth's claim that "this deede is but a playe" designed to offer pleasure and delight. As Viviana Comensoli has suggested, "writers of domestic drama reveal an interest in perversity and contrariety" as often as they reveal their allegiance to social conservatism.[33] Despite Yarington's commitment to a relatively straightforward process of mimesis which folds the past seamlessly into the present, and despite his positioning of the audience as a coherent, stable, and yet malleable group, Truth's severing of the relationship between emotion and memory unravels the play's didactic effectiveness. And yet Truth's description of contradictory emotions (fear, horror, pleasure), and their bewildering simultaneity, is surely a more accurate description of what happens when a trauma from the past is replayed. As Peter Holland has recently reminded us, in his study of memory in early modern drama, trauma damages our ability accurately to remember.[34] Yarington's sketch of Londoners' emotional confusion, detachment, and disorder, whether they are onstage or in the playhouse, is both chilling and mesmerizing in its perverse contrariety.

The 'Italian plot,' like the 'London plot,' deals with what happens when the affective work of remembering fails or is interrupted. Grief-stricken by the death of his parents, Pertillo sets out to create a "sad memoriall" (B2v); but the villainous Fallerio insists there will be no such lavish "stately ceremoniall pompe" (B2v). The stories of *Two Lamentable Tragedies* proceed in parallel, and this "two-folde Tragedie" (A3r), as Homicide calls it in the prologue, has offered a series of tempting binaries to recent scholarship on early modern theater and affect. These accounts tend to be fairly schematic – exploring, for example, the contrasting emotional lives of those who belong to higher and lower social classes, or in metropolitan and rural settings. The 'London plot,' based on real-life events, has been said to involve plain English feeling, whereas the 'Italian plot,' founded in fiction, involves sophisticated or high emotion. Such mappable schema provide a convenient framework for discussing the fugitive, spontaneous, and slippery nature of emotionality. But as this essay has explored, and despite its two-part structure, *Two Lamentable Tragedies* resists the binary oppositions that tend to inform critical accounts of early modern emotion. The play sketches a less schematic life for Londoners, past and present, and for audiences in the early modern playhouse. Yarington accepts the possibility of an audience's contradictory and absent feelings, and this is of a piece with his sense of London's complex, evolving, and discomforted urban psyche.

Two Lamentable Tragedies also offers a new approach to the acts of remembrance, and the risks of forgetting, involved in writing and experiencing historical drama. As the scenes set around the river demonstrate, the past seldom stays securely in the past, and cannot be projected easefully into the future. Instead, time works recursively, stopping and stalling unexpectedly, as Yarington evokes indistinct states between remembering and forgetting. At the conclusion of the play, Truth returns to the metaphor of water as she again addresses the audience directly:

> There is a Barke thats newly rigd for sea,
> Unmand, unfurnishd with munition . . .
> Would you be pleasd to man this willing barke
> With good conceits
>
> (K3v)

Here the play itself is figured as a "newly rigd" ship setting sail toward the ocean, and Truth seeks the audience's "smoothest smiles, and pleasing plaudiats" in order to repel the criticism of those who would "sincke her in reproches waves" (K3v).[35] This *captatio benevolentiae*, or closing appeal for audience goodwill, looks more or less conventional. But to describe the play as "Unmand, unfurnishd" suggests not only its insufficiency but also its radical provisionality. Truth herself is no transparently allegorical figure, and her interpellations scarcely illuminate what Rachel calls "our sceane of ruthe" (C3r). Truth's partiality, and her knowing manipulation of the audience, allows Yarington to disturb one of the fundamental assumptions of domestic tragedy: that the past acts bluntly on the present in order to repair it. The action of the 'London plot' does not resolve into homiletic stasis, partly because of the choppy ways in which recent historical events are felt or not felt. Instead, Yarington proposes new, unpredictable connections between urban emotionality, onstage acts of memory-making, and the reception of theatrical culture more generally at the turn of the seventeenth century.

Notes

The author would like to thank Catherine Richardson and the editors of this volume for their helpful feedback on earlier drafts of this essay.

1 For a summary of this debate, see Chiaki Hanabusa, ed., *Two Lamentable Tragedies* (Manchester: Malone Society Reprints, 2013), xxviii–xxix. All references to the play refer to this facsimile edition. Old spelling is retained although u/v and i/j have been updated.
2 See W. W. Greg, ed., *Henslowe's Diary* (London: A. H. Bullen, 1908), 209; for a useful summary of this debate, see Gemma Leggott's introduction to her unpublished edition of the play (8–13), https://extra.shu.ac.uk/emls/iemls/renplays/Two%20Lamentable%20Tragedies%20ed%20by%20Gemma%20Leggott.doc.
3 The play's first performance may have taken place as early as 1595, the year after the murders took place. See Martin Wiggins, ed., with Catherine Richardson, *British Drama, 1533–1642: A Catalogue* (Oxford University Press, 2013), vol. III, 304–8 (1015).
4 Compare the description of "domesticke hystories" in Thomas Heywood's *An Apology for Actors* (1612), B5r; quoted in Viviana Comensoli, *"Household Business": Domestic Plays of Early Modern England* (University of Toronto Press, 1996), 3.
5 See Ariane Balizet, *Blood and Home in Early Modern Drama: Domestic Identity on the Renaissance Stage* (London: Routledge, 2014), esp. chapter 2, "The Bleeding Husband: Cuckoldry and Murder in *Arden of Faversham* and *A Warning for Fair Women*," 53–88; Catherine Richardson, *Domestic Life and Domestic Tragedy in Early Modern England: The Material Life of the Household* (Manchester University Press, 2006), esp. chapter 4, "Two Lamentable Tragedies," 128–50; Emma Whipday and Freyja Cox Jensen, "'Original Practices,' Lost Plays, and Historical Imagination: Staging 'The Tragedy of Merry,'" *Shakespeare Bulletin*, 35.2 (2017), 289–307.
6 Richardson, *Domestic Life and Domestic Tragedy*, 129.
7 Alison Landsberg, *Prosthetic Memory: The Transformation of American Remembrance in the Age of Mass Culture* (New York: Columbia University Press, 2004), 19.
8 Henry Hitch Adams, *English Domestic or Homiletic Tragedy 1575–1642* (New York: Columbia University Press, 1943), 108–9. Richardson also discusses the play's determinedly "didactic project"; see *Domestic Life and Domestic Tragedy*, 138.
9 Caterina Guardini, "'The Lovely Nymph of Stately Thames': The Rhetoric of Water in the Creation of the Prince of Wales," in Luca Baratta and Alice Equestri, eds., *Forms of Nationhood: Selected Papers from the "Shakespeare and His Contemporaries" Graduate Conference* (Florence: British Institute, 2016), 81–109; 84. See also Andrew McRae, *Literature and Domestic Travel in Early Modern England* (Cambridge University Press, 2009), esp. chapter 1, "Rivers," 21–66.

10 Guardini, "'The Lovely Nymph of Stately Thames,'" 84. On the export industry associated with the port of London, see Jeremy Boulton, "London 1540–1700," in Peter Clark, ed., *The Cambridge History of Urban Britain*, 3 vols. (Cambridge University Press, 2000), vol. II, 1540–1840, 315–46; esp. 320–26.
11 On the collective memory-making undertaken by city pageants of the 1580s and 1590s, see Ian W. Archer, "Memorialization in Early Modern London," in J. F. Merritt, ed., *Imagining Early Modern London: Perceptions and Portrayals of the City from Stow to Strype, 1598–1720* (Cambridge University Press, 2001), 89–113; 90.
12 See Lawrence Manley, *Literature and Culture in Early Modern London* (Cambridge University Press, 1995), 177. Drayton's Sonnet 24 in *Ideas Mirrour* (1594) begins with a description of "Our floods-Queene *Thames*, for shyps and Swans is crowned" (D4v) before offering an encomium of other English rivers. The "silver streaming *Thamesis*" appears in *The Ruines of Time*, line 2, in William A. Oram et al., eds., *The Yale Edition of the Shorter Poems of Edmund Spenser* (New Haven, CT: Yale University Press, 1989), 232; the "silver streaming *Themmes*" is mentioned again in *Prothalamion*, line 11. Spenser describes the Thames' long courtship of Medway, and the celebratory "banquet of the watry Gods," in A. C. Hamilton, ed., *The Faerie Queene* (London: Longman, 1980), IV.xi.8–10.
13 Mark S. R. Jenner has written that London's conduits reveal "a moral economy of water" connected to social relationships, especially neighborliness. See "From Conduit to Commercial Network? Water in London, 1500–1725," in Paul Griffiths and Mark S. R. Jenner, eds., *Londinopolis: Essays in the Cultural and Social History of Early Modern London* (Manchester University Press, 2000), 250–72; 254.
14 For a discussion of early modern humoral fluidity and the early modern city, see the opening chapter of Gail Kern Paster's *The Body Embarrassed: Drama and the Disciplines of Shame in Early Modern England* (Ithaca, NY: Cornell University Press, 1993), 23–63.
15 In the 'Italian plot,' Pertillo's corpse, like Beech's, is "cast ... in some durtie ditch" (D1v) by a pair of ruffians who mirror the watermen of the 'London plot.'
16 On London's watermen, see Michael Leapman, *London's River: A History of the Thames* (London: Pavilion, 1991), 59–60; and Chris Roberts, *Cross River Traffic: A History of London's Bridges* (London: Granta, 2005), 5. John Evelyn records that Baynard's Castle, the seat of the Herbert family, was destroyed in the Great Fire of London; see Roy Porter, *London: A Social History* (London: Penguin, 1994; revised ed., 2000), 53, 106.
17 For the watermen as clowns, see Whipday and Jensen, "'Original Practices,'" 296.
18 Isabel Karremann, *The Drama of Memory in Shakespeare's History Plays* (Cambridge University Press, 2015), 7–8.
19 See, for example, George Chapman, Ben Jonson, and John Marston's *Eastward Ho* (1605) in which the butcher Slitgut compares the storm-tossed river to an overburdened horse: "What a coil the Thames keeps! She bears

some unjust burden, I believe, that she kicks and curvets thus to cast it" (4.1.11–12); see James Knowles, ed., *The Roaring Girl and Other City Comedies* (Oxford University Press, 2001), 109. Falstaff finds himself cast into the Thames "like a barrow of butcher's offal" (3.5.4); see David Crane, ed., *The Merry Wives of Windsor* (Cambridge University Press, 1997), 108.

20 On the idea that theater "plays a part in maintaining urban health" through offering tragic catharsis, see Marissa Greenberg's reading of Thomas Heywood's *An Apology for Actors* in "Women and the Theatre in Thomas Heywood's London," in Joan Fitzpatrick, ed., *The Idea of the City: Early-Modern, Modern and Post-Modern Locations and Communities* (Newcastle: Cambridge Scholars Publishing, 2009), 79–89; 80.

21 See Roslyn Knutson, David McInnis, and Matthew Steggle, eds., *Thomas Merry (Beech's Tragedy)*, in The Lost Plays Database, https://lostplays.folger.edu; Whipday and Jensen, "'Original Practices,'" 289; Marissa Greenberg, *Metropolitan Tragedy: Genre, Justice and the City in Early Modern England* (University of Toronto Press, 2015), 33 and 154 (n. 38); Roslyn L. Knutson, "'Toe to Toe across Maid Lane': Repertorial Competition at the Rose and Globe, 1599–1600," in Paul Nelson and June Schlueter, eds., *Acts of Criticism: Performance Matters in Shakespeare and His Contemporaries* (Madison, NJ: Fairleigh Dickinson University Press, 2006), 33.

22 The story of Thomas Arden's murder also circulated in a variety of media and genres. See Catherine Belsey, *The Subject of Tragedy: Identity and Difference in Renaissance Drama* (London: Routledge, 1985; repr. 2014), 129–48; 130.

23 See Karremann, *The Drama of Memory*, 1–35 and 90–91.

24 Frances E. Dolan, *Dangerous Familiars: Representations of Domestic Crime in England, 1550–1700* (Ithaca, NY: Cornell University Press, 1994), 3.

25 Holly Dugan offers a cultural history of the sense of smell in early modern London, arguing that rosemary in particular may have aroused "collective memories of shared urban experience of the plague." See *The Ephemeral History of Perfume: Scent and Sense in Early Modern England* (Baltimore, MD: Johns Hopkins University Press, 2011), 101.

26 On the play's performance history, including a possible reference to the Fortune, see Leggott, ed., *Two Lamentable Tragedies*, 48–53. For a discussion of early modern urban neighborliness, see Laura Gowing, *Domestic Dangers: Women, Words, and Sex in Early Modern London* (Oxford: Clarendon Press, 1996), esp. chapter 1, "Gender, Household, and City," 1–29; 13. See also Bernard Capp, *When Gossips Meet: Women, Family, and Neighbourhood in Early Modern England* (Oxford University Press, 2003), 342–43.

27 Landsberg, *Prosthetic Memory*, 19.

28 Jean E. Howard, "London and the Early Modern Stage," in Lawrence Manley, ed., *The Cambridge Companion to the Literature of London* (Cambridge University Press, 2011), 34–49; 42.

29 Sheila Coursey, "*Two Lamentable Tragedies* and True Crime Publics in Early Modern Domestic Tragedy," *Comparative Drama*, 53.3–4 (2019), 263–86; 265.

30 Balizet, *Blood and Home in Early Modern Drama*, 56.
31 Landsberg, *Prosthetic Memory*, 8.
32 The 'Italian plot' contains a similar metatheatrical device as Allenso dons a false beard "Such as our common actors use to weare" (H2v).
33 Comensoli, *"Household Business,"* 16. Gowing concurs in *Domestic Dangers* that "the moral vision behind the exercise of regulation was not uncontested," 263. For further discussion of how domestic tragedies complicate the "unequivocal moral judgements" of their pamphlet sources, see Leonore Lieblein, "Murder in English Domestic Plays, 1590–1610," *Studies in English Literature, 1500–1900*, 23.2 (1983), 181–96, esp. 181, 188.
34 Peter Holland, *Shakespeare and Forgetting* (London: Arden, 2021), chapter 1.
35 Leggott reads this speech as an extended metaphor on the Fortune Theatre; see Leggott, ed., *Two Lamentable Tragedies*, 49.

CHAPTER 9

Mourning Memory in Cymbeline

Daniel Normandin

Suppose "grief" or "mourning" are names we give to those instances when memory is most keenly, painfully felt. ("Nostalgia" is a gentler, bittersweet relative.) A mourning without memory seems paradoxical, impossible: How can felt grief lack a known object? Yet memory itself can be lost and mourned, as Shakespeare shows in his late romance *Cymbeline*. "I cannot delve him to the root" (1.1.28), an unnamed "Gentleman" says of the orphaned protagonist, Posthumus, referring to his uncertain lineage. He may as well be speaking of the play's general quest for origins – personal, familial, and national alike – in an ancient British setting far murkier than that of the medieval histories. Here, pasts are unknown, lineages askew, roots undelvable, memory enfeebled. The past's shadows are darkest in the subplot featuring the exiled courtier Belarius, who has abducted the titular king's two sons and raised them as noble savages in the wilds of Wales. In that marginal hinterland, memory becomes not so much the vehicle for mourning as its object. Isolated from any larger community, ignorant of their parentage, the princes bitterly feel the absence of known origins: they mourn memory itself. That grief takes on public resonance in a play so preoccupied with questions of nation and of historical memory. In what follows, I will therefore interpret the rustic princes' mourning as a political, national, and even colonial emotion that can illuminate how, and why, a newly imperial people imagined ancient forebears as memoryless "primitives." I locate this emotion at the convergence of two fledgling but transformative movements in England when the play was first staged around 1611: the antiquarian recollection of the nation's distant past and the colonial expansion of its territory.

My political reading follows the important work of affect theorists and scholars who have noted that, in Stephanie Trigg's words, "'emotion' is not only the response or expression of the individual romantic subject but can also refer to collective feelings and passions."[1] As the editors of *Historical Affects and the Early Modern Theater* argue, "in its relationship to institutional forces, affect might best be understood as an ideological and a potentially powerful political instrument, martialed in the name of racial identification, or feelings of civic belongingness."[2] The political affects of *Cymbeline* may seem fairly uncomplicated instruments. The king's climactic, and apparently sudden, decision to "submit to Caesar / And to the Roman empire" (5.4.458–59), and to "Let / A Roman and a British ensign wave / Friendly together" (5.4.477–79), may dramatize the *translatio imperii* through which the Roman Empire foreshadowed, and therefore licensed, a nascent "British" Empire in the early seventeenth century.[3] Yet if the play depicts a British nation's absorption of a Roman "heritage," it does so through an oblique, even inverted, vision of empire, its Britain occupied rather than occupier. In the chronicles of Raphael Holinshed, his main source, Shakespeare would have been reminded that the Romans "planted their forworne legions in the most fertile places of the realme."[4] Over the past two decades, Shakespeareans have accordingly emphasized the play's vision of the home nation as occupied territory, reflecting colonization as it was then being practiced in Virginia and Ulster, not merely imperial ideology as it was theorized in London.[5] From this perspective, the Welsh scenes invite a vision of ancient British primitive indigeneity, a homegrown but culturally dangerous parallel to Native Americans and the "wild Irish." With this stranger, less comfortable form of "racial identification" in mind, we might well understand Shakespeare's Globe theater as a piece of "affective technology," to use Steven Mullaney's term, that "helped the Elizabethan [here, Jacobean] present to understand its own shifting or ruptured relationship with the distant and immediate past."[6]

When Wales first appears in Act 3, scene 3, this primordiality immediately takes center stage. Belarius and the rustic princes, Guiderius and Arviragus, are introduced in a cave, and there is a hint of sun-worship in the former's avuncular morning commandment: "Stoop, boys; this gate / Instructs you how t'adore the heavens, and bows you / To a morning's holy office" (3.3.2–4).[7] True to romance form, Wales also houses a culture that is separate from, and explicitly opposed to, a degraded court. "O, this life / Is nobler than attending for a check, / Richer than doing nothing for a bribe, / Prouder than rustling in unpaid-for silk," Belarius declares (3.3.21–24). These lines tempt the reader to view Wales as yet another in the long Renaissance series of salutary pastoral spaces.

Yet the pastoral that first seems enticingly removed to the audience strikes the princes themselves as deathly dull. Removed from history, Wales has become literally unmemorable, and the princes register their desire to escape into some other, more eventful text – a text with a chronology rather than an eternal recurrence of the pastoral, primitive same. They seek an escape from the prehistory into which Belarius has plunged them and an entry into the sphere of recorded event. Guiderius complains to Belarius after the latter has finished one of his diatribes against court life:

> Out of your proof you speak. We, poor unfledged,
> Have never winged from view o' th' nest, nor know not
> What air's from home. Haply this life is best,
> If quiet life be best; sweeter to you
> That have a sharper known, well corresponding
> With your stiff age; but unto us it is
> A cell of ignorance, travelling abed,
> A prison for a debtor that not dares
> To stride a limit.
> (3.3.27–35)

Arviragus chimes in:

> What should we speak of
> When we are old as you? When we shall hear
> The rain and wind beat dark December, how,
> In this our pinching cave, shall we discourse
> The freezing hours away? We have seen nothing.
> We are beastly: subtle as the fox for prey,
> Like warlike as the wolf for what we eat.
> (3.3.35–41)

Arviragus helpfully simplifies his brother's rhetoric: the princes fear that memory's lack has rendered them bestial. By his lights, to "see nothing," to "know not," is to be subhuman; cultured humanity consists in the capacity to speak one's story and to fill empty pastoral time with the "discourse" of oneself. It consists, in other words, of memory, without which consciousness itself is rendered impotently primitive. To not know and to be unknown are identical problems, as Arviragus makes clear in the next act:

> I am ashamed
> To look upon the holy sun, to have
> The benefit of his blest beams, remaining
> So long a poor unknown.
> (4.4.40–43)

The prince's blunt confession of "shame," an emotion that guards the border between private and public, acknowledges the outside world (as well as the sun deity whom Belarius has taught him to worship). His shift here from knowing to known-ness reveals – albeit in negative terms – a connection between the personal and the communal, between the self's capacity for individual memory and the self's position within public memory, also known as history. "What the brothers protest," Jodi Mikalachki argues, "is their exclusion from history.... Confined to their pinching cave in Wales, they have, quite literally, no history to speak of."[8] "Speak" is the operative word, since the prince imagines not just the capacity of remembrance but also the media of its transmission: a primitive form of oral storytelling that circulates cave-fire fame.

As memorylessness takes emotional form in Arviragus's shame, it likewise shapes the affective performance of the princes' actual mourning rituals. Like their complaints to Belarius, these rites convey their desire to enter into history, to locate themselves within some coherent historical scheme with a past and future that might frame and contextualize their disappointingly eternal present. This is clearest, and most haunting, in their daily obeisance before the grave of the woman they suppose their mother. Belarius reveals all in an aside: "Euriphile, / Thou wast their nurse; they took thee for their mother, / And every day do honour to her grave" (3.3.103–5). The princes intend their graveside honors as a recognition of some past legacy, reflecting a profound longing for lineage and familial memory. In mourning a false mother, though, they unwittingly misplace their grief. Euriphile the nurse cannot grant them the genealogical access they crave, and so once again Shakespeare emphasizes the lack at the center of their mourning, structured as it is around memory's absence rather than its presence.

Such misplaced emotions, based on delusions, also guide their "burial" of Posthumus's wife Innogen, who has encountered the princes in Wales disguised as the boy Fidele. Through a series of plot contrivances, Innogen/Fidele has taken a potion that renders her lifeless but not dead, fooling the brothers. They place "his" body in telling proximity to Euriphile's: "And let us, Polydore, though now our voices / Have got the mannish crack, sing him to th' ground / As once to our mother; use like note and words, / Save that 'Euriphile' must be 'Fidele'" (4.2.234–37). It's troubling enough to bury and mourn a live person, even more so when that person is, in fact, somebody else. "Euriphile must be Fidele": the one error breeds the other. Shakespeare's dramatic irony marks the grave distance between emotion and object, exposing the double delusion under which the princes intone their famous dirge "Fear No More" (4.2.257–80). Yet these "obsequies" (4.2.281) still move us because emotion does not need to pass some rational verification test to become "real" or "true"; it does not need to be "proved." Beneath the layers of irony, Arviragus's critical side glance at "rich-left heirs that let their fathers lie / Without a monument" (4.2.225–26) establishes a truly felt, inherent connection between mourning and intergenerational memorial. The yearning for the maternal, the parental, the ancestral here colors all acts and monuments of grief. If mourning ritualizes the remembrance of – and, here, the seeking after – prior descent, so too does it suggest its corollary, the promise of future descent. As part of this broader yearning for lineage, then, mourning is the means by which the princes can insert themselves into legible history. In these scenes, though, history still refuses to admit them; missing its mark, their mourning returns them once again to oblivion.

By delving into Britain's archaic, primordial roots in his Welsh subplot – and finding there a disturbing deficiency in the capacity for remembrance – Shakespeare echoes the remarks of early modern antiquarians who were deeply troubled by the absence of documented memory among the nation's early inhabitants. John Speed bemoaned "the mistie darknesse of obscuritie and obliuion" shrouding this period; in a 1604 speech before the Society of Antiquaries, William Camden declared that the ancient nation was "cast so farr backward into darkness, that there is no hope for us so late born to discover them. The first Inhabitants, as being merely barbarous, never troubled themselves with care to transmitt their Originals to posterity, neither if they would, could they, being without lettres which only can preserve and transferr knowledge."[9] Without the reassuring but debunked legends of Geoffrey of Monmouth, Edmund Bolton complained in 1618, "there is a vast Blanck upon the Times of our Country, from the Creation of the World till the coming of Julius Caesar."[10] Elsewhere, Camden wrote, "As touching the very name and the first inhabitants of Britaine, I feare me greatly, that no man is able to fetch out the truth, so deeply plunged within the winding revolutions of so many ages."[11] Darkness, obscurity, oblivion: the trademark antiquarian emotions seem to include a deep fear of the shadowy unknown and a longing for some memorial presence that might retrieve lost pasts, the same feelings that motivate the rustic princes.[12]

In the Wales subplot, Shakespeare can likewise present "barbarousness" as a distinctly "oblivious" condition. When Belarius guiltily tells the princes that they

> find in my exile the want of breeding,
> The certainty of this hard life; aye hopeless
> To have the courtesy your cradle promised,

> But to be still hot summer's tanlings and
> The shrinking slaves of winter
>
> (4.4.26–30)

he is not only bemoaning their lack of proper upbringing, but also suggesting that they do indeed lack a "breed," a genealogy that might grant them a place in the lineal history ensured by the regular progression of generation to generation. This progression is honored and remembered in the act of familial mourning just as it is in the hope for generations to come. Belarius is aware that a "natural" life, a life in the Welsh wilds, denies the princes such a history because they are *too* natural, too affected by their savage environment. They are "hot summer's tanlings and / The shrinking slaves of winter," controlled by the climate rather than controlling it, and thus estranged – exiled – from the historical memory that cultured civilization supposedly guarantees. Belarius here worries about a form of primordiality in which human culture has not yet fully differentiated itself from the natural environment: a dangerously deep antiquity.

This ecological aspect of immemorial primordiality structures the scenes of mourning and burial. The play's Wales seems to foster an essential equality between mortal materiality, as Innogen, posing as Fidele, hints in a biblical paraphrase: "clay and clay differs in dignity, / Whose dust is both alike" (4.2.4–5). The image is reiterated throughout the scene: "mean and mighty rotting / Together have one dust," Belarius says; later, Arviragus sings, "The sceptre, learning, physic, must / All follow thee and come to dust" (4.2.245–46, 267–68). Such language nods, on the one hand, to the Anglican "ordre for the buriall of the dead" and, on the other, to Arviragus's invocation of the subtle fox and warlike wolf: What difference, after all, is there between human cave-dweller and animal?[13] Between human and plant, even? Burying Fidele, the princes emphasize precisely this form of bodily recomposition with the stuff of soil. Arviragus's lament for Fidele partakes in the conventions of pastoral elegy, but, set against the distinctly flattened Welsh ecological dynamic I have been describing, his catalog of vegetation becomes more than simply figurative. His mourning rite depicts a relationship between the human and the environment from a primitive perspective:

> With fairest flowers,
> Whilst summer lasts and I live here, Fidele,
> I'll sweeten thy sad grave. Thou shalt not lack
> The flower that's like thy face, pale primrose, nor
> The azured harebell, like thy veins; no, nor

> The leaf of eglantine, whom not to slander,
> Outsweetened not thy breath.
>
> (4.2.217–23)

His language yokes body to plant in similes intense enough to verge on a form of materialist metonymy: once ritualized, these "primroses like faces" and "harebells like veins" force an awareness of the continuities between primroses and faces, harebells and veins, corpses and ground. After the body of the villainous Cloten has been placed respectfully next to Innogen's, Belarius develops this conceit while addressing the corpses:

> You were as flowers, now withered; even so
> These herblets shall, which we upon you strow.
> Come on, away, apart upon our knees –
> The ground that gave them first has them again.
>
> (4.2.285–88)

"You *were* as flowers," he insists, completing the identification of human with nonhuman, of body with "ground."

Affect studies can supplement the resources of environmental criticism in our consideration of these chthonic moments of mourning. Recent ecocritical readings of the funeral rites have found in them a hopefully premodern ecological strain: the body enmeshed with its environment, an end to destructive human dominance over the land. Tom MacFaul argues that the burials end up "binding [the princes] to the land and its products," while Randall Martin claims that the princes' "theory of burial is naturally metabiotic: it presumes that Innogen will live beyond death not by transcending physical nature but by becoming biologically reintegrated into its perpetually renewing cycles and evolutionary adaptations."[14] Patricia Phillippy similarly argues that the "Fear No More" song "replaces religious and liturgical figurations with those of the natural, seasonal cycles of birth and death ... What is imagined in this act of remembrance is the body's gradual merger with earth."[15] From this perspective, the funereal sequences in *Cymbeline* seem to portray what affect theorists have termed the "intimately interlaced" relationship between the human and the non-human, in which "a body is as much outside itself as in itself – webbed in its relations – until ultimately such firm distinctions cease to matter."[16] The prevailing humoral conception of the body and its sensations encouraged such a "premodern ecology of the passions," in Gail Kern Paster's influential phrase.[17] Comparing this "ecology" with recent academic theorizations of "affect," David Landreth notes that "the model of embodiment that the Renaissance inherited from antiquity" stresses "the material continuity between an individual's interiority and the exterior world ... Feeling enacts the porosity of the self's contents to its environment and vice versa."[18] Thus when Belarius first glimpses "Fidele's" apparent corpse, he immediately guesses the cause of death: "Thou diedst a most rare boy, of melancholy" (4.2.207). The reference is telling here, since the melancholy humor was associated with earth, both being physically "cold and dry."[19] To grow melancholy is to become earthly, and so to die of melancholy is to be doubly reduced to the stuff of ashes and dust. Indeed, to mourn ritualistically is not even the special province of the human, as Arviragus notes in his reference to the ceremonial presence of a "ruddock," or robin, at Fidele's grave, who will "With charitable bill ... bring thee all this, / Yea, and furred moss besides, when flowers are none, / To winter-ground thy corpse" (4.2.224–28). These instinctive grave offerings suggest an ecological and affective network which entangles the human rather than being controlled by the human.

A similar form of bodily "reintegration" with earth shapes the series of events that lead to the burial of Cloten, wicked son of the wicked queen. After confronting and beheading – offstage – this representative of the fallen court culture at Lud's Town (primordial London), Guiderius reenters bearing his foe's head, vowing to "throw't into the creek / Behind our rock, and let it to the sea / And tell the fishes he's the Queen's son, Cloten" (4.2.150–52).[20] Guiderius reaffirms the materialist worldview developed throughout the Welsh scenes by throwing the head into the river to sleep with the fishes. Detached from the body, the head becomes a mere seriocomic object, "an empty purse" (4.2.112) destined to nestle alongside animal life in an undifferentiated community of matter, organic and nonorganic. However vicious, then, his decision takes its cue from the "merger" of human with environment shown in the burial sequences (including the burial of Cloten's headless trunk that immediately follows).

These brutal moments might induce us to read the naturally enmeshed human body as something other than an opportunity, seized by ecocriticism and affect theory alike, to celebrate monist fertility. Consider the case of Innogen, who, once in Wales as "Fidele," seems to absorb the rustic princes' attitudes about primitivistic burial. When she awakens from her near-death sleep to find the headless corpse of Cloten alongside her, she mistakes the body for that of her exiled husband, Posthumus, since Cloten had disguised himself as Posthumus in order to seek Innogen in Wales. Vowing to cover the grave "[w]ith wildwood leaves and weeds" (4.2.389), she delivers a grief-stricken monologue culminating in a shockingly savage act, smearing her face with his blood: "O, / Give colour to my pale cheek with thy blood, / That we the horrider might seem to those / Which chance to find us. O, my lord, my lord!" (4.2.328–31). *This* mourning ritual suggests a kind of regression, the king's daughter reduced to her basest primeval element in a mingling of blood and weeds. And the prospect of civilizational regression – the past irrupting into the present – once again returns us to the question of historical memory and its political formations.

How, then, might we view these staged minglings of the human and the nonhuman in the specific context of settler colonialism and the social constructions of "primitivism" it encouraged? Plunged in a "blank," the memory of ancient Britain became worryingly unrecoverable outside the reports from colonizing Romans of "barbarous," tattooed, near-naked primitives. To be primitive was to exist enmeshed within nature rather than controlling it: a "savage" existence, to adopt the ubiquitous colonial epithet whose Latin root means "of the woods." To be a colonist, meanwhile, was to manipulate nature productively: as a Virginia Company pamphlet declared, "A Colony is therefore denominated, because they should be Coloni, the Tillers of the Earth, and Stewards of fertilitie."[21] This contrast between English-style tillage and the pastoral nomadism of Native Americans and the native Irish served as a basis for territorial possession. Native nomads forfeited any rights to land by refusing to "improve" it, leaving it "waste" and "void," the *terra nullius* of colonialist legal doctrine.[22] This pastoral paradigm was read back onto the ancient British. According to Holinshed's *Chronicles*, "our predecessors" fed on milk and flesh "bicause they applied their cheefe studies vnto pasturage and feeding," while the "North Britons" were woods-dwellers who "liued with hearbes and rootes" and the Picts survived "by hunting and preie, and oftentimes with the fruit of their trees."[23] Camden, in his assemblage of quotations, includes Dio Nicaeus's assertion that "they till no ground: They live upon prey, venison, and fruits."[24] John Clapham cited Caesar to argue that the Britons "delighted in warre, neglecting husbandrie, or perhaps not then knowing the vse of it ... Their dyet was such as Nature yeelded of her selfe, without the industrie of man."[25]

For antiquarians, not to mention promoters and planters eyeing Ireland and America, the Roman colonizers' most instructive legacy was their perceived "improvement" of this (agri)cultural ignorance, a forcible, violent education to which the early modern English owed their civilization. "This yoke of the Romanes," Camden wrote, "although it were grievous, yet comfortable it proved and a saving health vnto them ... the brightnesse of that most glorious Empire, chased away all savage barbarisme from the Britans minds."²⁶ According to those advocating the aggressive planting of settlers and crops alike, human and environmental improvements proceeded alongside each other. William Strachey, for whom civilizing the Virginia Algonquian was akin to a father's "violence to his child, when he beats him, to bringe him to goodnes," insisted that "had not this violence, and this Iniury, bene offred vnto vs by the Romanis ... even by *Iulius Caesar* himself ... we might yet haue lyved overgrowne Satyrs, rude, and vntutred, wandring in the woodes, dwelling in Caues, and hunting for our dynners, (as the wyld beasts in the forrests for their prey)."²⁷ In a 1609 sermon before the Virginia Company, William Symonds preached that Caesar's Britain had been "as wilde a forrest, but nothing so fruitfull, as *Virginia*, and the people in their nakednes did arme themselues in a coate armor of *Woad*," but "by the ciuill care of conquerors and planters it is now become a very paradise in comparison of that it was."²⁸ From this ecological perspective, settler violence had transformed, and could transform again, landscapes even as it civilized people. "The Britons," John Stow noted, "had no townes but called that a town which had a thicke intangled wood," but thanks to "the Romaines, who sowed the seedes of ciuilitie ouer all Europe, this Citie [London] whatsoeuer it was before, began to bee renowned, and of fame." Stow aptly imagines a "sowing" of Britain that replaces primordial forests with prosperous towns, the pastoral with the arable: a portable model, since "the Irishmen our next neighbors doe at this day" favor rough settlements akin to those primitive British dwellings.²⁹ A 1612 ballad sponsored by the Virginia Company offered a pithier version of this environmental history: "Who knowes not England once was like / a Wildernesse and sauage place, / Till gouernment and vse of men, / that wildnesse did deface."³⁰

With this rhetoric of "improvement" in mind, and comparing the rustic princes to the ancient Britons imagined in antiquarian and colonial texts, we might see their various funeral rites as staging a form of primitivism on the cusp of attaining "culture," split between a "bestial" oblivion and a culture of memory. Through these dark visions of omnipresent wilderness, though, shine occasionally glimpsed forms of *improvable* wildness: a potential for acculturation that lies dormant but latent in the untamed human and the untamed land alike. After all, the princes' inherent nobility promises transformative potential. "How hard it is to hide the sparks of nature!" Belarius remarks; indeed, "nature prompts them / In simple and low things to prince it much / Beyond the trick of others" (3.3.79, 84–86). The faux father often relies on environmental imagery in his repeated variations on this theme; as in the burial scenes, these evocations of nature become more than merely figurative:

> 'Tis wonder
> That an invisible instinct should frame them
> To royalty unlearned, honour untaught,
> Civility not seen from other, valour
> That wildly grows in them, but yields a crop
> As if it had been sowed.
> (4.2.175–80)

The motif of environmental improvement culminates in agricultural rhetoric: Belarius notes a disparity between wildness and civility, but in terms that suggest the embryonic presence of planned husbandry already nascent in the wilderness, the cultivated field emergent in the wild. The distinction between outward form and inner worth is a convention of pastoral romance – Belarius speaks according to generic script when he remarks, "The time seems long; their blood thinks scorn, / Till it fly out and show them princes born" (4.4.53–54) – but the transition from "unknowing" to "knowing" blood is here cast specifically as a kind of improvement. Indeed, a code of natural amelioration extends beyond the Wales scenes; thus, the gentlemen in the opening scene relate how Posthumus, under Cymbeline's tutelage, absorbed "all the learnings [of] his time ... As we do air, fast as 'twas ministered, / And in's spring became a harvest" (1.1.43, 45–46). This harvest, as Derek Traversi notices, "has been carefully prepared for" in the line about "delving" to Posthumus's "root," so that the scene associates "virtue with lineage in a single process of spontaneous, overflowing fertility ... relat[ing] lineage to a conception of natural growth."[31] If Posthumus so thrives, he does so alongside his improving nation. Boasting of his fellow Britons while exiled in Italy, he claims that they are "more ordered" since Caesar's invasion, a "people such / That mend upon the world" (2.4.21, 25–26). Nations, landscapes, and individuals alike are malleable throughout, existing in a primordial state of emergence. As a perpetually "mending" people blessed with the capabilities of innate transformation, the play's Britons can exist in savagery even as they progress away from it.

It is Innogen, unknown sister to the brothers, who most fully articulates and embodies this form of progress in Wales. Once she journeys into the wild countryside and assumes the identity of "Fidele," she functions not only as a bridge between the plots in Lud's Town and Wales but also as a formative prototype of improvement, a model for the princes as they yearn to progress beyond the restrictive barrier of primitivism. Linking the quality of civility to the potential for language itself and, ultimately, for literacy, she emblematizes the promise of cultivation implanted in textuality. Consider her anxious call as she first approaches what she calls the "savage hold" (3.6.18) of the princes' cave: "If anything that's civil, speak; if savage, / Take or lend" (3.6.23–24). In this scene, Valerie Wayne argues, "*Cymbeline* registers its familiarity with [colonial] discourses by dramatizing the moment of a first encounter.... Innogen appears like an early modern who, with drawn sword and quaking limbs, is encountering New World peoples for the first time as well as looking in on her ancient past."[32] As Fidele, she quickly becomes a transforming force of domesticity, serving as "housewife" (as Belarius puts it in an oblivious gendered slip) and as "cave-keeper" (Innogen's own term) (4.2.45, 297). "But his neat cookery!" Guiderius exclaims. "He cut our roots in characters" – that is, he has carved the roots on which the boys basely feed into actual letters (4.2.49). Innogen's precious introduction of the stable human household into the prehuman suggests another mode of improving upon the bestial or vegetative life. Generating text from nature, she stages the eruption of textual culture, not only domestic culture, into a pre-textual society.

I have already mentioned the antiquarians' "ecological" reading of national history, but this developmental narrative also identified textuality, the presence of writing and letters, as an index of cultural advancement. Illiteracy was a marker of the primitive, and text joined husbandry as a crucial sign of civilization precisely because it was able to preserve the kind of historical, transgenerational memory that the princes lack. This conjunction is especially apparent in the Oxford geographer Nathanael Carpenter's 1625 reflection on the ancient British and German pasts:

> ... as we see all sortes of *Plantes* and *Hearbs* by good husbandrie, to grow better, but left to themselues to grow wilde and barren; So shall we find it, if not much more, in *mankind*; which though neuer so *Savage* & *barbarous*, haue by discipline bin corrected and reformed.... It is recorded by the ancients as well of the *Germans*, as of our *owne* nation, that they liued almost in the condition of *wilde beasts* in Woods and Desarts, feeding like swine on *hearbs* and *rootes*, without law or *discipline*: Insomuch as their *Bardes* or learned men (as they deem'd them) want[ed] the vse of *letters*.... Their onely law was nature, or some few customes preserued by tradition, not writing: Little differing from the present *Americans*, not yet reduced to civility. But *time* and *discipline* prevailing against *barbarisme*, they are (God be praised) reduced to such a height of civility.[33]

Carpenter blames the Britons' bestial, forest-dwelling existence on the want of letters, the same lack now dooming Native Americans to their oblivious state of nature.[34] The development ensured by writing is figured as a form of "good husbandrie," humans as "Plantes and Hearbs," and the farmer's "disciplined" management of the wilderness becomes the governing metaphor for the nation's progressive improvement over time. Just as farming improves wasted wilds, Carpenter suggests, text improves on mere "tradition," the fragile, fleeting oral memory of the ancient bards: plantations on empty, "unowned" land, *terra nullius*, suggest inscriptions on a tabula rasa. From this perspective, it is worth emphasizing that Innogen is a distinctly textual creature throughout; more than quoting Ovid, she visibly handles a volume of the *Metamorphoses* (2.2.3–4), and she becomes a central node in the busy network of ostentatious letter exchange that shapes the plot (3.2.35–39; 3.4.11–29, 78–82; 4.2.315–19, 383–85). As an emissary from a documented world, a realm of paper, she is especially enticing to the brothers and useful in their quest to enter history by obtaining memory. Hence their admiration of her root-letters: Innogen models the material production of historical memory at its germinal state as a progressive movement away from a base natural life.

Innogen cultivates text in Wales, and text reaches its apotheosis an act later in the mysterious book brought down to the stage by Jupiter himself, a "tablet" relating an obscure prophecy:

> Whenas a lion's whelp shall, to himself unknown, without seeking find, and be embraced by a piece of tender air; and when from a stately cedar shall be lopped branches which, being dead many years, shall after revive, be jointed to the old stock, and freshly grow; then shall Posthumus end his miseries, Britain be fortunate and flourish in peace and plenty. (5.3.202–7)

As in Shakespeare's other romances, genealogical reconciliations define Act 5, but the lineages restored in *Cymbeline* belong to nations themselves, not only to families. As the "tablet" suggests, the orphaned Posthumus and Britain will find good fortune together, and the soothsayer's interpretation similarly finds a national dimension in the restoration of the princes to their father:

> The lofty cedar, royal Cymbeline,
> Personates thee, and thy lopped branches point
> Thy two sons forth, who, by Belarius stol'n,
> For many years thought dead, are now revived,
> To the majestic cedar joined, whose issue
> Promises Britain peace and plenty.
>   (5.4.451–56)

Belarius himself has revealed and returned the princes to Cymbeline shortly after the boys miraculously defeat the invading Romans in battle with the sole help of their abductor. Informing the king that the two rustics are in fact "well descended" (5.4.303), he confesses:

> These two young gentlemen that call me father,
> And think they are my sons, are none of mine.
> They are the issue of your loins, my liege,
> And blood of your begetting.
>
> (5.4.328–31)

Cymbeline then makes his final, surprising agreement to resume paying tribute to the Romans: "Although the victor, we submit to Caesar / And to the Roman empire, promising / To pay our wonted tribute" (5.4.458–60).

It may seem that a hasty resolution has awkwardly ruined the moment of a moving family reunion, but the conjunction of Britain and Rome is itself such a reunion: a meeting of nations that each claim Aeneas as ancestor, according to the Brutus myth.[35] Just as the princes find their genealogical predecessor in Cymbeline, so too a renewed awareness of ultimate origins – yet another "delving to the root," now on a national scale – emerges from this "reunification of cousin states."[36] The resolution accomplishes the transvaluation of *translatio imperii* from a relationship defined by historical distance into one defined by familial proximity, a "unity" transcending centuries whose authorization derives ultimately from the common imperial parent, Troy. This renewed closeness of kin reaffirms a legitimating ancestral original, making legible a family line that must be delved to its source. The expected romance restoration of genealogical lines activates the archaeological imagination, and now excavation yields results, as it did not for the princes in Wales. The play's final moments accomplish the filling in of the primordial "blanck" that so worried the princes within the play and so frustrated antiquarian endeavor outside it.

Beneath the gnomic reference to a "stately cedar" in Jupiter's tablet, then, lies a rhetoric of planting and growth central to the colonial imagination of the early Jacobean era. For, as the soothsayer has it, the tablet has divined the restoration of the princes to Cymbeline in the "joining" of the "lofty cedar" with its "lopped branches," and as such it extends the language of natural amelioration that characterizes their scenes in Wales. According to the soothsayer, the cedar's "issue / Promises Britain peace and plenty" (5.4.455–56). As Jean Feerick emphasizes, the rejoining procedure described in the tablet is "an act of cultivation," a deliberate remaking of the land suitable for a play that "approach[es] the mechanisms of conquest and expansion through the motif of grafting."[37] The soothsayer's "plenty" thus functions here as the material guarantee of the *translatio imperii* between Brutus's reconciled descendants. It describes a future surfeit that can fill the gnawing lack of pastness in the boys' earlier, primitive lives. That primitivism manifested as undeveloped ecological imbrication: the princes were coextensive with their environment rather than ruling it as their domain. Now, though, they are depicted as part of the elevated, sovereign cedar that oversees, manages, and fructifies its environment. Vertical dominance overtakes horizontal continuity just as an articulated lineage fills in the "blank" of historical amnesia.

Jupiter's text describes and achieves the recovery of memory necessary in the transition from colonized to colonizer. As a document both past- and future-oriented, his tablet is a material construction of memory that can sooth the mourners of lost histories, whether the "blank" of ancient British history or the pastlessness of unrooted Posthumus and the unstoried princes. By play's end, memory has not only been supplied for those who lacked it; it has gained force, a westering directionality. It has become a technique of colonization. To improve their "savage" indigeneity, the princes have assumed a settler memory, the memory of Brutus, of the occupying Romans: a memory of plantation that demands to be planted once more in other "empty" lands.

Notes

1 Stephanie Trigg, "Introduction: Emotional Histories – Beyond the Personalization of the Past and the Abstraction of Affect Theory," in "Pre-Modern Emotions [Special Issue]," *Exemplaria: A Journal of Theory in Medieval and Renaissance Studies*, 26.1 (2014), 5. See also the pathbreaking work by Maurice Halbwachs on collective memory: "Collective frameworks are ... precisely the instruments used by the collective memory to reconstruct an image of the past which is in accord, in each epoch, with the predominant thoughts of the society"; Halbwachs, *On Collective Memory*, ed. and trans. Lewis A. Coser (University of Chicago Press, 1992), 40.
2 Editors' introduction, *Historical Affects and the Early Modern Theater*, ed. Ronda Arab, Michelle Dowd, Adam Zucker (New York: Routledge, 2015), 5.
3 According to Brian Lockey, "Cymbeline views himself as the new incarnation of Roman heroism and honor, the inheritor of a *translatio imperii* from Rome which obliquely promises to transform Cymbeline into a new Caesar and Britain into a new Roman empire"; Lockey, *Law and Empire in English Renaissance Literature* (Cambridge University Press, 2006), 162.

4 Raphael Holinshed, *The First and second volumes of Chronicles* (London: John Harrison, 1587), B2r.
5 Mary Floyd-Wilson, *English Ethnicity and Race in Early Modern Drama* (Cambridge University Press, 2003), 161–83; Ros King, *Cymbeline: Constructions of Britain* (Burlington: Ashgate, 2005), 109–16; Gordon McMullan, "The Colonisation of Early Britain on the Jacobean Stage," in Gordon McMullan and David Matthews, eds., *Reading the Medieval in Early Modern England* (Cambridge University Press, 2007), 119–40; Jean E. Feerick, *Strangers in Blood: Relocating Race in the Renaissance* (University of Toronto Press, 2010), 78–112; editor's introduction, William Shakespeare, *Cymbeline*, ed. Valerie Wayne, Arden Shakespeare Third Series (London: Bloomsbury, 2017), 59.
6 Steven Mullaney, *The Reformation of Emotions in the Age of Shakespeare* (University of Chicago Press, 2015), 4.
7 See also *Love's Labour's Lost*: who views Rosaline, Berowne asks, "That, like a rude and savage man of Ind / At the first opening of the gorgeous east, / Bows not his vassal head …?" (4.3.213–15). In *All's Well That Ends Well*, Helen describes her unrequited love for Bertram: "Thus Indian-like, / Religious in mine error, I adore / The sun that looks upon his worshipper, / But knows of him no more" (1.3.176–79).
8 Jodi Mikalachki, *The Legacy of Boadicea: Gender and Nation in Early Modern England* (London: Routledge, 1998), 106.
9 John Speed, *The theatre of the empire of Great Britaine* (London: Iohn Sudbury & George Humble, 1612), Oo2r. For Camden's speech, see Thomas Hearne, ed., *A Collection Of Curious Discourses, Written by Eminent Antiquaries Upon several Heads in our English Antiquities* (Oxford: Thomas Hearne, 1720), 149. Speed later closely paraphrased his remarks in *The theatre of the empire of Great Britaine*, Oo2r.
10 Edmund Bolton, "Hypercritica" (c. 1618), in *Critical Essays of the Seventeenth Century*, ed. J. E. Springarn, 3 vols. (Oxford: Clarendon Press, 1908), vol. I, 82–115, esp. vol. I, 86.
11 William Camden, *Britain*, trans. Philemon Holland (London: Impensis Georgii Bishop & Ioannis Norton, 1610), 6.
12 On similar terrain, Philip Schwyzer tracks early modern archaeological "examples of impermanence, loss, and dissolution" that "testif[y] to the impossibility of communicating with the dead" in *Archaeologies of English Renaissance Literature* (Oxford University Press, 2007), 4.
13 "I commende thy soule to God the father almighty, and thy body to the grounde, earth to earth, asshes to asshes, dust to dust …"; Brian Cummings, ed., *The Book of Common Prayer: The Texts of 1549, 1559, and 1662* (Oxford University Press, 2011), 82–83.
14 Tom MacFaul, *Shakespeare and the Natural World* (Cambridge University Press, 2015), 72; Randall Martin, *Shakespeare and Ecology* (Oxford University Press, 2015), 123.

15 Patricia Phillippy, *Shaping Remembrance from Shakespeare to Milton* (Cambridge University Press, 2018), 117–18.
16 Gregory J. Seigworth and Melissa Gregg, "Introduction: An Inventory of Shimmers," in Gregory J. Seigworth and Melissa Gregg, eds., *The Affect Theory Reader* (Durham, NC: Duke University Press, 2010), 6 and 3. The relevance of this "ecological" aspect of affect studies can be glimpsed in the very subtitle of a recent volume, Amanda Bailey and Mario DiGangi, eds., *Affect Theory and Early Modern Texts: Politics, Ecologies, and Form* (New York: Palgrave Macmillan, 2017). "Ecology" in this context doesn't necessarily connote the natural environmental as such, but one of the sections is titled "Affective Ecologies and Environment." See the introductory discussion by the editors on 8–13. See also the related concept of "cognitive ecology": "the multi-dimensional contexts in which we remember, feel, think, sense, communicate, imagine, and act," as Evelyn Tribble and John Sutton put it in "Cognitive Ecology as a Framework for Shakespearean Studies," *Shakespeare Studies*, 39 (2011), 94–103; 94.
17 Gail Kern Paster, *Humoring the Body: Emotions and the Shakespearean Stage* (University of Chicago Press, 2004), 9.
18 David Landreth, "How Does Matter Feel? Affect and Substance in Recent Renaissance Criticism," *The Spenser Review*, 44.3 (2015), www.english.cam.ac.uk/spenseronline/review/volume-44/443/how-does-matter-feel-1. Compare Martin's claim that in Wales the princes "have grown up immersed in its ecosystem," and that as a result their scenes depict a "non-traditional ontology" in which human culture is fully coextensive with nonhuman life and objects (Martin, *Shakespeare and Ecology*, 123).
19 Gail Kern Paster, "Melancholy Cats, Lugged Bears, and Early Modern Cosmology," in Gail Kern Paster, Katherine Rowe, and Mary Floyd-Wilson, eds., *Reading the Early Modern Passions: Essays in the Cultural History of Emotion* (Philadelphia: University of Pennsylvania Press, 2004), 113–29; 118.
20 See King, *Cymbeline: Constructions of Britain*, 27–29, and Wayne, ed., introduction, 62–63.
21 Virginia Company, *A true declaration of the estate of the colonie in Virginia* (London: William Barret, 1610), E4v.
22 Andrew Fitzmaurice, *Sovereignty, Property and Empire, 1500–2000* (Cambridge University Press, 2014), 1–124.
23 All descriptions by William Harrison, in "The description of England" and "The description of Scotland," collected, respectively, in Holinshed, *The First and second volumes*, vol. I, P4r–P4v and *The Second Volume of Chronicles* (London: John Harrison, 1586), B6r.
24 Camden, *Britain*, C3v.
25 John Clapham, *The historie of Great Britannie* (London: Valentine Simmes, 1606), B2v–B3r.
26 Camden, *Britain*, F2r.

27 William Strachey, *The Historie of Travell into Virginia Britania*, ed. Louis B. Wright and Virginia Freund (London: Hakluyt Society, 1953), 24.
28 William Symonds, *Virginia: A sermon* … (London: Eleazar Edgar and William Welby, 1609), D2r. A marginal note cites Caesar. Strachey takes his metaphor of paternal punishment from this sermon (C3v).
29 John Stow, *A suruay of London* (London: Iohn Wolfe, 1598), B2r–B2v.
30 Virginia Company, "Londons Lotterie" (broadside) (London: Henry Robards, 1612).
31 Derek Traversi, *Shakespeare: The Last Phase* (1955; Stanford University Press, 1965), 46.
32 Wayne, ed., Introduction, 61–62.
33 Nathanael Carpenter, *Geography delineated forth in two bookes* (Oxford: Henry Cripps, 1625), Nn1r–Nn1v.
34 In the Spanish New World, Walter Mignolo has shown, "people without letters were thought of as people without history," and therefore "Western literacy" became "a massive operation in which the materiality and ideology of Amerindian semiotic interactions were intermingled with or replaced by the materiality and ideology of Western reading and writing cultures"; *The Darker Side of the Renaissance: Literacy, Territoriality, and Colonization* (1995; Ann Arbor: University of Michigan Press, 2003), 3 and 76. See also Jonathan Baldo's discussion of the "forgetful native" trope in "Exporting Oblivion in *The Tempest*," *Modern Language Quarterly*, 56.2 (June 1995), 111–44, esp. 111–15.
35 Northrop Frye, *A Natural Perspective: The Development of Shakespearean Comedy and Romance* (New York: Columbia University Press, 1965), 88; Robert Miola, *Shakespeare's Rome* (Cambridge University Press, 1983), 233.
36 Paul Innes, "*Cymbeline* and Empire," *Critical Survey*, 19.2 (2008), 1–18; 9.
37 Feerick, "The Imperial Graft: Horticulture, Hybridity, and the Art of Mingling Races in *Henry V* and *Cymbeline*," in Valerie Traub, ed., *The Oxford Handbook of Shakespeare and Embodiment* (Oxford University Press, 2016), 211–27; 225 and 214.

PART IV

Memory, Affect, and Stagecraft

CHAPTER 10

The Tug of Memory
Affect and Invention in Shakespeare's Drama

William E. Engel

> No one can capture in a single instant the fullness of his entire past. The gift was never granted even to Shakespeare, so far as I know, much less to me, who was but his partial heir. A man's memory is not a summation; it is a chaos of vague possibilities. Saint Augustine speaks, if I am not mistaken, of the palaces and the caverns of memory. The second metaphor is the more fitting one. It was into those caverns that I descended.
> —Jorge Luis Borges, "Shakespeare's Memory"[1]

Borges's Shakespearean scholar, Hermann Sörgel, recounts here how he came to possess "Shakespeare's memory" and gradually realized that memories are "a good deal more auditory than visual,"[2] and not, as he had expected, orderly vignettes of fully fleshed-out experiences. Sörgel reports that he got more than he bargained for in taking on Shakespeare's memory: unmoored sounds, dislocated sites, contextless fragments of feelings. Part cautionary tale about any simplistic, reductive view of the workings of memory, part critique of modernist literary subjectivity, Borges's story ends with the narrator declining to write Shakespeare's biography and trying instead to pass on the burden of carrying Shakespeare's memory to someone else.

The epigraph above offers an ideal way to begin thinking about whether and the extent to which one's history can reemerge, captured "in a single instant." Shakespeare's mnemotechnically driven dramaturgical practices, I shall argue, affectively allow for the encapsulating and presentation of key moments when the "fullness" of a character's past momentarily comes rushing back, usually in response to some interpersonal onstage provocation. Potential threats to maintaining the integrity of an "identity front," performed in the course of presenting one's public persona, led pioneering

---

Preliminary versions of this chapter were presented at the Société Française Shakespeare Conference, "Shakespeare et les acteurs" (January 10, 2019), and the Shakespeare Association of America seminar, "Washed in Lethe: Renaissance Cultures of Remembering and Forgetting," organized by Jonathan Baldo and Isabel Karremann (April 18, 2019).

sociologist Erving Goffman to seize upon the dramaturgical perspective – involving the metaphor of stage, actors, and audience – to analyze the minutiae of everyday face-to-face interactions.[3] And, within the mimetic context of a stage production, Shakespeare plays off comparable self-reflective metatheatrical possibilities to represent memories being dredged up from a character's invented history so as to cue the past for all to observe.

This chapter approaches Shakespeare's plausibly invented histories of his characters from the other end of the telescope, though still keeping in view Borges's parable about the disarticulation of memory. I scrutinize representative instances of dramaturgical cueing of the past which direct the audience's attention toward some unlooked-for affective response to the situation being portrayed onstage. My goal is to clarify what is at stake in such particularized stagings of the tug of memory through spoken directives for the recalling of things preceding the chronology of the play. And I do so especially mindful of the age-old oratorical principles of invention (*inventio*, coming up with arguments) and memory (*memoria*, the stowage of things invented), the fourth canon of rhetoric.[4] As for *inventio*, Steele Nowlin has shown how, in medieval English poetics, "the relationship of affect to emotion functions analogously to the relationship of invention to invented text."[5] Accordingly, in my study, affect is not synonymous with emotion but part and parcel of the rhetorically grounded charge that informs and animates onstage revelations about a character's backstory, eliciting and guiding audience response to some tug of memory. This is in keeping with Renaissance rhetorical practices known as *progymnasmata* (derived from classical oratory, basically elemental exercises in the art of description), and grouped under the heading of *enargeia* – those figures concerned with creating lively and vivid word-pictures. The conveyance of affect, in this regard, is a result of the careful – indeed, highly artificial – use of the right words suited to the moment, by means of which the speaker aims to color the listener's assessment and judgment of the situation. Eliciting an emotional (or, more properly, an intrinsic) response is, of course, the speaker's goal. And regarding the latter (*memoria*), let us consider, for example, Iacomo's report given once back in Rome (*Cymbeline* 2.4.66–91), based on his fabricated *domus locorum* (his memory theater "noted" down in his table book but ultimately, he reflects, ensconced in his natural memory), of which Imogen constitutes the central image (2.2.43–44). His collocated memory images and suggestively urged associations affectively mark a place in the narrative which folds back on itself to plausibly move the jealousy plot forward.[6] Contemporary treatises on the art of memory advocate that all such "scriptile" notes and "hieroglyphics" should be situated in "an imaginary house or building" and that one should make use of the "innumerable examples" furnished by "emblems, written by Beza, Alciato, Peacham, and others."[7] So too in Renaissance drama,[8] for by such means the audience is primed to gain access to a "memory picture," much in the same way as emblems, blazons, proverbs, and other comparable components of mnemotechnical schemes enable one to invent and retain whole histories for future recollection and use.[9]

By way of setting up the rhetorical coordinates that will help us make sense of the different kinds of memory cues available to Shakespeare in his dramaturgical toolbox, I will analyze a pair of passages involving the tug of memory in *The Merchant of Venice* and *The Comedy of Errors*, and then present a sustained close reading of the use of proverbs in *Henry V*. First, though, in the interest of clarity, a few words are in order about the tug of memory as a hermeneutic tactic and about Shakespeare's cueing of the past. A tug is a quick or sharp pull, and, in the combined dramaturgical and mnemotechnical sense being used in this study, it is a pulling at something seemingly recessed or half-forgotten which, in an instant, is brought to the audience's attention. The word "tug" derives from an Old High German verb for "jerk" or "draw quickly" (*OED*), and by the sixteenth century denoted any sudden or powerful pull.[10] As with the classical art of memory, where invented images are stored in sequence for easy recollection and application,[11] the tug of memory here describes Shakespeare's presentation of a verbal cue to activate onstage the memory of some past instance. The concatenation of memory images in classical rhetoric treatises was figured as dancers linked hand in hand, each gently tugging on the hands of the others pulling one another along (Quintilian 11.2.20). Shakespeare's activation of the tug of memory works in a similar way: an articulated token of remembrance both initiates the tug and is itself the thing suddenly jerked center-stage. Audiences thereby are being made to remember something from a character's past, something that conveys telltale cues enabling a glimpse into that character's inner life.[12] Such a cueing of the past initiates this sudden pull insofar as it is tethered to some memory or story that will, in short order, be brought to the fore. Although the word "cue" principally is being used throughout in its rhetorical and, more strictly speaking, in its mnemotechnical sense, the term has a long history in the dramatic arts. While cues in theater and in rhetoric are not that far removed from one another, the word "cue" technically and traditionally belongs to theater, and its importance as such should not be overlooked.[13] Actors are prompted – or cued – to say their lines based on what the actor before them has just said. And actors play off one another's cues, a prerequisite for smooth delivery and coherent performances; this brings us back, metaphorically at least, to Quintilian's hand-clasping dancers where each needs the other to make the whole choreography of the scene come together and work as an ensemble. The tug of memory, moreover, cues the audience to become aware of some otherwise previously unseen connection that now – audibly and affectively – is being made a part of the play. The audience takes in what amounts to succinctly packaged "recovered histories," a production feature that William Dodd has discussed with reference to "discourse biographies."[14] An outstanding example of this is Enobarbus's expansive and lyrical account of Antony's momentous first meeting with Cleopatra when "she pursed up his heart upon the river of Cydnus" (*Ant.* 2.2.196–97).

Affectively Cueing the Past

A pair of passages from *The Merchant of Venice* will serve to illustrate the affective value of Shakespeare's ingenious approach to cueing an individual's past, which is of a different order from how proverbs in *Henry V* will be seen to cue a character's more universally appropriable shared collective past. Midway through *Merchant* we encounter a tug of memory that signals a decisive turning point in the play's coloring of audience perception of the character's history which, up to this point, has been fairly two-dimensional and straightforward. It begins innocently enough, as a report to Shylock about his missing daughter, Jessica, but then – suddenly and redolent with affective power – gives rise to a disclosure that brings into the open something otherwise unknowable to the audience about the character's backstory. Jessica has been seen in Genoa after having stolen away from her father's house in Venice with her Christian suitor, Lorenzo, and taken with her a portion of Shylock's treasure.

TUBAL: One of them showed me a ring that he had of your daughter for a monkey.
SHYLOCK: Out upon her! – thou torturest me Tubal, – it was my turquoise; I had it of Leah when I was a bachelor: I would not have given it for a wilderness of monkeys.

(3.1.93–97)

In the staging of this terse, revelatory episode, the audience is impelled to entertain the notion of a Shylock who has perhaps not always been so stern and unbending. The subliminal activation of this recollected image of a kinder, gentler Shylock is all the more resonant because of its lack of specificity – after all, it is someone else's memory we are being asked to share.¹⁵ In the blink of the mind's eye, we catch a glimpse of a youthful Shylock courting and perhaps even doting on the woman who would become his wife and Jessica's mother, Leah, otherwise absent from the play. This is a side of the Jewish moneylender the audience has not previously been given reason to consider. Moreover, its eruption on the stage at this point gives palpable credence to Shylock's rhetorically amplified expostulation earlier in the same scene to Salerio and Solanio, friends of the merchant Antonio (two seemingly interchangeable factotum characters, the "Rosencrantz and Guildenstern" of this play):

SHYLOCK: Hath not a Jew eyes? hath not a Jew hands, organs, dimensions, senses, affections, passions? fed with the same food, hurt with the same weapons, subject to the same diseases, healed by the same means, warmed and cooled by the same winter and summer, as a Christian is?
(3.1.46–50)

The deft limning of Shylock's inner character induces the audience to take note of an unlooked-for level of depth in this otherwise stereotypically depicted antagonist of the comedy who, consistent with theatrical conventions, is an impediment to young lovers getting together. In this role, Shylock thus is being tacitly paralleled to Portia's father, who sought to constrain his daughter's choice of a husband: "So is the will of a living daughter curbed by the will of a dead father" with "the lott'ry that he hath devised in these three chests" (1.2.20–25).

The next pair of passages, from *The Comedy of Errors*, both illustrates Shakespeare's evocative cueing of the past and sheds further light on the playwright's craft with respect to knowing when in the plot-arc to reveal the affective linchpin in a character's backstory to showcase the moment of maximum audience impact. Whereas the passages from *The Merchant of Venice* come from the midpoint of the play leading into the *peripeteia* or turning point, these passages from *The Comedy of Errors* come in the last act conducing to the *denouement* or unraveling and resolution . Up until this late moment in the comedy, Antipholus of Ephesus has remained a blank slate, playing the conventional hot-tempered husband of Plautine comedy who reacts to events in a fairly predictable way.¹⁶ This passage, however, in an instant at last explains – and gives deeper insight into – his fundamental character. It does so by bringing out what he was doing to make his way in the world from the time when he was found as a castaway in Ephesus to when he won the right, as granted by the Duke, to marry the wealthy, parentless Adriana. We learn nothing substantial about Antipholus of Ephesus during the first act of this play. The vital information about Antipholus of Ephesus's honorable military exploits is withheld until the last act and sets in train all the other revelations about who has been where and doing what all these many years, paving the way to the long-deferred and much-anticipated family reunion, restoration of civic order, and general sense of relief. After many madcap adventures and a dizzying series of misrecognitions, the patient and forbearing Adriana fears that her husband must be deranged. At last the Duke – not heard from since the first scene – appears, and Antipholus of Ephesus pleads to be heard:

> ANTIPHOLUS E.:   Justice, most gracious Duke, O, grant me justice,
>   Even for the service that long since I did thee
>   When I bestrid thee in the wars, and took
>   Deep scars to save thy life. Even for the blood
>   That then I lost for thee, now grant me justice.
>   . . .
>   Justice, sweet prince, against that woman there,
>   She whom thou gav'st to me to be my wife . . .
>   (5.1.190–98)

Up until this moment (and following the age-old dictum of comedy that twins can never be told apart until their proper identities are revealed in the denouement), everyone has taken Antipholus of Ephesus for Antipholus of Syracuse and vice versa. And yet still, Shakespeare subtly has portrayed them somewhat differently throughout, corresponding ostensibly to their differing life experiences after the shipwreck that caused the twins to be separated. Antipholus of Ephesus struck out boldly on his own and distinguished himself as a resourceful and courageous citizen previously indispensable to the Duke. His mercantile brother in the intervening years since their separation, appositively, found life unbearable in Syracuse without his brother and mother and went "[i]n quest of them," lamenting that he is "to the world . . . like a drop of water / That in the ocean seeks another drop" (1.2.35–40). From his first scene in the play, he is characterized as a malcontent; an acquisitive, seafaring bachelor ridiculously prone to superstition:

> ANTIPHOLUS S.:   They say this town is full of cozenage,
>   As nimble jugglers that deceive the eye,
>   Dark-working sorcerers that change the mind,
>   Soul-killing witches that deform the body,
>   Disguisèd cheaters, prating mountebanks,
>   And many suchlike liberties of sin.
>   If it prove so, I will be gone the sooner.

> I'll to the Centaur to go seek this slave.
> I greatly fear my money is not safe.
>
> (1.2.97–105)

In these two brothers, then, we can see Shakespeare deftly deploying the two main rhetorical means of information disclosure, namely, abbreviation and amplification. The terse phrasing used by Antipholus of Ephesus to sum up in an instant the service he has rendered the Duke at great peril to himself is characteristic of his taciturn soldierly humility, and it is the first time the audience learns anything of consequence about what he has done since coming to Ephesus. Conversely, the copious dilation on the anxiety experienced by Antipholus of Syracuse unfurls like a nervous merchant's list of things noted at a bustling market. These same two rhetorical techniques likewise are used in tandem to convey backstory elements of Shylock's character: Leah's ring exemplifies the trope of abbreviation, and his monologue "Hath not a Jew eyes," amplification. Both sets of representative passages affectively showcase something approaching the fullness of the past, adding depth, dimension, and a touch of pathos to the characters speaking the lines. In each case, the lines are delivered at a point in the play when the characters are at their wit's end, having been pushed to the extreme of what they can bear. Shakespeare's consummate staging of discrete tugs of memory to cue the past gives the audience reason to judge each character's situation differently now, seen in the light of what has just been filled in. Shakespeare sets in motion the recollection of some event or action in the past so that the audience can factor it in with their judgment of the character. Such proleptic statements by characters remembering and relating aspects of their own backstories serve to make their past viscerally present. Shakespeare's cueing up the past affectively sets memory to work, tugging at what is to be recalled and yanking it suddenly into view.

Affective Invention in *Henry V*

Recalling Erving Goffman's privileging of the "dramatic perspective," let us turn now to examine the boundary between the stage and lived experience which materializes with evocations of the invented backstories of Shakespeare's characters. As discussed in the previous section, this is what is implied by cueing the past through a well-placed tug of memory. It is realized through presenting cue information about a prior and always quite telling event, whether in a distilled or dilated form.

During the Renaissance these approaches to handling such cue information were expressed as and by means of rhetorical figures that, according to George Puttenham, were recognized in terms of abbreviation – exemplified through the figure of *paremia* (deploying "some common proverb or adage") – and "copious amplification."[17] They functioned as the twin poles of narrative description with a lineage going back to Aristotle,[18] elaborated with respect to oratory by Cicero and Quintilian,[19] sustained during the Middle Ages especially by Geoffrey of Vinsauf,[20] and further codified and catalogued in the Renaissance principally by Erasmus.[21] For Shakespeare as for other contemporary playwrights, amplification and abbreviation, or dilation and contraction as they sometimes were known in Renaissance rhetorical handbooks,[22] were the main modalities of copious expression – or *copia*.[23] The goal of *copia* was to cultivate a fulsome style through accumulating and having ready access to an abundant and expansive storehouse or treasury (whence the term *thesaurus*) for amplifying and augmenting one's speech and writing.

Allusions to these figures with reference to various types of narrative ploys, including tapping into the backlog of historical anecdotes (*exempla*) and excerpting famous sayings from classical texts (*sententiae*), were fundamental to the pedagogical practices in sixteenth-century England.[24] Two sides of the same rhetorical coin, these tropes of abbreviation and amplification are put on display – and, to some extent, slyly subverted – with exuberant transparency in *Henry V*, as will be disclosed more fully in what follows. As a preliminary case in point, though, to introduce how these tropes of *copia* (amplification and abbreviation) operated, let us consider two closely related moments in *Henry V* that speak directly to this theme. The first is the use of *exempla* (famous deeds of the ancients from which moral lessons were to be derived) on the part of the English camp, most notably by Fluellen, where recollected precedents and celebrated champions of warfare serve as the mnemic seeds of history, associated in Renaissance "faculty psychology" with memory.[25] As for the second, on the part of the French camp, we observe the marshaling of proverbs and *sententiae*, those pithy constituent elements of moral philosophy. With respect to the first, the bombastic Fluellen (Shakespeare's invented Welsh captain leading a contingent of troops in Henry's campaign in France during the Hundred Years' War) appears to be an avid if somewhat inattentive reader of deeds and legends of ancient worthies. Further, as was the case with many new readers of increasingly accessible humanist works of the day, Fluellen typifies the casual peruser of classical texts – or, more likely, of epitomes and anthologies – cherry-picking salient details to argue his point (*H5* 4.7.23–40). This was the aim of keeping a commonplace book – whether based on one's own reading[26] or in pre-digested print form[27] – filled with memorable entries so one might be stirred to recall what they referred to and be able to expand on any given theme, amplified copiously with references to choice classical works. Looking back to the exemplars of the past, Fluellen inadvertently makes a hash of the rhetorical tropes reserved for augmentation. His main talking point concerns establishing an analogy that parallels young Harry of Monmouth (Henry V) to Alexander the Great, and Falstaff (whose name he cannot quite recall) to Clytus (4.7.36–40).[28] Far from making this point, though, what is highlighted here is how his fumbled allusion extends and ornamentally presents but does not illuminate the topic.

Fluellen's failed tactic of amplification is given its own parallel in the French camp, albeit at the other end of the copiousness spectrum, namely, abbreviation, with the flight of proverbs and *sententiae* let loose by the Dauphin and his captains. Shakespeare showcases the extent to which recourse to copiousness in this game of one-upmanship is virtually inexhaustible – and hence potentially exhausting for the audience. The playwright tests just how long the jest can be sustained and still remain entertaining, while at the same time holding this kind of display up to ridicule as an indecorous display of *copia*. In this excerpt we witness a breakdown in the signifying power of proverbs, which ordinarily would be sufficient in and of themselves to convey the intended sense when applied to a specific case. Erasmus, for example, offers a succinct definition in his *Adages*, the gold standard of such rhetorical handbooks: "A proverb is a saying in popular use, remarkable for some shrewd and novel turn."[29] What we find in the French camp, though, is each proverb being countered by another, resulting in a ridiculous exchange devoid of any real meaning other than to reveal the contentious nature of the characters engaged in such foolish banter, using adages that are supposed to be compact receptacles of universal if commonplace wisdom.[30] The larger implication is that there is such an enormous reservoir of proverbial wisdom that when deployed *ad absurdum* there is no end to what could be constructed.

CONSTABLE: By my faith, sir, but it is. Never anybody saw it but his lackey.
    'Tis a hooded valour, and when it appears it will bate.
ORLEANS: Ill will never said well.
CONSTABLE: I will cap that proverb with "There is flattery in friendship."

ORLEANS: And I will take up that with "Give the devil his due."
CONSTABLE: Well placed. There stands your friend for the devil. Have at the very eye of that proverb with "A pox of the devil."
ORLEANS: You are the better at proverbs, by how much "a fool's bolt is soon shot."
CONSTABLE: You have shot over.
ORLEANS: 'Tis not the first time you were overshot.
Enter a Messenger.

(3.7.99–111)

Presumably, this banter in proverbs could have gone on for a while longer still but, conveniently and decorously (dramaturgically speaking), is cut off mid-quip by a messenger reporting the English vanguard has been sighted within fifteen hundred paces.

Certain verbal expressive forms, exemplarily proverbs, at once draw on and activate internalized memory images. Owing to their pithy if rudimentary summing-up of some grain of truth observable in the world of human experience, proverbs take on a kind of universalizing effect. On the surface, proverbs mean what they say and, depending on the context in which they are used, have the capacity to speak beyond themselves.[31] And yet, in all their venerable simplicity, proverbs in the sixteenth century found analogues in commonplace visual tropes – and vice versa. In 1559, for example, the painter Pieter Bruegel the Elder, in a complex visual *jeu d'esprit* based on popular everyday expressions, satirically literalized over a hundred proverbs.[32] It is a short step from here – with proverbs – to seeing how the same sorts of inventions draw on the reservoir of commonplace everyday truths resulting in the dramaturgical sketching out of probable histories. Construed as mnemotechnic placeholders, such proverbs set in train the recovery of ever finer details of larger narratives and specific stories.

Shakespeare's self-conscious use of these tropes of abbreviation and amplification reflects fairly standard rhetorical and textual habits of the period. And yet the ways these tropes end up being expressed by his characters – given what is intimated about their own implied histories – mark them as being productively recursive. The extended camp episode in *Henry V* (3.7) referenced above offers a representative test case indicating a preferred dramaturgical practice by means of which the identity of a character is constructed in terms of, and also is conditioned by, telltale figures of speech. What distinguishes the class of allusive rhetorical cues discussed here and in what follows from, say, the malapropisms of Dogberry in *Much Ado* or the fustian phrases characterizing Holofernes in *Love's Labour's Lost* is the extent to which they are charged with affectively cueing the past by evoking a specific element in one's personal backstory that plausibly motivates the intertheatrical stage business at hand.³³ The audience thereby is given ready access to a cache of assumed specific memories to be recalled concerning an event (or series of contingent events) preceding the temporal coordinates of the play. This class of abbreviated tugs of memory features significantly in Shakespeare's plays, whether Pompey's tethered bitter memory that Antony still has his "father's house," which he cannot help bringing up even as they toast a prospective alliance, "But what? We are friends" (*Ant.* 2.7.122); or in Beatrice's reminder to Benedick that they have a shared history and she is wise to his tricks: "I know you of old" (*Ado* 1.1.139).

With respect to this last example, the battle of wit between Beatrice and Benedick uses some of the same rhetorical quibbles found elsewhere in the Shakespeare canon, and especially in *Henry V* (3.7) – most notably the jest about eating all one kills:³⁴

DAUPHIN: 'Tis midnight. I'll go arm myself. [*Exit*]
ORLEANS: The Duke of Bourbon longs for morning.
RAMBURES: He longs to eat the English.
CONSTABLE: I think he will eat all he kills.

(3.7.81–84)

The wry implication, of course, is that the Dauphin will not have to eat any. The same holds for Beatrice's mocking of Benedick's martial prowess: "But how many hath he killed? – for indeed I promised to eat all of his killing" (*Ado* 1.1.32–33). This recycled joke, while a well-known commonplace of the period,³⁵ was deployed in these two instances as a kind of quick character sketch of Benedick and the Dauphin as blustering swaggerers. As such it suggests something of the same underlying eristic structure in both contests of proverb-grounded wit that momentarily takes center stage. Whereas the Constable of France genuinely thinks the Dauphin will not distinguish himself in battle (even though he will not say this to his face; the Dauphin has just exited as he says the line), Beatrice makes a public declaration of her spirited taunting of Benedick such that her uncle, Leonato, qualifies her jibe: "You must not, sir, mistake my niece: there is a kind of merry war betwixt Signor Benedick and her: they never meet but there's a skirmish of wit between them" (1.1.45–47). Here, the backstory of a kind of needling amity ("merry war") between Beatrice and Benedick is corroborated. Moreover, the word "skirmish" evokes a sense of the martial implications of the proverbial battle of the sexes played out in *Much Ado* and which, in the end, will flip to embrace the marital sense as well. Comparably, but in reverse in *Henry V*, the discourse associated with amorous sonnets and erotic blazons sets the scene for the French warriors' rhetorical wrangling, launched by the Dauphin's absurd encomium on his warhorse:

> DAUPHIN: What a long night is this! I will not change my horse with any that treads but on four pasterns. *Ch'ha!* He bounds from the earth as if his entrails were hairs – *le cheval volant*, the Pegasus, *qui a les narines de feu*! When I bestride him I soar, I am a hawk! He trots the air. The earth sings when he touches it. The basest horn of his hoof is more musical than the pipe of Hermes.
>
> . . .
>
> CONSTABLE: Indeed, my lord, it is a most absolute and excellent horse.
> DAUPHIN: It is the prince of palfreys. His neigh is like the bidding of a monarch, and his countenance enforces homage.
> ORLEANS: No more, cousin.
> DAUPHIN: Nay, the man hath no wit that cannot from the rising of the lark to the lodging of the lamb vary deserved praise on my palfrey. It is a theme as fluent as the sea. Turn the sands into eloquent tongues and my horse is argument for them all. 'Tis a subject for a sovereign to reason on, and for a sovereign's sovereign to ride on, and for the world, familiar to us and unknown, to lay apart their particular functions and wonder at him. I once writ a sonnet in his praise, and began thus: "Wonder of nature! . . ."
> ORLEANS: I have heard a sonnet begin so to one's mistress.
> DAUPHIN: Then did they imitate that which I composed to my courser, for my horse is my mistress.
> ORLEANS: Your mistress bears well.
>
> (3.7.11–41)

This extended display of *copia*, reflecting a heightened self-consciousness about the use of *copia* among the interlocutors, reveals more than just the Dauphin's shallow character as someone stuck in schoolboy mode, taking pride in his application of commonplace rhetorical exercises: "It is a theme as fluent as the sea. Turn the sands into eloquent tongues." Also disclosed here, in a nutshell, is what Shakespeare wants the audience to think about the flower of French chivalry, represented here as a rout of contentious, bickering backbiters. Moreover, the allusive recollection of a poem that the Dauphin once wrote to his horse (and is eager and ready to recite) exemplifies precisely the kind of tug of memory that Shakespeare activates time and again in his plays – though here to show that rote learning is not the same thing as the judicious application of that learning in a social setting. The audience thus is made to call to mind some presumed general circumstances surrounding a speaker's character that is disclosed through a telling moment recalled from his past that leads to (in this particular case) our still being able to conjure up the idea – if not the specifics – of just such a blazon. So yes, the Dauphin is a fop; but further, the sociable if eristic setting and the timely disclosure of this anecdote assures that a much more richly evocative and fully fleshed-out backstory emerges. While the audience cannot (and indeed need not) know all the details involved, we recognize the tug of memory along with the characters onstage. And, accordingly, we respond by imagining the conjectural fully-formed memory preceding, conditioning, and constituent of the world of the play with special reference to a submerged narrative that we have thus been cued to call to mind. Shakespeare's ingenious pastiche of proverbs in *Henry V* (3.8.99–111) constructs and delivers a backstory of mutual antagonism among leaders of the French camp at Agincourt by means of the humanist recreational exercising of wit through *copia*.

Within the world of the play, the present is shown to be informed by actions and discernible behavioral patterns collected from the past. These brief reminders, by way of ostensible "throwaway lines," are in fact dramaturgically expedient triggers for the recall of key elements in characters' backstories otherwise inaccessible to the audience. To use another example, this time from a tragedy, in the final moments of *Hamlet*, Fortinbras declares to the remnant of the Danish court that he has "some rights of memory in this kingdom, / Which now to claim my vantage doth invite me" (5.2.368–69). This declaration in fact chiastically bookends and recalls the preparatory corroborative information Horatio disclosed in the opening scene of the play about "the inheritance of Fortinbras" (1.1.92).[36] This sets up a more fully fleshed out and politically nuanced backstory that impels the audience to imagine and entertain a whole submerged history, and one that turns out to be fundamental to the main dynastic plot, and which is being dragged along implacably until, in an instant, the tug of memory snaps it to the present.

Proverbs and the Signaling of Shakespeare's Mnemotechnical Craft

The trade in proverbs was a pervasive feature of Renaissance literary and mnemonic culture. Erasmus, for example, explicitly recognized adages as an aide-mémoire, contending that "in the proverb ... almost all the philosophy of the Ancients was contained."[37] Indeed, most of the ancient writers Erasmus quoted as illustrations in his early modern compendium come from Quintilian's classical digest of works from his own day rather than directly from the original authors. The same applies to Shakespeare's lining up of proverbs in *Henry V* (3.8.59–111), most of which are identified by editors simply as "traditional" with a nod to Tilley's *Dictionary*.[38] What we find in Shakespeare's use of these mnemonic seeds of immemorial wisdom here is an index to the special kind of ingenuity signaled by his self-conscious activation of the tug of memory when it comes to cueing the past.

With this in mind, we can attend to *Henry V* (3.8) as presenting a concentrated and stunning display of proverbs mobilized as *topoi*, as memorable places of invention, set in the French camp during the restless night before the Battle of Agincourt. As already observed, it is touched off by the Dauphin's encomium to his horse in terms properly reserved for praising one's lady. His extravagant use of *copia* recalls an Erasmian catalogue of *periphrasis*. Although Erasmus gives examples of hundreds of ways to vary and ornament simple phrases (such as "thank you for your letter") in his handbooks, in his own scholarly writings he studiously avoids periphrasis to foreclose any possible misinterpretation or overinterpretation.[39] It is fitting then that it is a dominant trope used in the French camp. For, rather than deploying the usual terms of forensic oratory to score their points, the case is debated in proverbs punctuated by a series of sporting double entendres and barbs involving the visual lexicon of heraldry.

RAMBURES: My lord Constable, the armour that I saw in your tent tonight, are those stars or suns upon it?
CONSTABLE: Stars, my lord.
DAUPHIN: Some of them will fall tomorrow, I hope.
CONSTABLE: And yet my sky shall not want.
DAUPHIN: That may be, for you bear a many superfluously, and 'twere more honour some were away.

(3.8.63–68)

It is this easy commerce of rhetorical blazons, heraldic cant, and pointed proverbs to which I would direct our attention. Each of these figures of speech, tropes, and features of copiousness are used by the speakers obviously aware they are the constituent parts of an argument insofar as they comment on them as such. Each reference takes us back to a

Affect and Invention in Shakespeare's Drama 215

collocation of some prior repository, thus making a claim on memory – and wit.

DAUPHIN: *"Le chien est retourné à son propre vomissement, et la truie lavée au bourbier."* Thou makest use of anything.
CONSTABLE: Yet do I not use my horse for my mistress, or any such proverb so little kin to the purpose.

(3.8.59–62)

Of the many things one might say about this remarkable exchange, Shakespeare's Dauphin quotes from the vernacular French Huguenot version of the scriptural warning to backsliders, concerning the dog returning to its vomit and a washed pig to its mud (Proverbs 26:11, cf. 2 Peter 2:22).[40] What stands out most, though, is that the cited proverb comes from the ur-text of proverbially framed wisdom, namely, the biblical book of Proverbs attributed to wise King Solomon.

Here, more directly than in the other points scored in this otherwise typical display of the combative schoolroom exercise known as *contentio*,[41] we catch a glimpse of how proverbs are enlisted in the service of one's argument, smuggled into one's discourse. This applies especially to the rapid-fire matching of proverb for proverb at the end of this episode, which, like the whole passage, is a staged representation of the kind of everyday repartee one might use in conversation, composed out of the mnemonically grounded germs of experience distilled from and associated with proverbs. Moreover, the metacritical proverb from the scriptural book of Proverbs is cast in French, even as is the Dauphin's initial praise for his warhorse. This reference to the biblical book of Proverbs is one of several key moments in the play where the French language figures significantly as a way of magnifying the sense of onstage contention and capitalizing on the generation of risible misunderstandings.

The audience may not long remember the specific details of Shakespeare's witty setting up of a foolish barrage of proverbs (3.8.99–111) but will leave the episode with an indelible impression of the French as commonplace-dependent combatants, ridiculous in their feisty posturing. The audience furthermore is left with a sense of admiration at the playwright's deft handling of this densely packed rhetorical display; for admiration, after all, was the nominal theme setting off the whole exchange, albeit concerning a horse. We admire in this scene how pliant such shopworn tropes and proverbs actually are – or can be – when ingeniously deployed. These quips, and their swift overturning, are drawn from a well-stocked reservoir of commonplaces shared by characters and audience alike. This is why the proverbs, with their universal resonance, also have the power to convey the tense humor of a battle of wit prior to an actual historical battle memorialized in this play, which the audience knows was disastrous for the French.[42] Such choice inventions to cue the past with Shakespeare's tugs of memory induce the audience finally to recall and reflect on the very mnemotechnical operations to which, ultimately, all such collocated proverbs owe their origin.

Notes

1 Jorge Luis Borges, *The Book of Sand and Shakespeare's Memory*, trans. Andrew Hurley (New York: Penguin Books, 1998), 128.
2 Ibid., 127.
3 Erving Goffman, *The Presentation of Self in Everyday Life* (New York: Anchor Books, 1956), 27–30.
4 Derived from classical sources, the five canons of rhetoric are *inventio* (invention), *dispositio* (arrangement), *elocutio* (style), *memoria* (memory), and *pronunciatio* (delivery); see Frances A. Yates, *The Art of Memory* (London: Penguin, 1978), 20–22; cf. William E. Engel, Rory Loughnane, and Grant Williams, eds., *The Memory Arts in Renaissance England* (Cambridge University Press, 2016), 5.
5 Steele Nowlin, *Chaucer, Gower, and the Affect of Invention* (Columbus: Ohio State University Press, 2016), 2.
6 Patricia Phillippy, *Shaping Remembrance from Shakespeare to Milton* (Cambridge University Press, 2017), 100–104.
7 For the full passage, and analysis of the cultural context, see Engel et al., *The Memory Arts*, 84.
8 On the analogy between acting and the construction of memory images, see Lina Perkins Wilder, *Shakespeare's Memory Theatre* (Cambridge University Press, 2010), 54; and William E. Engel, *Death and Drama in Renaissance England* (Oxford University Press, 2002), 52–53.
9 Yates, *The Art of Memory*, 22.
10 E.g., Thomas Nashe, *Lenten Stuff* (London: Nicholas Ling and Cuthbert Burby, 1599), F1v: "tugging forth."
11 Yates, *The Art of Memory*, 12–26.
12 Cf. Jelena Marelj, "Re-characterizing Shakespearean Character," in *Shakespearean Character: Language in Performance* (London: Arden Shakespeare, 2019), 1–20; 5–14.
13 On "interpreting cues," see Simon Palfrey and Tiffany Stern, *Shakespeare in Parts* (Oxford University Press, 2007), 91–95; on "plot-scenarios," Tiffany Stern, *Documents of Performance in Early Modern England* (Cambridge University Press, 2012), 8–35.

14 William Dodd, "Character as Dynamic Identity," in Paul Yachnin and Jessica Slights, eds., *Shakespeare and Character* (New York: Palgrave Macmillan, 2009), 62–79; 63–64.
15 Of the many places in Shakespeare's plays where a similar tug of memory gives stunning if tantalizingly vague insight into a character's backstory, few can match Lady Macbeth's "I have given suck, and know / How tender 'tis to love the babe that milks me" (*Macbeth* 1.7.54–55); cf. Emma Smith, *This Is Shakespeare* (New York: Pantheon Books, 2019), 250–51.
16 Richard F. Hardin, "The Renaissance of Plautine Comedy and the Varieties of Luck in Shakespeare and Other Plotters," *Mediterranean Studies* 16 (2007), 143–56; 149.
17 George Puttenham, *The Arte of English Poesie* (London, 1598); for "*paremia*," see "Of figures and figurative speeches" (3.7); on "copious amplification," see "A division of figures, and how they serve in exornation of language" (3.10) and "Of figures sententious, otherwise called Rhetorical" (3.19).
18 Verne R. Kennedy, "Auxesis: A Concept of Rhetorical Amplification," *Southern Speech Communication Journal*, 37.1 (1971), 60–72; 60–64.
19 Alexander H. Sackton, *Rhetoric as Dramatic Language in Ben Jonson* (New York: Octagon Books, 1967), 13.
20 Jane Baltzell, "Rhetorical 'Amplification' and 'Abbreviation' and the Structure of Medieval Narrative," *Pacific Coast Philology*, 2 (1967), 32–39; 33–36.
21 Peter Mack, "The Classics in Humanism, Education, and Scholarship," in Patrick Cheney and Philip Hardie, eds., *The Oxford History of Classical Reception in English Literature* (Oxford University Press, 2015), vol. II, 29–55; 33–40.
22 Patricia Parker, *Shakespeare from the Margins: Language, Culture, Context* (University of Chicago Press, 1996), 185–90.
23 See Virginia W. Callahan, "The *De Copia*: The Bounteous Horn," in Richard L. DeMolen, ed., *Essays on the Work of Erasmus* (New Haven, CT: Yale University Press, 1978), 99–109.
24 Lynn Enterline, *Shakespeare's Schoolroom: Rhetoric, Discipline, Emotion* (Philadelphia: University of Pennsylvania Press, 2012), 85–93.
25 E. Ruth Harvey, *The Inward Wits: Psychological Theory in the Middle Ages and the Renaissance* (London: Warburg Institute, 1975), 58–60.
26 See Fred Schurink, "Manuscript Commonplace Books, Literature, and Reading in Early Modern England," *The Huntington Library Quarterly*, 73.3 (2010), 453–69.
27 Ann Moss, *Printed Commonplace-Books and the Structuring of Renaissance Thought* (Cambridge: Clarendon Press, 1996), 101–214.
28 On Fluellen's faulty memory, with special reference to Shakespeare's shoring up and consolidating notions of Tudor kingship in *Henry V*, see William E. Engel, "Handling Memory in the Henriad: Forgetting Falstaff," in Andrew Hiscock and Lina Perkins Wilder, eds., *The Routledge Handbook of*

Shakespeare and Memory (London: Routledge, 2017), 165–79; and on this scene reminding "the audience to resort to their own historical and theatrical memory in order to withstand the force of nationalist oblivion," see Isabel Karremann, *The Drama of Memory in Shakespeare's History Plays* (Cambridge University Press, 2015), 151.

29 Desiderius Erasmus, *Adages Ii1 to Iv100*, in *Collected Works of Erasmus*, ed. R. A. B. Mynors, trans. Margaret Mann Phillips (University of Toronto Press, 1982), 4.

30 None of the proverbs in the ensuing passage is attributable to any definite source, although printed compilations of such of proverbs were common in the period: "Proverbs or adages represent the testimony of many men" and "usually earn greater conviction, expressing as they do what generations have regarded as true"; Miriam Joseph, *Shakespeare's Use of the Arts of Language* (Philadelphia: Paul Dry, 2005), 98.

31 Wolfgang Mieder, *"Proverbs Speak Louder than Words": Wisdom in Art, Culture, Folklore, History, Literature and Mass Media* (New York: Peter Lang, 2008), 251–76.

32 Margaret A. Sullivan, *Bruegel and the Creative Process, 1559–1563* (New York: Routledge, 2017), 33.

33 On Renaissance rhetorical habits and the affective shaping of Shakespeare's characters, see Joel B. Altman, *The Improbability of Othello: Rhetorical Anthropology and Shakespearean Selfhood* (University of Chicago Press, 2010), 235–60; and on all theatrical gestures as stylized, codified, and coming "with pasts," see William West, "Intertheatricality," in Henry Turner, ed., *Early Modern Theatricality* (Oxford University Press, 2013), 151–72; 156.

34 R. W. Dent, *Shakespeare's Proverbial Language* (Berkeley: University of California Press, 1981), 48.

35 Randle Cotgrave, *Dictionarie of the French and English Tongues* (London: Adam Islip, 1611), Q2v; entry for *Charrette*, the idiom *mangeur de charrettes ferrées*: "A terrible cutter, swaggerer, bugbear, swashbuckler; one that will kill all he sees, and eat all he kills."

36 A commonly used structuring device in Renaissance dramas; see William E. Engel, *Chiastic Designs in English Literature* (New York: Routledge, 2016), 3–10.

37 Erasmus, *Adages Ii1 to Iv100*, 83.

38 On what Renaissance writers considered proverbial and where they thought proverbs came from, see Morris Palmer Tilley, *A Dictionary of the Proverbs in England in the Sixteenth and Seventeenth Centuries* (Ann Arbor: University of Michigan Press, 1950), v.

39 Erika Rummel, *Erasmus as a Translator of the Classics* (University of Toronto Press, 1985), 96.

40 See Andrew Gurr, ed., *Henry V*, New Cambridge Shakespeare (Cambridge University Press, 2012), 152; this is the wording in French Huguenot Bibles

of 1540, 1551, and 1556, "proverbial enough" to appear "in Holinshed's *Chronicle of Ireland* (1587), 133."
41 John F. Tinkler, "Renaissance Humanism and the *genera eloquentia*," *Rhetorica*, 5.3 (1987), 279–309; 283–97.
42 On Shakespeare's politics of memory and national consciousness, see Jonathan Baldo, *Memory in Shakespeare's Histories: Stages of Forgetting in Early Modern England* (New York: Routledge, 2012), 104–12.

CHAPTER 11

Memory, Text, Affect
The Deaths of Gloucester

Rory Loughnane

All early modern English history plays memorialize a selectively represented and imagined version of the past. Plays in this genre are not documentary accounts, but rather amount to a series of curated episodes that have more or less historical basis. What a dramatist or team of dramatists chose to include was not prescribed by any sense of obligation to authoritatively represent the historical past. They sought, rather, to create a selective representation of remembered, recorded, and made-to-fit quasi-historical materials, often tempered by the mythologies that accrued with temporal distance from the events depicted. Dramatists knew they could not veer too far from any accepted historical narrative, but, so too, they knew there was much room to play within such narratives. In writing history plays, dramatists often drew upon assorted historical accounts, borrowed from the burgeoning supply of narrative chronicle history in print and embedded folklore traditions and historical rumor, to create eclectic versions of an imagined past that did not necessarily adhere to any single source.

I introduce the idea of eclectically produced histories, drawn from disparate sources, to highlight an initial parallel with the history of editing of early modern drama, including the history plays I will describe in this chapter, which once tended toward the practice of conflating distinct textual witnesses to produce eclectic play editions. More recently, as demonstrated in major series and collected works editions, there has been a marked turn toward single version editing where more than one version is preserved.[1] One effect of this editorial evolution is that distinct play versions demand distinct critical engagement; that is, critics who have adopted some recent editions no longer study plays as unitary texts (e.g., studying *Hamlet* as *a* play) but, rather, engage with a distinct version or versions of a play (e.g., studying Q1, Q2, or Folio *Hamlet*).[2] The critical concomitants of single version editing are significant, forcing us to reconsider past arguments that were built on conflated editions and to think anew how a version might work, so to speak, in its own right.

Memory, Text, Affect: The Deaths of Gloucester 221

In this chapter, I will consider how the infamous murder of Humphrey, Duke of Gloucester, is variously represented in the preserved versions of the second play in Shakespeare's first tetralogy. The play best known as *2 Henry VI* is preserved in two substantive versions, each of which offers a radically different version of Gloucester's murder. These textual differences have practical implications for staging and performance but are also, as I will argue, transformative for the affective power and emotional tenor of the imagined history they memorialize. I will further describe how comparison of the versions is complicated by matters relating to their textual transmission and authorship.

By focusing on the dramatic representation of one historical episode, the murder of Gloucester, I wish to draw into dialogue some traditionally siloed areas of study: memory, text, and affect. While the affective turn in early modern scholarship has yielded rich insights into how early modern dramatists like Shakespeare conceptualized their lived experience and the emotional lives of their characters, there has been little work that recognizes how the history of text, seen through the lens of textual transmission and authorship, might intersect with the history of emotions.[3] Similarly, while recent early modern memory studies have demonstrated a cultural fascination with remembering and forgetting that is reflected within print culture, little consideration has been given to how the history of text, with its inclusions, omissions, and variations, contributes to early moderns' conceptual understanding of, and relationship with, their past.[4] And, prompting the present collection, although recent research in early modern memory studies has revealed the extent to which practices of memory conditioned everyday habits, rituals, and behaviors in the period, there has been surprisingly little work on the role of emotions in the making of memory or its representation. This chapter approaches memory through the lens of early modern history-making through print culture – what version of the recorded or imagined past is mediated to later generations of audiences and readers – and uses the different versions of *2 Henry VI*, and the different affective register they command through character speech and action, to attempt to illuminate the interplay and interdependencies of these siloed areas of study.

How to Murder Gloucester

Crucial to a tetralogy of plays about the Wars of the Roses written by Shakespeare, Marlowe, and others in the early 1590s is the death of Henry VI's trusted advisor, Humphrey, Duke of Gloucester.[5] The character is murdered at the midpoint of the second play in the cycle, leaving Henry at the mercy of his enemies. Until the murder, which is a direct betrayal of Henry's command, the whisperings of rebellion and unrest were merely that. Squabbles between the peers were relatively restrained, while other subplots, including Eleanor's necromancy, the Simpcox scheme, and the Peter-Horner fight, contributed little to the important passage of history the play memorializes: the lead-up to civil war. Richard Plantagenet's lineage speech draws in the support of Salisbury and Warwick, but no decisive action is taken until Gloucester's murder. Thereafter follows the death of Beaufort, Suffolk's banishment and murder, Cade's rebellion, the rise of Richard, and full-blooded civil war. Notwithstanding the dark comedy of Cade and his followers – and there is little comic about either his populist rise or his followers' propensity for violence – the play adopts a bleaker, more serious tone in its second half as the imagined history it represents moves to scenes of war, precipitating the horrors witnessed in its immediate sequel. The murder of Gloucester is, therefore, of particular importance for the affective power and mood of this part of the cycle, as described in the next section, a watershed moment in the selectively remembered dynastic history it dramatizes.

The second play in the first tetralogy is preserved in two alternative versions. The version most people know, read, and study is the play printed in the 1623 Folio edition of Shakespeare's *Comedies, Histories & Tragedies* (hereafter F or *2 Henry VI*). There is, however, an early alternative version of the play, about one third shorter in length, that was printed in quarto in 1594, entitled *The First part of the Contention betwixt the two famous Houses of Yorke and Lancaster* ... (hereafter Q1 or *Contention*), and reprinted in 1600 (Q2) and 1619 (Q3), that mirrors the later printed *2 Henry VI* in various ways.[6] The provenance of this shorter text, and the relationship between the two versions, is much debated, the details of which need not detain us at this juncture. What we need to know is that while in both Q1 and F the murder of Gloucester proves a crucial turning point for the plot, the murder is represented in a starkly different ways in the two versions.[7]

The circumstances surrounding the death of Gloucester were one of the enduring mysteries of early modern England. The chroniclers tended to agree that he was murdered, but lacked consensus on who ordered it and the method of execution. Fabian recounts how Gloucester was "founde deede in hys bedde" and that "hys corps was layd opyn y^t all me[n] might se hym, but no wonder was founde on hym." This might suggest that he died naturally, but Fabian observes that "dyuers reports" were made of

Gloucester's "murder ... which [he] passe[s] over."⁸ For Hall, "all indifferent persons well knewe, that he died of no natural death but of some viole[n]t force":

> Some iudged him to be strangled: some affirme, that a hote spitte was put in his foundement: other write, that he was stiffeled or smoldered between two fetherbeddes.⁹

Holinshed, drawing on Hall's account, supplies the following description of events, which the dramatists most likely consulted:

> The duke the night after he was thus committed to prison, beeing the .xxiiij. of February was founde deade in his bedde, and his body shewed to the lordes and commons, as though hee had dyed of a palsey, or of an impostume: but all indifferent persons (as saithe Hall) well knewe, that hee dyed of some violent deathe: some iudged him to be strangled, some affirme that an hotte spit was put in at his fundement: other write that he was smouldered betwene .ij. fetherbeds, and some haue affirmed that hee dyed of verye griefe, for that he might not come openly to his answere.¹⁰

Hall and Holinshed advert to three forms of murder: strangling, penetration, and smothering. Holinshed, via Hall, notes the possibility of palsey or an impostume (abscess) or, more simply, dying from grief. Neither seems to favor this possibility, however, and in the *de casibus* tradition of historical writing, these more benign possibilities were ruled out explicitly. The downfalls of Eleanor and Gloucester were first included in the 1578 edition of *A Mirror for Magistrates*. Gloucester's ghost narrates his "secret murther" in this somewhat opaque manner:

> Then shaking and quaking, for dread of a Dreame,
> Halfe waked al naked in bed as I say,
> What tyme strake the chime of mine hower extreame,
> Opprest was my rest with mortal affray,
> My foes did vnclose, I know not which way
> My chamber dores, and boldly they in brake,
> And had me fast before I could awake.¹¹

Quite how they "had" him "fast" is unclear, but the narrator Gloucester insists on the following:

> But be thou sure by violence it was
> ...
> For when these wolues, my bodie once did cease,
> Vsed I was, but smally to myne ease:
> With tormentes strong, which went so nerethe quicke,
> As made me dye before that I was sicke.¹²

Gloucester-as-narrator concludes his account by noting that no evidence of the means of his murder could be seen on his corpse:

> Dead was I found, by such as best did know,
> The maner how the same was brought to passe.
> And than my corps, was set out for a show,
> By view whereof, nothing perceiued was:[13]

The reticence to reveal quite how he died is striking but we are left in little doubt as to the violence implied by "With tormentes strong, which went so nerethe quicke." It is not so explicit in detail as Hall or Holinshed but "G[eorge] F[errers]," who wrote this section, certainly leaves open the possibility that Gloucester was fatally penetrated rather than smothered or strangled.

For those recalling Gloucester's death from editions of Shakespeare's works, the means of murder described in Hall and Holinshed – a hot spit inserted into Gloucester's fundament or anal passage – may seem somewhat surprising. There are no editions of the play I am aware of where this possibility is even suggested. But this particular means of murder may also seem familiar from other sources. There is, of course, a remarkable correspondence between what is described in Hall and Holinshed and that which happens to Edward II in Marlowe's historical tragedy, drawn also from Hall and Holinshed . This correspondence has largely evaded critical commentary, which is surprising given the temporal proximity of the two plays.

I shall return to Marlowe's history in due course but let us first compare how the murder is represented in *Contention* (Q1) and *2 Henry VI* (F), beginning with the less familiar quarto text. The scene preceding the murder ends with a soliloquy by York. He has just listened to Queen Margaret, Suffolk, and Cardinal Beaufort form a plan to kill Gloucester following his arrest, a plan which York agrees with, and Suffolk and Beaufort accept this "charge" or responsibility (E1^r). Somerset and Buckingham are present also but say nothing while the plot is hatched; rather, they figure prominently once the conversation turns to the Irish rebellion. Left alone at last, York says he must think of himself and "rouse [himself] up" for the "time" is "offered [to him] so faire"; that is, in three short lines, he recognizes the time is opportune for him (E1^v). He then moves to the practicalities, explaining that he has "seduste" (seduced) John Cade to "raise commotion" and "by that meanes" York "shall perceiue how the common people / Do affect the claime and house of Yorke" (E1^v–E2^r). It is an important speech, outlining York's personal agenda and ambition,

Memory, Text, Affect: The Deaths of Gloucester 225

but also functional in that it creates space between the murder plot and its actualization. York ends his speech in rhyme by saying that when Gloucester is "made well away," then there is nothing to "stop the light to Englands Crowne" (that is, no one to prevent him from becoming King); the couplet ending with "But Yorke can tame and headlong pull them downe" (E2ʳ).

York exits, clearing the stage, and the next scene begins with the following stage action:

> *Then the Curtaines being drawne, Duke* Humphrey *is discouered in his bed, and, two men lying on his brest and smothering him in his bed. And then enter the Duke of* Suffolke *to them.* (E2ʳ)

This stage direction prescribes not simply movement but also playhouse resources. A backstage curtain is required that conceals a recess, the discovery space, which must be large enough for a bed in which Gloucester and the two murderers can be seen. The action begins *in media res* with the murder attempt already underway. Quite how Gloucester is being smothered, or with what, is unclear, but the two men are supposed to be on top of him ("lying on his brest"). Gloucester is killed at this time "And then" Suffolk enters – that is, after the murder – and addresses the murderers: "How now sirs, what haue you dispatch him?" The first murderer says that they have, and Suffolk instructs them to make sure that Gloucester's "cloathes [are] laid smooth about him" so that all "perceiue ... that he dide [died] of his owne accorde" (E2ʳ). Suffolk then orders them to "draw the Curtaines againe" (E2ʳ). Gloucester is hidden from view and the murderers depart. Suffolk remains onstage. Then there is a mass entry of Henry, Margaret, Buckingham, Somerset, and Beaufort. Significantly, there is no scene break between the murder and entrance, and the entering party encounter Suffolk. Henry orders Suffolk to "go call our vnkle Gloster" and "Tell him this day we will that he do cleare himself"; that is, Henry hopes Gloucester can that day clear himself of any accusations (E2ʳ). Yet there is some implied temporal shift from the nighttime murder to the "day" of Gloucester's trial. Suffolk returns, announces that Gloucester is "dead in his bed," and Henry, overcome by the news, "falles in a swoone" (E2ᵛ).

In *2 Henry VI*, the scene preceding Gloucester's murder (scene 9 or 3.1 in some modern editions) follows a similar overall pattern to Q1 in that Gloucester is arrested, and Margaret, Suffolk, Beaufort, and York (Richard Plantagenet) conspire and agree to have him killed. Yet the discussion about this is much more protracted, and York, speaking in asides, can be seen to be manipulating the situation to his advantage. Somerset and Buckingham are silent throughout the murder plot, and, unlike Q1, Buckingham is never reintegrated into the dialogue thereafter. York's scene-ending soliloquy is more than twice as long in F (52 lines as opposed to 24 in Q1), greatly expanding on the theme of ambition and his need to quell any of his personal fears. In some of the most memorable lines of the Folio version, he says:

> Now *Yorke*, or neuer, steele thy fearfull thoughts,
> And change misdoubt to resolution;
> Be that thou hop'st to be, or what thou art;
> Resigne to death, it is not worth th' enioying:
> Let pale-fac't feare keepe with the meane-borne man,
> And finde no harbor in a Royall heart.
>
> (9.331–36)[14]

It is an extraordinarily metatheatrical, if not meta-historiographical moment, as York recognizes that he must self-consciously step into the role he believes history has prepared for him. To do so, he must ward off fear of death, which has no place in his royal-born heart. He follows this with an extended set of natural metaphors explaining that he will do everything it takes to succeed: first, he is a spider weaving traps for his enemies, and, second, he self-identifies as the "starued Snake" (9.343) who, thought dead, stings the hearts of those that help it recover. His soliloquy ends with this couplet:

> For Humphrey being dead, as he shall be,
> And Henry put apart, the next for me
>
> (9.382–83)

– a striking transfer of emphasis and agency between the two versions from the politically motivated "crown-down" rhyme to the personal agency of "be-me." The next scene opens, as per Q1, with some prescribed stage action:

> *Enter two or three running ouer the Stage, from the Murther of Duke Humfrey.*
> (10.0.1–2)

The two murderers are running to find Suffolk having already killed Gloucester. They note that they have killed Gloucester, but include an important additional detail: "didst ever hear a man so penitent?" That is, while we do not see the murder, we learn that before Gloucester's death he made penance. Suffolk asks the murderers if they have "layd faire the Bed," which they say they have, and then they are dismissed. Unlike Q1, there is a clear scene break before the entrance of the King and party: an "*Exeunt*" (10.14.1) direction covers both Suffolk and the murderers.[15]

The next scene opens with this entrance:

> *Sound Trumpets. Enter the King, the Queene, Cardinall, Suffolke, Somerset, with Attendants.* (11.0.1–2)

The entrance of Suffolk here would appear to break the so-called law of reentry. This is an unwritten law that characters should not enter at the beginning of a scene if they have exited at the end of the preceding scene.[16] It is possible that the ceremonial entrance, with its pronounced aural cue ("*Sound Trumpets*"), implies some temporal lapse, from night to day, or some slight shift of scene. Suffolk is once more called on by Henry to fetch Gloucester, but, perhaps significantly, the King says nothing about his hope for Gloucester's pardon and rather that all must ensure that Gloucester is tried fairly "from true evidence" (11.7). Suffolk returns, looking pale and trembling, and announces that he has found Gloucester "Dead in his Bed" (11.15), and after Margaret and Beaufort feign shock, the "King sounds" (11.18.1).

Parsing Difference

I have identified some key differences between the two play versions to highlight how the same essential plot details can be rendered in demonstrably different ways. Each version leads from the conspiracy against Gloucester to York's soliloquy to the murderers' dialogue with Suffolk to the royal entry to King Henry swooning at the news of Gloucester's death. Textual variation can be easily established (what is in x but not y and in y but not x) but its significance has been only rarely pursued in criticism. Yet much of the variation I have described frames the represented history in ways that necessarily alter our interpretative engagement with the play version and characters in question. For example, in the longer Folio text, York's character emerges more fully, not simply outlining his plan but also his reasoning. Buckingham, on the other hand, is better integrated into the shorter quarto text, but left silently present in the Folio version while others conspire. If we think the quarto is a shorter version of the text underlying the Folio or the Folio is an extended version of the text underlying the quarto – and these have been the slightly misguided battle lines drawn in some textual scholarship about the versions – reading such variants in terms of cuts and additions forces consideration of the selectivity of historical representation. York's variant speeches are merely indicative of how textual absence or presence of dialogue can condition the affective register of a play, an idea pursued more fully below. York is more developed as a character, because, in a blunt sense, he is assigned more dialogue to expand on the personal emotional significance of his embrace of this opportunity. The textual variation surrounding Gloucester's murder operates at a different level, however. Here we can identify a choice, or set of choices, to stage the murder or not. Just as there was some underlying decision to include it in the version preserved by *Contention*, there was a similar decision made in the version preserved by the Folio to exclude it.

More recent thinking on the relationship between both texts may help illuminate the timeline for such decision-making. Influential early twentieth-century scholarship identified *Contention* as a memorial reconstruction of the Folio text, therefore positing that the manuscript underlying *Contention* postdated the manuscript underlying *2 Henry VI*.[17] The concept of memorial reconstruction became subject to much dispute in later decades, and in the most important and comprehensive study of so-called bad quartos, Laurie Maguire ruled against this possibility for *Contention*.[18] Two further article studies by Lawrence Manley and Barbara Kreps, although reaching starkly different conclusions about the relationship between the versions, produced compelling evidence that *Contention* and the Folio text ought to be treated as separate texts, rather than simply labeling *Contention* as a 'bad' report of the other.[19] More recently still, in my edition of *2 Henry VI*, I argue that the Folio text was revised by Shakespeare at some point after the formation of the Lord Chamberlain's Men in the mid-1590s and, therefore, postdating the version preserved by *Contention*.[20] This means that I think at least some of the writing found in the Folio text represents a later stage in the genesis of the text than that which could have been transmitted by the 1594 quarto. Any variations between both versions might then originate in either earliest composition or later revision.[21] Thus, we must consider not only textual variation between *Contention* and *2 Henry VI* but also textual stratification, between original and revised, in *2 Henry VI*. This situation is complicated even further by attribution analysis which has identified the hands of Shakespeare, Marlowe, and at least one anonymous author in the Folio text.[22] Thus far, such attribution work has focused on the canonical Folio text rather than *Contention*. The agreement of language and phrasing in passages found across both versions at least suggests that *Contention* also includes mixed writing, but a more systematic analysis is required to determine the authorship of the shorter version.

Regardless of our view about its textual provenance, what *Contention* reveals is that in some iteration of the play Gloucester's murder was, in fact, supposed to be staged.[23] Whether what is included in the dialogue of *Contention* has been corrupted in some way, the stage directions, and the actions they prescribe, indicate that in some version of the play it was decided that the backstage discovery space should be used to contain the body and bed. Indeed, Maguire notes that *Contention* has "very detailed S[tage] D[irection]s, with careful attention to stage action, character relationships, and attitude," and describes the text as being "very sensitive theatrically."[24] This does not mean that the language of the stage directions has any greater authorial authority than the rest of the dialogue but simply that it gestures toward an alternative staging history where the murder was enacted before an audience. Whoever writes the stage direction is thinking of a specific way of staging the scene and may even be thinking of a specific venue. In several ways, the version staged in *Contention* makes good practical sense. The curtain is still drawn to conceal Gloucester when the royal party enters. Henry revives from his swoon and Warwick and Salisbury enter to say that the commons are angry because they have heard that Gloucester was killed by Suffolk and Cardinal Beaufort. Warwick suggests to Henry that they should "Enter [Gloucester's] priuy chamber my lord, and view the body" (E2ᵛ), and a stage direction supplies the next action:

Warwicke drawes the curtaines and shewes Duke Humphrey in his bed. (E3ʳ)

The body is then visible for some undetermined amount of time before the curtains must be necessarily drawn closed. An obvious opportunity for this stage action would be when Cardinal Beaufort exits. This long scene in *Contention* then continues with the commons calling for Suffolk's death and ends with Suffolk and Margaret, alone, and kissing before he departs. It seems certain that Gloucester's body is no longer visible throughout these lengthy exchanges, and it would be morbidly absurd if still visible during Suffolk and Margaret's farewell. The very next scene begins with the curtains being drawn back open again. "*and then the curtaines be drawne, and the Cardinall is discouered in his bed, rauing and staring as if he were mad*" (F1ᵛ). *Contention* is markedly different in practical terms from what is required in *2 Henry VI*, where the bed is "put forth" by some unknown party ("*Bed put forth*"; 11.132.1) some 113 lines after Henry swoons. The Folio text also does not offer any provision for when the bed should be withdrawn, but, as I have suggested with *Contention* and in my edition of *2 Henry VI*, the exit of Cardinal Beaufort marks a natural terminus in the action.

Having worked through the practicalities of staging for both plays, we can now consider how the versions employ different affective registers, conditioning how audiences might respond to the represented history. I shall focus here on the aftermath to the murder, similar in both versions, where the body of Gloucester is seen in the bed (whether revealed in Q or wheeled on as in F). It is Warwick who provides the commentary on Gloucester's appearance in both versions. In a short speech in Q, Warwick deduces that "violent hands were laid" on Gloucester's life (E3ʳ). Speaking from past experience, Warwick offers the following evidence for murder:

> Oft haue I seene a timely parted ghost,
> Of ashie semblance, pale and bloudlesse:
> But loe, the bloud is setled in the face,
> More better coloured, then when he liude,
> His well proportioned beard made rough and sterne,
> His fingers spread abroad as one that graspt for life,
> Yet was by strength surprisde, the least of these are probable,
> It cannot chuse but he was murthered.
>
> (E3ʳ)

With the version of the script transmitted by *Contention* an audience would, of course, have seen Gloucester's fingers spread out as he grasped for life. Whatever method of murder was chosen in performance, they would have seen it enacted and watched the blood blush on Gloucester's face during his fatal struggle. In performance, the reappearance of Gloucester amounts, in effect, to a sort of postmortem inspection of a scene already witnessed. The deduction merely recounts what an audience would already know to have occurred, and there is little need for Warwick to expand any more on what he sees.

Contrast this, then, with the Folio text, where the murder has taken place off stage. In the version of the script transmitted by this version, an audience would have heard that Gloucester made penance before his death but know nothing of how the murder was effected. Warwick's much longer set of deductions in *2 Henry VI*, works, in effect, to create a scene in the minds of the audience for that which has not been witnessed:

> See how the blood is setled in his face.
> Oft haue I seene a timely-parted Ghost,
> Of ashy semblance, meager, pale, and bloodlesse,
> Being all descended to the labouring heart,
> Who in the Conflict that it holds with death,
> Attracts the same for aydance 'gainst the enemy,
> Which with the heart there cooles, and ne're returneth,

> To blush and beautifie the Cheeke againe.
> But see, his face is blacke, and full of blood:
> His eye-balles further out, than when he liued,
> Staring full gastly, like a strangled man:
> His hayre vprear'd, his nostrils stretcht with strugling:
> His hands abroad display'd, as one that graspt
> And tugg'd for Life, and was by strength subdude.
> Looke on the sheets his haire (you see) is sticking,
> His well proportion'd Beard, made ruffe and rugged,
> Like to the Summers Corne by Tempest lodged:
> It cannot be but he was murdred heere,
> The least of all these signes were probable.
>
> (11.146–64)

Warwick's set of imploring instructions to his listeners ("See how … But see … Looke on") and his affective description of what Gloucester's appearance must mean ("ashy semblance … face is blacke … eyeballes further out … full gastly … nostrils stretcht … tugg'd for Life"), induces an imaginative leap for audiences akin to that invited by the Chorus's opening speech in *Henry V*. Regardless of how the actor playing the corpse of Gloucester appears onstage, Warwick's blazon-like cataloguing of the unseen horrors implied by its strange appearance produces an emotionally arresting and visceral remembering of an unwitnessed past. Here, an episode from the past, which has not been selected to be represented in the drama, is instead memorialized vividly through a sort of historical reconstruction from slight evidence.

De-siloing Critical Practice

I began with the question of choice with the representation of historical episodes in early modern drama. While the murder of Gloucester is crucial to the plot of both *Contention* and *2 Henry VI*, its depiction represents a series of choices by the dramatist or dramatists writing their respective set of scenes that are at once highly pragmatic, setting out what is required in terms of personnel and properties, and attuned to the audience experience. They amount to two different authorial visions for Gloucester's murder: while *Contention* shows, *2 Henry VI* tells. *Contention* favors the instantly gratifying spectacle of staged violence, while *2 Henry VI* favors speech and inducing the power of imagination. The shift in the affective tenor and power such a choice makes in the Folio text should not be understated: Warwick's speech in *2 Henry VI*, in substance and effect, replaces the murder scene from *Contention*, enabling the audience to 'watch' the murder through the deductions drawn from the material witness; indeed, such history-making by Warwick functions as a synecdoche for the genre of early modern historical dramatic writing at large. Shakespeare's choice to tell rather than show is a choice to delay the gratification of the audience, building both suspense and emotional import.

Earlier I noted the textual argument that Shakespeare revised all three parts of *Henry VI* after the formation of the Chamberlain's Men. Might the treatment of the murder of Gloucester belong to this later phase of revision? Certainly, scenes 9–12 (3.1–3.4) in *2 Henry VI* – that is, the plotting scene, the fleeing from the murder scene, the discovery of the murder scene, and Beaufort's bedridden death scene – were primarily written by Shakespeare. The independent statistical studies of Craig-Burrows and Segarra et al. agree on Shakespeare's authorship.[25] This is the largest section of sustained writing in the Folio text that the two studies agree on for Shakespeare, and thus it seems plausible that this might be a section which has been reworked thoroughly.[26] If belonging to a revision by Shakespeare, then why might he have focused on the murder of Gloucester as a site for changes?

Here we might return to Marlowe's *Edward II* and the correspondences between the means of death suggested for Gloucester and Edward II in the chronicle sources. Writing about this correspondence, Claire Saunders settled on the idea that what is implied by the stage directions in *Contention* and in the dialogue of the Folio text is that Gloucester was simply smothered.[27] Saunders observed, however, that the editorial tradition has helped blur the line between the deaths of Gloucester and Edward: "This obvious link with the chronicled murder of Duke Humphrey is obscured in Dover Wilson's and Cairncross's editions of *2 Henry VI*. Both editors bowdlerize Hall, omitting 'some affirme that a hote spitte was put in his foundement.'"[28] Such editorial prudence alters our framework for interpretative engagement with the murder in the Folio text. Editors and critics working from the Folio are necessarily influenced by the *presence* of the murder scene, and its method, in the quarto; thus, an editor of the Folio might at least note how the murder was achieved in the quarto: smothering. Yet the Folio is remarkably silent about how Gloucester dies, detailing only the signs of an extreme physical experience, and leaving open the possibility that Gloucester died by a means more brutal than smothering.

It is perhaps instructive in this light to consider the vague nature of the stage action recorded in the early quarto of *Edward II* (1594). Lightborne, the murderer, asks his accomplices for a "spit, and let it be a red hote" as well as "a table and a featherbed." In the passage containing the murder itself, however, no stage direction was included:

Light.   Runne for the table.
Edw.   O spare me, or dispatch me in a trice.
Light.   So, lay the table downe, and stampe his body.
   But not too hard, least that you bruse his body.
Matreuis.   I feare mee that this crie will raise the towne,
   And therefore let vs take horse and away.²⁹

Editors of Marlowe have sought to resolve the staging uncertainties by interpolating their own stage directions or supplying extended glossarial notes, often drawing on Holinshed, to supply the imagined sequence of action. The "crie" that will "raise the towne," also recorded in Holinshed's vivid description of Edward II's death, suggests that no smothering was involved in early performance. Quite what exactly was performed when the play was first staged in the early 1590s is unknown, but the textual opacity of the printed quarto alerts us to the sensitivities of conveying such information via print. The officially approved copy of the script was likely similarly sparse in detail. After all, the only people who truly needed to know how to perform the scene were the actors. The copy which eventually found its way to print could have been censored, but it also need not explain how the scene worked exactly in performance.

The stage directions included in *Contention* note that Gloucester is smothered by two men lying on his breast. As we have only this prescribed stage action in either the quarto or Folio – and because of the vexed relationship between the two texts – then perhaps it is natural for readers, editors, and critics to assume that the stage action prescribed in one is that which is missing in the other. But this need not necessarily be the case. Saunders makes the valuable point that the absence of the death scene in the Folio text "encourages the audience's imagination to prepare for this visual climax, the display of the body," and that "until the bed and its occupant are actually presented to the view, they exert a powerful hold on the imagination; the power lies precisely in the hidden presence, elaborated by anticipation."³⁰ The audience must wait, as Saunders notes, some 150 lines for the body to appear and they have no idea what has happened to cause Gloucester's death. Earlier in the Folio text, the murderers' comments about Gloucester's good penance – offering a glimpse of a good death drawn from a horrible murder – introduce a lived experience left unseen.³¹ Warwick's deductions establish a historical opacity about Gloucester's death which mirrors the uncertainties of chronicle history. The revelation of Gloucester's corpse memorializes an unstaged past that can be reconstructed only through Warwick's commentary. The moment in history to be remembered – Gloucester's murder – has, after all, already passed in the timeline of the play, just as night turned to day.

Saunders imagines a scenario whereby the death of Gloucester might influence Marlowe's depiction of the death of Edward II. This is possible, perhaps, in the context of the performed murder as transmitted by the quarto text, not least given what we now know about Shakespeare and Marlowe's coauthorship. But given the nature of Shakespeare's later revisions to the Folio text, it is also possible that the staging of Edward's death in Marlowe's play influenced Shakespeare's decision to not show Gloucester's death in the version represented by the Folio. I am not suggesting that we should imagine that Gloucester, in the world of the Folio play, was necessarily killed in the same way as Marlowe's protagonist. Rather, I want to note that the Folio version works very hard to ensure that such horrors are not precluded.

What we do not know is often more terrifying than what we do, and the decision to tell rather than show, or, at least, to restrict that which is shown to Gloucester's corpse, introduces a level of uncertainty about the circumstances of death that had been resolved more concretely in *Contention*.[32] That is, Shakespeare recognized that playing on the forces of an audience's imagination about what might have happened was potentially more effective in heightening the emotional distress of Gloucester's death than the blunt force of showing the murder on stage. Thus, Shakespeare seems to believe, perhaps in revising the version underlying the Folio text, that once we rid ourselves of the certainty of circumstance that the version underlying the quarto presents, then the imagined possibilities for how Gloucester may have died become even more affective; that is, the historical uncertainty of what Gloucester endured is worse than a performed representation of one version of an imagined past. This chapter has sought to explore how studies in text (what is transmitted) might speak to studies in affect (what is experienced) and memory (what is remembered). The disparity in the representation of Gloucester's murder between *Contention* and *2 Henry VI* presents an unusually acute example of how these areas might intersect, with textual variation illuminating how different versions of a history play not only variously memorialize an imagined version of the past but also deploy distinct affective registers in doing so.

Notes

1. See, for instance, the Arden 3 editions of *Hamlet*, ed. Ann Thompson and Neil Taylor, which prints all three versions of *Hamlet* in two volumes (London: Thompson Learning, 2006), or the multiple volumes of the *New Oxford Shakespeare* (Oxford University Press, 2016–17) and forthcoming *New Oxford Shakespeare: Complete Alternative Versions*, which includes editions of all of the substantive versions of Shakespeare's works.
2. See, for example, the articles in the recent *Critical Survey* special issue "Canonizing Q1 *Hamlet*," 31.1–2 (2019), guest edited by Terri Bourus.
3. On the affective turn in early modern studies, see this volume's Introduction, 00–00.
4. Indicative work in this area, sometimes expressly about Shakespeare's works, includes Jonathan Baldo, *Memory in Shakespeare's Histories: Stages of Forgetting in Early Modern England* (New York: Routledge, 2012); Isabel Karremann, *The Drama of Memory in Shakespeare's History Plays* (Cambridge University Press, 2015); and William E. Engel, Rory Loughnane, and Grant Williams, eds., *The Memory Arts in Renaissance England: A Critical Anthology* (Cambridge University Press, 2016). On the relationship between studies in memory and early modern historiography and antiquarianism, see the latter critical anthology, 185–89.
5. On the coauthorship of *1*, *2*, and *3 Henry VI*, see the play entries in Gary Taylor and Rory Loughnane, "The Canon and Chronology of Shakespeare's Works," in Gary Taylor and Gabriel Egan, eds., *The New Oxford Shakespeare: Authorship Companion* (Oxford University Press, 2017), 417–602.
6. Q3 introduces some significant variants and is not a straightforward reprinting. For discussion of these variants, see William Montgomery, "'Textual Introduction' to 'The First Part of the Contention (2 Henry VI),'" in Stanley Wells and Gary Taylor, eds., with John Jowett and William Montgomery, *William Shakespeare: A Textual Companion* (Oxford University Press, 1987), 175–77; and Rory Loughnane, "Shakespeare, Marlowe, and Traces of Authorship," in Andrew J. Power, ed., *The Birth and Death of the Author: A Multi-Authored History of Authorship* (New York: Routledge, 2020), 54–78.
7. Indeed, signaling the importance of Gloucester's murder in the early printed versions, the primary section of the full print title of Q1 continues as "... *with the death of the good Duke Humphrey*" (STC 26100).
8. I quote from Part 7 of the 1533 reprinting, *Fabyans cronucle* (London: Wyllyam Rastell, 1533; STC 10660), Ii2r. An early version of the Chronicles was first published in 1516 (STC 10659) as *Newe cronycles of Englande and of Fraunce*.
9. Edward Hall, *The vnion of the two noble and illustre famelies of Lancastre* [and] *Yorke* (London: Richard Grafton, 1548), Bb3v. Hall's account is repeated verbatim in Richard Grafton's *A chronicle at large* (London: Richarde Tottle and Humffrey Toye, 1569; STC 12147), Fff6r, alerting us to the recycling of historical narrative.

10 Raphael Holinshed and others, *The firste volume of the chronicles of England, Scotlande, and Irelande* (London: Lucas Harrison, 1577; STC 13568b), Hh5r.
11 *The last part of the Mirour for magistrates* (London: Thomas Marsh, 1578; STC 1252), G&H5v.
12 Ibid.
13 G&H6r; Fol. 4[8]r (the printing accidentally duplicates "Fol. 47"; there are several errors in foliation in the text).
14 Rory Loughnane, ed., *2 Henry VI*, in Gary Taylor, John Jowett, Terri Bourus, and Gabriel Egan, eds., *New Oxford Shakespeare: Critical Reference Edition* (Oxford University Press, 2017). All citations from the Folio text are to this edition.
15 For this scene break, see "Textual Introduction," in Loughnane, ed., *2 Henry VI*, 2742–43.
16 For some instances in later drama where this law is broken, see David Nicol, "'Exit at one door and enter at the other': The Fatal Re-entrance in Jacobean Drama," *Shakespeare Bulletin*, 37.2 (2019), 205–29.
17 A. S. Cairncross, the editor of *2 Henry VI* for Arden 2, thought *Contention* showed the following signs of being a reported text: "abbreviation, transposition of material, the use of synonyms, recollections external and internal; with inferior metre, and verse wrongly divided as prose"; see *King Henry VI Part I* (London: Methuen, 1962), xxi. Also cited in Laurie Maguire, *Shakespearean Suspect Texts: The "Bad" Quartos and Their Contexts* (Cambridge University Press, 1996), 9.
18 Ibid., 237–38.
19 While we should be cautious in treating character studies as evidence for textual provenance and transmission, both scholars observe rather puzzling alterations in character between *Contention* and the Folio text and use these to advance contrasting theories of transmission. Using Margaret for her case study, Kreps proposes that the Folio text represents a revised and enlarged version of the earlier *Contention* version. Using Eleanor, Manley claims that *Contention* represents a revised and abridged version of the earlier Folio text. See Barbara Kreps, "Bad Memories of Margaret? Memorial Reconstruction versus Revision in *The First Part of the Contention* and *2 Henry VI*," *Shakespeare Quarterly*, 51:2 (2000), 154–80; and Lawrence Manley, "From Strange's Men to Pembroke's Men: *2 Henry VI* and *The First Part of the Contention*," *Shakespeare Quarterly*, 54.3 (2003), 253–87.
20 See "Textual Introduction," in Loughnane, ed., *2 Henry VI*, 2742–43.
21 Gary Taylor and I argue that these revisions were part of a set of revisions he undertook with *1, 2,* and *3 Henry VI* to create a play sequence, with *Richard III*, for the newly formed company. See play entries in Taylor and Loughnane, "The Canon and Chronology," 417–602.
22 On Marlowe as coauthor, see Hugh Craig, "The Three Parts of *Henry VI*," in Hugh Craig and Arthur F. Kinney, eds., *Shakespeare, Computers, and the Mystery of Authorship* (Cambridge University Press, 2009), 40–77; Santiago Segarra, Mark Eisen, Gabriel Egan, and Alejandro Ribeiro, "Attributing the

Authorship of the 'Henry VI' Plays by Word Adjacency," *Shakespeare Quarterly*, 67.2 (2016), 232–56; and Taylor and Loughnane, "The Canon and Chronology," 417–602. For *3 Henry VI*, see Hugh Craig and John Burrows, "A Collaboration about a Collaboration: The Authorship of King Henry VI, Part Three," in Marilyn Deegan and Willard McCarty, eds., *Collaborative Research in the Digital Humanities: A Volume in Honour of Harold Short, on the Occasion of His 65th Birthday and His Retirement, September 2010* (Farnham: Ashgate, 2012), 27–65.

23 See Maguire, *Shakespearean Suspect Texts*, on the specificity of staging requirements and its relationship to theories about memorial reconstruction: "The New Bibliographers glossed over the difficulty of presenting those suspect texts which require complicated or sophisticated staging facilities such as balconies, discovery spaces, and trapdoors (certainly in combination) in other than well-equipped theatres," 212. *Contention*, as Maguire notes, specifies the use of two doors and a curtained recess (for the murder of Gloucester and death of Beaufort).

24 Maguire, *Shakespearean Suspect Texts*, 238. Maguire further notes that Jane Howell's BBC film version of *2 Henry VI* often adopts readings and action from *Contention*, 238.

25 See Taylor and Loughnane, "The Canon and Chronology," 496.

26 Of course, contrariwise, it could be a set of scenes that Shakespeare wrote and was satisfied with in the version preceding any act of revisions. Neither possibility can be excluded.

27 Claire Saunders, "'Dead in His Bed': Shakespeare's Staging of the Death of the Duke of Gloucester in *2 Henry VI*," *The Review of English Studies*, 36.141 (1985), 19–34.

28 Ibid., 24 n.

29 Christopher Marlowe, *The troublesome raigne and lamentable death of Edward the second* (London: William Iones, 1594; STC 17437), M1r.

30 Ibid., 28.

31 On dying well in the early modern period, see Maggie Vinter, *Last Acts: The Art of Dying on the Early Modern Stage* (New York: Fordham University Press, 2019).

32 See also Frederika Bain, "The Affective Scripts of Early Modern Execution and Murder," in Richard Meek and Erin Sullivan, eds., *The Renaissance of Emotion: Understanding Affect in Shakespeare and His Contemporaries* (Manchester University Press, 2015), 221–40.

CHAPTER 12

Memory, Affect, and the Multiverse
From the History Plays to The Merry Wives of Windsor

Evelyn Tribble

The characters in Shakespeare's English chronicle histories are obsessed with and oppressed by memory. They return time and again to affect-laden recollections of painful moments in the past. In the *Henry VI* plays and *Richard III*, characters continually advert to the death of children, especially Rutland's death in *3 Henry VI*. Throughout *Richard III*, characters time and again recall the moment at which Margaret proffers the bloody handkerchief "steeped in Rutland's blood" (4.4.278) to his father York. Likewise, the characters in *1 and 2 Henry IV* constantly ruminate, brood on, and rehearse the past. They hark back continually to Richard's deposition, recalling with vivid particularity (and, often, with great inaccuracy) the events that have led to the present debacle. The characters often seem trapped within their past traumas, which they rehearse with sometimes obsessive attention.

In the context of this almost pathological co-rumination, in which past pain is cultivated, carried about, rehearsed, distorted, and amplified, *The Merry Wives of Windsor* demonstrates the attraction of amnesia. While scholars have tried to shoehorn the events of *Merry Wives* into timelines of the Henriad plays, these schemes do not account for the complete erasure of the past of the Henry plays that characterizes *Merry Wives*, the sense that the characters are both immediately recognizable and somehow altered. I argue that one way of approaching the relationship is to think of the plays as a multiverse. In contrast to storyworlds, which retain a shared backstory for the characters, the multiverse "is a set of mutually incompatible storyworlds."[1] In *The Shakespeare Multiverse: Fandom as Literary Praxis*, Valerie M. Fazel and Louise Geddes argue that "the Shakespeare multiverse is an infinite variety of discrete, developed, developing and nascent worlds and universes, each built from circulations of Shakespeare."[2] Their expansive and optimistic view of the Shakespeare multiverse provocatively positions the 1623 Folio publication as "the first material evidence of Shakespeare fandom,"[3] a founding act in the Shakespearean multiverse. In this chapter, I argue that Shakespeare himself creates the multiverse, or perhaps it is more accurate to say that the fan energy that accrues around an unexpectedly magnetic character – Falstaff – propels the character out of the cycle of rumination of the history plays. In fact, this transition begins with *2 Henry IV*, which might be seen as a work of fan fiction/nostalgia still tethered to the trajectory of English chronicle history. Once ensconced within the comic parameters of *Merry Wives*, the characters confine their memories to the immediate fiction of the play itself, and even within this framework they often forget rather than remember.

Rumination in the History Plays

As Jonathan Baldo and Isabel Karremann have established, the characters in Shakespeare's histories are burdened by memory.[4] One response to the overpowering weight of memory is strategic forgetting, a subject both Baldo and Jooni Koonce Dunn have explored.[5] Yet for many characters in the histories, especially those on the losing side, such strategies fail; instead, the characters ruminate and brood on the past, continually repeating accounts of traumatic events. In some cases, they have not witnessed the events of which they speak firsthand, but they nevertheless return to them almost obsessively. Psychologists who have studied the process of rumination have established that victims of traumatic experience often reexperience these events in "intrusive recollections, distressing dreams, memory flashbacks, or overreactions when exposed to cues remembering the traumatic situations" and that they "commonly evidence an insatiable need to talk about their negative emotional experience."[6]

One example of such obsessive remembering is Hotspur's continual rehearsal of the events that led to the Percy/Northumberland support of Bullingbroke in *Richard II*. In Act 2, scene 3, of *Richard II*, Northumberland escorts Henry to Berkeley Castle; the two are joined by "young Harry Percy" (2.3.21), who meets the then-Duke of Herford for the first time. As it is presented in *Richard II*, the meeting is relatively unremarkable. Percy at first fails to acknowledge Bullingbroke, leading to his father's rebuke: "Have you forgot the Duke of Herford, boy?" (2.3.36). Harry replies that he has never met the Duke: "[T]hat is not forgot / Which ne'er I did remember" (2.3.37–38). At this point he formally acknowledges him:

> My gracious lord, I tender you my service,
> Such as it is, being tender, raw and young,
> Which elder days shall ripen and confirm
> To more approvèd service and desert.
> (2.3.41–44)

Bullingbroke replies:

> I thank thee, gentle Percy, and be sure
> I count myself in nothing else so happy
> As in a soul remembering my good friends,
> And as my fortune ripens with thy love
> It shall be still thy true love's recompense.
> My heart this covenant makes, my hand thus seals it.
> (2.3.45–50)

Within the context of the larger dynamics in *Richard II*, on its face this moment seems much less memorable than the subsequent events of the scene. The primary focus of Act 2, scene 3, is the shifting allegiance of the Archbishop of York, who upbraids his nephew for his disloyalty but later relents in the face of Bullingbroke's assurances and the barely veiled threats from Northumberland, Ross, and Willoughby. York's ostensibly offhand offer of hospitality, in which he invites Bullingbroke and his companions to "enter in the castle / And there repose you for this night" (2.3.159–60), is rightly seen as the decisive turning point for Henry's bid for the throne. Only in retrospect – or, proleptically, from the knowledge of the subsequent unraveling of the alliance – can the significance of the moment for Hotspur be grasped.

This moment is remembered with advantages at a crucial juncture in *1 Henry IV*. The confrontation between King Henry and the Northumberland faction about Hotspur's prisoners and the fate of Mortimer in *1 Henry IV* triggers a cascade of memories of Bullingbroke's status as a "poor unminded outlaw" (4.3.58) prior to gaining the support of the Northumberland faction. Now king in Act 1, scene 3, of *1 Henry IV*, Henry is intent on asserting his authority. He expels Worcester from the court for reminding him that his "greatness" is due to their efforts: "which our own hands / Have helped to make so portly" (1.3.12–13). Rejecting Hotspur's attempt to justify refusing the prisoners, Henry humiliates him by a deliberately insulting address: "Art thou not ashamed? But sirrah, henceforth / Let me not hear you speak of Mortimer" (1.3.116–17). "Sirrah" of course is a form of address reserved for inferiors, servants, and recalcitrant boys and as such reminds Hotspur of his inferior status.

Hotspur is propelled into a tailspin of emotion; "[d]runk with choler" (1.3.127), he reminds his uncle and father that they "set the crown / Upon the head of this forgetful man" (1.3.158–59). Some 100 lines later, he returns to that moment, so "beyond the bounds of patience" (197) that he forgets the name of the place "where I first bowed my knee / Unto this king of smiles, this Bullingbrooke" (241–42):[7]

> Why, what a candy deal of courtesy
> This fawning greyhound then did proffer me!
> "Look when his infant fortune came to age,"
> And "gentle Harry Percy," and "kind cousin."
> O, the devil take such cozeners.
>
> (1.3.246–50)

This account is accurate in its general outlines, but it omits, conflates, and adds a good deal, at least as compared with Act 2, scene 3, of *Richard II*. Henry refers to Hotspur as an "infant warrior" (3.2.113) when upbraiding Hal in *1 Henry IV*; however, in *Richard II* he mentions only his own "infant fortune" (2.3.66). And although Henry is indeed courteous to the Northumberland faction – of necessity, given his unfriended state – in *Richard II* much of the "fawning" and "candy courtesy" that Hotspur describes comes from Northumberland himself, who compares Bullingbroke's "fair discourse" to "sugar, / Making the hard way sweet and delectable" (2.3.6–7), a bit of flattery comically at odds with Henry's apparent taciturnity in that scene. And while Hotspur recalls that he kneeled or "bowed my knee" to the king, the stage action in *Richard II* is by no means clear. The editor of the Cambridge edition, Andrew Gurr, notes that "[w]ith such an offer [of service] Percy might be expected to kneel to Bullingbrook. At [line] 50 however they shake hands. It is likely that at this point he does not make to the 'Duke' the gesture of loyalty he could make to the king."[8] Hotspur's humiliation in the present, then, may color his recollection of the past.

Such misremembering, conflation, and confabulation are typical of what we know of the fundamentally reconstructive nature of memory. Each act of recollection is new; memory is not a replay of an original event but a palimpsest of past moments of recollection, overlaid with the emotions and memories of subsequent events.[9] Thus Hotspur's outrage, anger, and hurt pride at Henry's treatment of him in the present fuels his memory of the past capitulation, adding emotional color and layering subsequent events into the act of recollection. The narrow focus of this memory – focusing not on the historical turning point but on Henry's words to him and his act of fealty – is also characteristic of the intensely personal and affective nature of recollection; Hotspur focuses on a moment that may have little meaning to anyone but him. Yet Shakespeare also frames the mnemonic moment within a much wider pattern of national memory which locates Richard's deposition as the originary moment of civil war. As the Bishop of Carlisle asks in *Richard II*, "[w]hat subject can give sentence on his king?" (4.1.121).

These recollections overwhelm and engulf the present; Hotspur seems compelled to ruminate on his grievances even in the face of imminent danger. On the eve of battle, Sir Walter Blunt visits to ask the rebels to name "[t]he nature of your griefs" (*1H4*, 4.3.42) for a possible pardon. Hotspur takes the invitation all too literally, launching into a prolix recollection of Henry's treachery and ingratitude to his father, speaking for thirty-six lines before Sir Walter interrupts him impatiently: "Tut, I came not to hear this" (4.3.88). Hotspur simply finishes his rant, claiming that the king "[b]roke oath on oath, committed wrong on wrong" (4.3.101), forgoing the opportunity to avert the conflict and leaving himself vulnerable to Worcester's lies. The "insatiable need to talk"[10] that characterizes rumination maroons Hotspur in the past.

King Henry himself is equally stranded; he continually adverts to the past in self-interested and self-regarding ways. In *2 Henry IV*, Henry indulges in a prolonged reminiscence of the events on the past ten years, in which nearly all the details he recounts are wrong:

> But which of you was by –
> [*to Warwick*] You, cousin Nevil, as I may remember –
> When Richard, with his eye brimful of tears,
> Then checked and rated by Northumberland,
> Did speak these words, now proved prophecy:
> "Northumberland, thou ladder by the which
> My cousin Bullingbrooke ascends my throne"?
> Though then, God knows, I had no such intent
>   (3.1.64–71)

Warwick was in fact not present in Shakespeare's *Richard II*, and Henry recasts Richard's words "The mounting Bullingbrook" (*R2*, 5.1.56) into the more neutral "cousin Bolinbroke." Moreover, the disclaimer "then, God knows, I had no such intent" utterly misremembers the context of the scene, which takes place *after* the deposition scene of Act 4, scene 1, and concludes with Henry's announcement of the day of his coronation. Consistent with the self-serving nature of recollection, Henry conflates this moment with the disingenuous disavowals of his intention after he lands at Ravensburgh, in particular, his kneeling to Richard once the King has effectively conceded to him.

"As I may remember" could almost serve as a subtitle for *2 Henry IV*, since the play consistently traffics in nostalgia.[11] Henry ruminates and misremembers his past; Shallow recalls seeing Falstaff when he was a young page, "a crack not thus high" (3.2.24), and Mistress Quickly indulges in obsessive recollection of the moment that Falstaff proposed to her "sitting in my Dolphin chamber at the round table by a sea-coal fire, upon Wednesday in Wheeson week, when the prince broke thy head for liking his father to a singing man of Windsor" (2.1.67–70).[12] In his Arden edition, James Bulman argues that the tavern scene in *2 Henry IV* "has made generation of playgoers nostalgic for the vibrant comedy of the tavern scene in *Part One*."[13]

These recollections are part of a wider pattern of reminiscence that pervades *2 Henry IV*, which may contribute to the perception that the play is a "diminished shadow of its predecessor."[14] As Bulman points out, this perspective reflects "the problem of being second-born," an assumption that the play is "an uninspired sequel,"[15] unaccountably backtracking from the apparent reformation of the Prince at the end of Part 1. Bulman argues that Shakespeare may have originally intended a two-part structure along the lines of the anonymous play *The Famous Victories*, with Part 1 ending with the Battle of Shrewsbury and the death of Hotspur, and the second tracing the arc from Henry IV's death to Henry V's victory at Agincourt. Bulman suggests that "when *Henry IV* proved hugely successful in performance, [Shakespeare] decided to write a sequel which would foreground the exploits of Falstaff and his followers."[16] This "opportunistic sequel" sheds much of the historical material and allows Falstaff to become a "free agent,"[17] up until the point at which history must have its way and expel him at the play's conclusion. Similarly, Giorgio Melchiori, who edited *Merry Wives* for the Arden 3 series as well as *2 Henry VI* for the Cambridge edition, argues that the latter is an "unplanned sequel."[18]

In this account of *2 Henry IV* Falstaff and his orbit are both free from and tethered to history. Bulman argues that "sequels do not demand consistency of plot to be effective";[19] indeed, Falstaff operates as what Shane Denson has described as a "serial figure" who "exists *as* a series – as the concatenation of instantiations that evolves, not within a homogeneous diegetic space, but *between* or *across* such spaces of narration." Isabel Karremann has argued that Falstaff is a quintessential example of a such a figure, possessing "conspicuously accumulating traces" that render him recognizable across time, space, and media.[20] If Bulman's account of the origins of *2 Henry IV* is correct, Falstaff could be seen as an early example of "fan practice."[21] In response to fan enthusiasm for Falstaff, Shakespeare takes a step toward the multiverse, partially unloosing Falstaff from history and expanding his orbit to include other figures such as Mistress Quickly and Pistol, both of whom are afforded a greater range of recognizable "traces" that they carry into *The Merry Wives of Windsor*.

Falstaff and Forgetting

In *2 Henry IV* Falstaff is still connected to history; it is he who must provide the final redemptive arc for Harry through the final rejection. If *2 Henry IV* is moored in reminiscence, nostalgia, and repetition, *The Merry Wives of Windsor* seems to have forgotten history altogether. Indeed, the place of the Falstaff of *Merry Wives of Windsor* in the Shakespearean canon has been subject to critical debate. Editors and critics have struggled to place *Merry Wives* within the framework of the histories, and it is often said that the Falstaff of *Merry Wives* is a different character from that of the histories.²² Those who admire the Falstaff of the history plays tend to be the fiercest critics of the Falstaff of *The Merry Wives*. A. C. Bradley remarked that "Falstaff was degraded by Shakespeare himself," and Anne Barton argued that "[t]he comedy itself constitutes a betrayal of Falstaff even worse than the one inflicted by Henry V."²³ The story that John Dennis told in his dedication to *The Comical Gallants: or The Amours of John Falstaff* (1702) that the "comedy was written at [Elizabeth's] demand ... and finished in fourteen days," repeated by Rowe in 1709 with the additional embellishment that Elizabeth wished to see "Falstaff in love," lingers in the critical tradition.²⁴ While most are skeptical of the story, it still lives on, attesting to its staying power as a way of accounting for the play's perceived departure from the Falstaff of the Henriad. The story's stickiness is interesting in itself, and it is often invoked by those who see the comic Falstaff as illegitimate, misremembered, or betrayed by his own creator. As Phyllis Rackin and Evelyn Gajowski write, "The myth of rapid composition to satisfy a royal command provided a convenient way to reconcile the play's supposed imperfections with the critics' faith in Shakespeare's transcendent genius."²⁵

Is one of the reasons that the "written at the command of the Queen" story still has such currency a resentment that a powerful woman is trying to dictate to Shakespeare? Harold Goddard writes, "Poets ... do not like commissions. It would be quite like Shakespeare, ordered by the Queen to write another play about Falstaff, to have his playful revenge by writing one about another man entirely, under the same name."²⁶ Harold Bloom, in his fan-fiction book entitled *Falstaff: Give Me Life*, describes *Merry Wives* "as a ghastly comedy that is an unacceptable travesty of Falstaff," composed by a grudging author engaged in "obedience and self-parody" at the behest of the Queen.[27] Elsewhere Bloom asserts that the Falstaff of *Merry Wives* is "a nameless imposter masquerading as the great Sir John Falstaff. Rather than yield to such usurpation, I shall call him pseudo-Falstaff throughout this brief discussion."[28] Bloom describes himself as a "Falstaffian" and refers to the plays in which the figure appears, omitting *Merry Wives*, as the "Falstaffiad." Like many ardent fans, Bloom is irate about the violation of the rules of his beloved storyworld. No Star Wars fanboy could be more outraged about the intrusion of women and ethnic minorities into their universe than Bloom is about the assault that *Merry Wives* represents to his conception of Falstaff.[29] Bloom's is a form of fandom that attempts to police boundaries rather than expand them, to delimit a canon rather than revel in multiplicity. Fazel and Geddes describe such attitudes as "antefandom," which they define as a "defensive strategy designed to keep out anything that might contaminate the fan object and, by extension, the attached fan."[30]

As Harriet Phillips suggests, "The paradox is that Falstaff is chronically out of place in a play to which he is nevertheless indispensable."[31] Some editors and critics have attempted to invent a timeline that might fit Falstaff, Bardolph, Pistol, and Mistress Quickly within the fictional universe of the history plays. In the note on Mistress Quickly in his edition, Giorgio Melchiori suggests that Shakespeare imagined that "after the rejection of Falstaff in *Two Henry IV* and before the French campaign in *Henry V*, Quickly had moved with Falstaff, Bardolph, and Pistol to Windsor, taking a job as a private housekeeper."[32] Perhaps. But they seem to have become amnesiacs in the process, as though subjected to a *Men in Black*–style neuralyzer that has erased their memory of past events. Sandwiching the characters into a plausible timeline does not account for the complete erasure of the past of the *Henry* plays that characterizes *Merry Wives*, the sense that the characters are both immediately recognizable and somehow altered. In one sense, Bloom is correct to see the disjuncture between the Falstaff he so prizes and the characters who inhabit *Merry Wives*. But rather than policing the Falstaffian storyworld, as Bloom advocates, we might instead imagine the characters inhabiting a Shakespeare multiverse in the spirit of Fazel and Geddes. In contrast to storyworlds, which retain a shared backstory for the characters, the multiverse "is a set of mutually incompatible storyworlds."[33] Characters enter alternative realities, in which, for example, Batman might be able to fly rather than simply mess about with gadgets, or in which their backstories and/or some essential features are altered.

Navigating multiverses is not easy for readers/viewers, who must hold in memory the rules of the original storyworld while negotiating an altered reality. As Kukkonen notes, multiverses create cognitive demands on their audiences. Although inhabiting alternative universes that ignore and rewrite their histories, the characters must be memorable enough to be recognizable as somehow the same: "because a baseline reality is often difficult to discern within this constellation of worlds, the multiverse poses considerable processing challenges."[34] She argues that creators of such fictions "deploy a range of strategies to help readers navigate this multiverse of mutually incompatible realities." One of these is the use of iconographic elements in their representation, which work as a kind of "cognitive shortcut" or heuristic to help readers to navigate the newly unfamiliar world: "This strategy enabl[es] them to keep different character versions distinct and connect them to their original storyworlds."[35] The use of such iconographic mnemonic markers has, I believe, useful analogues to the particular practices of early modern theater.

Falstaff doesn't wear a superhero cape, of course, but he nevertheless possesses a highly memorable iconography, which William Engel has described as his "egregious silhouette."[36] Early in *Merry Wives* Falstaff proudly surveys his "portly belly" (1.3.45), reminding the audience of his most salient characteristic in the histories. As Wilder points out, the physicality of the actor playing Falstaff renders him unmistakable, both to audiences and to the other characters in the cycle. Both Wilder and Engel note that in *Henry V*, Fluellen recalls Falstaff not by his name but by his distinctive kinesthetic and verbal signatures: he tells Gower that Henry "turned away the fat knight with the great belly doublet. He was full of jests and gypes and knaveries and mocks – I have forgot his name" (4.7.38–40). In a repertory system, audiences were used to seeing the same actors play different parts on a daily basis; this must have been – and still is – one of the real pleasures of recognition in the theater. But actors had to create the *same* character, in a multiverse in which the familiar trappings of the plays – the Boar's Head tavern, the court, the battlefields – are missing, and from which the familiar, larger cast of characters in the histories is absent.

So, the materials of theater from which the 'same' characters inhabit a different universe are these: the body of the actor, the costumes, and their kinesthetic and affective signatures. As I have discussed elsewhere, kinesthetic signatures are those little ways of moving, taking a breath, pausing, walking, holding one's head, handling a weapon, moving a hand.[37] These are all the subtle yet unmistakable movements that enable acts of recognition of the actor behind the character. So telling are they that they can be used as a form of allusion. Will West has termed some moments "intertheatricality," physical business that moves across parts and also across actors, as distinctive physical styles and gestures are imitated.[38] These physical signatures, I argue, are closely tied to the characteristic mode of speech of each character. Shakespeare often seems to suggest bearing and gesture from the distinctive speech patterns he writes for his characters. Late in *Cymbeline*, for example, Belarius recognizes Cloten because "[t]he snatches in his voice, / And burst of speaking were as his" (4.2.104–5).[39] For an expert actor, especially in Shakespeare's time, this verbal tic would be part of a package of traits of gesture and gait. Action and accent are conjoined, so that "snatches" and "bursts of speaking" may well cue an equal lack of control over the body in movement – which fits well with Cloten's poor swordplay, his incontinent sweating, and his swearing. They are also closely linked to their affective signatures, to the pleasures of repetition, recognition, and variation that mark fan practice. Fazel and Geddes note that "affective attachment" can be a "driving force for new creations."[40] It is possible that the affective attachment of the public to Falstaff is behind both the peculiar structure of *2 Henry IV* and the comedic multiverse explored in *The Merry Wives of Windsor*. While the story of Queen Elizabeth desiring to see "Falstaff in love" is no doubt apocryphal, the impulse to see a beloved character in an unfamiliar setting, taking paths closed off in the original storyworld, is a hallmark of fan practice.

Indeed, particular kinesthetic and verbal signatures may provide insight into which features of the characters were especially valued. The characters of *Merry Wives* are transported from their history-world into a comic genre with a different set of expectations and possibilities. They may have lost their personal histories but they retain distinctive kinesthetic and verbal signatures. As in *2 Henry IV*, Shallow's manner of speaking is marked by repetitions and hesitancies: "Sir, he's a good dog and a fair dog. Can there be more said? He is good, and fair" (*MW*, 1.1.75–76). He retains also his reminiscing about physical feats from his younger days, combined with sententiousness: "though I now be old and of the peace, if I see a sword out, my finger itches to make one ... we have some salt of our youth in us. We are the sons of women, Master Page" (2.3.34–38).

Pistol similarly retains his characteristic explosive style of speech, his choler, and his swagger. He is known in *2 Henry IV* for taglines from bombastic plays from the late 1580s and early 1590s, such as his parody of the *Muly Mahomet* line, "feed and be fat, my fair Calipolis" (2.4.143). His first line in the folio *Merry Wives* is a similar tagline from an old play:

"How now, Mephostophilus?" (1.1.105). The staccato rhythms of his speech and his use of fricatives and affricates are part of his recognizable "iconography" that is consistent across the multiverse: "I combat challenge of this latten bilbo! / Word of denial in thy *labras* here! / Word of denial! Froth and scum, thou liest" (1.1.128–30). The language here propels the character into a series of aggressive gestures that produce his on-brand swagger. Bardolph retains his characteristic red face, and Mistress Quickly, despite being placed in a completely different profession and environment, retains her malapropisms and her intended or unintended double entendres. Taken together, these verbal and kinesthetic signatures, embedded in the actors' bodies, would have acted as powerful memory traces that link them across the plays, making them instantly recognizable despite their altered environment. Claims that they are somehow 'different' characters neglect the overriding mnemonic salience of theatrical, embodied presentation – as opposed to a textually oriented assessment of the characters' consistency. This point perhaps explains the continual popularity of the play on stage even during its critical eclipse in the twentieth century.

By way of conclusion, let us consider how attractive the prospect of amnesia is. As we have seen, the history plays carry a heavy burden of memory; rumination is painful and blocks action in the present. Moving the characters into a comic multiverse allows them, at least within the parameters of this fiction, to forget the past grievances and searing memories, including the devastating renouncing of Falstaff at the end of *2 Henry IV*. The characters in *Merry Wives* confine their memories to the immediate fiction of the play itself, and even within this framework often forget rather than remember. The quarrel that begins the play between Shallow and Slender, on the one side, and Falstaff, Pistol, and Nim, on the other, is never alluded to again after the first scene. Falstaff's repeated acceptance of invitations to dally with Mistress Page and Mistress Ford, even after they have taken their first revenge, seem to indicate forgetfulness, irrepressible optimism, or perverse desire.[41] The terrifying punishment of Falstaff at the end of the play is determinedly forgotten by the characters, as Mistress Page invites all home to "laugh this sport o'er by a country fire / Sir John and all" (5.5.213–14). Only forgetting guarantees the happy ending of the comic genre. Perhaps the appeal of the multiverse to fans is similar: a chance to forget the constraints and accretions of the past. But I would not necessarily then consign *Merry Wives* to the realm of pure nostalgia; the anger of Falstaff stans such as Bloom at the toppling of their bad-boy hero points to more complex implications of transporting Falstaff to a multiverse ruled, at least temporarily, by women.

Notes

1. Karin Kukkonen, "Navigating Infinite Earths: Readers, Mental Models and the Multiverse of Superhero Comics," *Storyworlds: A Journal of Narrative Studies*, 2 (2010), 39–58, 40. See also Marie Laurie Ryan and Jan-Noel Thon, *Storyworlds across Media: Toward a Media-Conscious Narratology* (Lincoln: University of Nebraska Press, 2014). I'd like to give credit for my thinking along these lines to the students in my Fall 2018 Shakespeare and contemporaries class, and in particular to Julia Wold.
2. Valerie E. Fazel and Louise Geddes, *The Shakespeare Multiverse: Fandom as Literary Praxis* (New York: Routledge, 2022), 5.
3. Ibid, 42.
4. Jonathan Baldo, *Memory in Shakespeare's Histories: Stages of Forgetting in Early Modern England* (London: Routledge, 2012); Isabel Karremann, *The Drama of Memory in Shakespeare's History Plays* (Cambridge University Press, 2015).
5. Jonni Koonce Dunn, "The Functions of Forgetfulness in *1 Henry IV*," *Studies in Philology* 113:1 (2016), 82–100.
6. Bernard Rimé, "Mental Rumination, Social Sharing, and the Recovery from Emotional Exposure," in J. W. Pennebaker, ed., *Emotion, Disclosure, and Health* (Washington, DC: American Psychological Association, 1995), 271.
7. Karremann suggests that in this moment of forgetting, Hotspur "seeks to repress a shameful action in the past that is at odds with his exalted notion of honour" (*Drama of Memory*, 97).
8. Andrew Gurr, ed., *Richard II*, The New Cambridge Shakespeare (Cambridge University Press, 2003), note to 2.3.41.
9. This view of memory is well established; for an accessible introduction to the reconstructive view of memory, see Charles Fernyhough, *Pieces of Light: How the New Science of Memory Illuminates the Stories We Tell about Our Pasts* (New York: Harper, 2012).
10. Rimé, "Mental Rumination," 272.
11. See Harriet Phillips, *Nostalgia in Print and Performance, 1510–1613: Merry Worlds* (Cambridge University Press, 2019), for a discussion of nostalgia as a "market-driven process," 3.
12. Lina Perkins Wilder discusses Mistress Quickly's "capacious memory" in *Shakespeare's Memory Theatre: Recollection, Properties, and Character* (Cambridge University Press, 2010), 100.
13. James Bulman, ed., *King Henry IV, Part 2*. Arden Shakespeare Third Series (London: Bloomsbury, 2016), 59.
14. Stephen Booth, "Shakespeare in the San Francisco Bay Area," *Shakespeare Quarterly*, 29.2 (1978), 267–78; 270.
15. Bulman, *King Henry IV, Part 2*, 1.
16. Ibid., 15–16.
17. Ibid., 7.
18. See Giorgio Melchiori, ed., *The Merry Wives of Windsor*, Arden Shakespeare Third Series (London: Bloomsbury 2000), 15.

19 Bulman, *King Henry IV, Part 2*, 5.
20 Isabel Karremann, "Falstaff, Again (and Again): Configurations of Serial Memory in Early Modern Culture," unpublished paper, SAMEMES, Neuchâtel 2021, 3.
21 Fazel and Geddes, *The Shakespeare Multiverse*, 9.
22 See Rebecca Ann Bach, "Falstaff Becomes the (Hu)man at the Expense of *The Merry Wives of Windsor*," in Phyllis Rackin and Evelyn Gajowski, eds., *The Merry Wives of Windsor: New Critical Essays* (London: Routledge, 2015), 171–83, for a discussion of this phenomenon.
23 A. C. Bradley, "The Rejection of Falstaff," *Fortnightly Review*, 71(1904), 849; Anne Barton, "Falstaff and the Comic Community," in Barton, ed., *Essays, Mainly Shakespearean* (Cambridge University Press, 1994), 315.
24 See Melchiori, *The Merry Wives*, 2.
25 Rackin and Gajowski, "Introduction," in *Merry Wives of Windsor*, 9.
26 Harold Goddard, *The Meaning of Shakespeare* (University of Chicago Press, 1951), vol. I, 182.
27 Harold Bloom, *Falstaff: Give Me Life* (New York: Scribner, 2017), 53.
28 Harold Bloom, *Shakespeare: The Invention of the Human* (New York: Riverhead, 1998), 315.
29 An account of fan outrage at what is referred to as the "social justice warrior" subtext in J. J. Abrams's *The Last Jedi* can be found in Kate Erbland, "J. J. Abrams: 'Star Wars' Fans Who Didn't Like 'Last Jedi' Are 'Threatened' by Women Characters – Exclusive," IndieWire, February 16, 2018, www.indiewire.com/2018/02/jj-abrams-star-wars-last-jedi-women-1201929593/.
30 Fazel and Geddes, *The Shakespeare Multiverse*, 173.
31 Harriet Phillips, "Late Falstaff, the Merry World, and *The Merry Wives of Windsor*," *Shakespeare*, 10.2 (2014), 111–37; 112.
32 Melchiori, *The Merry Wives*, 123.
33 Kukkonen, "Navigating Infinite Earths," 55.
34 Ibid., 42.
35 Ibid., 43.
36 William E. Engel, "Handling Memory in the Henriad: Forgetting Falstaff," in Andrew Hiscock and Lina Perkins Wilder, eds., *The Routledge Handbook of Shakespeare and Memory* (New York: Routledge, 2018), 165–79; 166.
37 Evelyn Tribble, "Kinesic Intelligence on the Early Modern English Stage," in Kathryn Banks and Timothy Chesters, eds., *Movement in Renaissance Literature* (London: Palgrave Macmillan, 2018), 213–24.
38 William N. West, "Intertheatricality," in Henry S. Turner, ed., *Early Modern Theatricality* (Oxford University Press, 2018), 151–72.
39 I discuss this scene at some length in *Early Modern Actors and Shakespeare's Theatre: Thinking with the Body* (London: Bloomsbury, 2018).
40 Fazel and Geddes, *The Shakespeare Multiverse*, 5.
41 For the latter possibility, see Carol Thomas Neely, "Strange Things in Hand," in Valerie Traub, ed., *The Oxford Handbook of Shakespeare and Embodiment* (Oxford University Press, 2016).

CHAPTER 13

Cut Short All Intermission
Sound, Space, Memory, and Macduff's Grief

Lina Perkins Wilder

At the very end of Act 4 of Shakespeare's *Macbeth*, Ross arrives in England to meet the exiled Malcolm and Macduff, who has recently fled Macbeth's court and joined Malcolm's rebellion. Ross brings the news that the audience already knows: Macduff's family has been slaughtered on Macbeth's orders. Malcolm tries to make immediate use of this news, urging Macduff to speak his grief and then turn it into motivation for revenge:

MALCOLM: Be comforted.
  Let's make us med'cines of our great revenge
  To cure this deadly grief.
MACDUFF: He has no children. All my pretty ones?
  Did you say all? O hell-kite! All?
  What, all my pretty chickens and their dam
  At one fell swoop?
MALCOLM: Dispute it like a man.
MACDUFF: I shall do so;
  But I must also feel it as a man;
  I cannot but remember such things were
  That were most precious to me.
                                                    (4.3.215–26)

"Be comforted": Malcolm rushes through the creation of a motivating memory, which he doesn't even name as memory. Malcolm's perspective on past trauma is essentially medicinal: he treats the possibility of traumatic memory with violent action. Malcolm is oddly anxious to thrust the past into the past. The news of the murders – a new thing, new information – has only just arrived, and Malcolm is already trying to purge it from Macduff's mind, or at least make this news into something that will serve Malcolm's purposes. If Macduff will not simply "be comforted" in his grief, Malcolm offers him the expedient of revenge, a gendered, past-oriented action that transforms strong emotion into violence. However, like Hamlet, Macduff balks at the prospect of expressing his love for his family through revenge. Macduff might anticipate that he will eventually be able to achieve Malcolm's gendered ideal and combat his feelings, but for the moment, those feelings are subject to the involuntary power of an emotionally charged memory: he "cannot but remember." Like Hamlet ("Must I remember?"), he finds the gravitational pull of memory keeps him from moving toward any potential future action.

In this exchange, Malcolm attempts to create an instant, intentional, purpose-driven, future-oriented memory for Macduff, which will serve to motivate the killing that will heal both Macduff and the state. But this instant conversion of experience to purpose-driving memory is not possible for Macduff. The difference between Malcolm's idea of memory and Macduff's experience of it is analogous to Proust's voluntary and involuntary memories: the one goal-oriented and intentional, the other produced by sensory experience and separate from the will. In the early modern period, a similar distinction was marked in terms of gender, class, and race.[1] For Malcolm, memory is self-fashioning; love and grief only the materials for a revenge that allows for psychic repair. Revenge, and nothing else, will "cure this deadly grief" (4.3.217). Macduff's response demonstrates how difficult it is to convert traumatic news into knowledge and knowledge into memory, and it demonstrates the impossibility of assimilating new knowledge so quickly into a preexisting, stable selfhood. Although Macduff eventually effects this conversion, its difficulty is imprinted in the language of his exchange with Ross and Malcolm, not in semantic content but in sound. Repetition, enjambment, and most importantly the poetic meter comprise an affective dramaturgy in which grief, disbelief, and anger can be felt and made into the materials for memory.

From one perspective, the messenger's arrival seems tailor-made to serve the plot by providing intense personal motivation for Macduff to kill Macbeth. The audience does not yet know that Macduff is the solution to the riddle posed by the weird sisters, but this information too will arrive at the moment when it is required. However, other than adding intensity to Macduff's rebellion, the additional motivation is superfluous: committed enough to rebellion against Macbeth that he flees Scotland to join Malcolm's army, Macduff already has all the motivation he requires. One might suggest that the need for revenge renews Macduff's determination after it has been diminished by Malcolm's bizarre test of his loyalties. However, the news of the murders does not immediately turn into motivation nor turn Macduff to revenge; in fact, the news stops him from acting. The "intermission," as Macduff calls it, is temporary, but it is also disruptive. Macduff could, as Malcolm urges him to do, turn immediately from grief to anger and take revenge on Macbeth. However briefly, Macduff's grief, and his involuntary memory, stop the forward motion of the plot at a crucial juncture.

In plot terms, Macduff's grief does nothing. In a play as busy with plotting as *Macbeth*, this is remarkable. Moreover, the pause in action created by Macduff's grief allows for a brief glimpse of a different way of being. This is particularly notable not in the exchange between Malcolm and Macduff but in the immediately preceding exchange between Macduff and Ross. The model of feeling and memory in this exchange is relational and collaborative, not limited to the kind of centralized executive control that Macbeth demands and by which Malcolm also seems bound.

This chapter reads Macduff's exchange with Ross through the work of three affect theory scholars: Julian Henriques, Lauren Berlant, and Sara Ahmed, all of whom point toward the necessity of nonpurposive, non-semantic registers of expression. Ultimately, I argue that Macduff's unstable, language-shattering reaction to the news of the killings reveals the limits of the dramatic plot. Macduff's refusal to shift immediately from grief to violence is a rejection of a specific type of plot, revenge tragedy. Revenge tragedy does provide a model for using violence to assuage grief. Macduff shares with Hamlet a resistance to the equivalences created in revenge tragedy. But beyond this resistance to the genre, I argue that Macduff's affective response reflects the inadequacy of plot itself to give logical form to human actions. Plot, as a literary device, cannot provide Macduff with the space for a grief that is at once unbearably large and imperceptible.

I. Sound, Time, Henriques's Vibrations, and Macduff's Meter

In the 1983 BBC series *Playing Shakespeare*, actors from the Royal Shakespeare Company, with RSC director John Barton, describe how Shakespeare's blank verse shapes their work. A baby-faced Ian McKellen demonstrates how he would approach Antonio's speech at the beginning of *The Merchant of Venice*. The speech contains a short line, which McKellen describes as a pause structured by the surrounding verse:

MCKELLEN: I think when the rhythm of the blank verse enters an actor's soul, as it were, and that rhythm is interrupted because there are no words to complete the line –

"I am to learn," de dum, de dum, de dum –
It just indicates that the mind is going on ticking although words are not coming out to explain what the thoughts are.

BARTON: That's right.

MCKELLEN: Then of course you come into the next line with a bit more of a push because of that.[2]

McKellen's use of the formal qualities of Shakespeare's language is typical of RSC actors. The RSC has a long practice of encouraging actors to recognize the possibilities of metrical stresses and to derive meaning from rhythmic patterns in both speech and silence. (This general approach to Shakespeare's text is articulated more thoroughly in the work of former RSC voice director Cicely Berry and famed voice coach Kristin Linklater, among others.)[3] In a way, McKellen's statement about meter leads to a fairly basic observation about subtext, an analogy between the conventions of early modern verse drama and the different conventions of twentieth- and twenty-first-century scripts, where silence might be scripted in stage directions. The difference is that in Shakespeare's verse drama, as McKellen describes it, the pause is timed by the felt, remembered sound of the iambic pentameter line.

The relationship between the verse and McKellen's performance is multisensory and dynamic. McKellen describes the rhythm of the line not as something that he hears but rather as something that "enters [his] soul." Rhythm, which is temporal, becomes an entity that can move through space, from the lines on the page and into his soul (and not his mind or ear). The rhythm does not "live" in his soul; it "enters." It is in motion, not static. This rhythm marks out the time that the missing words would take, as well as their missing metrical emphases. The timed pause, in turn, produces subtext: the pause "indicates that the mind goes on ticking," as if it were a clock (and perhaps specifically as if it were a Timex watch, which "takes a licking and keeps on ticking"). The mind's action, too, is timed; in fact, it all but *is* time, or a measurement of time, ticking into the silence left by the missing words. Although the "ticking" implies mental activity, it does not necessarily indicate that the activity is language-based, or even that it has semantic content. The ticking pause is one of continuing activity, timed and rhythmically marked by iambic pentameter.

I give McKellen's account of an actor's experience of using iambic pentameter to introduce my reading of the verse in Macduff's exchange with Ross and Malcolm in terms of what sounds studies scholar Julian Henriques calls *vibrational affect*. Focusing on a crowd dancing on a Wednesday night in Kingston, Jamaica – an example of the famous

Jamaican "dancehall scene" – Henriques describes affect as vibration that creates waves in "corporeal, or material, or sociocultural" mediums.[4] Distinct from language and other forms of signification, vibrational affects travel between and among human and nonhuman actors:

> As with the "vibes" of the [dancehall] scene, waves and rhythms hardly restrict themselves to a particular medium or channel. Instead, their intensities vary, sometimes "spilling over" into violence.... The rhythmic patterning of vibrations thus helps dissolve the autonomous individual as a distinct self-consistent object in space and time, as it is often considered.[5]

Vibrational affect moves through crowds via "propagation," the rhythmic patterning and spreading of waves. "The propagation model," Henriques writes, "is valuable insofar as it offers an organizing principle for the transmission of affect – that eludes the prism of representation – and for the meaning of affect – that eludes the prison house of language."[6] Something like Henriques's vibrational affect can be seen in Shakespeare's manipulation of the iambic pentameter line.

In terms of semantic content, Ross's initial response to Macduff's queries is a study in avoidance. (Come in, equivocator.)

MACDUFF: How does my wife?
ROSS: Why, well.
MACDUFF: And all my children?
ROSS: Well, too.
MACDUFF: The tyrant has not battered at their peace?
ROSS: No, they were well at peace, when I did leave 'em.
MACDUFF: Be not a niggard of your speech: how goes't?

(4.3.178–82)

Ross responds to Macduff's last question by describing the state of the country of Scotland rather than the state of Macduff's family. This distraction, rather than any of Ross's answers to his direct questions, leads Macduff away from the topic of his family.

But why are Ross's answers unsatisfactory? Editors dutifully point out that "well" and "at peace" can both conventionally describe the dead.[7] Nothing else in the meaning of Ross's words prompts Macduff to look for this secondary sense. How does Macduff know that something is wrong, without language, or feel without knowing? How does he sense unease in the absence of lexical sense? And how is it that Ross's words prove more difficult to speak and more difficult for Macduff to hear and absorb than the feeling of foreboding that Macduff so clearly reflects? The answer, I think, lies with the sound of the lines.

Sound is crucial to *Macbeth*, a play punctuated by animal cries, offstage voices, knocking, and distinctive metrical effects in the utterances of the weird sisters.[8] This exchange is hardly the most obvious example of the play's engagement with sound, but nonetheless, sound provides the clearest expression of Ross's reluctance and Macduff's unease as they contemplate the unspeakable news of the massacre. Henriques writes: "The energetic patterning of vibrations offers a way of understanding meaning that is not tied to ideas of representation, encoding, inscription, or even Aristotelian logic."[9] Affect provides a way of conceptualizing meaning that does not depend on signification.[10] While their exchange is a much simpler example of vibrational affect than the dancehall scene instanced by Henriques, Macduff and Ross and the audience create meaning through a similar kind of "energetic patterning." As Paul Pellikka writes, effects of sound in *Macbeth* "overlap and blend in ways which the audience will probably apprehend more than comprehend."[11] This is a moment where the sound of the verse takes over from sense as the primary means of expression and connection.

In fact, Henriques uses the sonic qualities of language as a way of illustrating his broader point about the complex musical and interpersonal environment of the dancehall scene. "Through the prosodic inflections of an utterance," Henrique writes, "a person may express intentions, subtext and feelings, that give the listener clues on how to interpret what they say, possibly at odds from its literal meaning.... Such inflections may be consciously patterned as a rhythm, to create further rhetorical effects, as the MCs do on the sound system mike."[12] Like the MC over the sound system, the metrical structure of verse drama formalizes "prosodic inflections," precisely as prosody.

Metrical analysis draws attention to nonrepresentational aspects of language. Henriques writes: "[T]he transmission of affect should be considered as the dynamic patterning of frequencies, as distinct from the circulation or traffic of objects, the flow of particles, or the kinetic movement of bodies" as well as from meaning-bound concepts such as representation or discourse.[13] The distinction between a stressed and an unstressed syllable is vibrational. An iamb has a distinct rhythm, short-long. In addition to duration, the stressed syllable is also distinguished by pitch (lower, or, usually, higher than the unstressed syllable) and sometimes volume (louder, usually, than the unstressed syllable).

The shared lines at the beginning of the exchange between Ross and Macduff use sound to create an affective connection. They illustrate a key principle from affect studies, which is that affect is collective rather than individual. Notably, this collective effect is missing from Malcolm's exchange with Macduff: Malcolm completes Macduff's verse lines, but Macduff does not complete Malcolm's. The performance of a shared line can produce a frisson (another kind of vibration) among the audience as complex interactions are compressed into the line's seemingly unitary structure. In "Using the Verse," from the *Playing Shakespeare* series directed by Barton, Patrick Stewart and David Suchet work through the famous shared line from *King John*:[14]

KING JOHN:	Death.			
HUBERT:		My lord.		
KING JOHN:			A grave.	
HUBERT:				He shall not live.
KING JOHN:				Enough.

(3.3.66)

The actors first deliver the line without a pause and without much in the way of nuance or shading. After this swift delivery, the other actors on set are briefly silent, and then stir in surprise. Stewart and Suchet's final version of this exchange adds a pause after "Death," but little else changes – and if anything, the contrast in speed between the portentous single syllable and the swift and partly unspoken plan made in the next line is even more breathtaking. The RSC's typical approach of "playing the lines" rather than "playing the pauses" emphasizes the unitary and unifying quality of a shared line. Shared between two actors, the line is both a unit of thought in itself and a conversation, a versified illustration of the complex interchange of trained and skilled performers in the drama.

Macduff picks up the end of Ross's unfinished line to ask after his wife. The next line is shared between the two speakers. Often, such lines are spoken quickly, each speaker picking up the rhythm of the previous speaker so that the whole line scans audibly as one. This line, however, trips up at the beginning with the spondee –

$\bar{}\ \bar{}$
Why, well.

– and while Macduff then reestablishes the iambic rhythm, Ross slows it again with a second spondee at the end of the line:

$\bar{}\ \bar{}$
Well, too.

In fact, Macduff's intervention notwithstanding, the line is missing at least one syllable. There is a pause where a stressed syllable should be.

```
 -    -   / x    -    / x   -   / x      - / -  -
Why, well. / And all   / my chil- / dren? [pause] / Well, too.
```

Ross's pause, the repetition of "well" (a third time in the following lines), and the spondee all combine to create a small tug or nudge of unease.[15] Ross states that Macduff's family is "well," but the semantic content of this word is emptied as he speaks it, and the crumbling of sense is signaled by the rhythm of the lines.

Ross does not speak, but asserts words that he should speak and that require both excessive noise and inaudibility: "I have words / That would be howled out in the desert air, / Where hearing should not latch them" (4.3.195–97). Control of the voice is a crucial component of early modern masculinity, as Gina Bloom demonstrates.[16] Ross's hesitation to speak the words that would communicate semantically what has happened to Macduff's family might be construed as a failure in this gendered sense, just as Lear's spoken or wailed "howls" might represent a capitulation to feeling in spite of gendered expectations of control. Ross's hesitation might also, however, be construed as a complicated demonstration of a different kind of control, one that takes into account not only the content of words but their effect on hearers. The hearers are his focus in these lines: he does not say that the words are unspeakable, although he does say that they should only be spoken in a specific manner and context, "howled" in a broad and empty space. But here, it is not so much the howling that Ross rejects as the hearing. He suggests that the proper context for his news is an empty place where hearers cannot "latch," or receive, it. (Lear again: the heath.)

This announcement aligns the news of the murders with the play's binary of noise and sound, which, as David Sterling Brown and Jennifer Stoever argue in a talk at the Folger Shakespeare Library, "The Sound of Whiteness," is further aligned with binaries of gender, race, and class.[17] In their talk, Brown and Stoever argue that binary division between sound and noise in the play is a form of racialized thinking: noise is disorderly, takes place at night, and aligns with cultural ideas about blackness; sound (of which speech is a subset) is orderly, happens in the daytime, and aligns with cultural ideas about whiteness.[18] The noise that Ross imagines as the only means of expressing the devastating news of the murders is Macbeth-like; it is Malcolm's antithesis. Malcolm seems to think that grief is harmful, even deadly, if it is not expressed in language. Speech is purgation: "Give sorrow words; the grief that does not speak, / Whispers the o'erfraught heart and bids it break" (4.3.211–12). Noise, in contrast, represents disorder, instability, and darkness.

The violent death of the hero's wife and children is a staple, even a cliché, of narratives that center on white masculinity. António Ferreira's (1528–1569) play *A Castro*, among the first true "Renaissance" plays written in the vernacular, is a crucial early example. The play concerns the historical narrative of Inês de Castro (1325–1355), who was killed on the orders of the King of Portugal, Alfonso IV, so that his son and heir, later King Peter I, would not legitimate their marriage and her children. On the English stage, *The Revenger's Tragedy* provides one example. Modern examples of the trope are abundant. (Among Scottish historical fantasies, *Braveheart* springs to mind.)[19] In narratives such as these, the hero's love for his wife or lover separates him from the concerns of a dominant group, often the state, and provides fuel for a violent revenge. The wife and children are figured as essentially vulnerable, shielded from a dangerous world only by the hero, whose violence is morally good because it protects a white woman and white offspring from external dangers. The deaths of Lady Macduff and the Macduff children fit easily into this narrative tradition. Macduff's ultimate response to their deaths is also very much in line with such narratives.

In the "intermission" between Ross's arrival and the rebels' departure for Scotland, however, other narrative possibilities almost emerge. Given Brown and Stoever's argument, it seems significant to me that these possibilities emerge alongside something that does not happen: an impossible, norm-shattering noise, "words / That would be howled out in the desert air, / Where hearing should not latch them" (4.3.195–97). This is not quite the trope of inexpressibility. Ross does not say that he cannot speak the words, but that they require an environment that he cannot provide and that they should be "howled out," not simply spoken aloud. Lear's norm-shattering howls represent his best alternative. A means of expression is available for the words he has to speak, but to use it, like Lear, he would have to flee civilization for the "desert air" and allow the words to turn his speech into animal noise. The news is not unspeakable or inexpressible but uncommunicable, at least under the auspices of a society that despises noise.

Ross's reluctance to give the words the affective qualities that he considers their due also falls into the narrative tradition that treats the deaths of women and children as the most extreme violation of white patriarchal order. But for a moment, Ross seems to glimpse an alternative system of mourning and self-expression, where howling might be a way to speak. This possibility disappears almost immediately, however, and is replaced by a form of speech that conveys the unspeakable, periphrasis.

The strongest expression that Macduff gives his grief is periphrastic, and, crucially for the theme of this collection of essays, it is an emerging and unbidden memory: "I cannot but remember such things were / That were most precious to me" (4.3.225–26). The periphrasis covers both the nature of his memories ("such things were") and their affect ("which were most precious to me"). Periphrasis allows Macduff to speak what cannot be spoken, to do precisely what Malcolm wants him to do – speak his grief – while still honoring the unspeakability of his thoughts.

II. Space, Movement, Berlant's *Impasse*, and Macduff's *Intermission*

Temporally, Macduff's memory stretches its wings in the brief gap of time created by emotional turbulence. Ross's news halts the forward action of Malcolm's planned attack on Macbeth, and it interrupts and dismantles easy communication. A disruption in language and action like this is a phenomenon that Lauren Berlant calls an *impasse*. The impasse represents an interruption of the normal structures of desire and fulfillment or nonfulfillment, with a resulting shift in action:

> [T]he impasse is a stretch of time in which one moves around with a sense that the world is at once intensely present and enigmatic, such that the activity of living demands both a wandering absorptive awareness and a hypervigilance that collects material that might help to clarify things, maintain one's sea legs, and coordinate the standard melodramatic crises with those processes that have not yet found their genre of event.[20]

Glossing Berlant's impasse, Taylor Schey writes:

> Within a schema of temporal or historical movement, an impasse marks a point at which the unceasing reproduction of the status quo is brought to a halt, enabling one to sense both the contingency and the brutality of the conditions in which they dwell; it opens the possibility, though not the inevitability, of something else.[21]

While a revolution is already underway when Ross arrives, the interruption of his news and Macduff's grief represent a more fundamental challenge to the structures of class and gender that remain untouched by a change from one king to another. When he temporarily refuses to subordinate his grief to Malcolm's cause, Macduff pulls away from these structures. He has a name for this response: "intermission" (4.3.235).

Where Berlant finds *impasse*, Macduff finds *intermission*. Such pauses are common in Shakespeare's plays; for example, in *Richard II*, where

Richard's loss of power leads to a cessation of physical movement and a change in how language is used: "For God's sake," Richard demands, "let us sit upon the ground / And tell sad stories of the death of kings" (3.2.155–56). Berlant's *impasse* and Macduff's *intermission* are both spatial: *intermission* is placed-between; *impasse* is a place from which there is no movement. Both are also temporal: *impasse* involves a suspension of time conceptualized as forward momentum while also cutting off retreat toward the past. An intermission is a "temporary pause" (*OED*), a time placed between other time, a time that does not "count" toward the main action. The Latin root, *mittere*, can mean to *let go* as well as to *send* or to *put*.[22]

But Macduff's *intermission*, even more than Berlant's *impasse*, implies that action is halted only temporarily. An impasse may be escaped or resolved, but only through some kind of change. The same thing won't do. Not so with the intermission, which ends merely with a resumption of the same action as before. Nothing must change as a result of an intermission. (Theaters did not yet have intermissions – or intervals, the more usual term in British English – but the sense of a pause in otherwise continuous action remains.) In contrast to Macduff, Hamlet manages to extend the time of his own intermission by filling it with language. His "words, words, words" (*Hamlet*, 2.2.189) skirt the line between sense and nonsense, obliquely or, sometimes, pointedly conveying his memory of his father to a bewildered audience. There is no Malcolm to urge him back to task. Even the violent resolution of Hamlet's inaction takes place not due to an intentional act of revenge but due to Hamlet's willingness to allow himself to be buffeted by circumstances. When Hamlet kills Claudius, he does not give Old Hamlet's murder as his reason. Instead, he tosses out an accusation grounded in the present: "follow my mother!" Hamlet's "revenge," if you can call it that, occurs only because he abandons any attempt to dictate the manner of Claudius's death or his own. John Kerrigan suggests that Hamlet remains silent on the topic of Old Hamlet in this scene because "memory [is] private," but the whole point of revenge tragedy is to bring the private memory of a hidden crime into the public sphere in a violent and spectacular fashion.[23] The duel is spectacular, but its significance is obscured for all but a few onstage spectators. Even as he enacts something like the revenge demanded by the Ghost, Hamlet essentially remains inactive as a revenger, stalled in a psychologically generative impasse of grief and memory.

For Macduff, however, memory remains a temporary intermission. Macduff does not name the intermission before it is over. He is already returning to the work of masculinity, to waging war and maintaining the hereditary monarchy, when he reflexively describes what has happened:

MACDUFF: But gentle heavens,
 Cut short all intermission. Front to front
 Bring thou this fiend of Scotland and myself;
 Within my sword's length set him. If he scape,
 Heaven forgive him too!

(4.3.234–38)

Approval for Macduff's resumption of a more acceptable affective register is evident in Malcolm's response: "This tune goes manly" (4.3.238). Masculinity, it seems, can be located again simply by changing the way one sounds. Those musical effects that form a nonrepresentational means of shared expression between Ross and Macduff are replaced here by resounding iambs, boastful but not too boastful, periphrastic only in avoiding the central spectacle of violence that the play itself also ultimately avoids when Macbeth's death at Macduff's hands takes place offstage.

III. Speaking What We Feel: Sara Ahmed and Sharing Pain

In "The Contingency of Pain," Sara Ahmed writes about the difficult work of sharing the pain of others. At first, this is a practical problem: drawing from Merleau-Ponty, Ahmed invites her readers to imagine her own foot, pressed against a corner of her desk as she writes, until it goes numb and then begins to hurt. While we can imagine or even remember a similar sensation, we cannot share her pain. Then, Ahmed extends the practical difficulty to include the ethical problems of feeling even the pain of those closest to us. She gives the example of her own mother's pain from a chronic illness. Ahmed lived with this pain, shared it in the sense of being in its orbit, but it was not hers. Finally, Ahmed turns to the political problem of witnessing and responding to a pain inflicted on members of a social group to which one does not belong.

In the last section of her essay, Ahmed responds to a 1997 document produced by the Australian government, called *Bringing Them Home*, which describes the "stolen generation" of Aboriginal Australian and Torres Strait Island children, who were removed from their homes to be forcibly assimilated into white society. The document is an attempt to act as witness to this trauma, but Ahmed objects to its language of *healing*, where the body being healed is the body of the nation of Australia. If this pain should not be generalized in this way and cannot be healed, what is to be the response? But if the other's pain is appropriated as the nation's pain, and the "wound" is

> fetishized as the broken skin of the nation, is the answer to forget the other's pain, to admit to the impossibility of hearing that pain by refusing to hear? No. That's all I can say. No. Our task instead is *to learn how to hear what is impossible*, to allow ourselves to be moved by a pain that we cannot feel, and to get closer to others only so that we can move away. This is about taking responsibility for forming a different kind of national body, where the healing is not the bringing of the other's pain into the body, and the use of their pain to seal the skin of the nation. Such a responsible response, one that moves and is moving, is only responsible when it moves us beyond guilt or shame *and into a different way of inhabiting or dwelling in the world with indigenous others.*[24]

The practice of removing Native children from their families and housing them in government or religious institutions was common around the world, and the often horrific treatment of these children, on top of the trauma of separating them from their families, is only now beginning to be brought to light. Feeling her way through the challenges of responding to this pain, Ahmed does not so much invite her readers to adopt a particular stance toward it, but uses the form of the essay to work through her own feelings about a trauma that she does not fully share. Living with others, Ahmed suggests, requires an impossible kind of hearing and an equally impossible empathy. Feeling with others is both something that cannot be done and that must be done.

But now my argument is beginning to break down. Ross and Macduff may feel one another's feelings in a way that resonates with some part of Ahmed's argument about pain and community, but with this last part, where Ahmed tries to feel with a mother and daughter separated by a cruel and racist government policy, there is no real resonance to my argument. The difference between the scenario described by Ahmed and the exchange between Ross and Macduff is reminiscent of something Declan Donnellan, cofounder of the theater group Cheek by Jowl, says about the difference between sympathy and empathy:

> When we put on a piece of theatre we are a group of people looking at other people doing something, and that really couldn't be more important. It's very important politically. We're facing very frightening times, and we need to develop our empathy. And the best way to develop our empathy is to make a sharp distinction between that and our sympathy [in the sense] "I feel the same as you." This is the complete opposite of empathy, by my definition. Empathy is understanding we have no idea what the other person is feeling.[25]

Ross and Macduff feel together so well partly because they are so alike, because their experience of tyranny and pain involves a common enemy, and because while their power within the Scottish court may have changed, their status has not. If their masculinity, whiteness, and high social status seem inadequate to the task of responding to the deaths of Macduff's family, they do not ultimately challenge those systems; in fact, the disruption only allows them to return to their previous situation with renewed vigor. The ethical action that could be enabled by empathy is simply not available to them.

IV. Conclusion

Macduff's grief is, ultimately, assimilable within the preexisting systems of his society. This is the difference between Macduff and Hamlet: Macduff's grief and involuntary remembering stops the play only for a moment; Hamlet's grief and memory lead to a genuine impasse. It takes only a few lines for Macduff to convert the unspeakably huge weight of feeling from an impediment to action to a factor that motivates action. Malcolm celebrates not only because Macduff renews his commitment to the cause but because his recommitment is a triumph of masculinity and a triumph of the kind of decorum and control that mark the play's alternative to the norm-shattering actions of Macbeth. Macduff will return shortly with his trauma refashioned into the form that provides the answer to the weird sisters' riddling prophecy. It seems no accident that the peculiarity of Macduff's birth is a rupture between parent and child; it almost seems as though Macduff's involuntary memory of his wife and their children is rearranged in this scenario, with Macduff himself still surviving the death of his family as a child without a mother. Control over one's memory was thought of as a masculine characteristic, and disorderly or involuntary memory was correspondingly feminized.[26] But if "Macduff was from his mother's womb / Untimely ripped" (5.8.15–16), that pain only allows him to act more effectively within the society that is reasserting control over government, war, and masculine rituals of succession.

To apply the work of Henriques, Berlant, and Ahmed to this text – a Black scholar of Black Caribbean culture, a queer nonbinary scholar, and a scholar of color who is writing about the experiences of Aboriginal and Torres Strait Island people of Australia – is a kind of appropriation. What I hope to convey, however, is that the work of such scholars, who are on the vanguard of thinking about self, society, trauma, happiness, and all the things that go into human experiences, can intervene powerfully to clarify the all but invisible moments in a canonical author such as Shakespeare, like this one, in which Macduff almost finds himself abandoning the system of decorum that governs his performance of whiteness and masculinity.

Maynard Mack suggests that moments like the one I have been discussing are typical of Shakespeare's tragedies:

> Toward the close of a tragic play, or if not toward the close, at the climax, will normally appear a short scene or episode (sometimes more than one) of spiritual cross purposes: a scene in which the line of tragic speech and feeling generated by commitment is crossed by an alien speech and feeling very much detached. There will appear a moment of spiritual cross-purposes.... Shakespeare here lays open to us, in an especially poignant form, what I take to be the central dialogue of tragic experience[,] ... a dialogue in which each party makes its case in its own tongue, incapable of wholly comprehending what the other means.[27]

Shakespeare does, often, move abruptly into a different affective register toward the end of his tragedies. The graveyard scene in *Hamlet* is one example discussed by Mack; another is the scene between Desdemona and Emilia in *Othello*. With the possibilities of the tragic plot rapidly shutting down, such moments can provide relief, or amplify the consequences of the tragic conclusion, or otherwise remove the audience from the unfolding action and show them the alternatives that will no longer be available in a few scenes. Shakespeare's discomfort with emplotment is perhaps more obvious in his comedies than in the tragedies: the marriage-plot ending becomes increasingly untenable for him as his career progresses, to the point that the comedy genre itself breaks apart in the late plays. One could argue that these "moments of spiritual cross-purposes" represent the tragic answer to the discomfort with the marriage plot in the comedies.

But if Shakespeare's tragedies hover on the edge of new possibilities in such moments, they usually close off those possibilities very quickly. In the end, opposition to the dominant way of thinking in any given tragedy is very quiet and sometimes easy to miss. (Some may "speak what we feel, not what we ought to say" (5.3.298), as Albany/Edgar urges at the end of *King Lear*, but they will speak it in rhyme.) The elegiac feel of intermissions like Macduff's allows whatever challenge is represented in these temporary pauses to be assimilated as a sad, but faintly pleasurable sense of loss. The resumption of the tragic machinery feels inevitable, even in the face of affective difference. Cutting short any intermission, anything placed between, Shakespeare's plays return to the main action, leaving other possibilities behind.

Notes

1 The element of race is discussed below. On gender and class, see Garrett A. Sullivan, Jr., *Memory and Forgetting in English Renaissance Drama: Shakespeare, Marlowe, Webster* (Cambridge University Press, 2005), 32–39; Lina Perkins Wilder, *Shakespeare's Memory Theatre: Recollection, Properties, and Character* (Cambridge University Press, 2010), 2–8, 61; see also the chapter on *Macbeth*, 156–70.
2 RSC, "Using the Verse," www.youtube.com/watch?v=H3rMaHqH2TE&t=1246s, 19:20–21:10.
3 On Shakespeare's verse, see Cicely Berry, *The Actor and the Text*, revised ed. (London: Virgin Books, 2000); Kristin Linklater, *Freeing Shakespeare's Voice: The Actor's Guide to Talking the Text* (New York: Theatre Communications Group, 1992). See also Mort Paterson, "Stress and Rhythm in the Speaking of Shakespeare's Verse: A Performer's View," *Shakespeare Bulletin*, 33.3 (2015), 469–88.
4 Julian Henriques, "The Vibrations of Affect and Their Propagation on a Night Out on Kingston's Dancehall Scene," *Body & Society*, 16.1 (2010), 57–89; esp. 58. On the history of Jamaican dancehall music, see Sonjah Stanley Niaah, *Dancehall: From Slave Ship to Ghetto* (University of Ottawa Press, 2010); Jordan Chung, "Choppa Rising: A History of Jamaican Trap Dancehall," *Afropunk*, October 22, 2019, https://afropunk.com/2019/10/choppa-rising-a-history-of-jamaican-trap-dancehall/.
5 Henriques, "Vibrations," 83.
6 Ibid.
7 See, e.g., Kenneth Muir, ed., *Macbeth* (London: Methuen, 1951), 133 n.
8 On sound in *Macbeth*, see, among many others, David L. Kranz, "The Sounds of Supernatural Soliciting in *Macbeth*," *Studies in Philology*, 100.3 (2003), 346–83; Ling-chiao Lin, "'Every Noise Appals Me': Macbeth's Plagued Ear," *Tamkang Review*, 43.2 (2013), 131–50; Paul Pellikka, "'Strange things I have in head, that will to hand': Echoes of Sound and Sense in *Macbeth*," *Style*, 31.1 (1997), 14–33; Evelyn Tribble, "'When Every Noise Appalls Me': Sound and Fear in *Macbeth* and Akira Kurosawa's *Throne of Blood*," *Shakespeare*, 1.1 (2005), 75–90; and the address by David Sterling Brown and Jennifer Stoever, "Sound of Whiteness, or Teaching Shakespeare's Other 'Race Plays'," Critical Race Conversations, Folger Shakespeare Library, July 16, 2020, www.youtube.com/watch?v=iBGSh4h-74U&t=960s. On Shakespeare and sound studies, see Gina Bloom, *The Voice in Motion* (Philadelphia: University of Pennsylvania Press, 2007); Bruce R. Smith, *The Acoustic World of Early Modern England: Attending to the O-Factor* (University of Chicago Press, 1999); Wes Folkerth, *The Sound of Shakespeare* (London: Routledge, 2002); Kenneth Gross, *Shakespeare's Noise* (University of Chicago Press, 2001); Sonia Massai, *Shakespeare's Accents: Voicing Identity in Performance* (Cambridge University Press, 2020); Jennifer Richards, *Voices and Books in the English Renaissance* (Oxford University Press, 2019); Scott Trudell, *Unwritten Poetry:*

Song, Performance, and Media in Early Modern England (Oxford University Press, 2019); Jennifer Linhart Wood, *Sounding Otherness in Early Modern Drama and Travel: Uncanny Vibrations in the English Archive* (London: Palgrave Macmillan, 2019); and the essays in the special issue of *The Upstart Crow*, 29 (2010), "Shakespearean Hearing," ed. Leslie Dunn and Wes Folkerth.
9. Henriques, "Vibrations," 76.
10. Ibid.
11. Pellikka, "Strange Things," 16.
12. Henriques, "Vibrations," 77.
13. Ibid., 58.
14. RSC, "Using the Verse," www.youtube.com/watch?v=H3rMaHqH2TE, 16:43–19:09.
15. On the pause, see Muir's second-series Arden edition: *Macbeth*, 133 n.
16. Bloom, *The Voice in Motion*, 10–12.
17. Brown and Stoever, "The Sound of Whiteness."
18. Ibid.
19. Other examples on film include *Lethal Weapon*, *Patriot Games*, *The Fugitive*, and *Gladiator*. Television examples include plotlines in many police-procedural dramas (*NCIS*, *CSI*, and their spinoffs; *24*) and the *Star Trek* franchise, among others. Comic-book examples are also numerous. See "Crusading Widower," *TV Tropes: The All-Devouring Pop Culture Wiki*, https://tvtropes.org/pmwiki/pmwiki.php/Main/CrusadingWidower.
20. Lauren Berlant, *Cruel Optimism* (Durham, NC: Duke University Press, 2011), 4.
21. Taylor Schey, "Impasse? What Impasse? Berlant, de Man, and the Intolerable Present," *Comparative Literature*, 72.2 (2020), 180–202; esp. 181.
22. Patricia Ticineto Clough, "Afterword: The Future of Affect Studies," *Body & Society*, 16.1 (2010), 222–30; 224–26.
23. John Kerrigan, *Revenge Tragedy: Aeschylus to Armageddon* (Oxford: Clarendon Press, 1996), 187.
24. Sara Ahmed, "The Contingency of Pain," *Parallax*, 8.1 (2002), 17–34; esp. 29; emphasis in original.
25. Qtd. in Peter Kirwan, *Shakespeare in the Theatre: Cheek by Jowl*, Shakespeare in the Theatre Series (London: Bloomsbury, 2019), 156.
26. Sullivan, *Memory and Forgetting*, 32–39; Wilder, *Shakespeare's Memory Theatre*, 2–8.
27. Maynard Mack, *Everybody's Shakespeare: Reflections Chiefly on the Tragedies* (Lincoln: University of Nebraska Press, 1993), 241–42.

Coda

CHAPTER 14

Remembering Shakespeare

Peter Holland

I cannot remember not remembering Shakespeare. And I remember too how others have remembered him, how they have shown what they have remembered. Passages in the plays automatically conjure up for me the memory of someone's voice, that person's rhythms of speaking Shakespeare. Often it is an actor's voice, sometimes a relative's or a friend's. As I remember those voices turning text to sound, so I can repeat their way of repeating, recite their reciting, and, in doing so, the text is suffused by complex emotions of memory, of the where and the when and the who and the what that attaches to those people in general, and especially to their demonstrations of having remembered their Shakespeare, the Shakespeare they have chosen or been made to choose.

In such cases, where the emotions of the memory of their memories are so strong, it is not usually the actor that induces emotion. Yes, I can – and occasionally do – speak some Shakespeare passages in what seems to me still a fairly precise imitation of an actor's delivery of those lines. Almost the only spoken-word vinyl record that my parents had bought (along with the *Homage to Dylan Thomas*,[1] the only modern poet whose poems were in their modest library) was of Olivier performing speeches from *Hamlet* and *Henry V*, a recording that was not all taken from the soundtracks for the films, for it included Olivier speaking some parts of the Chorus to Act 4, the Duke of Burgundy's "My duty to you both" in Act 5, scene 2, and the epilogue, these less performed, presumably, than read, created in the recording studio, not on the film set or in post-production.[2] I played the LP, especially the *Henry V* side, endlessly, loving the sound of Olivier's voice and of Walton's music, especially for the charge of the French knights at Agincourt, a scene that was always the highlight of seeing Olivier's film, as I did at the Academy Cinema on Oxford Street in London every year for a decade, growing up with the film. I remember the sound and I recall Olivier's delivery. I remember enjoying it and also that the speeches got themselves memorized without my ever settling down to commit them to memory. Like a child requiring a favorite bedtime story always to be read the same way, this was, for me at that time, unarguably the right way to speak those speeches from *Henry V*, and the frequent repetition fixed them in my memory so that I hear that voice still and replicate it whenever these passages come to mind, again warmly coddled in that childhood memory.

Another memory is built on that one: my being taken by my parents to the Mermaid Theatre in 1960 to see a production of *Henry V* in modern dress, with the text adjusted to suit that costume choice, so that I still have stuck in my mind the emendation they made: "Think when we talk of *tanks* that you see them / Printing their proud *tracks* i' th' receiving earth" (Prol. 26–27). I recall my memory of hearing and instantly disliking the change, an awareness that this was plain wrong, not because of some sacrosanct notion of the Shakespeare text but of the equally sacrosanct memory of it in Olivier's film – and the moment of hearing their change now seems like some bizarre early prefiguration of my future career decades later.

Two additional memories of others speaking Shakespeare now come immediately and uncontrollably to mind. First, there is Cassius' response to Brutus: "Then must I think you would not have it so" (*Julius Caesar*, 1.2.81). I hear this in the voice of my Uncle Alec, a gentle, fragile man who left school aged about thirteen but who, till the end of his long life, remembered this scene and enjoyed speaking it to me. The line was spoken quickly, evenly, unstressed, the monosyllables all of equal weight, a sign of his learning them by rote at school and speaking them without interpretation, without offering meaning, but always with his smile at his still remembering them half a century later. So, every performance of *Julius Caesar* becomes a memory of my uncle, a happy remembering of his kindness. Hearing *Caesar* cannot, for me, be detached from him, however much the Cassius may in a particular production be far better.

Then, a remembering I did not hear. The Shakespeare scholar Anne Barton, my dissertation supervisor and mentor, had a prodigious memory for poetry throughout her life, able to recall many hundreds of poems at will and speak them with perfect accuracy.[3] In her last days, as she lay in her hospital bed, she astonished and delighted the nurses and other patients by reciting Shakespeare sonnets by the dozen. She found the act of memory comforting, her confidence in her memory rightly never shaken, and the *Sonnets* themselves became a space in which to pass the tedious time, as she was unable now to read because of the onset of macular degeneration (though she had taken her copy of Stephen Orgel's

2001 Pelican edition of the *Sonnets* with her). She was able always to remember and to enjoy the unending and demanding complexity of Shakespeare's thought as her memory traced the rhythm of those lines. To think of her there then is painful but also comforting. Her pride in her memory is well worth remembering, even though it is full of her absence now.

If the opening pages of this chapter have seemed to any of my readers self-indulgent – for why should my memories matter to you? – then I hope that they have provoked your memories of remembering, yours or others', for one person's speaking of memories encourages us to remember remembering. As John Smith put it, in *The Mysterie of Rhetorique Unvail'd* (1657), "*Anamnesis* is a figure whereby the speaker calling to mind matters past, whether of sorrow, joy, &c. doth make recital of them for his own advantage, or for the benefit of those that hear him."[4] These "matters past" may, if you are annoyed by my writing about them, seem to have been recited "for [my] own advantage," or, if you have not been, then it has been "for the benefit of those that" read them.

The classic (and classical) encouragement of the future benefits of memory is Aeneas' confident statement to his men in Virgil's *Aeneid*: "forsan et haec olim meminisse iuvabit" (1.203). As Tom Jenkins notes in his commentary on the passage, after calling it "arguably Virgil's most famous line," the line "may be familiar to modern readers as the dedication to innumerable high school yearbooks."[5] There is, though, a difficulty in translating Virgil here, caused by the semantic field of the verb *iuvo*, whose primary meaning is "help, assist, benefit" but which can also carry the sense of "delight, gratify, please."[6] In a fascinating exploration of translations of the line, Dani Bostick asks, "Why don't more translators think it will be helpful to remember in Aeneid 1.203?"[7] Thomas Phaer, in a translation that Shakespeare might have known, translates the line as "To thinke on thys may pleasure be, perhaps another day."[8] And ever since, as Bostick comments as she lists many translators' results, "'please' has become a reflexive choice." So John Dryden (1697) had "An hour will come, with pleasure to relate / Your sorrows past"; Robert Fagles (2006) offered "A joy it will be one day, perhaps, to remember even this"; Robert Fitzgerald (1981) made it "Some day, perhaps, remembering this even will be a pleasure"; and, to add one Bostick does not include, Fairclough's Loeb edition, revised by Goold (1999), produced "Perhaps even this distress it will some day be a joy to recall."[9] Critics as well as translators tend to read the line the same way: what has been painful in the moment may become pleasurable later in remembering.

Bostick's response to her students whenever they reached for "help" as they translated the line had been to reply firmly "Here *iuvo* means 'please.'" But her view has changed. Some translations did choose "help," as in Gavin Douglas' version in Scots (completed in 1513, printed 1553): "Sum tyme heiron to think may help perchance." As we learn how to respond to trauma, so we accept that repression of the memory is profoundly damaging and only remembering will *help*. Aeneas (and Virgil) may presciently be in line with such contemporary responses, offering the hope that at a future time the transformation of involuntary nightmare into voluntary memory helps healing and that Aeneas "provides an alternative to suppressing these memories and deleting part of their personal and collective history."[10]

The translations, then, move between a therapeutic and an affective possibility. None of the ones Bostick quotes or that I have found elsewhere offers a version in which both possibilities coexist, a version in which the memory might be conceptualized as offering in the future something helpful in coping with the trauma and pleasing in seeing how far the memory has shifted from the immediacy of pain. Help as healing and pleasing as transformative distancing in surviving create a combination that is complexly paradoxical. So, too, my two examples of remembering individuals remembering Shakespeare have pain in the thought of their deaths and pleasure in the joy they took in those acts of remembering. These affects of memory are here intertwined with contrary emotions in different areas of consideration of the memory of memory. Understanding that paradox is a help to me as I work with what these memories mean to me and how they mean it.

Shakespeare probably read the *Aeneid* at school. It is equally probable that Virgil's line hovers behind Romeo's assertion, as he leaves Juliet, that "all these woes shall serve / For sweet discourses in our times to come" (3.5.52–53). As T. W. Baldwin puts it, in a schoolmasterish tone, "if Shakspere read this first part of the *Aeneid* in the detail with which he should have read it, and from other characteristics appears to have read it, then he is likely to be echoing this particular passage."[11] Perhaps the memory is designed to be noticed. So familiar is Virgil's line to some of us even now and to all of Shakespeare's playgoers who have had some schooling that I see the echo as one he deliberately wants us to know, forming the gap between what will prove to be the impossibility of Romeo and Juliet ever having "sweet discourses," of their having "times to come," set against the very different history of Aeneas and his men.

Of course, the phrase or something like it was more broadly proverbial. So, for instance, R. W. Dent has examples for "The remembrance of past sorrows (dangers) is joyful."[12] M. P. Tilley, Dent's predecessor in the charting of early modern proverbial language, listed numerous sources for this same thought, such as Marston's version in *Jack Drum's Entertainment* (1601), "Sad sorrow past, delights to be rehearsed," or Goffe's in *The Raging Turk* (1631), "After an age of woes it proves at last / A sweet content to tell of dangers past."[13] It did not need Virgil for the concept to circulate. But the controlling version is about joy, delight, pleasure, not *help*, for which, so far as I can see, neither Tilley nor Dent offer an entry connecting the affect to *memory* or *remembering*.

The pleasure of remembering is everywhere palpable in the interviews that make up *Remembering Shakespeare*, a beautiful, moving documentary film by Cecilia Rubino, Peter Lucas, and Will Lucas.[14] Take a moment from the most famous segment in the film, an interview with Justice Ruth Bader Ginsburg: "Did I memorize Shakespeare in P.S. 238 in Brooklyn, New York? Yes! I think the first piece was Polonius' advice to Laertes, 'Neither a borrower nor a lender be,' and it was not only recitation in English classes but in our Music class, we sang 'Who is Sylvia?'" RBG also remembered memorizing "The quality of mercy is not strained," but she moves on to a powerful indictment of Portia, noting the difference between the speech in isolation and the speech in context:

> Yes, that was a favorite of mine until I read the play because that speech excerpted gives a very favorable portrait of Portia but the rest of *The Merchant* does not. A few pages later she forgets all about the quality of mercy in her dealings with Shylock. She shows him no mercy. She is a very difficult character ... [She] gives a kind of reading of the law that no jurist would ever give ... She's full of tricks ... So she is not my favorite Shakespeare woman.

One has only to watch RBG's face as she remembers memorizing to see her pleasure in the recollection, a different response from her analysis of why a contract that enabled a creditor to commit murder was unenforceable "in any court of law – maybe a Mafia court but no other."

Near the beginning of the film, Rubino, in the film's only moment of voice-over, narrates how she was giving lectures on Shakespeare at Jefferson Market Library and, after the last lecture, asked her audience if they had "memories of Shakespeare they wanted to share and all of these elderly New Yorkers, most of whom had no connection to the theater, stood up and they were able to speak verbatim all these lines of Shakespeare that they'd memorized back when they were at school."

She realized that there was "this huge cross-section of New Yorkers that have Shakespeare's words embedded into their everyday lives."

The next interviewee is Mordecai Rosenfeld, a retired lawyer, who grew up in Brooklyn, and recalled his experiences, aged ten or eleven in the fifth or sixth grade at P.S. 152, a school that prided itself on having a poetry class. Each child of the thirty-five to thirty-eight in the class was required to memorize the same poem, often a Shakespeare sonnet, and recite it in front of the whole class, one after another. To relieve the boredom of the endless repetition, he recalls, the boys decided to see who could say it the fastest. And then he's off, reciting Sonnet 18 at breakneck speed, the rhythm intact but with the same flat (albeit much faster) intonation that I recalled in Uncle Alec's recitation from *Caesar*. As Rubino herself recalls, in an article on the film, "he can still, with stunning virtuosity, speak the lines of a number of them at lightning speed" at the age of eighty-five.[15] Rosenfeld described how he would prepare:

> I would read the assigned sonnet the night before, over and over and then start to say it to myself out loud as fast as I could. And my father would ask me what I was doing and I would say I was just memorizing Shakespeare and he would ask what does it mean and I would say I didn't know. I didn't know it was supposed to mean anything ... The goal was to say the sonnet in less than 14 seconds, a second a line. I was often the fastest but sometimes you would miss a line or cough or sneeze and loose a second.[16]

On camera, with no cough or sneeze, it takes him twenty-eight seconds by my timing and I am left wondering what it would have sounded like twice as fast as that.

Proudly, Rosenfeld remembers that, on Parents' Night, Miss Curtis, the poetry teacher, would tell his parents that he "was one of the best Shakespeare scholars she had and my mother would beam for weeks."[17] In his parents' small library, mostly of books on Jewish religion and philosophy, there was a ten-volume edition of Shakespeare, the Henley Edition, which he still owns and shows off on camera.[18] The dominant emotion is pride: pride in the memory of Parents' Night, pride in still remembering the sonnet, and pride in the volumes that his parents so valued and that he still does too. The affect of memory here is a quiet joy, but there is also Rosenfeld's sharp self-awareness that "We look at ourselves through the prism of memory and make ourselves better than we were." His humility and his eloquence remake the emotion (here hardly a sin) of pride into something admirable in its recollection of a childhood pleasure.

What does one do with the memorized passage? For Donna Robin, another of the film's interviewees, Shakespeare was a central part of caring for her husband through his last illness and then in her grieving. "To be or not to be," which she mentions with a tinge of embarrassment for its apparently clichéd obviousness, has become vital to her life, to the choice that she is always making, something somehow all the more acute for her professional understanding, as a psychotherapist, of what she is experiencing: "that [speech] explores my dilemma – that's it ... It speaks to me. I recite it almost every day, sometimes many times a day." The act of reciting is here not a triumphant memory of something achieved in the past and sustained ever since but instead an exploration of the choices of the present, neither pleasurable nor helpful in Virgilian terms but instead with an immediacy and urgency about how – indeed, whether – to face the next moments of her life.

Like Rosenfeld, Robin sees the language functioning as a transformation of its source, using the same image of the prism: the speech's words are "prismatic, they are on an axle that keeps turning, the light keeps coming through them and reflecting."[19] My examples from the film so far have been of voluntary recalling, people choosing actively and consciously to remember, but another of its subjects, David Lehman, sees that not all recall is controlled: "Knowing a poem by heart means that you can revisit it either willingly or by chance ... In a city like New York you find yourself in a crowd all the time and the lines of a poem memorized or a soliloquy memorized may recur to you and, when they do recur to you, you will see them in a new light." Again, there is that knowledge that the object, the memorized words, stays the same but its meaning can be both accessed and transformed in the moment by the act of reciting what has been learned.

So completely is remembering, for me, bound up with affect that I find it immediately striking that emotion has virtually no part to play in the excellent recent critical anthology on the early modern arts of memory.[20] Even the finely detailed index to the collection offers only one emotion, "pleasure," and that is listed under "history," its index-points revealing that Thomas Fuller in his *History of the Worthies of England* (1662) saw that biography sought to entertain and that John Beadle, in *The Journal or Diary of a Thankful Christian* (1656), asserted that "Of all histories, the history of men's lives is the most pleasant."[21] This is not, I must emphasize, in any way intended as a criticism of the anthology's editors but rather as a recognition of the extent of the dissociation of affect from memory in the materials that the anthology gathers. If we – or at least I – cannot separate memory from emotion, we are in that precisely unlike those early modern writers, whether theorists of the memory arts or practitioners of the theories in their applications across every field of writing from religion to education, from poetry to science, who sought to explore early modern mnemo-techniques.

There is one other exception to the absences of emotion in the anthology, one emotion that is cleverly associated with memory itself (actually, *him*self): laughter. Thomas Tomkis' *Lingua* (1607) is a play so successful that it had gone through six editions by 1657, probably in part because it is an academic play that bucked the norm and was written in English rather than Latin. One of its many threads concerns a character named Memoria and his servant Anamnestes, who have, as it were, wandered into Tomkis' play from the House of Temperance in Book 2 of Spenser's *Faerie Queene*. We might see this as a kind of early modern mash-up in its transposition from one work to a very different other. As Engel and his coeditors rightly suggest, the two characters "personify the Aristotelian relationship between memory as recorder of images and recollection as retriever of them."[22]

The comedy here is often of a stereotypical kind with Memoria as the *senex* set against his lackadaisical and put-upon young servant, whose name, the play suggests, translates precisely as "Remembrance" (D3v). But Memoria has and is a memory strikingly full of forgetfulness, losing his purse and at one point announcing, "I Remember that I forgot my spectacles, I left them in the 349. page of *Halls* Chronicles" (F3r). As Stewart and Sullivan gleefully point out, "For the curious, in none of the editions of Hall's *Chronicles* does pagination reach 349."[23] A memory that forgets more than it remembers is here the stuff of comic *lazzi*, a part of the mad world Tomkis exhilaratingly creates.

But for the most part the arts of memory are apparently too serious a matter to involve early modern emotions. If the comedy of memory in Tomkis is a source of pleasure, and elsewhere the arts of memory are about helping, not pleasing, the worth of learning these arts and displaying them lies in what they enable, not the affects they conjure up . The same seriousness is apparently true for the experience of going to watch a play. Hence there is the insistence with which Simon Forman, our earliest extant extensive reviewer of Shakespeare in performance (in the four reports of productions, three by Shakespeare and one not, that he wrote about in his "Bocke of Plaies" in 1611), writes, as it were to and for himself, so repeatedly the aggressive command "Remember," five times in his account of the non-Shakespearean play about Richard II alone. The report becomes a series of instructions to himself, injunctions couched so emphatically in the imperative mode to "Remember therein how ... Also remember how ... Remember also ... Remember therein also how ... Remember also how ...," an aggregation of memories through the conscious act of remembering in the writing of the performance into memory. And Forman, almost as frequently, writes an instruction to "observe," where the imperative is also a memory of what has been observed: note what it signifies but also note what I saw. So "Observe there how" in his account of *The Winter's Tale* parallels "Remember how" and also, in his notes on the *Macbeth* performance, becomes "there was to be observed," memory as a record of the act of spectatorship.[24]

The fragments of what Forman chooses to record bear witness to his awareness of the inadequacy of the writing as observation and as remembrance. Forman's record leaves the play dissolved into summary of plot (often messy, especially, though unsurprisingly, with *Cymbeline*, which ends, rather desperately, with "and how she was found by Lucius, etc."), summations of moral learning achieved or reinforced (his account of *The Winter's Tale* ends with "Beware of trusting feigned beggars or fawning felons"), and so on.

At no point in his memoranda of play-going does Simon Forman directly express an emotion of response, even though at times his choice of what to record seems to indicate that he found something striking. So, for instance, the very extent of his account of what happened when Banquo's ghost appeared seems to me to indicate that he was excited by this piece of stage-business that he so carefully writes down after seeing *Macbeth*:

> The next night being at supper with his noblemen, whom he had bid to a feast (to the which also Banquo should have come), he began to speak of noble Banquo and to wish that he were there. And as he thus did, standing up to drink a carouse to him, the ghost of Banquo came and sat down in his chair behind him. And he turning about to sit down again saw the ghost of Banquo which fronted him so that he fell into a great passion of fear and fury, uttering many words about his murder, by which when they heard that Banquo was murdered they suspected Macbeth.[25]

This implicit emotional response apart, there is nothing in Forman's fairly extensive documenting of what he wanted to remember that hints at the pleasure of playgoing.

Next to Forman's stern imperatives, it is a relief to turn to the emotions of response, positive and negative, that dominate the brief comments that Samuel Pepys so frequently attaches to his detailing of his playgoing in his diary. On December 31, 1660, for instance, he bought a copy of Shakespeare's *Henry IV Part 1* in Paul's Churchyard and then went on to the Theatre Royal in Vere Street "and there saw it acted; but my expectation being too great, it did not please me as otherwise I believe it would; and my having a book I believe did spoil it a little."[26] As usual,

Pepys records whether he enjoyed the play or not, here affected by anticipation and by having the book – perhaps he was reading along with the performance. When he saw the play again on June 4, 1661, he thought it "a good play" (II:115). He did not see the play again until November 6, 1667, this time with his wife and her maid: "and contrary to expectation, was pleased in nothing more than in Cartwright's speaking of Falstaffe's speech about *What is Honour?*" (VIII:516). None of his records of dozens of playhouse visits is more famous than his account of his first visit, with his wife and a friend, to *A Midsummer Night's Dream*, which, he reports, "I have never seen before, nor shall ever again, for it is the most insipid ridiculous play that ever I saw in my life. I saw, I confess, some good dancing and some handsome women, which was all my pleasure" (September 29, 1662, III:208). No question here about the emotion the performance created. If this is the reverse of the future pleasure of memory that Aeneas promises, it is also a help, a firm reminder never to go to see *Dream* again – and, at least for the duration of the diary, he never did.

What was somehow a necessity for Pepys and, as it were, never occurs to Forman – the need to define the response to the theater event not as moral instruction but as a site of intellectual interest and the pleasures of entertainment – was something with which I grew up. I hear in my memory my father's voice saying, often, as we made our way out of the theater, his most damning comment: "That was very interesting but I wasn't entertained." Playgoing itself and the memory of our spectatorship share the pleasure. While there are times that these memories are a help, as I recall in class a production I saw decades before my students were born, they are most powerfully a delight, as the affects of remembering make Shakespeare immediately and thrillingly present.

Notes

1 As I type this, I immediately hear in my head Emlyn Williams' voice reading the opening of Thomas's "A Visit to Grandpa's" on that LP: "It was the first time I had stayed at Grandpa's house."
2 Laurence Olivier, *Scenes from Shakespeare's "Hamlet" and "Henry V,"* RCA Red Seal LP, LM-1924, first released in 1955.
3 See my memoir, "Anne Barton, 1933–2013," *Biographical Memoirs of Fellows of the British Academy*, 14 (2015), 15–35, esp. 35.
4 John Smith, *The Mysterie of Rhetorique Unvail'd* (London: George Eversden, 1657), 249. It is the epigraph to my chapter "Going to Shakespeare: Memory and Anamnesis," in William McKenzie and Theodora Papadopoulou, eds., *Shakespeare and I* (London: Continuum Books, 2012), 87–106, a piece that

touches on some of the same issues as this chapter, though from a very different perspective.
5 See https://sites.fas.harvard.edu/~classics/poetry_and_prose/Aeneid.1.195-207.html.
6 See s.v. *juvo*, in Charlton T. Lewis and Charles Short, eds., *A New Latin Dictionary* (New York: American Book Company, 1907), 1021.
7 Dani Bostick, "Forsan et haec olim meminisse iuvabit: Will Remembering Help or Please?," *In Medias Res*, posted April 1, 2019, https://medium.com/in-medias-res/forsan-et-haec-olim-meminisse-iuvabit-will-remembering-help-or-please-d631c8829886.
8 Thomas Phaer, *The Seven First Bookes of the Eeneidos of Virgill* (London: Richard Iugge, 1558), A3v.
9 Virgil, *Eclogues, Georgics, Aeneid I–VI*, trans. H. Rushton Fairclough, revised by G. P. Goold, Loeb Classical Library (Cambridge, MA: Harvard University Press, [1916], revised ed., 1999), 277.
10 Bostick, "Forsan et haec."
11 T. W. Baldwin, *William Shakespere's Small Latine & Lesse Greeke*, 2 vols. (Urbana: University of Illinois Press, 1944), vol. II, 487.
12 R. W. Dent, *Shakespeare's Proverbial Language: An Index* (Berkeley: University of California Press, 1981), R73, quoted *ad loc.*, in René Weis' Arden 3 edition of *Romeo and Juliet* (London: Arden Shakespeare, 2012).
13 Maurice Palmer Tilley, ed., *A Dictionary of the Proverbs in England in the Sixteenth and Seventeenth Centuries* (Ann Arbor: University of Michigan Press, 1950), R73, 568.
14 For *Remembering Shakespeare*, see the film website: www.rememberingshakespearefilm.com/. The film was made available on demand in 2020 at https://vimeo.com/ondemand/rememberingshakespeare and the RBG segment is free at https://vimeo.com/460404469. All transcriptions from the film are my own. My thanks to Cecilia Rubino for information about the film and much friendly conversation. See also her chapter, "If It Live in Your Memory: On Memory, Memorization and Shakespeare," in Petar Penda, ed., *The Whirlwind of Passion: New Critical Perspectives on William Shakespeare* (Newcastle-upon-Tyne: Cambridge Scholars Publishing, 2016), 324–44.
15 Cecilia Rubino, "The Making of *Remembering Shakespeare*," *Altre Modernità*, (2017), special issue: "Will Forever Young! Shakespeare & Contemporary Culture," 169–86; 172–73.
16 Ibid., 173.
17 Ibid., 174.
18 This is presumably the set published by P. F. Collier and Son (New York, 1912), edited by William Ernest Henley.
19 Rubino, "The Making of *Remembering Shakespeare*," 181.
20 William E. Engel, Rory Loughnane, and Grant Williams, eds., *The Memory Arts in Renaissance England: A Critical Anthology* (Cambridge University Press, 2016).

21 Ibid., 367, 213, 183.
22 Ibid., 336.
23 Alan Stewart and Garrett A. Sullivan Jr., "'Worme-eaten, and full of canker holes': Materializing Memory in *The Faerie Queene* and *Lingua*," *Spenser Studies*, 17 (2003), 215–38; 223.
24 Modernized versions of the transcriptions are taken from the Folger's excellent *Shakespeare Documented* website: https://shakespearedocumented.folger.edu/resource/document/formans-account-seeing-plays-globe-macbeth-cymbeline-winters-tale.
25 Ibid.
26 Samuel Pepys, *The Diary*, ed. Robert Latham and William Matthews, 11 vols. (London: G. Bell and Sons, 1970–83), vol. I, 325.

Bibliography

All quotations from Shakespeare's works are taken from the New Cambridge Shakespeare edition, unless stated otherwise. References to the single volume editions are given parenthetically in the text.

PRIMARY SOURCES

Agricola, *De inventione dialectica*, trans. in Wayne A. Rebhorn, ed., *Renaissance Debates on Rhetoric* (Ithaca, NY: Cornell University Press, 2000).
Anon., *Il Sacrificio de gl'intronati, celebrato nei givochi d'vn carnevake in Siena et Gl'Ingannati, commedia de I medisimi* (Venezia: Plinio Peitrasanta, 1554).
  The last part of the Mirour for magistrates (London: Thomas Marsh, 1578).
  Oh read ouer D. iohn bridges, for it is worthy worke: Or an epitome of the fyrste booke, of that right worshipfull volume, written against the puritanes, in the defence of the noble cleargie, by as worshipfull a priest, iohn bridges, presbyter, priest or elder, doctor of diuillitie, and deane of sarum wherein the arguments of the puritans are wisely prevented (Fawsley: Robert Waldegrave, 1588).
Aquinas, St. Thomas, *Summa theologiae*, ed. and trans. Thomas Gilby (London: Blackfriars, 1972).
Aristotle, *The Nicomachean Ethics*, trans. David Ross, Oxford World's Classics (Oxford University Press, 2009).
Aristotle on Memory, ed. and trans. Richard Sorabji (Providence, RI: Brown University Press, 1971).
Armstrong, Archie, *A Banquet of Jest* (1657), in P. M. Zall, ed., *A Nest of Ninnies and Other English Jestbooks of the Seventeenth Century* (Lincoln: University of Nebraska Press, 1970).
Augustine, *Confessions*, trans. R. S. Pine-Coffin (London: Penguin, 1961).
Bacon, Francis, "Of Discourse," in Brian Vickers, ed., *The Major Works*, Oxford World's Classics (Oxford University Press, 1996).
Bandello, M., *Certaine tragicall discourses*, trans. Geoffrey Fenton (London: Thomas Marshe, 1567; STC 1356.1).

Bolton, Edmund, "Hypercritica," in J. E. Springarn, ed., *Critical Essays of the Seventeenth Century*, 3 vols. (Oxford: Clarendon Press, 1908).
The Book of Common Prayer: The Texts of 1549, 1559, and 1662, ed. Brian Cummings (Oxford University Press, 2011).
Bracciolini, Poggio, *The Facetiae or Jocose Tales of Poggio*, 2 vols. (Paris: Isidore Liseux, 1879).
Camden, William, *Britain*, trans. Philemon Holland (London: Impensis Georgii Bishop & Ioannis Norton, 1610).
Carpenter, Nathanael, *Geography delineated forth in two bookes* (Oxford: Henry Cripps, 1625).
Castiglione, Baldesar, *The Book of the Courtier*, ed. Daniel Javitch, A Norton Critical Edition (New York: W. W. Norton, 2002).
Cavendish, George, *Metrical Visions*, ed. A. S. G. Edwards, The Newberry Library (Columbia: University of South Carolina Press, 1980).
Cicero, *De oratore; or, On the Character of the Orator*, in *Cicero on Oratory and Orators*, trans. J. S. Watson (Carbondale: Southern Illinois University Press, 1970).
  On the Ideal Orator, trans. James M. May and Jakob Wisse (New York: Oxford University Press, 2001).
  Orator, trans. G. L. Hendrickson and H. M. Hubbell, Loeb Classical Library (Cambridge, MA: Harvard University Press, 1939).
  Rhetorica ad Herennium, ed. and trans Harry Caplan, Loeb Classical Library (Cambridge, MA: Harvard University Press, 1954).
Clapham, John, *The historie of Great Britannie* (London: Valentine Simmes, 1606).
Conti, Natale, *Natale Conti's Mythologiae*, trans. John Mulryan and Steven Brown, 2 vols. (Tempe, AZ: ACMRS, 2006).
Cotgrave, Randle, *Dictionarie of the French and English Tongues* (London: Adam Islip, 1611).
Dekker, Thomas, and George Wilkins, *Iests to make you Merie* (London: Nathaniell Butter, 1607).
Erasmus, Desiderius, *Adages IIı to IV100, Collected Works of Erasmus*, ed. R. A. B. Mynors, trans. Margaret Mann Phillips (University of Toronto Press, 1982).
  Apophthegmata, trans. and annotated by Betty I. Knott and Elaine Fantham, in Betty I. Knot, ed., *Collected Works of Erasmus* (Toronto University Press, 2014).
Fabian, Robert, *Fabyans cronucle* (London: Wyllyam Rastell, 1533; STC 10660).
  Newe cronycles of Englande and of Fraunce (London: Richard Rynson, 1516; STC 10659).
Foxe, John, *Acts and Monuments* (London: John Day, 1563).
Fuller, Thomas, *Historie of the Worthies of England* (London: Thomas Williams, 1661).

Grafton, Richard, *A chronicle at large* (London: Richarde Tottle and Humffrey Toye, 1569; STC 12147).
Hall, Edward, *The vnion of the two noble and illustre famelies of Lancastre [and] Yorke* (London: Richard Grafton, 1548).
Hearne, Thomas, ed., *A Collection Of Curious Discourses, Written by Eminent Antiquaries Upon several Heads in our English Antiquities* (Oxford: Thomas Hearne, 1720).
Holinshed, Raphael, *The Chronicles of England, Scotland and Ireland*, 2 vols. (London: Lucas Harrison, 1577).
   The First and Second Volumes of Chronicles (London: Lucas Harrison, 1587).
Johnson, Richard, *The Pleasant Conceites of Old Hobson the merry Londoner, full of humorous discourses, and witty meriments* (London: Iohn Wright, 1607).
Machyn, Henry, *Diary of Henry Machyn, Citizen and Merchant-Taylor of London*, ed. J. G. Nichols, Camden Record Society Old Series (London: Camden Society, 1848).
Marlowe, Christopher, *The troublesome raigne and lamentable death of Edward the second* (London: William Iones, 1594; STC 17437).
Marston, John, *The Scourge of Villainy* (London: Iohn Buzbie, 1598).
Marston, John, et al., *The Insatiate Countess*, ed. by Giorgio Melchiori (Manchester University Press, 1984).
Nashe, Thomas, *A countercuffe giuen to martin iunior by the ventruous, hardie, and renowned pasquill of england caualiero* (London: [John Charlewood], 1589).
   Lenten Stuff (London: Nicholas Ling and Cuthbert Burby, 1599).
   The Works of Thomas Nashe, ed. Ronald B. McKerrow, revised edition F. P. Wilson, 5 vols. (New York: Barnes and Noble, 1966).
Niccholes, Alexander, *A discourse of marriage and wiving* (London: Leonard Becket, 1620).
Painter, William, *The second tome of the palace of pleasure* (London: Nicholas England, 1567).
Pepys, Samuel, *The Diary of Samuel Pepys*, ed. Robert Latham and William Matthews, 11 vols. (London: G. Bell, 1970–83).
Perkins, William, *A Direction for the Government of the Tongue according to Gods word* (London: Abraham Kitson, 1593).
   The Foundation of Christian Religion (London: Iohn Porter and Iohn Legat, 1595).
Phaer, Thomas, *The Seven First Bookes of the Eeneidos of Virgill* (London: Richard Iugge, 1558).
Plato, *The Collected Dialogues of Plato*, ed. Edith Hamilton and Huntington Cairns (Princeton University Press, 1961).
Plautus, *The Two Menaechmuses*, ed. and trans. Wolfgang de Melo, Loeb Classical Library (Cambridge, MA: Harvard University Press, 2011).
Pontano, Giovanni Gioviano, *The Virtues and Vices of Speech*, ed. and trans. G. W. Pigman III, The I Tatti Renaissance Library (Cambridge, MA: Harvard University Press, 2019).

Puttenham, George, *The arte of english poesie contriued into three bookes: The first of poets and poesie, the second of proportion, the third of ornament* (London: Richard Field, 1589).
Quintilian, *The Orator's Education*, trans. H. E. Butler (Cambridge, MA: Harvard University Press, 1979).
Raleigh, Walter, *Sir Walter Raleighs instructions to his sonne and to posterity* (London: Beniamin Fisher, 1632; STC 20641.5).
Rich, Barnabe, *Faultes, faults, and nothing else but faultes* (London: Ieffrey Chorleton, 1606).
Sidney, Philip, *An Apology for Poetry*, ed. Forrest G. Robinson (New York: Macmillan, 1970).
Smith, John. *The Mysterie of Rhetorique Unvail'd* (London: George Eversden, 1657).
Speed, John, *The theatre of the empire of Great Britaine* (London: Iohn Sudbury & George Humble, 1612).
Spenser, Edmund, *The Faerie Queene*, 2nd ed., ed. A. C. Hamilton et al. (Harlow: Pearson Education, 2007).
Stow, John, *A suruay of London* (London: Iohn Wolfe, 1598).
Strachey, William, *The Historie of Travell into Virginia Britania*, ed. Louis B. Wright and Virginia Freund (London: Hakluyt Society, 1953).
Stubbes, Philip, *The anatomie of abuses containing, a discouerie, or briefe summarie of such notable vices and imperfections, as now raigne in many countreyes of the world* (London: John Kingston for Richard Jones, 1583).
Swetnam, Joseph, *The araignment of leuud, idle, froward, and vnconstant women* (London: Thomas Archer, 1615).
Symonds, William, *Virginia: A sermon preached at White-Chappel, in the presence of many, honourable and worshipfull, the aduenturers and planters for Virginia* (London: Eleazar Edgar and William Welby, 1609).
Taylor, John, *Taylors Wit and Mirth*, in William Carew Hazlitt, ed., *Shakespeare's Jest Books* (1864; New York: Barnes and Noble, 2007).
Tofte, Robert, *Alba* (London: Matthew Lownes, 1598).
Virgil, *Eclogues, Georgics, Aeneid I–VI*, trans. H. Rushton Fairclough, revised by G. P. Goold, Loeb Classical Library (Cambridge, MA: Harvard University Press, 1916, revised ed., 1999).
Virginia Company, *A true declaration of the estate of the colonie in Virginia* (London: William Barret, 1610).
"Londons Lotterie" (broadside) (London: Henry Robards, 1612).
Willis, John, *Mnemonica, or The Art of Memory* (London: Henry Seely, 1621).
Wilson, Thomas *Art of Rhetoric (1560)*, ed. Peter E. Medine (University Park: Pennsylvania State University Press, 1994).
Wright, Thomas, *The Passions of the Minde in Generall*, ed. Thomas O. Sloan (London, 1604; reprint, Urbana: University of Illinois Press, 1971).
Yarington, Robert, *Two Lamentable Tragedies*, ed. by Chiaki Hanabusa (Manchester: Manchester University Press, 2013).

SECONDARY TEXTS

Adams, Henry Hitch, *English Domestic or Homiletic Tragedy 1575–1642* (New York: Columbia University Press, 1943).
Agócs, Peter, "Speaking in the Wax Tablets of Memory," in Luca Castagnioli and Paola Ceccarelli, eds., *Greek Memories: Theories and Practices* (Cambridge University Press, 2019), 68–90.
Ahmed, Sara, "The Contingency of Pain," *Parallax*, 8.1 (2002), 17–34.
Alexander, Jeffrey C., *Trauma: A Social Theory* (Malden, MA: Polity Press, 2012).
Altman, Joel B., *The Improbability of Othello: Rhetorical Anthropology and Shakespearean Selfhood* (University of Chicago Press, 2010).
Alvarez-Recio, Leticia, *Fighting the Antichrist: A Cultural History of Anti-Catholicism in Tudor England* (Brighton: Sussex Academic Press, 2011).
Anderson, Miranda, "Distributed Cognition in the Early Modern Era," in D. Jalobeanu and C. T. Wolfe, eds., *Encyclopedia of Early Modern Philosophy and the Sciences* (Cham: Springer, 2021), https://doi.org/10.1007/978-3-319-20791-9_586-2.
Anderson, Thomas P., *Performing Early Modern Trauma from Shakespeare to Milton* (Burlington, VT: Ashgate, 2006).
Arab, Ronda, Michelle Dowd, and Adam Zucker, eds., *Historical Affects and the Early Modern Theater* (New York: Routledge, 2015).
Archer, Ian W., "Memorialization in Early Modern London," in J. F. Merritt, ed., *Imagining Early Modern London: Perceptions and Portrayals of the City from Stow to Strype, 1598–1720* (Cambridge University Press, 2001), 89–113.
Assmann, Aleida, *Cultural Memory and Western Civilization: Functions, Media, Archives* (Cambridge: Cambridge University Press, 2011).
  Is Time out of Joint? On the Rise and Fall of the Modern Time Regime, trans. Sarah Clift (Ithaca, NY: Cornell University Press, 2020).
Assmann, Jan, "Communicative and Cultural Memory," in Astrid Erll and Ansgar Nünning, eds., *Cultural Memory Studies: An International and Interdisciplinary Handbook* (Berlin: De Gruyter, 2010), 109–18.
  Cultural Memory and Early Civilization: Writing, Remembrance, and Political Imagination (Cambridge: Cambridge University Press, 2011).
Assman, Jan, and John Czaplicka, "Collective Memory and Cultural Memory," *New German Critique*, 65 (1995), 125–33.
Babb, Lawrence, *The Elizabethan Malady: A Study of Melancholia in the English Literature from 1580 to 1642* (East Lansing: Michigan State College Press, 1951).
Bach, Rebecca Ann, "Falstaff Becomes the (Hu)man at the Expense of *The Merry Wives of Windsor*," in Phyllis Rackin and Evelyn Gajowski, eds., *The Merry Wives of Windsor: New Critical Essays* (London: Routledge, 2015), 171–83.
Bailey, Amanda, "*Hamlet* without Sex. The Politics of Regenerate Loss," in John S. Garrison and Kyle Pivetti, eds., *Sexuality and Memory in Early*

Modern England: Literature and the Erotics of Recollection (Routledge, 2016), 220–36.

Bailey, Amanda, and Mario DiGangi, eds., *Affect Theory and Early Modern Texts: Politics, Ecologies, and Form* (New York: Palgrave Macmillan, 2017).

Bain, Frederika, "The Affective Scripts of Early Modern Execution and Murder," in Richard Meek and Erin Sullivan, eds., *The Renaissance of Emotion: Understanding Affect in Shakespeare and His Contemporaries* (Manchester University Press, 2015), 221–40.

Baldo, Jonathan, "Exporting Oblivion in *The Tempest*," *Modern Language Quarterly*, 56.2 (June 1995), 111–44.

Memory in Shakespeare's Histories: Stages of Forgetting in Early Modern England (New York: Routledge, 2012).

Baldwin, T. W., *William Shakespere's Small Latine and Lesse Greeke*, 2 vols. (Urbana: University of Illinois Press, 1944).

Balizet, Ariane M., "'Amend Thy Face': Contagion and Disgust in the *Henriad*," in Darryl Chalk and Mary Floyd-Wilson, eds., *Contagion and the Shakespearean Stage* (Cham: Palgrave, 2019), 127–46.

Blood and Home in Early Modern Drama: Domestic Identity on the Renaissance Stage (London: Routledge, 2014).

Baltzell, Jane, "Rhetorical 'Amplification' and 'Abbreviation' and the Structure of Medieval Narrative," *Pacific Coast Philology*, 2 (1967), 32–39.

Barber, C. L., *Shakespeare's Festive Comedies: A Study of Dramatic Form and Its Relation to Social Custom* (Princeton University Press, 1972).

Barikin, Amelia, "After the End: The Temporality of Melancholia," in Andrea Bubenik, ed., *The Persistence of Melancholia in Arts and Culture* (New York: Routledge, 2019), 107–21.

Barret, J. K., "The Crowd in Imogen's Bedroom: Allusion and Ethics in *Cymbeline*," *Shakespeare Quarterly*, 66.4 (2015), 440–62.

Barton, Anne, "Falstaff and the Comic Community," in Barton, *Essays, Mainly Shakespearean* (Cambridge University Press, 1994), 70–91.

Shakespeare and the Idea of the Play (London: Chatto & Windus, 1962).

Beard, Mary, *Laughter in Ancient Rome: On Joking, Tickling, and Cracking Up* (Berkeley: University of California Press, 2014).

Belsey, Catherine, *The Subject of Tragedy: Identity and Difference in Renaissance Drama* (London: Routledge, 1985; repr. 2014).

Benjamin, Walter. "Theses on the Philosophy of History," in Hannah Arendt, ed., *Illuminations. Essays and Reflections* (New York: Schocken, 2007), 253–264.

Berlant, Lauren, *Cruel Optimism* (Durham, NC: Duke University Press, 2011).

Berlant, Lauren, and Jordan Greenwald, "Affect in the End Times: A Conversation with Lauren Berlant," *Qui Parle*, 20 (2012), 71–89.

Berry, Cicely, *The Actor and the Text*, revised ed. (London: Virgin Books, 2000).

Berry, Philippa, *Shakespeare's Feminine Endings. Disfiguring Death in the Tragedies* (London: Routledge, 1999).

Bertelsen, Lone, and Andrew Murphie, "An Ethics of Everyday Infinities and Power: Félix Guattari on Affect and the Refrain," in Melissa Gregg and Gregory J. Seigworth, eds., *The Affect Theory Reader* (Durham, NC: Duke University Press, 2010), 138–57.
Bialo, Caralyn, "Popular Performance, the Broadside Ballad, and Ophelia's Madness," *Studies in English Literature, 1500–1900*, 53.2 (2013), 293–309.
Birth, Kevin, "Calendars: Representational Homogeneity and Heterogenous Time," *Time & Society*, 22.2 (2013), 216–36.
Bloom, Gina, *The Voice in Motion* (Philadelphia: University of Pennsylvania Press, 2007).
Bloom, Harold, *Falstaff: Give Me Life* (New York: Scribner, 2017).
  Shakespeare: The Invention of the Human (New York: Riverhead, 1998).
Bolzoni, Lina, *The Gallery of Memory: Literary and Iconographic Models in the Age of the Printing Press*, trans. Jeremy Parzen (University of Toronto Press, 2001).
Boose, Lynda E., "Othello's Handkerchief: 'The Recognizance and Pledge of Love,'" *English Literary Renaissance*, 5.3 (1975), 360–74.
Booth, Stephen, "Shakespeare in the San Francisco Bay Area," *Shakespeare Quarterly*, 29.2 (1978), 267–78.
Borges, Jorge Luis, *The Book of Sand and Shakespeare's Memory*, trans. Andrew Hurley (New York: Penguin Books, 1998).
Bostick, Dani, "Forsan et haec olim meminisse iuvabit: Will Remembering Help or Please?," *In Medias Res*, April 1, 2019, https://medium.com/in-medias-res/forsan-et-haec-olim-meminisse-iuvabit-will-remembering-help-or-please-d631c8829886.
Boulton, Jeremy, "London 1540–1700," in Peter Clark, ed., *The Cambridge History of Urban Britain*, 3 vols. (Cambridge University Press, 2000), vol. II (1540–1840), 315–46.
Bourus, Terri, "Canonizing Q1 *Hamlet*," *Critical Survey*, 31.1–2 (2019).
Bowen, Barbara C., *One Hundred Renaissance Jokes: An Anthology* (Birmingham, AL: Summa Publications, 1988).
Bradshaw, Graham, *Misrepresentations: Shakespeare and the Materialists* (Ithaca, NY: Cornell University Press, 1993).
Brewer, S. Derek, "Prose Jest-Books Mainly in the Sixteenth to Eighteenth Centuries in England," in Jan Bremmer and Herman Roodenburg, eds., *A Cultural History of Humour: From Antiquity to the Present Day* (Cambridge: Polity, 1997), 90–111.
Broomhall, Susan, ed., *Early Modern Emotions: An Introduction* (London: Routledge, 2017).
  Gender and Emotions in Early Modern Europe: Destroying Order, Structuring Disorder (Farnham: Ashgate, 2015).
Broomhall, Susan, and Sarah Finn, eds., *Violence and Emotion in Early Modern Europe* (Abingdon: Routledge, 2016).

Brown, David Sterling, and Jennifer Stoever, "Sound of Whiteness, or Teaching Shakespeare's Other 'Race Plays,'" Critical Race Conversations, Folger Shakespeare Library, July 16, 2020, www.youtube.com/watch?v=iBGSh4h-74U&t=960s.
Brown, Pamela, *Better a Shrew than a Sheep: Women, Drama, and the Culture of Jest in Early Modern England* (Ithaca, NY: Cornell University Press, 2002).
Budra, Paul, *"A Mirror for Magistrates" and the de casibus Tradition* (University of Toronto Press, 2000).
Buelens, Gert, et al., eds., *The Future of Trauma Theory: Critical Literary and Cultural Criticism* (New York: Routledge, 2014).
Burgess, Clive, "A Service for the Dead: The Form and Function of the Anniversary in Late Medieval Bristol," *Transactions of the Bristol and Gloucestershire Archeological Society*, 105 (1987), 183–212.
Burke, Peter, *Popular Culture in Early Modern Europe* (New York University Press, 1978).
  The Renaissance, 2nd ed., Studies in European History (Basingstoke: Palgrave Macmillan, 1997).
Cahill, Patricia, "The Feel of the Slaughterhouse: Affective Temporalities and Marlowe's *The Massacre at Paris*," in Amanda Bailey and Mario DiGangi, eds., *Affect Theory and Early Modern Texts* (New York: Palgrave, 2017), 155–74.
Callahan, Virginia W., "The *De Copia*: The Bounteous Horn," in Richard L. DeMolen, ed., *Essays on the Work of Erasmus* (New Haven, CT: Yale University Press, 1978), 99–109.
Capp, Bernard, *When Gossips Meet: Women, Family, and Neighbourhood in Early Modern England* (Oxford University Press, 2003).
Carroll, Noel, *Humour: A Very Short Introduction* (Oxford University Press, 2014).
Carruthers, Mary, *The Book of Memory: A Study of Memory in Medieval Culture* (Cambridge University Press, 1990).
  The Craft of Thought: Meditation, Rhetoric, and the Making of Images, 400–1200, Cambridge Studies in Medieval Literature 34 (Cambridge: Cambridge University Press, 1998).
Carruthers, Mary, and Jan M. Ziolkowski, eds., *The Medieval Craft of Memory: An Anthology of Texts and Pictures* (Philadelphia: University of Pennsylvania Press, 2002).
Caruth, Cathy, *Unclaimed Experience: Trauma, Narrative, and History* (Baltimore, MD: Johns Hopkins University Press, 1996).
Cave, Terence, *Recognitions: A Study in Poetics* (Oxford: Clarendon Press, 1988).
Chambers, E. K., *The Elizabethan Stage*, 4 vols. (Oxford: Clarendon Press, 1924).
  The Medieval Stage, 2 vols. (Oxford: Clarendon Press, 1903).
  William Shakespeare: A Study of Facts and Problems, 2 vols. (Oxford: Clarendon Press, 1930).
Charnes, Linda, "Anticipating Nostalgia: Finding Temporal Logic in a Textual Anomaly," *Textual Cultures*, 4.1 (2009), 72–83.

Charney, Maurice, and Hanna Charney, "The Language of Madwomen in Shakespeare and His Fellow Dramatists," *Signs* 3.2 (1977), 451–60.
Chedgzoy, Kate, Elspeth Graham, Katharine Hodgkin, and Ramona Wray, "Researching Memory in Early Modern Studies," *Memory Studies*, 11 (2018), 5—20.
Clegg, Cyndia, *Press Censorship in Elizabethan England* (Cambridge University Press, 1997).
Clough, Patricia Ticineto, "Afterword: The Future of Affect Studies," *Body & Society*, 16.1 (2010), 222–30.
Clough, Patricia Ticineto, and Jean Halley, *The Affective Turn: Theorizing the Social* (Durham, NC: Duke University Press, 2007).
Cohen, Adam Max, "*Hamlet* as Emblem: The *Ars Memoria* and the Culture of the Play," *Journal for Early Modern Cultural Studies*, 3.1 (2003), 77–112.
Coleman, Janet, *Ancient and Medieval Memories: Studies in the Reconstruction of the Past* (Cambridge University Press, 2010).
Colie, Rosalie L., *Paradoxia Epidemica: The Renaissance Tradition of Paradox* (Princeton University Press, 1966).
Collins, Stephen, "A Kind of Lawful Adultery: English Attitudes to the Remarriage of Widows, 1550–1800," in Peter C. Jupp and Glennys Howarth, eds., *The Changing Face of Death: Historical Accounts of Death and Disposal* (London: Macmillan and St. Martin's Press, 1997), 34–47.
Comensoli, Viviana, *"Household Business": Domestic Plays of Early Modern England* (University of Toronto Press, 1996).
Connolly, William, *Identity/Difference: Democratic Negotiations of Political Paradox* (Minneapolis: University of Minnesota Press, 2002).
Coursey, Sheila, "*Two Lamentable Tragedies* and True Crime Publics in Early Modern Domestic Tragedy," *Comparative Drama*, 53.3–4 (2019), 263–86.
Craig, Hugh, "The Three Parts of *Henry VI*," in Hugh Craig and Arthur F. Kinney, eds., *Shakespeare, Computers, and the Mystery of Authorship* (Cambridge University Press, 2009), 40–77.
Craig, Hugh, and John Burrows, "A Collaboration about a Collaboration: The Authorship of *King Henry VI, Part Three*," in Marilyn Deegan and Willard McCarty, eds., *Collaborative Research in the Digital Humanities: A Volume in Honour of Harold Short, on the Occasion of His 65th Birthday and His Retirement, September 2010* (Farnham: Ashgate, 2012), 27–65.
Craik, Katharine A., ed., *Shakespeare and Emotion* (Cambridge University Press, 2020).
  "Shakespeare's *A Lover's Complaint* and Early Modern Criminal Confession," *Shakespeare Quarterly*, 53.4 (2002), 437–59.
Craik, Katharine A., and Tanya Pollard, *Shakespearean Sensations: Experiencing Literature in Early Modern England* (Cambridge University Press, 2013).
Cressy, David, *Birth, Marriage, and Death: Ritual, Religion, and the Life-Cycle in Tudor and Stuart England* (Oxford University Press, 1997).
  Bonfires and Bells: National Memory and the Protestant Calendar in Elizabethan and Stuart England (Berkeley: University of California Press, 1989).

Cummings, Brian, and Freya Sierhuis, *Passions and Subjectivity in Early Modern Culture* (Farnham: Ashgate, 2013).
Daniell, Christopher, *Death and Burial in Medieval England, 1066–1550* (London: Routledge, 1997).
Daybell, James, *The Material Letter in Early Modern England* (Houndmills: Palgrave Macmillan, 2012).
Dent, R. W., *Shakespeare's Proverbial Language* (Berkeley: University of California Press, 1981).
Depledge, Emma, *Shakespeare's Rise to Cultural Prominence: Politics, Print and Alteration, 1642–1700* (Cambridge University Press, 2018).
Dodd, William., "Character as Dynamic Identity," in Paul Yachnin and Jessica Slights, eds., *Shakespeare and Character* (New York: Palgrave Macmillan, 2009), 62–79.
Dodds, Madeleine Hope, and Ruth Dodds, *The Pilgrimage of Grace, 1536–37, and the Exeter Conspiracy 1539*, 2 vols. (1915; revised ed., London: Frank Cass and Co., 1971).
Dolan, Frances E., *Dangerous Familiars: Representations of Domestic Crime in England, 1550–1700* (Ithaca, NY: Cornell University Press, 1994).
  Twelfth Night: Language and Writing (London: Bloomsbury Arden Shakespeare, 2014).
  Whores of Babylon: Catholicism, Gender, and Seventeenth-Century Print Culture (Ithaca, NY: Cornell University Press, 1999).
Douglas-Fairhurst, Robert, "Tragedy and Disgust," in Sarah Annes Brown and Catherine Silverstone, eds., *Tragedy in Transition* (Malden, MA: Blackwell, 2007), 58–77.
Dubrow, Heather, *Echoes of Desire: English Petrarchism and Its Counterdiscourses* (Ithaca, NY: Cornell University Press, 1995).
Dugan, Holly, *The Ephemeral History of Perfume: Scent and Sense in Early Modern England* (Baltimore, MD: Johns Hopkins University Press, 2011).
Duncan, Sophie, *Shakespeare's Props: Memory and Cognition* (London: Routledge, 2019).
Dunn, Jonni Koonce, "The Functions of Forgetfulness in *1 Henry IV*," *Studies in Philology* (2016), 82–100.
Eaton, Sarah, "Defacing the Feminine in Renaissance Tragedy," in Valerie Wayne, ed., *The Matter of Difference: Materialist Feminist Criticism of Shakespeare* (Ithaca, NY: Cornell University Press, 1991), 181–98.
Eliot, T. S., "*Hamlet*," in Frank Kermode, ed., *Selected Prose of T. S. Eliot* (London: Faber & Faber, 1975), 45–49.
Enderwitz, Anne, "Modernist Melancholia and Time: The Synchronicity of the Non-synchronic in Freud, Tylor and Conrad," in Martin Middeke and Christina Wald, eds., *The Literature of Melancholia: Early Modern to Postmodern* (Houndmills: Palgrave, 2011), 173–86.
Enenkel, Karl A. E., and Anita Traninger, eds., *Discourses of Anger in the Early Modern Period* (Leiden: Brill, 2015).

Engel, William E., *Chiastic Designs in English Literature* (New York: Routledge, 2016).
  Death and Drama in Renaissance England (Oxford University Press, 2002).
  "Handling Memory in the Henriad: Forgetting Falstaff," in Andrew Hiscock and Lina Perkins Wilder, eds., *The Routledge Handbook of Shakespeare and Memory* (London: Routledge, 2017), 165–79.
  "Mnemonic Criticism and Renaissance Literature: A Manifesto," *Connotations*, 1.1 (March 1991), 12–33.
Engel, William E., Rory Loughnane, and Grant Williams, eds., *The Memory Arts in Renaissance England: A Critical Anthology* (Cambridge University Press, 2016).
Enterline, Lynn, *Shakespeare's Schoolroom: Rhetoric, Discipline, Emotion* (Philadelphia: University of Pennsylvania Press, 2012).
Erikson, Amy Louise, *Women and Property in Early Modern England* (London: Routledge, 1993).
Erll, Astrid, *Memory in Culture*, trans. Sara B. Young (Houndmills: Palgrave, 2011).
Eschenbaum, Natalie K., and Barbara Correll, eds., *Disgust in Early Modern Literature* (London: Routledge, 2016).
Escolme, Bridget, *Emotional Excess on the Shakespearean Stage: Passion's Slaves* (London: Bloomsbury Arden Shakespeare, 2014).
Essary, Kirk, "The Renaissance of *affectus*? Biblical Humanism and Latin Style," in Juanita Feros Ruys, Michael W. Champion, and Kirk Essary, eds., *Before Emotions: The Language of Feeling 400–1800* (New York: Routledge, 2019).
Fazel, Valerie E., and Louise Geddes, *The Shakespeare Multiverse: Fandom as Literary Praxis* (New York: Routledge, 2022).
Feerick, Jean, "The Imperial Graft: Horticulture, Hybridity, and the Art of Mingling Races in *Henry V* and *Cymbeline*," in Valerie Traub, ed., *The Oxford Handbook of Shakespeare and Embodiment: Gender, Sexuality, and Race* (Oxford University Press, 2016), 211–27.
  Strangers in Blood: Relocating Race in the Renaissance (University of Toronto Press, 2010).
Fernyhough, Charles, *Pieces of Light: How the New Science of Memory Illuminates the Stories We Tell about Our Pasts* (New York: Harper, 2012).
Ferrand, Jacques, *A Treatise on Lovesickness*, ed. Donald Beecher and Massimo Ciavolella (Syracuse, NY: Syracuse University Press, 1990).
Ficino, Marsilio, *Commentary on Plato's Symposium on Love*, 2nd ed., trans. Sears Reynolds Jayne (Woodstock, CT: Spring Publications, 1999).
Fineman, Joel, *Shakespeare's Perjured Eye: The Invention of Poetic Subjectivity in the Sonnets* (Berkeley: University of California Press, 1986).
Fischer, Sandra K., "Hearing Ophelia: Gender and Tragic Discourse in *Hamlet*," *Renaissance and Reformation*, 14.1 (1990), 1–10.
Fitzmaurice, Andrew, *Sovereignty, Property and Empire, 1500–2000* (Cambridge University Press, 2014).

Floyd-Wilson, Mary, *English Ethnicity and Race in Early Modern Drama* (Cambridge University Press, 2003).
Folkerth, Wes, *The Sound of Shakespeare* (London: Routledge, 2002).
Freud, Sigmund, "Screen Memories," trans. David McLintock, in Adam Phillips, ed., *The Penguin Freud Reader* (London: Penguin Books, 2006).
Frye, Northrop, *A Natural Perspective: The Development of Shakespearean Comedy and Romance* (New York: Columbia University Press, 1965).
Glennie, Paul, and Nigel Thrift, *Shaping the Day: A History of Timekeeping in England and Wales, 1300–1800* (Oxford University Press, 2009).
Goddard, Harold, *The Meaning of Shakespeare* (University of Chicago Press, 1951).
Goffman, Erving, *The Presentation of Self in Everyday Life* (New York: Anchor Books, 1956).
Gordon, Andrew, "Material Fictions: Counterfeit Correspondence and the Culture of Copying in Early Modern England," in James Daybell and Andrew Gordon, eds., *Cultures of Correspondence in Early Modern Britain* (Philadelphia: University of Pennsylvania Press, 2016), 85–109.
Gowing, Laura, *Domestic Dangers: Women, Words, and Sex in Early Modern London* (Oxford: Clarendon Press, 1996).
Gray, Ronald, *Shakespeare on Love in the Sonnets and Plays in Relation to Plato's Symposium, Alchemy, Christianity and Renaissance Neo-Platonism* (Newcastle upon Tyne: Cambridge Scholars Publishers, 2011).
Greenberg, Marissa, *Metropolitan Tragedy: Genre, Justice and the City in Early Modern England* (University of Toronto Press, 2015).
  "Women and the Theatre in Thomas Heywood's London," in Joan Fitzpatrick, ed., *The Idea of the City: Early-Modern, Modern and Post-modern Locations and Communities* (Newcastle upon Tyne: Cambridge Scholars Publishing, 2009), 79–89.
Greenblatt, Stephen, *Shakespearean Negotiations: The Circulation of Social Energy in Renaissance England* (Oxford: Clarendon Press, 1988).
Greene, Thomas, *The Light in Troy: Imitation and Discovery in Renaissance Poetry* (New Haven, CT: Yale University Press, 1982).
Greg, W. W., ed., *Henslowe's Diary* (London: A. H. Bullen, 1908).
Gregory, Brad S., *Salvation at Stake: Christian Martyrdom in Early Modern Europe* (Cambridge, MA: Harvard University Press, 1999).
Gross, Kenneth, *Shakespeare's Noise* (University of Chicago Press, 2001).
Guardini, Caterina, "'The Lovely Nymph of Stately Thames': The Rhetoric of Water in the Creation of the Prince of Wales," in Luca Baratta and Alice Equestri, eds., *Forms of Nationhood: Selected Papers from the "Shakespeare and His Contemporaries" Graduate Conference* (Florence: British Institute, 2016), 81–109.
Gumbrecht, Hans Ulrich, *Production of Presence: What Meaning Cannot Convey* (Stanford University Press, 2004).
Halbwachs, Maurice, *On Collective Memory*, ed. and trans. Lewis A. Coser (University of Chicago Press, 1992).

Hardin, Richard F., "The Renaissance of Plautine Comedy and the Varieties of Luck in Shakespeare and Other Plotters," *Mediterranean Studies*, 16 (2007), 143–56.
Harris, Barbara Jean, *English Aristocratic Women, 1450–1550: Marriage and Family, Property and Careers* (Oxford University Press, 2002).
Harris, Jonathan Gil, *Untimely Matter in the Time of Shakespeare* (Philadelphia: University of Pennsylvania Press, 2009).
Harvey, E. Ruth, *The Inward Wits: Psychological Theory in the Middle Ages and the Renaissance* (London: Warburg Institute, 1975).
Hassel, R. Chris, "Hamlet's 'Too, Too Solid Flesh,'" *Sixteenth Century Journal*, 25.3 (1994), 609–22.
Helfer, Rebeca, *Spenser's Ruins and the Art of Recollection* (University of Toronto Press, 2012).
  "The State of the Art of Memory and Shakespeare Studies," in Andrew Hiscock and Lina Perkins Wilder, eds., *The Routledge Handbook of Shakespeare and Memory* (London: Routledge, 2018), 315–28.
Henriques, Julian, "The Vibrations of Affect and Their Propagation on a Night Out on Kingston's Dancehall Scene," *Body & Society*, 16.1 (2010), 57–89.
Hiscock, Andrew, and Lina Perkins Wilder, eds., *The Routledge Handbook of Shakespeare and Memory* (London: Routledge, 2018).
Hobgood, Allison P., *Passionate Playgoing in Early Modern England* (Cambridge University Press, 2014).
Höfele, Andreas, "Der Prinz und das Fleisch. Hamlets Ekel," in Ortrud Gutjahr, ed., *Hamlet: Theatralität und Tod in Michael Thalheimers Inszenierung am Thalia Theater Hamburg* (Würzburg: Königshausen & Neumann, 2009), 95–109.
Holcomb, Chris, *Mirth Making: The Rhetorical Discourse on Jesting in Early Modern England* (Columbia: University of South Carolina Press, 2001).
Holland, Peter, "Anne Barton, 1933–2013," *Biographical Memoirs of Fellows of the British Academy*, 14 (2015), 15–35.
  "Going to Shakespeare: Memory and Anamnesis," in William McKenzie and Theodora Papadopoulou, eds., *Shakespeare and I* (London: Continuum Books, 2012), 87–106.
  "On the Gravy Train: Shakespeare, Memory and Forgetting," in Holland, ed., *Shakespeare, Memory and Performance* (Cambridge University Press, 2006), 207–34.
  Shakespeare and Forgetting (London: Bloomsbury Publishing, 2021).
Hotson, Leslie, *The First Night of Twelfth Night* (London: Rupert Hart-Davis, 1954).
Howard, Jean E., "London and the Early Modern Stage," in Lawrence Manley, ed., *The Cambridge Companion to the Literature of London* (Cambridge University Press, 2011), 34–49.
Hui, Andrew, *The Poetics of Ruin in Renaissance Literature* (New York: Fordham University Press, 2017).

Hutton, Ronald, *The Rise and Fall of Merry England: The Ritual Year 1400–1700* (Oxford University Press, 1994).
Huyssen, Andreas, *Twilight Memories: Marking Time in a Culture of Amnesia* (New York: Routledge, 1995).
Ingram, Martin, "Reformation of Manners in Early Modern England," in Paul Griffiths, Adam Fox, and Steve Hindle, eds., *The Experience of Authority in Early Modern England* (Basingstoke: Macmillan, 1996), 47–88.
Innes, Paul, "*Cymbeline* and Empire," *Critical Survey*, 19.2 (2008), 1–18.
Irigaray, Luce, *This Sex Which Is Not One*, trans. Catherine Porter and Carolyn Burke (Ithaca, NY: Cornell University Press, 1985).
Jankowski, Theodora A., *Women in Power in the Early Modern Drama* (Urbana: University of Illinois Press, 1992).
Jenner, Mark S. R., "From Conduit to Commercial Network? Water in London, 1500–1725," in Paul Griffiths and Mark S. R. Jenner, eds., *Londinopolis: Essays in the Cultural and Social History of Early Modern London* (Manchester University Press, 2000), 250–72.
Johanson, Kristine, "On the Possibility of Early Modern Nostalgias," *Parergon*, 33.2 (2016), 1–15.
Johnson, Laurie, John Sutton and Evelyn Tribble, eds., *Embodied Cognition and Shakespeare's Theatre: The Early Modern Body-Mind* (New York: Routledge, 2014).
Jones, Ann Rosalind, and Peter Stallybrass, *Renaissance Clothing and the Materials of Memory* (Cambridge University Press, 2000).
Jones, Joseph M., *Affects as Process: An Inquiry into the Centrality of Affect in Psychological Life* (Hillsdale, NJ: Analytic Press, 1995).
Joseph, Miriam, *Shakespeare's Use of the Arts of Language* (Philadelphia: Paul Dry, 2005).
Kambaskovic, Danijela, "'Of comfort and dispaire': Plato's Philosophy of Love and Shakespeare's *Sonnets*," in R. S. White, Mark Houlahan, and Katrina O'Loughlin, eds., *Shakespeare and Emotions: Inheritances, Enactments, Legacies* (Basingstoke: Palgrave Macmillan, 2015), 17–28.
Karremann, Isabel, *The Drama of Memory in Shakespeare's History Plays* (Cambridge University Press, 2015).
  "A Passion for the Past: The Politics of Nostalgia on the Early Jacobean Stage," in Brian Cummings and Freya Sierhuis, eds., *Passions and Subjectivity in Early Modern Culture* (Ashgate, 2013), 149–64.
Kennedy, Verne R., "Auxesis: A Concept of Rhetorical Amplification," *Southern Speech Communication Journal*, 37.1 (1971), 60–72.
Kerrigan, John, *Motives of Woe: Shakespeare and "Female Complaint"* (Oxford: Clarendon Press, 1991).
  Revenge Tragedy: Aeschylus to Armageddon (Oxford: Clarendon Press, 1996).
Kimbro, Devori, *Trauma, Typology, and Anti-Catholicism in Early Modern England, 1579–1625* (Tempe: Arizona State University Press, 2015).
King, John, *English Reformation Literature* (Princeton University Press, 1982).

"Fact and Fiction in Foxe's *Book of Martyrs*," in David Loades, ed., *John Foxe and the English Reformation* (Aldershot: Ashgate, 2002).

"Introduction," in King, ed., *Foxe's Book of Martyrs: Selected Narratives* (Oxford University Press, 2009), xi–xii.

King, Ros, *Cymbeline: Constructions of Britain* (Farnham: Ashgate, 2005).

Kirwan, Peter, *Shakespeare in the Theatre: Cheek by Jowl*, Shakespeare in the Theatre Series (London: Bloomsbury, 2019).

Knutson, Roslyn L., "'Toe to Toe across Maid Lane': Repertorial Competition at the Rose and Globe, 1599–1600," in Paul Nelson and June Schlueter, eds., *Acts of Criticism: Performance Matters in Shakespeare and His Contemporaries* (Madison, NJ: Fairleigh Dickinson University Press, 2006), 21–37.

Knutson, Roslyn L., David McInnis, and Matthew Steggle, eds., *Thomas Merry (Beech's Tragedy)*, The Lost Plays Database, https://lostplays.folger.edu.

Kolnai, Aurel, *On Disgust* (Chicago: Open Court, 2004).

Korsmeyer, Carolyn, *Savoring Disgust: The Foul and the Fair in Aesthetics* (Oxford University Press, 2011).

Kranz, David L., "The Sounds of Supernatural Soliciting in *Macbeth*," *Studies in Philology*, 100.3 (2003), 346–83.

Kreps, Barbara. "Bad Memories of Margaret? Memorial Reconstruction versus Revision in *The First Part of the Contention* and *2 Henry VI*," *Shakespeare Quarterly*, 51.2 (2000), 154–80.

Kristeva, Julia, "Women's Time," *Signs*, 7.1 (1981), 13–35.

Kukkonen, Karin, "Navigating Infinite Earths: Readers, Mental Models and the Multiverse of Superhero Comics," *Storyworlds: A Journal of Narrative Studies*, 2 (2010), 39–58.

Kundera, Milan, *The Curtain: An Essay in Seven Parts*, trans. Linda Asher (New York: HarperCollins, 2007).

Lacan, Jacques, *The Language of the Self: The Function of Language in Psychoanalysis*, trans. Anthony Wilden (Baltimore, MD: Johns Hopkins University Press, 1968).

Lake, Peter, and Michael Questier, *The Antichrist's Lewd Hat: Protestants, Papists, and Players in Post-Reformation England* (New Haven, CT: Yale University Press, 2002).

Lakoff, George, and Mark Johnson, *Philosophy in the Flesh* (New York: Basic Books, 1999).

Landreth, David, "How Does Matter Feel? Affect and Substance in Recent Renaissance Criticism," *The Spenser Review*, 44.3 (2015), www.english.cam.ac.uk/spenseronline/review/volume-44/443/how-does-matter-feel-1.

Landsberg, Alison, *Prosthetic Memory: The Transformation of American Remembrance in the Age of Mass Culture* (New York: Columbia University Press, 2004).

LaPerle, Carol Mejia, ed., *Race and Affect in Early Modern English Literature* (Tempe, AZ: ACMRS Press, 2022).

Leapman, Michael, *London's River: A History of the Thames* (London: Pavilion, 1991).

Lees-Jeffries, Hester, *Shakespeare and Memory*, Oxford Shakespeare Topics (Oxford University Press, 2013).
Leet, Leonora, *Elizabethan Love Tragedy, 1587–1625* (New York University Press, 1971).
Leminus, Levinus, *The Touchstone of Complexions*, trans. Thomas Newton (London, 1576; STC 15446).
Levine, Caroline, *Forms: Whole, Rhythm, Hierarchy, Network* (Princeton University Press, 2015).
Lewis, Rhodri, "Hamlet, Metaphor, and Memory," *Studies in Philology*, 109.5 (2012), 609–41.
Leys, Ruth, "The Turn to Affect: A Critique," *Critical Inquiry*, 37.3 (2011), 434–72.
Lieblein, Leanore, "Murder in English Domestic Plays, 1590–1610," *Studies in English Literature, 1500–1900*, 23.2 (1983), 181–96.
Limon, Jerzy, "The Archaeology of Memory," *Cahiers Élisabéthains*, 73.2 (2008), 39–47.
Lin, Ying-chiao, "'Every Noise Appals Me': Macbeth's Plagued Ear," *Tamkang Review*, 43.2 (2013), 131–50.
Lindfors, Bernth, "Ira Aldrich at Covent Garden, April 1833," *Theatre Notebook*, 61.3 (2007), 144–69.
Linklater, Kristin, *Freeing Shakespeare's Voice: The Actor's Guide to Talking the Text* (New York: Theatre Communications Group, 1992).
Little, Arthur L., "'An Essence that's Not Seen': The Primal Scene of Racism in *Othello*," *Shakespeare Quarterly*, 44.3 (1993), 304–24.
Loades, David, *John Foxe and the English Reformation* (Aldershot: Ashgate, 2002).
Lockey, Brian, *Law and Empire in English Renaissance Literature* (Cambridge University Press, 2006).
Loughnane, Rory, "Shakespeare, Marlowe, and Traces of Authorship," in Andrew J. Power, ed., *The Birth and Death of the Author: A Multi-Authored History of Authorship* (New York: Routledge, 2020), 54–78.
Lucas, Scott, *"Mirror for Magistrates" and the Politics of the English Reformation* (Amherst: University of Massachusetts Press, 2009).
Luck, George, "*Vir Facetus*: A Roman Ideal," *Studies in Philology*, 55.2 (April 1958), 107–21.
Lund, Mary Ann, *A User's Guide to Melancholy* (Cambridge University Press, 2021).
MacFaul, Tom, *Shakespeare and the Natural World* (Cambridge University Press, 2015).
Mack, Maynard, *Everybody's Shakespeare: Reflections Chiefly on the Tragedies* (Lincoln: University of Nebraska Press, 1993).
Mack, Peter, "The Classics in Humanism, Education, and Scholarship," in Patrick Cheney and Philip Hardie, eds., *The Oxford History of Classical Reception in English Literature*, (Oxford University Press, 2015), vol. II, 29–55.

Maguire, Laurie, *Shakespearean Suspect Texts: The "Bad" Quartos and Their Contexts* (Cambridge University Press, 1996).
Manley, Lawrence, "From Strange's Men to Pembroke's Men: *2 Henry VI* and *The First Part of the Contention*," *Shakespeare Quarterly*, 54.3 (2003), 253–87.
  Literature and Culture in Early Modern London (Cambridge University Press, 1995).
Marelj, Jelena, *Shakespearean Character: Language in Performance* (London: Arden Shakespeare, 2019).
Marotti, Arthur F., "'Love Is Not Love': Elizabethan Sonnet Sequences and the Social Order," *ELH*, 49.2 (1982), 396–428.
  Religious Ideology and Cultural Fantasy: Catholic and Anti-Catholic Discourses in Early Modern England (University of Notre Dame Press, 2005).
Martin, Randall, *Shakespeare and Ecology* (Oxford University Press, 2015).
Maslen, R. W., "The Afterlife of Andrew Borde," *Studies in Philology*, 100.4 (2003), 463–91.
Massai, Sonia, *Shakespeare's Accents: Voicing Identity in Performance* (Cambridge University Press, 2020).
Massumi, Brian, "The Autonomy of Affect," *Cultural Critique*, 31 (1995), special issue: "The Politics of Systems and Environments," 83–109.
Mayer, Thomas F., *Reginald Pole: Prince and Prophet* (Cambridge University Press, 2000).
Mazzola, Elizabeth, *The Pathology of the English Renaissance: Sacred Remains and Holy Ghosts* (Leiden: Brill, 1998).
McMullan, Gordon, "The Colonisation of Early Britain on the Jacobean Stage," in Gordon McMullan and David Matthews, eds., *Reading the Medieval in Early Modern England* (Cambridge University Press, 2007), 119–40.
McRae, Andrew, *God Speed the Plough: The Representation of Agrarian England, 1500–1660* (Cambridge University Press, 1996).
  Literature and Domestic Travel in Early Modern England (Cambridge University Press, 2009).
Meek, Richard, and Erin Sullivan, *The Renaissance of Emotion: Understanding Affect in Shakespeare and His Contemporaries* (Manchester: Manchester University Press, 2015).
Menninghaus, Winfried, *Disgust: The Theory and History of a Strong Sensation*, trans. Howard Eiland and Joel Golb (Albany: State University of New York Press, 2003).
Mentz, Steve, "Is Compassion an Oceanic Feeling?," *Emotions: History, Culture, Society*, 4.1 (2020), 109–27.
Mieder, Wolfgang, *"Proverbs Speak Louder than Words": Wisdom in Art, Culture, Folklore, History, Literature and Mass Media* (New York: Peter Lang, 2008).
Mignolo, Walter, *The Darker Side of the Renaissance: Literacy, Territoriality, and Colonization* (1995; Ann Arbor: University of Michigan Press, 2003).
Mikalachki, Jodi, *The Legacy of Boadicea: Gender and Nation in Early Modern England* (London: Routledge, 1998).

Miller, William Ian, *The Anatomy of Disgust* (Cambridge, MA: Harvard University Press, 1997).
Miola, Robert, *Shakespeare and Classical Comedy: The Influence of Plautus and Terence* (Oxford University Press, 1994).
  Shakespeare's Rome (Cambridge University Press, 1983).
Montgomery, William, "'Textual Introduction' to *The First Part of the Contention (2 Henry VI)*," in Stanley Wells and Gary Taylor, eds., *William Shakespeare: A Textual Companion* (Oxford University Press, 1987), 175–77.
Moss, Ann, *Printed Commonplace-Books and the Structuring of Renaissance Thought* (Cambridge: Clarendon Press, 1996).
Mullaney, Steven, "Affective Technologies: Toward an Emotional Logic of the Early Modern Stage," in Mary Floyd-Wilson and Garrett A. Sullivan, Jr., eds., *Environment and Embodiment in Early Modern England* (Basingstoke: Palgrave, 2007), 71–89.
  The Reformation of Emotions in the Age of Shakespeare (University of Chicago Press, 2015).
Munro, Ian, and Anne Lake Prescott, "Jest Books," in Andrew Hadfield, ed., *The Oxford Handbook of English Prose 1500–1640*, (Oxford University Press, 2013), 343–59.
Murray, Daisy, *Twins in Early Modern English Drama and Shakespeare* (London: Routledge, 2017).
Murrin, Michael, *The Veil of Allegory* (University of Chicago Press, 1969).
Neely, Carol Thomas, "Strange Things in Hand," in Valerie Traub, ed., *The Oxford Handbook of Shakespeare and Embodiment* (Oxford University Press, 2016).
Neill, Michael, "Unproper Beds: Race, Adultery, and the Hideous in *Othello*," *Shakespeare Quarterly*, 40.4 (1989), 383–412.
Niaah, Sonjah Stanley, *Dancehall: From Slave Ship to Ghetto* (University of Ottawa Press, 2010).
Nicol, David, "'Exit at one door and enter at the other': The Fatal Re-entrance in Jacobean Drama," *Shakespeare Bulletin*, 37.2 (2019), 205–29.
Nolan, Maura, "'Now wo, Now Gladnesse': Ovidianism in *The Fall of Princes*," *ELH*, 71.3 (2004), 531–58.
Nora, Pierre, "Between Memory and History: *Les lieux de memoire*," trans. Marc Roudebush, in Genevieve Fabre and Robert O'Meally, eds., *History and Memory in African-American Culture* (Oxford: Oxford University Press, 1994).
Nowlin, Steele, *Chaucer, Gower, and the Affect of Invention* (Columbus: Ohio State University Press, 2016).
O'Neil, John, ed., *Freud and the Passions* (University Park: Pennsylvania State University Press, 1996).
Palfrey, Simon, and Tiffany Stern, *Shakespeare in Parts* (Oxford University Press, 2007).
Panek, Jennifer, *Widows and Suitors in Early Modern English Comedy* (Cambridge University Press, 2004).

Parker, K. R., "Wassailing and Festive Music in Shakespeare's *Twelfth Night*," *Australasian Drama Studies*, 76 (2020), 160–82.
Parker, Patricia, *Shakespeare from the Margins: Language, Culture, Context* (University of Chicago Press, 1996).
Paster, Gail Kern, *The Body Embarrassed: Drama and Disciplines of Shame in Early Modern England* (Ithaca, NY: Cornell University Press, 1993).
  Humoring the Body: Emotions and the Shakespearean Stage (University of Chicago Press, 2004).
Paster, Gail Kern, Katherine Rowe, and Mary Floyd-Wilson, eds., *Reading the Early Modern Passions: Essays in the Cultural History of Emotion* (Philadelphia: University of Pennsylvania Press, 2004).
Paterson, Mort, "Stress and Rhythm in the Speaking of Shakespeare's Verse: A Performer's View," *Shakespeare Bulletin*, 33.3 (2015), 469–88.
Pellikka, Paul, "'Strange things I have in head, that will to hand': Echoes of Sound and Sense in *Macbeth*," *Style*, 31.1 (1997), 14–33.
Peters, Erin, and Cynthia Rogers, "Reading Historical Trauma: Moving Backward to Move Forward," in Peters and Rogers, eds., *Early Modern Trauma: Europe and the Atlantic World* (Lincoln: University of Nebraska Press, 2021).
Petrarch, *Petrarch's Lyric Poems: The Rime Sparse and Other Lyrics*, trans. Robert M. Durling (Cambridge, MA: Harvard University Press, 1976).
Phillippy, Patricia, *Shaping Remembrance from Shakespeare to Milton* (Cambridge University Press, 2018).
Phillips, Harriet, "Late Falstaff, the Merry World, and *The Merry Wives of Windsor*," *Shakespeare*, 10.2 (2014), 111–37.
  Nostalgia in Print and Performance, 1510–1613: Merry Worlds (Cambridge University Press, 2019).
Pierce, Hazel, *Margaret Pole: Countess of Salisbury 1473–1541: Loyalty, Lineage, and Leadership* (Cardiff: University of Wales Press, 2003).
Pincombe, Mike, "A Place in the Shade: George Cavendish and *De casibus* Tragedy," in Mike Pincombe and Cathy Shrank, eds., *The Oxford Handbook of Tudor Literature* (Oxford University Press, 2009), 372–88.
Pollmann, Judith, *Memory in Early Modern Europe, 1500–1800* (Oxford University Press, 2017).
Poole, Robert, *Time's Alteration: Calendar Reform in Early Modern England* (London: UCL Press, 1998).
Porter, Roy, *London: A Social History* (London: Penguin, 1994; rev. 2000).
Prescott, Anne Lake, "Humanism in the Tudor Jestbook," *Moreana*, 24.95–96 (1987), 5–16.
Prince, Kathryn, "Misremembering *Hamlet* at Elsinore," in Paul Megna et al., eds., *Hamlet and Emotions* (Cham: Palgrave, 2019), 253–70.
Rastell, John, *A Hundred Merry Tales: The Shakespeare Jest Book*, ed. John Thor Ewing (London: Welkin Books, 2018).
Richards, Jennifer, *Voices and Books in the English Renaissance* (Oxford University Press, 2019).

Richardson, Catherine, *Domestic Life and Domestic Tragedy in Early Modern England: The Material Life of the Household* (Manchester University Press, 2006).
Rimé, Bernard, "Mental Rumination, Social Sharing, and the Recovery from Emotional Exposure," in J. W. Pennebaker, ed., *Emotion, Disclosure, and Health* (Washington, DC: American Psychological Association, 1995).
Roberts, Chris, *Cross River Traffic: A History of London's Bridges* (London: Granta, 2005).
Robinson, Benedict S., "Disgust, c. 1600," *ELH*, 81.2 (2014), 553–83.
  "Thinking Feeling," in Amanda Bailey and Mario DiGangi, eds., *Affect Theory and Early Modern Texts* (New York: Palgrave, 2017), 109–27.
Roche, Thomas P., Jr., *Petrarch and the English Sonnet Sequences* (New York: AMS Press, 1989).
Rosenwein, Barbara, *Generations of Feeling: A History of Emotions, 600–1700* (Cambridge University Press, 2016).
Rossi, Paolo, *Logic and the Art of Memory: The Quest for a Universal Language*, trans. Stephen Clucas (University of Chicago Press, 2000).
Rubino, Cecilia, "If It Live in Your Memory: On Memory, Memorization and Shakespeare," in Petar Penda, ed., *The Whirlwind of Passion: New Critical Perspectives on William Shakespeare* (Newcastle-upon-Tyne: Cambridge Scholars Publishing, 2016), 324–44.
  "The Making of Remembering Shakespeare," *Altre Modernità*, (2017), special issue: "Will Forever Young! Shakespeare & Contemporary Culture," 169–86.
Rummel, Erika, *Erasmus as a Translator of the Classics* (University of Toronto Press, 1985).
Ryan, Marie Laurie, and Jan-Noel Thon, *Storyworlds across Media: Toward a Media-Conscious Narratology* (Lincoln: University of Nebraska Press, 2014).
Sackton, Alexander H., *Rhetoric as Dramatic Language in Ben Jonson* (New York: Octagon Books, 1967).
Salingar, Leo, *Shakespeare and the Traditions of Comedy* (Cambridge University Press, 1974).
Saunders, Claire, "'Dead in His Bed': Shakespeare's Staging of the Death of the Duke of Gloucester in *2 Henry VI*," *The Review of English Studies*, 36.141 (1985), 19–34.
Saunders, Corinne, and Charles Fernyhough, "The Medieval Mind," *The Psychologist: Journal of the British Psychological Association*, 29.11 (2016).
Scarr, Richard, "Insatiate Punning in Marston's Courtesan Plays," in T. F. Wharton, ed., *The Drama of John Marston: Critical Re-Visions* (Cambridge University Press, 2000), 82–99.
Schey, Taylor, "Impasse? What Impasse? Berlant, de Man, and the Intolerable Present," *Comparative Literature* 72.2 (2020), 180–202.
Schiffer, James, "Mnemonic Cues to Passion in *Hamlet*," *Renaissance Papers* (1995), 65–80.

Schlegel, Johannes, "'Disjoint and Out of Frame': *Hamlet* and the Problem of Synchrony," *Zeitschrift für Anglistik und Amerikanistik*, 66.2 (2018), 163–79.
Schneider, Rebecca, *Performing Remains: Art and War in Times of Theatrical Reenactment* (London: Routledge, 2011).
Schurink, Fred, "Manuscript Commonplace Books, Literature, and Reading in Early Modern England," *The Huntington Library Quarterly*, 73.3 (2010), 453–69.
Schwyzer, Philip, *Archaeologies of English Renaissance Literature* (Oxford University Press, 2007).
  "Fallen Idols, Broken Noses: Defacement and Memory after the Reformation," *Memory Studies*, 11.1 (2018), 21–35.
Sedgwick, Eve K., "Paranoid and Reparative Reading, or, You're So Paranoid You Probably Think This Essay Is about You," in Sedgwick, ed., *Touching Feeling: Affect, Pedagogy, Performativity* (Durham, NC: Duke University Press, 2003), 123–51.
Segarra, Santiago, et al., "Attributing the Authorship of the *Henry VI* Plays by Word Adjacency," *Shakespeare Quarterly*, 67.2 (2016), 232–56.
Seigworth, Gregory J., and Melissa Gregg, eds., *The Affect Theory Reader* (Durham, NC: Duke University Press, 2010).
Shell, Alison, *Catholicism, Controversy and the English Literary Imagination, 1558–1660* (Cambridge University Press, 1999).
  Oral Culture and Catholicism in Early Modern England (Cambridge University Press, 2007).
Sherman, Anita Gilman, *Skepticism in Early Modern English Literature: The Problems and Pleasures of Doubt* (Cambridge University Press, 2021).
Shouse, Eric, "Feeling, Emotion, Affect," *M/C Journal*, 8.6 (2005), http://journal.mediaculture.org.au/0512/03-shouse.php.
Simpson, James, *Reform and Cultural Revolution* (Oxford University Press, 2002).
Skinner, Quentin, *The Foundations of Modern Political Thought*, 2 vols. (Cambridge University Press, 1978).
Smith, Bruce R., *The Acoustic World of Early Modern England: Attending to the O-Factor* (University of Chicago Press, 1999).
  Twelfth Night: Texts and Contexts (Boston: St Martin's Press, 2001).
Smith, Emma, *This Is Shakespeare* (New York: Pantheon Books, 2019).
Smith, Rosalind, Michelle O'Callaghan, and Sarah C. E. Ross, "Complaint," in Catherine Bates, ed., *A Companion to Renaissance Poetry* (Hoboken, NJ: Wiley Blackwell, 2018), 339–53.
Smyth, Adam, "Divines into dry Vines': Forms of Jesting in Renaissance England," in Allison K. Deutermann and András Kiséry, eds., *Formal Matters: Reading the Materials of English Renaissance Literature* (Manchester University Press, 2013), 56–72.
Snow, Edward A., "Sexual Anxiety and the Male Order of Things in *Othello*," *English Literary Renaissance*, 10.3 (1980), 384–412.
Sohmer, Steve, "The 'Double Time' Crux in *Othello* Solved," *ELR*, 32.2 (2002), 214–38.

Soler, Colette, *Lacanian Affects: The Function of Affect in Lacan's Work*, trans. Bruce Fink (London: Routledge, 2016).
Spiller, Michael R. G., *The Development of the Sonnet: An Introduction* (New York: Routledge, 1992).
Starks-Estes, Lisa S., *Violence, Trauma, and Virtus in Shakespeare's Roman Poems and Plays: Transforming Ovid* (London: Palgrave Macmillan, 2014).
Steggle, Matthew, *Laughing and Weeping in Early Modern Theatres* (Aldershot: Ashgate, 2007).
Stegner, Paul, "A Reconciled Maid: *A Lover's Complaint* and Confessional Practices in Early Modern England," in Shirley Sharon Zisser, ed., *Critical Essays on Shakespeare's A Lover's Complaint* (Aldershot: Ashgate, 2006), 79–90.
Stern, Tiffany, *Documents of Performance in Early Modern England* (Cambridge University Press, 2012).
Stewart, Alan, and Garrett A. Sullivan, "'Worme-eaten, and full of canker holes': Materializing Memory in *The Faerie Queene* and *Lingua*," *Spenser Studies*, 17 (2003), 215–38.
Strier, Richard, *The Unrepentant Renaissance: From Petrarch to Shakespeare to Milton* (University of Chicago Press, 2011).
Stuart, Robin S., "From Last Judgement to Leviathan: The Semiotics of Collective Temporality in Early Modern England," in Lauren Shohet, ed., *Temporality, Genre and Experience in the Age of Shakespeare: Forms of Time* (Bloomsbury, 2018), 223–46.
Sullivan, Erin, *Beyond Melancholy: Sadness and Selfhood in Renaissance England* (Oxford University Press, 2016).
Sullivan, Garrett A., Jr., *Memory and Forgetting in English Renaissance Drama: Shakespeare, Marlowe, Webster* (Cambridge University Press, 2005).
  "Voicing the Young Man: Memory, Forgetting, and Subjectivity in the Procreation Sonnets," in Michael Schoenfeldt, ed., *A Companion to Shakespeare's Sonnets* (Malden, MA: Blackwell, 2007), 331–42.
Sullivan, Margaret A., *Bruegel and the Creative Process, 1559–1563* (New York: Routledge, 2017).
Taylor, Gary, John Jowett, Terri Bourus, and Gabriel Egan, eds., *The New Oxford Shakespeare: Critical Reference Edition* (Oxford University Press, 2017).
Taylor, Gary, and Rory Loughnane, "The Canon and Chronology of Shakespeare's Works," in Gary Taylor and Gabriel Egan, eds., *The New Oxford Shakespeare: Authorship Companion* (Oxford University Press, 2017), 417–602.
Thomas, Keith, "The Perception of the Past in Early Modern England," in David Bates, Jennifer Wallis, and Jane Winters, eds., *The Creighton Century, 1907–2007* (University of London Press, Institute of Historical Research, 2009), 181–218.
  "The Place of Laughter in Tudor and Stuart England," *Times Literary Supplement*, January 21, 1977, 77–81.

Tilley, Morris Palmer, *A Dictionary of the Proverbs in England in the Sixteenth and Seventeenth Centuries* (Ann Arbor: University of Michigan Press, 1950).

Tinkler, John F., "Renaissance Humanism and the *genera eloquentia*," *Rhetorica*, 5.3 (1987), 279–309.

Todd, Barbara J., "The Virtuous Widow in Protestant England," in Sandra Cavallo and Lyndan Warner, eds., *Widowhood in Medieval and Early Modern Europe* (New York: Addison Wesley Longman, 1999), 66–83.

Traversi, Derek, *Shakespeare: The Last Phase* (Stanford University Press, 1965 [1955]).

Tribble, Evelyn, *Cognition in the Globe: Attention and Memory in Shakespeare's Theatre* (New York: Palgrave, 2011).

 Early Modern Actors and Shakespeare's Theatre: Thinking with the Body (London: Bloomsbury, 2018).

 "Kinesic Intelligence on the Early Modern English Stage," in Kathryn Banks and Timothy Chesters, eds., *Movement in Renaissance Literature* (London: Palgrave Macmillan, 2018), 213–24.

 "Memory in the Early Modern Context: Practices and Theories," in D. Jalobeanu and C. T. Wolfe, eds., *Encyclopedia of Early Modern Philosophy and the Sciences* (Cham: Springer, 2021), https://doi.org/10.1007/978-3-319-20791-9_601-1.

 "Minds in and out of Time: Memory, Embodied Skill, Anachronism, and Performance," *Textual Practice*, 26.4 (2012), 587–607.

 "'When Every Noise Appalls Me': Sound and Fear in *Macbeth* and Akira Kurosawa's *Throne of Blood*," *Shakespeare*, 1.1 (2005), 75–90.

Tribble, Evelyn, and Nicholas Keene, *Cognitive Ecologies and the History of Remembering: Religion, Education and Memory in Early Modern England* (London: Palgrave Macmillan, 2011).

Tribble, Evelyn, and John Sutton, "Cognitive Ecology as a Framework for Shakespearean Studies," *Shakespeare Studies*, 39 (2011), 94–103.

Trigg, Stephanie, "Introduction: Emotional Histories – Beyond the Personalization of the Past and the Abstraction of Affect Theory," in "Pre-Modern Emotions [Special Issue]," *Exemplaria: A Journal of Theory in Medieval and Renaissance Studies*, 26.1 (2014).

Trudell, Scott, *Unwritten Poetry: Song, Performance, and Media in Early Modern England* (Oxford University Press, 2019).

Vaughn, Jennifer C., *Masculinity and Emotion in Early Modern English Literature* (London: Routledge, 2008).

Vendler, Helen, *The Art of Shakespeare's Sonnets* (Cambridge, MA: Harvard University Press, 1997).

Vickers, Brian, ed., *English Renaissance Literary Criticism* (Oxford: Clarendon Press, 1999).

Vinter, Maggie, *Last Acts: The Art of Dying on the Early Modern Stage* (New York: Fordham University Press, 2019).

Waddington, Raymond B., "Shakespeare's Sonnet 15 and the Art of Memory," in Thomas O. Sloan and Raymond B. Waddington, eds., *The Rhetoric of*

Renaissance Poetry: From Wyatt to Milton (Berkeley: University of California Press, 1974), 96–122.
Walker, Greg, *Church Papists: Catholicism, Conformity and Confessional Polemic in Early Modern England* (London: Royal Historical Society Studies in History, 1993).
  John Heywood: Comedy and Survival in Tudor England (Oxford University Press, 2020).
Walsham, Alexandra, *The Reformation of the Landscape: Religion, Identity and Memory in Early Modern Britain and Ireland* (Oxford University Press, 2019).
Watson, Amanda, "'Full character'd': Competing Forms of Memory in Shakespeare's *Sonnets*," in Michael Schoenfeldt, ed., *A Companion to Shakespeare's Sonnets* (Malden, MA: Blackwell, 2007), 343–60.
Weber, Samuel, *Return to Freud: Jacques Lacan's Dislocation of Psychoanalysis*, trans. Michael Levine (Cambridge University Press, 1991).
Weissbourd, Emily, "'Search This Ulcer Soundly': Sex as Contagion in *The Changeling* and *Othello*," in Darryl Chalk and Mary Floyd-Wilson, eds., *Contagion and the Shakespearean Stage* (Cham: Palgrave Macmillan, 2019), 105–25.
Welsford, Enid, *The Fool: His Social and Literary History* (London: Faber & Faber, 1935).
West, William N., "Intertheatricality," in Henry S. Turner, ed., *Early Modern Theatricality* (Oxford University Press, 2013), 151–72.
Whipday, Emma, and Freyja Cox Jensen, "'Original Practices,' Lost Plays, and Historical Imagination: Staging 'The Tragedy of Merry,'" *Shakespeare Bulletin*, 35.2 (2017), 289–307.
White, Helen Constance, *Tudor Books of Saints and Martyrs* (Madison: University of Wisconsin Press, 1963).
Wiggins, Martin, ed., with Catherine Richardson, *British Drama, 1533–1642: A Catalogue* (Oxford University Press, 2013).
Wilder, Lina Perkins, *Shakespeare's Memory Theatre: Recollection, Properties, and Character* (Cambridge University Press, 2010).
Williams, Grant, "Monumental Memory and Little Reminders: The Fantasy of Being Remembered by Posterity," in Andrew Hiscock and Lina Perkins Wilder, eds., *The Routledge Handbook of Shakespeare and Memory* (London: Routledge, 2018), 297–311.
Williams, Grant, and Christopher Ivic, "Introduction," in Williams and Ivic, eds., *Forgetting in Early Modern English Literature and Culture: Lethe's Legacies* (London: Routledge, 2004), 1–18.
Wilson, F. P., "The English Jestbooks of the Sixteenth and Early Seventeenth Centuries," *Huntington Library Quarterly*, 2 (1938–39), 121–58.
Winkler, Amanda Eubanks, and Richard Schoch, *Shakespeare in the Theatre: Sir William Davenant and the Duke's Company* (London: Arden Shakespeare, 2022).

Withington, Phil, "The Sociable Self," in Withington, ed., *Society in Early Modern England: The Vernacular Origins of Some Powerful Ideas* (Cambridge: Polity, 2010), 171–201.
Wood, David, *Time, Narrative and Emotion in Early Modern England* (Farnham: Ashgate, 2009).
Wood, Gillian, *Shakespeare's Unreformed Fictions* (Oxford University Press, 2013).
Wood, Jennifer Linhart, *Sounding Otherness in Early Modern Drama and Travel: Uncanny Vibrations in the English Archive* (London: Palgrave Macmillan, 2019).
Woodward, Jennifer, *Theatre of Death: The Ritual Management of Royal Funerals in Renaissance England, 1570–1624* (Woodbridge: Boydell Press, 1997).
Woolf, Daniel R., "From Hystories to the Historical: Five Transitions in Thinking about the Past, 1500–1700," in *Huntington Library Quarterly*, 68.1–2 (2005), 33–70.
Yates, Frances A., *The Art of Memory* (University of Chicago Press, 1966; repr. London: Penguin, 1978).
Young, Alan R., *Tudor and Jacobean Tournaments* (London: George Philip & Son, 1987).
Zall, P. M., "The Natural History of Jestbook: An Introduction," in Zall, ed., *A Hundred Merry Tales and Other English Jestbooks of the Fifteenth and Sixteenth Centuries* (Lincoln: University of Nebraska Press, 1963).
Žižek, Slavoj, *The Parallax View* (Cambridge, MA: MIT Press, 2006).

Index

Abbott, George, Archbishop of Canterbury, 56
Adams, Henry Hitch, 164
adaptation, 45–46, 91, 187
Aesop, 127
affect, 91
affect studies/affect theory, 1, 3–5, 11, 13, 15, 187–88, 253, 256
affection, 2, 6–7, 49, 79, 205
affective
  communities, 137, 156
  dramaturgy, 14, 201, 204, 211, 251–65
  power, 5, 11–12, 27–28, 34, 164, 172–74, 204, 231, 234
  register, 155, 169, 228, 230, 234, 253, 262, 265
  relation with the past, 5, 11, 14, 164–65, 171
  resonance, 91, 101–2
  response, 13–16, 27, 95, 102, 144, 146–47, 150, 156, 166, 202, 253
  turn, 1, 3, 10
Agricola, Rudolph, 60–61
  De inventione dialectica, 60
Ahmed, Sara, 253, 262–64
Alciato, Andrea, 203
Alexander, Jeffrey C., 91–92
Alfonso IV, King of Portugal, 259
allegory, 29–35, 37–40
amnesia, 15, 29, 31, 195, 238, 248
Anderson, Miranda, 8–9
anger, 17, 110, 118, 241, 248, 252–53
antiquarianism, 181, 185, 190, 194
antiquity, 27, 32–38, 126, 131, 186–87
Aquinas, Thomas, 130
Aristotelian logic, 256
Aristotle, 1, 7, 72, 126, 130–32, 208, 278
  Nicomachean Ethics, 130–31
Armin, Robert, 130
  Nest for Ninnies, A, 130
Armstrong, Archie, 133
  Banquet of Jests, A, 133
ars amatoria, 11, 27

ars memoriae, 9, 11, 27–28
Assmann, Aleida, 4
Assmann, Jan, 4, 102
audience, 131, 147, 205
  (discrepant) awareness, 230, 232–33, 251–52
  affective engagement of, 5, 10, 60–61, 73, 78, 96, 107, 137, 156, 163–64, 170–71, 173–76, 202, 232, 234, 247, 256
  cognitive demands on, 246–47
  members, 96–97, 170, 173
  memory, 14–15, 40, 80, 144, 170, 174, 202–4, 207, 211–13, 215–16, 246, 275
  response, 202, 230
Augustine, Saint, 31–32, 201
  Confessions, 31
Averroes (Mohammed Ibn Rushd), 1
Aylmer, John, 57

Bacon, Francis, 133
Bailey, Amanda, 9, 11
Baldo, Jonathan, 239
Baldwin, T. W., 274
Bale, John, 94, 97
Balizet, Ariane, 163, 172
Bandello, Matteo, 68
  Novelle, 68
Barber, C. L., 45–46, 53, 56, 59
Barret, J. K., 144
Barton, Anne, 60, 244, 272
Barton, John, 253, 257
Baudelaire, Charles, 16
Bayly, Lewis, 56
  Practice of Pietie, The, 56
Beadle, John, 277
  Journal or Diary of a Thankful Christian, The, 277
Becket, Thomas, 93
Belleforest, François de, 68
  Histoires Tragiques, 68
Berlant, Lauren, 3, 253, 260–61, 264
Berry, Cicely, 254

308

Index

Betterton, Thomas, 45
Bevis of Southampton, 126
Beza, Theodore, 203
Bible, 92–93, 95
Bloom, Gina, 258
Bloom, Harold, 244–45, 248
Boccaccio, Giovanni, 127
bodily fluids, 56
bodily recomposition, 186, 188
body, 2–3, 6–10, 25, 27, 33–34, 48–50, 55, 68–69, 71–76, 78–79, 82, 145, 147, 150–51, 155, 166, 169, 172–73, 184, 187–88, 223, 229–30, 233, 247, 262–63
Bolton, Edmund, 185
Boose, Lynda E., 154
Borde, Andrew, 124
  Scoggin's Jests, 124, 126, 128
Borges, Jorge Luis, 201–2
Bostick, Dani, 273–74
Bracciolini, Poggio, 127, 129, 131–32
  Facetiae, 127–28
Bradley, A. C., 244
Bradshaw, Graham, 152
Brown, David Sterling, 258–59
Bruegel, Pieter (the Elder), 210
Bulman, James, 243–44
Burrows, John, 232

Caesar, Julius, 189–91, 194
Cahill, Patricia, 11
Cairncross, Andrew S., 232
Caius, John, 125
Camden, William, 185, 189
Carpenter, Nathanael, 192–93
Carruthers, Mary, 1
Cartwright, William, 280
Cassius Dio, Lucius, 53, 189
Castiglione, Baldassare, 132
  Book of the Courtier, 132
Castro, Inês de, 259
catharsis, 14, 165
Catherine of Aragon, 111, 117–18
Cave, Terence, 63
Cavendish, George, 13, 15, 107–12, 116–17, 119
  Life of Cardinal Wolsey, The, 110
  Metrical Visions, 13, 107–10, 118–20
Caxton, William, 127
  Fables of Alfonce and Poge, The, 127
Chambers, E. K., 50, 53, 56
Charles I, King of England, 45, 56, 133
Charles II, King of England, 45
Charnes, Linda, 143–44
Chaucer, Geoffrey, 110, 124

Cheek by Jowl, 263
Cicero, Marcus Tullius, 1, 11, 29, 31, 126, 131–32, 208
  De Oratore, 1, 29, 131–32
  Rhetorica ad Herennium, 1, 50
civility, 13, 125, 132, 136–37, 191–92
Clapham, John, 189
Clough, Patricia Ticineto, 3
Cobbler of Canterbury, The, 128
cognition, 2, 4, 6–11, 49–50, 62, 70, 148, 246
  distributed, 7–9, 147
cognitive turn, 49
comedy, 15, 45–47, 50, 58, 60, 164, 169, 205–6, 243–45, 265, 278
Comensoli, Viviana, 175
commemoration, 4, 10, 69, 77–78, 80, 91–92, 143, 145
commonplaces, 209, 211, 215
compassion, 17
complaint poetry, 13, 106–20
copia, 208–9, 212–14
Copley, Anthony, 130
  Wits, Fits, and Fancies, 130
Coursey, Sheila, 171
Courtenay, Henry, 112–16
Craig, Hugh, 232
Cressy, David, 52
Cromwell, Thomas, 112
Cummings, Brian, 8, 10

Daniel, Samuel, 164
  Tethys Festival, 164
Dante (Alighieri), 31–32
  Divine Comedy, 32
  Vita Nuova, 32
Davenant, Sir William, 45–46
  Love and Honour, 45
Day, John, 170
Dekker, Thomas, 130, 133
  Jests to Make You Merry, 130, 133
Deleuze, Gilles, 3
delight, 126, 175, 273, 275, 280
Dennis, John, 244
  Comical Gallants, The, 244
Denson, Shane, 243
Dent, R. W., 275
desire, 6, 11–12, 15, 27, 30–31, 33–39, 48–49, 69, 74, 78, 80, 82, 133, 149, 151, 162, 169, 171, 183–84, 248, 260
DiGangi, Mario, 9, 11
Diogenes Laertius, 126
  Lives of the Eminent Philosophers, 127
disgust, 13, 144–52, 154–56
Dodd, William, 204

Dolan, Frances E., 170
domestic tragedy, 162–65, 169–76
Donne, John, 32
  Canonization, The, 32
Donnellan, Declan, 263
Douglas, Gavin, 274
Dover Wilson, John, 151
drama, 14–17, 60, 76, 113, 119, 131, 144, 162, 169, 175–76, 203, 220, 231–32, 254, 256–57
Drayton, Michael, 165
  Poly-Olbion, 165
Dryden, John, 46, 273
Dudley, Lord Robert, 44
Duncan, Sophie, 9
Dunn, Jooni Koonce, 239
Dürer, Albrecht, 148
  Melancholia I, 148

Eaton, Sara, 76
education, 28, 31, 131, 189, 278
Edward II, King of England, 54, 232–33
Edward III, King of England, 54
Edward IV, King of England, 124
Edward VI, King of England, 54, 94, 96, 98, 110
Eliot, T. S., 146–47
Elizabeth I, Queen of England, 44–45, 47–50, 54, 56–57, 59–60, 92–99, 101–2, 125, 134–35, 244, 247
embodied
  cognition, 7–8, 148
  emotion, 48
  experience, 8, 10
  knowledge, 6–9
  memory, 10
  mind, 2, 49
  perception, 8
  soul, 7
  subject, 9
embodiment, 8–9, 11, 75, 77, 79, 97, 147, 156, 187
emotional
  arousal, 6, 60–61
  contagion, 12, 16, 120
  detachment, 2, 168, 175, *see also* indifference
  disturbance, 6, 51, 60, 175, 260
  excess, 48, 174
  extremity, 166
  force, 27, 112
  landscapes, 163
  mobilization, 148
  regulation, 148
  responsiveness, 48, 202, 279
emotions
  expression of, 2, 60, 78, 149, 166, 253, 256, 260, 279

history of, 5, 8–9, 176
and memory, 1–12, 17, 26–27, 92, 106, 175, 207, 274–77, 280
and recollection, 2
and rhetoric, 5, 60
and sense perception, 49
empathy, 263–64
Engel, William, 246, 278
environment, 8–10, 147, 162, 186–88, 195, 248, 256, 259
envy, 6, 128
Erasmus of Rotterdam, 11, 57–58, 62, 126–31, 208–9, 213–14
  Adagia, 126, 209
  Apophthegmata, 126–28, 130
  De Copia, 12
Erikson, Amy, 81
Erll, Astrid, 143
Eusebius of Caesarea, 98–99
experience, 2, 8–13, 15–16, 46, 49–50, 52, 61–64, 70, 74, 96–97, 108, 111, 120, 143, 146–47, 149–50, 166, 169, 201, 206–7, 210, 215, 230–33, 239, 252, 254, 264–65, 276, 278

Fabian, Robert, 222
faculty psychology, 5, 7–8, 208
Fagles, Robert, 273
Fairclough, H. Rushton, 273
Famous Victories, The, 243
Fastolf, John, 124
Fazel, Valerie M., 238, 245–47
fear, 5–6, 13, 69, 79, 92, 107–8, 110, 168, 175, 185, 226, 279
feeling, 3, 5, 60–61, 64, 107, 111–14, 120, 148, 152, 155, 163–64, 166–70, 174–75, 181, 185, 188, 201, 252–53, 255–56, 258, 262–65
Feerick, Jean, 194
Fenton, Geoffry, 68, 76
Fernyhough, Charles, 1
Ferreira, António, 259
  A Castro, 259
Ferrers, George, 224
Ficino, Marsilio, 72–73
Fitzgerald, Robert, 273
Fletcher, John, 46
  Island Princess, The, 46
Florio, John, 144
  Worlde of Wordes, A, 144
forgetting, 11–12, 14–16, 26, 29, 32, 36, 40, 54, 69–71, 74–75, 80, 82, 143, 148, 164, 169, 173–74, 176, 239, 248
Forman, Simon, 278–80
Foxe, John, 12, 15, 89–102
  Acts and Monuments, 12, 15, 89, 92–95, 97–98, 100–2, 120
  Rerum in ecclesia gestarum, 97

Frazer, Sir James, 53
  Golden Bough, The, 53
Freud, Sigmund, 4, 51–52, 62, 90
Fuller, Thomas, 53, 277
  History of the Worthies of England, 277

Gaius Julius Caesar Strabo, 131
Gajowski, Evelyn, 244
Galenic humoralism, 7–9, 71–73, 169
Geddes, Louise, 238, 245, 247
genre, 12–14, 16, 50, 89, 94, 96, 101–2, 107–8, 114–15, 133, 220, 232, 247–48, 253, 260, 265
George Plantagenet, Duke of Clarence, 111, 117
ghost, 147–48, 223, 230, 261, 279
Ginsburg, Ruth Bader, 275
Gl'Ingannati, 47
Goddard, Harold, 244
Goffe, Thomas, 275
  Raging Turk, The, 275
Goffman, Erving, 202, 207
Goold, George Patrick, 273
Greenblatt, Stephen, 4, 46
Gregory, Brad S., 91
grief, 6, 15, 48, 54, 64, 110, 144, 164, 166, 181, 184–85, 223, 251–53, 258–61, 264
Grindal, Edmund, 48, 56
Guareschi, Giovannino, 134
Guattari, Félix, 3
guilt, 13, 107, 120, 148, 263
Gurr, Andrew, 241

hagiography, 12, 96, 98
Halbwachs, Maurice, 4–5
Hall, Edward, 223–24, 232, 278
  Union of the Two Noble and Illustre Families of Lancastre and Yorke, The, 278
happiness, 17, 48, 106, 264
Hardt, Michael, 3
Harris, Jonathan Gil, 153
Haughton, William, 170
Henriques, Julian, 253–54, 256, 264
Henry Frederick, Prince of Wales, 164
Henry VII, King of England, 117
Henry VIII, King of England, 54, 96, 98, 108, 110–11
Henslowe, Philip, 170
Heywood, John, 128, 131
historical phenomenology, 9
historiography, 12, 91, 98, 102
history play, 5, 14–15, 108, 170, 220, 234, 239, 244–45, 248
Holinshed, Raphael, 53, 182, 189, 223–24, 233
  Holinshed's Chronicles of England, Scotland and Ireland, 53, 189

Holland, Peter, 59, 175
Homer, 50–51
  Iliad, 50
  Odyssey, 63, 69
Horace, 35
Hotson, Leslie, 44, 47
Howard, Jean, 171
humors, 2, 8, 58, 70, 73
Humphrey, Duke of Gloucester, 110, 222, 224, 232
Hutton, Leslie, 45, 54
Hutton, Ronald, 45

Il Sacrificio, 47
imagination, 2, 7–8, 28, 34, 51, 62, 72, 91, 93, 96, 149–50, 170, 194, 231, 233–34
indifference, 14, 61, 165, 168–69
Irigaray, Luce, 73

James I, King of England, 45, 56, 133, 164
Jeffrey C., Alexander, 94–96
Jenkins, Tom, 273
jestbooks, 12–13, 124–25, 127, 129–30, 133–35
jests, 13, 47–48, 124, 127–30, 132–37, 246
Johnson, Mark, 49–50, 60
Jones, Ann Rosalind, 10
Jonson, Ben, 45
  Christmas His Masque, 45

Karremann, Isabel, 150, 169, 239, 243
Kemble, John Philip, 50
Kerrigan, John, 148, 261
King, John N., 98
King, John, Bishop of London, 56
Knox, John, 97
Kolnai, Aurel, 146
Kreps, Barbara, 228
Kristeva, Julia, 151
Kukkonen, Karin, 246
Kundera, Milan, 16
Kyd, Thomas
  Arden of Faversham, 164

Lacan, Jacques, 155
LaCapra, Dominick, 91–92, 100–1
Lakoff, George, 49–50, 60
Landreth, David, 187
Landsberg, Alison, 4–5, 164, 171, 173
Langland, William
  Piers Ploughman, 38
laughter, 5, 11, 126, 129–31, 133, 136–37, 278
Lees-Jeffries, Hester, 143, 145
Lehman, David, 277
Levine, Caroline, 107–9
Lewis, Rhodri, 147
Leys, Ruth, 3

Limon, Jerzy, 144
Linklater, Kristin, 254
Little, Arthur L., 154
Loades, David, 93
London, 162–63, 165, 170–71, 173, 176
love, 5–6, 11–12, 15–16, 25–40, 44, 47–49, 52, 60, 62–63, 69, 71, 78, 81, 149, 153, 240, 244, 247, 251–52, 259
Lucas, Peter, 275
Lucas, Will, 275
Lucian of Samosata, 129
Lucius Mallius, 127
lust, 6, 38, 68–80
Lydgate, John, 107, 109–11
　Fall of Princes, The, 107, 110
Lyly, John, 56
　Euphues, 56

MacFaul, Tom, 187
Machyn, Henry, 54
Mack, Maynard, 265
Macrobius Ambrosius Theodosius, 127, 131
　Saturnalia, 127, 131
Maguire, Laurie, 228–29
Manley, Lawrence, 228
Manningham, John, 46–47, 50
Mantel, Hilary, 116, 118
marital law, 80–81
Marlowe, Christopher, 11, 224, 228, 232–34
　Edward II, 232
　Massacre at Paris, The, 11
Marprelate, Martin, 57–58
Marston, John, 12, 68–70, 75–80, 82, 275
　Insatiate Countess, The, 12, 68–70, 75–76, 78–79, 81–82
　Jack Drum's Entertainment, 275
Martin, Randall, 187
martyrdom, 89, 94, 98–102
martyrology, 15, 92, 94–98, 102
Mary I, Queen of England, 56, 93–94, 97–101, 110–11, 117–18
Massumi, Brian, 3
matter, 2, 25, 73, 130, 150, 188
Mazzola, Elizabeth, 96
McKellen, Ian, 1–15
medieval, 1–2, 5, 33, 38–39, 50, 52, 57, 107–10, 126–28, 136–37, 145, 181, 202
melancholy, 13, 48, 71, 148–50, 188
Melchiori, Giorgio, 68, 76, 243, 245
memorialization, 13, 34, 54, 59, 69–70, 80, 89, 91–93, 97, 102
memorization, 27
memory
　art of, 1, 6, 9–11, 25–40, 69, 80, 202–3, 277–78

　artificial, 27, 30–31
　and the body, 2, 150, 173
　collective, 3–4, 13–14, 17, 137, 204, 274
　crisis of, 143, 145
　cue, 203–5, 207, 211, 214, 216
　cultural, 3–5, 10, 53, 102, 109, 125–26, 129, 137, 164
　emotional, 2, 10, 46, 163, 170, 172, 252, 271
　historical, 181, 186, 189, 193
　individual, 3–4, 107, 183
　intentio, 2
　involuntary, 253, 264
　national, 13, 242
　natural, 6, 26, 30, 202
　object, 147
　objects, 9, 147–48, 150–51, 153–56
　practices of, 10–11, 170
　selective, 143
　and selfhood, 3–4, 12, 61–62, 70, 75, 79, 114, 155, 183, 188
　and space, 13, 27, 162–76
　transfer of, 62, 106, 108, 112, 114–15, 118–20
　and text, 192–93, 195, 208–9
memory studies, 1, 3–5, 9
memory theater, 9, 26, 202
Menninghaus, Winfried, 149, 152
Merleau-Ponty, Maurice, 262
metaphor, 7, 37, 49–50, 55–56, 176, 193, 201–2, 226
Middleton, Thomas
　Revenger's Tragedy, The, 259
Mikalachki, Jodi, 184
mimesis, 46, 53, 59, 64, 175
mimetic form, 46, 50, 60–61, 202
Mirror for Magistrates, A, 107–9, 111, 223–24
mnemonic
　culture, 69, 76, 81–82, 213
　dramaturgy, 14, 201–16, 238–48
　metaphor, 25, 33, 35
　poetics, 12, 26, 28, 30–32
mnemonics, 14, 27, 31, 37, 143–44, 201–3, 210, 216
Molloy, Charles
　Half-Pay Officers, The, 45
Monmouth, Geoffrey of, 185
More, Sir Thomas, 128–29
mourning, 6, 48, 51, 54, 64, 77–78, 145, 184–87, 189, 259
Mullaney, Steven, 182
multiverse, 15, 238–39, 243, 245–48
Munday, Anthony, 164
　London's Love to the Royal Prince Henrie, 164

Nashe, Thomas, 58–59
  Summer's Last Will and Testament, 58–59, 63
Neill, Michael, 154
network (Levine), 107–9, 111–12, 116, 119–20
Niccholes, Alexander, 79
Nolan, Maura, 110
Nora, Pierre, 5
nosce te ipsum, 69–70, 75, 80
nostalgia, 4–6, 10, 13–14, 45, 54, 124–25, 127, 129, 133, 137, 143, 150, 181, 239, 242, 244, 248
Nowlin, Steele, 202

oblivion, 5, 11–12, 25–26, 33, 40, 54, 68–69, 72, 75–77, 81–82, 170, 174, 185, 190
Oldcastle, John, 124
Olivier, Laurence, 271–72
Orgel, Stephen, 273
Orsini, Virginio, 44
Ovid (Publius Ovidius Naso), 7, 108–9, 115, 193
  Ars amatoria, 7
  Metamorphoses, 193

pain, 5, 15, 32, 92, 107–9, 113, 120, 238, 262–64, 274
Painter, William, 68, 76
Panek, Jennifer, 79
Parker, Patricia, 154
passions, 3, 6–8, 10, 27, 29, 38, 59, 125, 181, 205
  ecology of, 8, 187
  theory of, 49
Paster, Gail Kern, 2, 8, 71, 187
pastoral, 151, 182–83, 186, 189–91
Peacham, Henry, 203
Pellikka, Paul, 256
Pepys, Samuel, 45–46, 53, 279–80
perception, 4, 6–8, 10, 49, 243
performance, 15–16, 27, 29, 31, 44–46, 56, 59, 254
  play in, 50, 59, 61, 233, 257, 272, 278
Perkins, William, 6, 125–26
  Arte of Prophecying, The, 6
  Foundation of Christian Religion, The, 125
Peter I, King of Portugal, 259
Peters, Erin, 90
Petrarch (Francesco Petrarca), 31–32, 34, 38
Petrus Alphonsus, 127, 130
  Disciplina Clericalis, 127
Phaer, Thomas, 273
Phillippy, Patricia, 10, 187
Phillips, Harriet, 1, 4, 245

philosophy, 2, 6, 26, 29–31, 47, 208, 214, 276
Pierce, Hazel, 107
Pincombe, Mike, 109, 119
Plato, 11, 26, 29–31, 34, 127
  Phaedrus, 11, 26, 29–31, 33–34, 36, 39
  Republic, 29
  Symposium, The, 11, 26, 29–31, 33–34, 36, 39, 127
Platonism, 26, 31, 33, 40
  Platonic allegory, 27, 31–32, 38–39
  Platonic bargain, 36–37
  Platonic love, 11, 27, 31–40
Plautus, Titus Maccius, 47, 51, 54
  Menaechmi, 47
playhouse, 9, 171, 175, 225, 280
Playing Shakespeare (BBC series 1983), 253, 257
pleasure, 13, 17, 32, 34, 45, 48, 59, 74, 124–25, 129–30, 133, 136–37, 154, 156, 169, 175, 246, 273–80
Plutarch, 126, 131
  Moralia, 126
  Quaestiones convivales, 131
poetic meter, 252
poetics, 11–12, 26–35, 37, 39–40, 53, 202
poetry, 25–40, 106–8, 110, 120
Pole, Henry, 112–16
Pole, Margaret Countess of Salisbury, 111–12, 116–20
Pole, Reginald, 112
Pole, Sir Geoffrey, 112–16
politics, 5, 10, 12, 15, 107–12, 116, 120, 133, 143, 147, 182
Pollmann, Judith, 90
Pontano, Giovanni, 132–33
  De Sermone, 132
Prince, Kathryn, 148, 150
Protestant/Protestantism, 12, 48, 70, 80, 89–102, 117, 136, 153
Proust, Marcel, 252
proverbs, 131, 203–4, 208–10, 213–16
psyche, 5, 9, 90, 162, 176
Puttenham, George, 50, 208
  Arte of English Poesie, The, 50

Quintilian, Marcus Fabius, 1, 126, 131–32, 203–4, 208, 214
  Institutio Oratoria, 1, 132

Rackin, Phyllis, 244
Raleigh, Walter, 81
Rastell, John, 128
  Hundred Merry Tales, A, 128
recollection, 1, 4, 9–12, 15–16, 26–34, 39–40, 106, 148, 203, 207, 212, 238–39, 241–43, 275–76, 278

Reformation, 4, 10, 13, 45, 78, 89–102, 108, 110, 112, 125
  Counter-Reformation, 94, 98, 125
religion, 54, 57, 59, 80, 90, 92, 94, 99–100, 110, 125, 133, 276–77
remembering, 2, 10–12, 14–16, 26, 30–31, 35, 37, 40, 51–52, 70, 80, 82, 106, 111, 113, 147–48, 162, 169–70, 174–76, 207, 231, 239, 264, 271–80
remembrance, 40, 153, 184–85, 187, 203, 278
  acts of, 156, 165, 176
  and affect, 17, 46, 78, 91, 107, 110, 113, 144–45, 147, 162, 169, 241, 275, 277
  of the dead, 162–63, 172
  as ethical, 70, 75, 82
  and male identity, 69, 75, 77, 80
  in mnemonics, 27, 30–31
  internal, 26
  poetic, 27, 33–34
  practices of, 148
  and temporality, 143–44
  and trauma, 15
  in religion, 30
  ritualized, 6, 185
  self-remembrance, 70, 75, 80, 82
revision of playtext, 45, 228–34
rhetoric, 5–6, 8–9, 11, 27–30, 49, 60–62, 94–95, 116, 126, 129, 131–32, 183, 190–91, 194, 202–3, 207–12, 214–15
Rich, Barnabe, 132
Richard II, King of England, 124
Richardson, Catherine, 163
ritual, 46, 53, 55–57, 59–60, 64, 69, 184, 189
  and theater, 46, 53
  games, 48
  religious, 4, 46, 59, 63–64, 77–78, 80, 110–11, 120
  social, 45, 50, 53, 74, 264
Robert Devereux, 2nd Earl of Essex, 44
Robin, Donna, 276
Robinson, Benedict, 7, 144
Rogers, Cynthia, 90
Rogers, John, 99
Rosenfeld, Mordecai, 276
Rowe, Nicholas, 244
Rubino, Cecilia, 275–76
ruin, 13, 25–26, 28, 30, 32–40, 110
rumination, 238–39, 242, 248

Salingar, Leo, 47
Saunders, Claire, 232–34
Scarr, Richard, 75
Schey, Taylor, 260
Schneider, Rebecca, 147
Scogan, Henry, 124

Scoggin, John, 124
Segarra, Santiago, 232
self/selfhood, 3, 17, 252, 264
Seneca the Younger, 60
  Oedipus, 60
sensation, 49, 149, 173, 187, 262
sense(s), 7–8, 16, 48, 61–62, 145, 170, 205
Servilius Geminus, 127
Shakespeare, William, 2, 5–6, 11, 15, 25–27, 32–34, 37–40, 44–51, 53, 58–59, 61–62, 70, 78, 117–18, 120, 124, 143–47, 152, 181–82, 184–85, 193, 201–16, 224, 228, 232, 234, 238–39, 241, 243–47, 251, 253–55, 260, 264–65, 271–80
  Antony and Cleopatra, 5, 204, 211
  Comedy of Errors, The, 203, 205–7
  Cymbeline, 14, 181–82, 187, 192–93, 202, 247, 279
  Hamlet, 5, 9, 13, 25, 40, 45, 78, 113, 144–52, 156, 213, 220, 252, 261, 265, 271
  Henry IV, Part 1, 238, 240–43, 279
  Henry IV, Part 2, 124, 238–39, 242–45, 247–48
  Henry V, 5, 14, 45, 106, 115, 124, 203–4, 208–14, 231, 245–46, 271–72
  Henry VI, Part 2, 14, 224–34, 243
  Henry VI, Part 3, 238
  Julius Caesar, 272, 276
  King John, 257
  King Lear, 259, 265
  Love's Labour's Lost, 211
  Macbeth, 6, 15, 45, 251–62, 264, 279
  Merchant of Venice, The, 203–5, 253
  Merry Wives of Windsor, The, 15, 238–48
  Midsummer Night's Dream, A, 280
  Much Ado About Nothing, 210–12
  Othello, 9, 13, 147, 152–56, 265
  Richard II, 239–42, 260
  Richard III, 5, 75, 117, 120, 238
  Romeo and Juliet, 148, 274
  Sonnets, The, 11, 25–27, 32–40
  Tempest, The, 6, 45–46, 144
  Twelfth Night, 5, 12, 44, 46, 48, 50, 58–59, 61, 63–64
  Winter's Tale, The, 12, 15, 279
shame, 5, 10, 13, 17, 38, 40, 74, 77, 107, 109, 114–15, 119, 148, 152, 166, 171, 183, 240, 263
Shell, Alison, 4
Sidney, Philip, 8, 28
  Defense of Poesie (Apology for Poetry), 8, 28
Sierhuis, Freya, 8, 10
Simonides of Ceos, 11, 27–31, 34
Smith, John, 273
  Mysterie of Rhetorique Unvail'd, The, 273
Snow, Edward A., 154

Index

Socrates, 26, 29–31, 33–34, 36, 39
Sohmer, Steve, 152–53
soul, 7–8, 26–27, 30–33, 38, 60–61, 64, 69–70, 73, 76, 78, 240, 253–54
sound, 16, 48, 149, 227, 252, 254–56, 258, 271
space, 15, 31–32, 34, 59, 101–2, 225, 243, 253–55, 258, 272
Speed, John, 185
Spenser, Edmund, 70, 98, 164, 278
   Faerie Queene, The, 70, 165, 278
   Prothalamion, 164
   Ruines of Time, The, 164
spirits transmitting affect, 8
Stallybrass, Peter, 10
Stesichorus, 30
Stewart, Alan, 278
Stewart, Patrick, 257
Stoever, Jennifer, 258–59
Stow, John, 190
Strachey, William, 190
Stuart, Robin S., 144
Stubbes, Phillip, 57
   Anatomy of Abuses, The, 57
Sturken, Marita, 5
Suchet, David, 257
suffering, 5, 91, 93, 101, 106, 110–11, 114, 119
Sullivan, Garrett A., 10, 69, 278
Swetnam, Joseph, 72
Symonds, William, 190
sympathy, 58, 168, 175, 263–64

Tales and Quick Answers, 127, 129, 135
Taylor, John, 130, 134, 136
   Wit and Mirth, 134
temperance, 278
temporality, 13–14, 34–36, 39, 113, 143–45, 147, 150, 152–55
testimony, 6, 106, 110–11, 118, 120
Thames, 14, 162, 164–69, 172
theater
   and affect, 16, 175, 182
   and ritual, 60
   defense of, 8
   materials of, 246
   religious context, 45
Thomas, Keith, 125, 133
Tilley, Morris Palmer, 214, 275
Time (allegorical figure), 35–36, 39
Tofte, Robert, 77
Tomkis, Thomas, 278
   Lingua, 278
tragedy, 6, 13, 60, 68, 107, 109, 111, 117–18, 145–46, 152, 156, 170, 213, 224, 253, 259, 261, 265

translation, 76, 93, 95, 127, 144, 273
trauma, 89–102
   as performance, 96
   traumatropism, 91, 100–2
Traversi, Derek, 191
Tribble, Evelyn, 144
Trigg, Stephanie, 181
True Discourse of a Most Cruell and Barbarous Murther Committed by one Thomas Merrey, A, 170
Tyndale, William, 95

urbanity, 132

Vinsauf, Geoffrey of, 208
Virgil (Publius Vergilius Maro), 273–75, 277
   Aeneid, 273–74

Walker, Greg, 131
Walsham, Alexandra, 4, 10
Walton, William, 271
Warning for Faire Women, A, 164
Wayne, Valerie, 192
Weber, Max, 94, 96
Weber, Samuel, 155
Weissbourd, Emily, 154
Welsford, Enid, 58
West, Will, 247
Whipday, Emma, 163
White, Helen Constance, 95
Whitgift, John, 57
widow, 68, 72, 78–82
Wilder, Lina Perkins, 246
Wilkins, George, 130, 133
   Jests to Make You Merry, 130, 133
William, Duke of Cleves, 130
Willis, John, 6, 203
Wilson, Dover, 232
wit, 34, 58, 124, 126–29, 131–33, 136–37, 211–15
Wood, Gillian, 4
Woolf, Daniel R., 101
World of Wonders, A Mass of Murders, A, 170
Wright, Thomas, 7–8
   Passions of the Minde, 7
Wright, Thomas, 7
Wycliffe, John, 93, 95

Yarington, Robert, 13, 162–66, 169–72, 174–76
   Two Lamentable Tragedies, 13, 162–64, 167, 170–76

Žižek, Slavoj, 75

For EU product safety concerns, contact us at Calle de José Abascal, 56–1°, 28003 Madrid, Spain or eugpsr@cambridge.org.